Emerging Perspectives in Big Data Warehousing

David Taniar
Monash University, Australia

Wenny Rahayu
La Trobe University, Australia

A volume in the Advances in Data Mining and
Database Management (ADMDM) Book Series

Published in the United States of America by
    IGI Global
    Engineering Science Reference (an imprint of IGI Global)
    701 E. Chocolate Avenue
    Hershey PA, USA 17033
    Tel: 717-533-8845
    Fax: 717-533-8661
    E-mail: cust@igi-global.com
    Web site: http://www.igi-global.com

Library of Congress Cataloging-in-Publication Data

Names: Taniar, David, editor. | Rahayu, Johanna Wenny, editor.
Title: Emerging perspectives in big data warehousing / David Taniar and Wenny
  Rahayu, editors.
Description: Hershey, PA : Engineering Science Reference, [2019] | Includes
  bibliographical references and index.
Identifiers: LCCN 2018058989| ISBN 9781522555162 (hc) | ISBN 9781522555179
  (eISBN) | ISBN 9781522591948 (sc)
Subjects: LCSH: Data warehousing. | Data mining. | Big data.
Classification: LCC QA76.9.D37 E44 2019 | DDC 006.3/12--dc23 LC record available at https://lccn.loc.gov/2018058989

This book is published in the IGI Global book series Advances in Data Mining and Database Management (ADMDM) (ISSN: 2327-1981; eISSN: 2327-199X)

British Cataloguing in Publication Data
A Cataloguing in Publication record for this book is available from the British Library.

The views expressed in this book are those of the authors, but not necessarily of the publisher.

For electronic access to this publication, please contact: eresources@igi-global.com.

Advances in Data Mining and Database Management (ADMDM) Book Series

David Taniar
Monash University, Australia

ISSN:2327-1981
EISSN:2327-199X

Mission

With the large amounts of information available to organizations in today's digital world, there is a need for continual research surrounding emerging methods and tools for collecting, analyzing, and storing data.

The **Advances in Data Mining & Database Management (ADMDM)** series aims to bring together research in information retrieval, data analysis, data warehousing, and related areas in order to become an ideal resource for those working and studying in these fields. IT professionals, software engineers, academicians and upper-level students will find titles within the ADMDM book series particularly useful for staying up-to-date on emerging research, theories, and applications in the fields of data mining and database management.

Coverage

- Database Security
- Neural Networks
- Educational Data Mining
- Information Extraction
- Profiling Practices
- Data Warehousing
- Database Testing
- Association Rule Learning
- Sequence analysis
- Predictive Analysis

IGI Global is currently accepting manuscripts for publication within this series. To submit a proposal for a volume in this series, please contact our Acquisition Editors at Acquisitions@igi-global.com or visit: http://www.igi-global.com/publish/.

Titles in this Series

For a list of additional titles in this series, please visit: www.igi-global.com/book-series

Online Survey Design and Data Analytics Emerging Research and Opportunities
Shalin Hai-Jew (Kansas State University, USA)
Engineering Science Reference • copyright 2019 • 226pp • H/C (ISBN: 9781522585633) • US $215.00 (our price)

Handbook of Research on Big Data and the IoT
Gurjit Kaur (Delhi Technological University, India) and Pradeep Tomar (Gautam Buddha University, India)
Engineering Science Reference • copyright 2019 • 568pp • H/C (ISBN: 9781522574323) • US $295.00 (our price)

Managerial Perspectives on Intelligent Big Data Analytics
Zhaohao Sun (Papua New Guinea University of Technology, Papua New Guinea)
Engineering Science Reference • copyright 2019 • 335pp • H/C (ISBN: 9781522572770) • US $225.00 (our price)

Optimizing Big Data Management and Industrial Systems With Intelligent Techniques
Sultan Ceren Öner (Istanbul Technical University, Turkey) and Oya H. Yüregir (Çukurova University, Turkey)
Engineering Science Reference • copyright 2019 • 238pp • H/C (ISBN: 9781522551379) • US $205.00 (our price)

Big Data Processing With Hadoop
T. Revathi (Mepco Schlenk Engineering College, India) K. Muneeswaran (Mepco Schlenk Engineering College, India) and M. Blessa Binolin Pepsi (Mepco Schlenk Engineering College, India)
Engineering Science Reference • copyright 2019 • 244pp • H/C (ISBN: 9781522537908) • US $195.00 (our price)

Extracting Knowledge From Opinion Mining
Rashmi Agrawal (Manav Rachna International Institute of Research and Studies, India) and Neha Gupta (Manav Rachna International Institute of Research and Studies, India)
Engineering Science Reference • copyright 2019 • 346pp • H/C (ISBN: 9781522561170) • US $225.00 (our price)

Intelligent Innovations in Multimedia Data Engineering and Management
Siddhartha Bhattacharyya (RCC Institute of Information Technology, India)
Engineering Science Reference • copyright 2019 • 316pp • H/C (ISBN: 9781522571070) • US $225.00 (our price)

Data Clustering and Image Segmentation Through Genetic Algorithms Emerging Research and Opportunities
S. Dash (North Orissa University, India) and B.K. Tripathy (VIT University, India)
Engineering Science Reference • copyright 2019 • 160pp • H/C (ISBN: 9781522563198) • US $165.00 (our price)

IGI Global
DISSEMINATOR OF KNOWLEDGE

701 East Chocolate Avenue, Hershey, PA 17033, USA
Tel: 717-533-8845 x100 • Fax: 717-533-8661
E-Mail: cust@igi-global.com • www.igi-global.com

Table of Contents

Detailed Table of Contents

Xiufeng Liu, Technical University of Denmark, Denmark
Huan Huo, University of Technology Sydney, Australia
Nadeem Iftikhar, University College of Northern Denmark, Denmark
Per Sieverts Nielsen, Technical University of Denmark, Denmark

Data warehousing populates data from different source systems into a central data warehouse (DW) through extraction, transformation, and loading (ETL). Massive transaction data are routinely recorded in a variety of applications such as retail commerce, bank systems, and website management. Transaction data record the timestamp and relevant reference data needed for a particular transaction record. It is a non-trivial task for a standard ETL to process transaction data with dependencies and high velocity. This chapter presents a two-tiered segmentation approach for transaction data warehousing. The approach uses a so-called two-staging ETL method to process detailed records from operational systems, followed by a dimensional data process to populate the data store with a star or snowflake schema. The proposed approach is an all-in-one solution capable of processing fast/slowly changing data and early/late-arriving data. This chapter evaluates the proposed method, and the results have validated the effectiveness of the proposed approach for processing transaction data.

Francisca Vale Lima, University of Minho, Portugal
Carlos Costa, University of Minho, Portugal
Maribel Yasmina Santos, University of Minho, Portugal

The large volume of data that is constantly being generated leads to the need of extracting useful patterns, trends, or insights from this data, raising the interest in business intelligence and big data analytics. The volume, velocity, and variety of data highlight the need for concepts like real-time big data warehouses (RTBDWs). The lack of guidelines or methodological approaches for implementing these systems requires further research in this recent topic. This chapter presents the proposal of a RTBDW architecture that includes the main components and data flows needed to collect, process, store, and analyze the available data, integrating streaming with batch data and enabling real-time decision making. Using Twitter data, several technologies were evaluated to understand their performance. The obtained results were satisfactory and allowed the identification of a methodological approach that can be followed for the implementation of this type of system.

Chapter 3

Kornelije Rabuzin, University of Zagreb, Croatia

This chapter presents the concept of "deductive data warehouses." Deductive data warehouses rely on deductive databases but use a data warehouse in the background instead of a database. The authors show how Datalog, as a logic programming language, can be used to perform on-line analytical processing (OLAP) analysis on data. For that purpose, a small data warehouse has been implemented. Furthermore, they propose and briefly discuss "Datalog by example" as a visual front-end tool for posing Datalog queries to deductive data warehouses.

Chapter 4

Marwa Manaa, University of Tunis, Tunisia
Thouraya Sakouhi, University of Tunis, Tunisia
Jalel Akaichi, University of Bisha, Saudi Arabia

Mobility data became an important paradigm for computing performed in various areas. Mobility data is considered as a core revealing the trace of mobile objects displacements. While each area presents a different optic of trajectory, they aim to support mobility data with domain knowledge. Semantic annotations may offer a common model for trajectories. Ontology design patterns seem to be promising solutions to define such trajectory related pattern. They appear more suitable for the annotation of multiperspective data than the only use of ontologies. The trajectory ontology design pattern will be used as a semantic layer for trajectory data warehouses for the sake of analyzing instantaneous behaviors conducted by mobile entities. In this chapter, the authors propose a semantic approach for the semantic modeling of trajectory and trajectory data warehouses based on a trajectory ontology design pattern. They validate the proposal through real case studies dealing with behavior analysis and animal tracking case studies.

Chapter 5

Olfa Layouni, ISG Tunis, Tunisia
Jalel Akaichi, University of Bisha, Saudi Arabia

Spatio-temporal data warehouses store enormous amount of data. They are usually exploited by spatio-temporal OLAP systems to extract relevant information. For extracting interesting information, the current user launches spatio-temporal OLAP (ST-OLAP) queries to navigate within a geographic data cube (Geo-cube). Very often choosing which part of the Geo-cube to navigate further, and thus designing the forthcoming ST-OLAP query, is a difficult task. So, to help the current user refine his queries after launching in the geo-cube his current query, we need a ST-OLAP queries suggestion by exploiting a Geo-cube. However, models that focus on adapting to a specific user can help to improve the probability of the user being satisfied. In this chapter, first, the authors focus on assessing the similarity between spatio-temporal OLAP queries in term of their GeoMDX queries. Then, they propose a personalized query suggestion model based on users' search behavior, where they inject relevance between queries in the current session and current user' search behavior into a basic probabilistic model.

Chapter 6

In the big data warehouses context, a column-oriented NoSQL database system is considered as the storage model which is highly adapted to data warehouses and online analysis. Indeed, the use of NoSQL models allows data scalability easily and the columnar store is suitable for storing and managing massive data, especially for decisional queries. However, the column-oriented NoSQL DBMS do not offer online analysis operators (OLAP). To build OLAP cubes corresponding to the analysis contexts, the most common way is to integrate other software such as HIVE or Kylin which has a CUBE operator to build data cubes. By using that, the cube is built according to the row-oriented approach and does not allow to fully obtain the benefits of a column-oriented approach. In this chapter, the main contribution is to define a cube operator called MC-CUBE (MapReduce Columnar CUBE), which allows building columnar NoSQL cubes according to the columnar approach by taking into account the non-relational and distributed aspects when data warehouses are stored.

Chapter 7

A big data warehouse enables the analysis of large amounts of information that typically comes from the organization's transactional systems (OLTP). However, today's data warehouse systems do not have the capacity to handle the massive amount of data that is currently produced. Business intelligence (BI) is a collection of decision support technologies that enable executives, managers, and analysts to make better and faster decisions. Organizations must make good use of business intelligence platforms to quickly acquire desirable information from the huge volume of data to reduce the time and increase the efficiency of decision-making processes. In this chapter, the authors present a comparative analysis of commercial and open source BI tools capabilities, in order to aid organizations in the selection process of the most suitable BI platform. They also evaluated and compared six major open source BI platforms: Actuate, Jaspersoft, Jedox/Palo, Pentaho, SpagoBI, and Vanilla; and six major commercial BI platforms: IBM Cognos, Microsoft BI, MicroStrategy, Oracle BI, SAP BI, and SAS BI & Analytics.

Chapter 8

With the ongoing increasing amount of data, these data have to be processed to gain new insights. Data mining techniques and user-driven OLAP are used to identify patterns or rules. Typical OLAP queries require database operations such as selections on ranges or projections. Similarly, data mining techniques require efficient support of these operations. One particularly challenging, yet important property, that an efficient data access has to support is multi-dimensionality. New techniques have been developed taking advantage of novel hardware environments including SIMD or main-memory usage. This includes sequential data access methods such SIMD, BitWeaving, or Column Imprints. New data structures have been also developed, including Sorted Projections or Elf, to address the features of modern hardware and multi-dimensional data access. In the context of multidimensional data access, the influence of modern hardware, including main-memory data access and SIMD instructions lead to new data access techniques. This chapter gives an overview on existing techniques and open potentials.

Chapter 9

Salman Ahmed Shaikh, National Institute of Advanced Industrial Science and Technology (AIST), Japan

Kousuke Nakabasami, University of Tsukuba, Japan

Toshiyuki Amagasa, University of Tsukuba, Japan

Hiroyuki Kitagawa, University of Tsukuba, Japan

Data warehousing and multidimensional analysis go side by side. Data warehouses provide clean and partially normalized data for fast, consistent, and interactive multidimensional analysis. With the advancement in data generation and collection technologies, businesses and organizations are now generating big data (defined by 3Vs; i.e., volume, variety, and velocity). Since the big data is different from traditional data, it requires different set of tools and techniques for processing and analysis. This chapter discusses multidimensional analysis (also known as on-line analytical processing or OLAP) of big data by focusing particularly on data streams, characterized by huge volume and high velocity. OLAP requires to maintain a number of materialized views corresponding to user queries for interactive analysis. Precisely, this chapter discusses the issues in maintaining the materialized views for data streams, the use of special window for the maintenance of materialized views and the coupling issues of stream processing engine (SPE) with OLAP engine.

Chapter 10

Marko Petrović, University of Belgrade, Serbia

Nina Turajlić, University of Belgrade, Serbia

Milica Vučković, University of Belgrade, Serbia

Sladjan Babarogić, University of Belgrade, Serbia

Nenad Aničić, University of Belgrade, Serbia

ETL process development is the most complex and expensive phase of data warehouse development so research is focused on its conceptualization and automation. A new solution (model-driven ETL approach – M-ETL-A), based on domain-specific modeling, is proposed for the formal specification of ETL processes and their implementation. Several domain-specific languages (DSLs) are introduced, each defining concepts relevant for a specific aspect of an ETL process (primarily, languages for specifying the data flow and the control flow). A specific platform (ETL-PL) technologically supports the modeling (using the DSLs) and automated transformation of models into the executable code of a specific application framework. ETL-PL development environment comprises tools for ETL process modeling (tools for defining the abstract and concrete DSL syntax and for creating models in accordance with the DSLs). ETL-PL execution environment consists of services responsible for the automatic generation of executable code from models and execution of the generated code.

Chapter 11

This chapter introduces a method that discovers characteristic sequential patterns from sequential data based on background knowledge. The sequential data is composed of rows of items. This chapter focuses on the sequential data based on the tabular structured data. That is, each item is composed of an attribute and an attribute value. Also, this chapter focuses on item constraints in order to describe the background knowledge. The constraints describe the combination of items included in sequential patterns. They can represent the interests of analysts. Therefore, they can easily discover sequential patterns coinciding to the interests of the analysts as characteristic sequential patterns. In addition, this chapter focuses on the special case of the item constraints. It is constrained at the last item of the sequential patterns. The discovered patterns are used to the analysis of cause, and reason and can predict the last item in the case that the sub-sequence is given. This chapter introduces the property of the item constraints for the last item.

Preface

In the context of the dynamic business environment which exists nowadays, it is increasingly critical that organizations use only quality and up to date information, in order to make successful business decisions. Data warehouses are built with the aim of providing integrated and clean chronological data. Additionally, they are accompanied by tools which allow business users to query and analyse the warehoused data. The purpose of this book is to present and disseminate new concepts and developments in the areas of data warehousing in the era of Big Data.

The concept of data warehouse was defined by Inmon (2005) as a "subject-oriented, integrated, time-variant and non-volatile collection of data in support of management's decisions". Another definition was given by Marakas (2003), that a data warehouse is "a copy of transaction data specifically structured for querying, analysis and reporting".

It has been shown that for relational database systems, the operational and historical data cannot exist within the same structure because neither of them would perform well. Several reasons have been enumerated to support the need for a separate data warehouse to collect data for decisional support:

- A data warehouse is subject-oriented, which means that it is built around the major focus of an application: customer, product, sales etc. Conversely, an operational system contains all data produced by daily transaction processing and, depending on the application, might include data not required by the decision process;
- A data warehouse might contain information integrated from multiple sources (e.g. relational database, other files of different formats, emails, etc.), whereas operational systems always contain data produced by the application, most usually in the form of data in relational tables;
- A data warehouse is time variant and reflects the collection of data during a large period of time (e.g., 5-10 years or more), while operational systems do not keep data for such a long period of time;
- A data warehouse is used for the decision process only, and not for daily transaction processing. This means that a low number of queries are applied on larger volumes of data, compared with operational systems which are queried very often but for low volumes of data (e.g., to respond customer enquires);
- Finally, a data warehouse is non-volatile, which means that after the warehouse is built, data is uploaded and never deleted; new data arrives periodically and expands the data warehouse; queries are usually applied by the data analysts and therefore a data warehouse does not require concurrent transaction processing features; comparatively, operational systems are updated frequently, should allow multiple users, and hence should allow concurrent transaction processing.

Generic data warehouse architecture as proposed by Kimball and Ross (2002) contains the following four main areas:

- **Operational Source Systems:** These contain the transactional data, used in day to day operations, by a large number of users (possible hundreds or thousands in large applications). The data in these systems needs to be current, guaranteed up to date and the priority is high performance and high availability of the information;
- **Data Staging Area:** This is the area where the ETL (Extract – Transform – Load) process takes place. As the name says, the data is extracted from the operational source systems, then it is cleaned, transformed and integrated, and finally it is sent to be loaded into the data warehouse. Note that data staging area does not provide presentation services to the business users, in other words business users are not the direct consumers of the ETL process' output;
- **Data Presentation Area:** This is where the data is organised and stored, ready to be accessed by the business users. The storage is modelled as a series of data marts, depending on the specific business requirements, all conforming to the data warehouse bus architecture. For more details on *data marts* and *bus architecture* we refer the reader to Kimball and Ross (2002), whose authors have actually introduced these concepts in the warehousing literature;
- **Data Access Tools:** This is a collection of ad hoc query tools, report writers, data mining applications, etc., all designed to query, report or analyse data stored in the data warehouse;

The data warehouse architecture described above was proposed for traditional relational databases, where the data is structured and therefore easier to manipulate. In the case of other types of complex data though, this architecture might need some alterations to support the complex scenario.

EMERGING DOMAINS IN DATA WAREHOUSING

Nowadays the information is very dynamic and many applications create huge amounts of data everyday. For example, millions of transactions are completed continuously in large online shops (e.g., Amazon, eBay, etc.), many banking systems, share markets etc. Companies in the entire world are in a tight competition to provide better services and attract more clients. Hence, an easy customer access to web applications and the ability to perform transactions anytime from anywhere has been the fastest growing feature of the business applications in the last few years.

More, the data itself cannot be labelled as "simple" anymore (that is, numerical or symbolic) but it can now be expressed in different formats (structured, unstructured, images, sounds, etc.), it can come from different sources, or can be temporal (that is, it would change its structure and/or values in time) (Darmont & Boussaïd, 2006). Consequently, different types of storage, manipulation and processing are required in order to manage this complex data. New visions on data warehousing and data mining are therefore required.

During the last few years we could witness a growing amount of research work, determined by the growing size of the data warehouses which need to be build, the more and more heterogeneous data which needs to be integrated and stored, and the complex tools needed to query it. This section discusses therefore some of the trends in the area.

Spatial Data Warehousing

This is an area concerned with integration of spatial data with multidimensional data analysis techniques. The term 'spatial' is used in a geographical sense, meaning data that includes descriptors about how objects are located on Earth. Mainly, this is done using coordinates.

There are quite a few types of data which can be considered as spatial, as follows: data obtained via mobile devices (e.g., GPS), geo-sensory data, data about land usage etc. These types of data are collected either by private companies (e.g., mobile data) or by public governmental bodies (e.g., land data). Because this type of information could be used to take security decisions, spatial data warehousing becomes therefore a key technique in enabling access to data and data analysis for decision making support.

Spatial data warehousing can be seen as an integration of two main techniques: spatial data handling and multidimensional data analysis (Damiani & Spaccapietra, 2006).

Spatial data handling can be done using two types of systems:

- **Spatial Database Management Systems:** These extend the functionality of regular DBMS by including features for efficient storage, manipulation and querying of spatial data. Two such commercial spatial DBMS are Oracle Spatial and IBM DB2 Spatial Extender (Damiani & Spaccapietra, 2006). Note that spatial DBMS are not for direct end-user usage, but would be interrogated by database specialists to produce reports, various analyses, etc.;
- GIS (Geographical Information System) is an integration of computer programs written to read and represent information from a spatial DBMS, and present it in a nice visual way to the end-user. Note that, in this case the end-user would be the direct consumer of the GIS output, without the need of a database specialist's help;

Multidimensional data analysis is a leading technique in many domains, where various quantitative variables are measured against dimensions, such as time, location, product etc. Information is stored in cubes, at the intersection between selected dimensions, and offers the possibility of analysis by drilling-down, rolling-up, slicing, dicing etc.

By integrating spatial data with multidimensional data analysis technique, spatial information can be studied from different perspectives, including a spatial dimension. This integration is already very powerful in existing business systems, for example in warehousing enterprise information, where localisation of data could be decisive. Nevertheless, spatial data warehousing is still a young research area, where multidimensional models are yet to be determined and implemented. The reason why this area is a step behind the business domains is because spatial data is peculiar and complex, and spatial data management technology has only recently reached maturity (Damiani & Spaccapietra, 2006).

Research work in this area started ten years ago with the introduction of concepts of 'spatial dimension' and 'spatial measure' by Han et al. (1998). Following that, most recent research literature in spatial data warehousing includes: Rivest et al. (2001), Fidalgo et al. (2004), Scotch and Parmantoa (2005), and many others. A comprehensive and formal data model for spatial data warehousing was still a major research issue. Damiani and Spaccapietra (2006) proposed a novel spatial multidimensional data model for spatial objects with geometry, called Multigranular Spatial Data Warehouse (MuSD) where they suggest representing spatial information at multiple levels of granularity.

Future work and trends identified in spatial data warehousing are related to storage, manipulation and analysis of complex spatial objects. These are objects that cannot be represented using geometries such as lines, polygons, etc., but they are spatio-temporal and continuous object: an example is the concept of trajectory of a moving entity. Research is focused nowadays on obtaining summarised data out of database of trajectories, by using the concept of similarity and proposing new methods of measuring this similarity.

Text Data Warehousing

Recently, this area has known more and more research interest, because in an enterprise setting the data which needs to be stored in a data warehouse does not usually come only from the operational database systems, but also from a range of other sources (such as email, documents, reports). Generally, it can be said that in an enterprise environment the information lives in structured, unstructured and semi-structured sources. In order to integrate data from structured systems (relational databases) with the structured or unstructured data, current approaches use Information Retrieval techniques. Other approaches propose to use Information Extraction paradigms. We present here some of the research work which use these approaches.

In order to incorporate text documents into a data warehouse where the data from structured systems is also stored, the same components and steps of the warehousing process, including ETL (Extract-Transform-Load), need to be followed (Kimball & Ross, 1996, 2002). The source documents need to be identified, then the documents need to undergo some transformations (e.g., striping emails of their header and storing them as separate entities, or striping documents of their format and storing only the text component); eventually, the documents are physically moved into the data warehouse.

For each document, two components need to be stored in the data warehouse: the document itself and the metadata (this is, information about the document which can be read by the computer, e.g., size, title, subject, version, author, etc.). The metadata is stored in the data warehouse in a separate section, called metadata repository. Kimball (2002) deems that, for highly complex metadata, even a small star schema can be constructed, where the fact table would store the actual documents, while the different types of metadata would be stored in dimensions.

To store the document content itself, Information Retrieval approaches treat it as a "bag of words". Each word from the document is scanned and tokenised, the linking and stop words are removed, and the output of the procedure is a list of words - where each word receives a weight, based on the number of its appearances in the initial text. The output is used in so called "inverted index", where an index is created by sorting the list of terms and, for each term, a list of documents which contain each term is kept. Other more complex indexes also keep the number of appearances, or the position(s) where the term appears, in order to support proximity queries (Badia, 2006). In a vector-space approach, queries are represented as vectors of query terms (where the non-content words have been removed) and answering those queries actually means to find the document vectors of terms which are closest to the query vector.

The IR (Information Retrieval) approaches are criticised because they only utilise the physical terms appearing in the documents, while these terms are "(at best) second-order indicators of the content of a document". More, the vector-space approach has some issues related to the usage of words as such, especially where synonyms, homonyms, and other relationships can appear (research work has proposed to solve these issues by employing the concept of 'thesaurus') (Badia, 2006).

Information Extraction (IE) is another approach employed to solve text data warehousing problem. In this case, the input collection of documents are analysed using "shallow parsing" to perform entity extraction (to determine which entities are referred to in the text), link extraction (to determine which entities are in any sort of relationships) and event extraction (to determine what events are described by the entities and links discovered). The information extracted would then be integrated into a data warehouse.

It is possible that IR-oriented techniques would dominate the text warehousing area for a while, because there is still a lot of research work proposing solutions to deal with the identified issues. However, it is prognosed that IE approaches will see a rapid growing in the near future, fuelled by the boost in requests for text mining and consequently for more efficient text warehousing techniques (Badia, 2006).

Web Data Warehousing

Web data has been an increasing presence nowadays, because the World Wide Web offers the foundation for many large-scale web applications to be developed.

One area of research is XML warehousing. It has been predicted that soon most of the stored data will be in XML format (Pardede, 2007). Other authors also predict that XML will become the 'lingua franca' of the web (Mignet et al., 2003). It is therefore critical that efficient and scalable XML warehousing techniques should exist. At the same time, the great flexibility of the XML format for data representation and the dynamicity of available XML data increase the difficulty which is naturally associated with the task of storing huge amounts of information.

ORGANIZATION OF THE BOOK

The book is organized into 11 chapters. A brief description of each of the chapters follows:

Chapter 1 addresses a classical data warehousing problem which involves transactional databases. Data warehousing is often thought as a transformation from transaction and operational databases. This chapter describes a two-tiered segmentation approach for transaction data warehousing.

Chapter 2 focuses on real-time data warehousing. As opposed to traditional data warehousing which is static, a real-time data warehousing focuses on how data warehousing is maintained for real-time databases. This includes various kinds of update techniques for data warehousing.

Chapter 3 introduces a new kind of data warehousing based on deductive logic. Various access methods and aggregation of logic data are described using some examples. A query language: Datalog is also explained.

Chapter 4 studies trajectory data warehousing, particularly for behaviour analysis and tracking. This covers trajectory ontology design patterns using trajectory semantic. A case study on animal tracking is used in this chapter.

Chapter 5 describes spatio-temporal data warehousing, and the use of spatio-temporal OLAP queries. This also focuses on user behaviour to find similarity among users. The complexity of spatio-temporal OLAP is also examined.

Chapter 6 introduces the concept of NoSQL in data warehousing. NoSQL is a new wave of database management system, and the impact of NoSQL in data warehousing is still in the process of maturity. This chapter discusses the main concepts of NoSQL data warehousing.

Chapter 7 introduces the concept of Big Data in data warehousing. Big Data is a new emerging technology in data management and processing. This chapter evaluates commercial and open source Business Intelligence platforms for big data warehousing.

Chapter 8 focuses specifically on the index structure, also in the context of big data and data warehousing. Indexing is an important part of efficient data access, and consequently, indexing in big data warehousing is a critical part of the success of adoption of big data warehousing.

Chapter 9 focuses on a different aspect of big data, namely multidimensional analysis. As big data involves high dimensional data, the impact to data warehousing becomes enormous.

Chapter 10 discusses the traditional, and yet still important, in data warehousing, namely ETL (Extract-Transform-Load). This chapter discusses the ETL processes using a domain specific modelling approach.

Finally, chapter 11 studies how sequential patterns are discovered in the presence of item constraints. Pattern discovery is an ultimate goal of data warehousing, and this chapter highlights these characteristics.

David Taniar
Monash University, Australia

Wenny Rahayu
La Trobe University, Australia

REFERENCES

Badia, A. (2006). Text Warehousing: Present and Future. In *Processing and Managing Complex Data for Decision Support*. Idea Group Publishing. doi:10.4018/978-1-59140-655-6.ch004

Damiani, M. L., & Spaccapietra, S. (2006). Spatial Data Warehouse Modelling. In *Processing and Managing Complex Data for Decision Support*. Idea Group Publishing. doi:10.4018/978-1-59140-655-6.ch001

Darmont, J., & Boussaïd, O. (2006). *Processing and Managing Complex Data for Decision Support*. Idea Group Publishing. doi:10.4018/978-1-59140-655-6

Fidalgo, R. N., Times, V. C., Silva, J., & Souza, F. (2004), GeoDWFrame: a framework for guiding the design of geographical dimensional schemas. *Proceedings of the 6th International Conference on Data Warehousing and Knowledge Discovery (DaWaK 2004), 3181*, 26-37. 10.1007/978-3-540-30076-2_3

Inmon, W. H. (2005). *Building the Data Warehouse*. Wiley.

Kimball, R. (1996). *The Data Warehouse Toolkit*. Wiley & Sons.

Kimball, R., & Ross, M. (2002). *The Data Warehouse Toolkit*. Wiley & Sons.

Marakas, G. M. (2003). *Modern Data Warehousing, Mining, and Visualisation*. Prentice-Hall.

Mignet, L., Barbosa, D., & Veltri, P. (2003). The XML Web: A first study. In *Proceed. of the 12th International World Wide Web Conference (WWW 2003)* (pp. 500-510). ACM. 10.1145/775152.775223

Pardede, E. (2007). *eXtensible Markup Language (XML) Document Update in XML Database Storages* (PhD thesis). LaTrobe University, Australia.

Rivest, S., Bedard, Y., & Marchand, P. (2001). Towards better support for spatial decision making: Defining the characteristics of spatial on-line analytical processing (SOLAP). *Geomatica*, *55*(4), 539–555.

Scotch, M., & Parmantoa, B. (2005). SOVAT: Spatial OLAP visualisation and analysis tool. *Proceedings of the 38th Hawaii International Conference on System Sciences*.

Chapter 1
A Two–Tiered Segmentation Approach for Transaction Data Warehousing

Xiufeng Liu
Technical University of Denmark, Denmark

Huan Huo
University of Technology Sydney, Australia

Nadeem Iftikhar
University College of Northern Denmark, Denmark

Per Sieverts Nielsen
Technical University of Denmark, Denmark

ABSTRACT

Data warehousing populates data from different source systems into a central data warehouse (DW) through extraction, transformation, and loading (ETL). Massive transaction data are routinely recorded in a variety of applications such as retail commerce, bank systems, and website management. Transaction data record the timestamp and relevant reference data needed for a particular transaction record. It is a non-trivial task for a standard ETL to process transaction data with dependencies and high velocity. This chapter presents a two-tiered segmentation approach for transaction data warehousing. The approach uses a so-called two-staging ETL method to process detailed records from operational systems, followed by a dimensional data process to populate the data store with a star or snowflake schema. The proposed approach is an all-in-one solution capable of processing fast/slowly changing data and early/ late-arriving data. This chapter evaluates the proposed method, and the results have validated the effectiveness of the proposed approach for processing transaction data.

DOI: 10.4018/978-1-5225-5516-2.ch001

INTRODUCTION

A data warehouse is the decision-making database which holds the data extracted from transaction systems, operational data stores, or other external source systems. The process of processing the data from source systems into a central data warehouse is traditionally referred as data warehousing (Kimball & Caserta, 2004). The transformed data in a data warehouse (Inmon, 2002) are typically saved into the tables with a star schema and accessed by decision-support systems, such as Online Analytical Processing (OLAP) tools and Business Intelligence (BI) applications (March & Hevner, 2007). Data warehousing systems run ETL jobs at a regular time interval, such as daily, weekly or monthly. Operational data management systems create dynamic data through transactions. Transaction data are increasingly common across a variety of applications, such as telecommunications, bank systems, retail commerce, and website management. Transaction data consist of the records of individuals and events, and can be changed during business operations, e.g., add new orders, update or cancel existing orders. These changes are updated to the data warehouse to support decision-making purposes. The detailed transaction records in a data warehouse can trace the operations of an operational processing system, called System of Record (SOR) (Inmon, 2003). Usually, an ETL processes transaction records according to the arriving order of records, e.g., the timestamps, and the dependencies between records (if they exist). For example, when loading data to the data warehouse with a star schema, the dimension records are usually loaded first, then fact records, due to their foreign-key referencing relationship. If a fact record arrives first, the looking-up of a dimensional key will fail. Another example is to load data into snowflake schema tables where the foreign-key references also exist between normalized tables. The standard approach for loading snowflake schema tables is to load parent tables first (referenced tables), then to load child tables (referencing tables). As this approach loads data according to table dependency, there are some weaknesses: It requires extra space for storing early-arriving data; fact data loading cannot proceed until the dimension data have been loaded; and parallel loading becomes difficult, due to table dependency. Besides, another challenge in data warehousing is how to deal with loading fast-/slowly-changing data. For example, for loading of slowly changing dimension data (SCDs) (Kimball & Caserta, 2004), the traditional approach is first to check history records in the DW, then update the date attributes of the records, finally add a new record. All of the above are the challenges for a transaction data warehousing system.

This chapter proposes a two-tiered segmentation solution for a transaction data warehousing system. The proposed solution first uses a two-staging ETL to process detailed transaction records towards an SOR data warehouse (Tier-1 segmentation), then uses a second ETL process to populate the dimensional data store (DDS), which is called DDS process (Tier-2 segmentation). The two-staging ETL is responsible for populating the data from operational source systems into an SOR data warehouse, while the DDS process is responsible for populating the data from SOR into a multi-dimension data store. The two segmentations have a similar structure in which an additional data store is introduced for the ETL. The purpose of this design is to ease ETL optimizations, for example, implement parallelization and lower the complexity of data transformation. Moreover, this design is a one-stop solution to deal with early/late-arriving data, and fast/slowly-changing data (It will be discussed shortly). This solution is more efficient and less intrusive compared with the standard approach, which is, particularly, favorable for processing transaction data.

In summary, this chapter makes the following contributions: 1) The authors propose a novel 2-tier segmentation approach for a transaction data warehousing system; 2) The authors propose an all-in-one method for handling fast/slowly-changing data, and early/late-arriving data, which is easy for the maintenance and optimization of an ETL; 2) The authors propose a less-intrusive ETL method with a fast loading step, which can effectively reduce the downtime of a business intelligence system; 3) The authors propose an augmentation process for handling early/late-arriving data; and 4) the proposed approach can decouple ETL dependencies, which makes it possible to parallelize data loading.

The remainder of the chapter is structured as follows. Section 2 gives an overview of the proposed solution; Section 3 and 4 present the details of the proposed solution, including two-staging ETL process and DDS data process, respectively; Section 5 presents the evaluation; Section 6 discusses some issues; Section 7 presents related work; and the final section concludes the chapter and presents the future work.

SOLUTION OVERVIEW

Figure 1 shows an overview of the proposed solution where the whole ETL is divided into two segments, *Tier 1 and Tier 2*. The tier-1 segmentation is a two-staging ETL process consisting of two staging areas, SSA Lv1 and SSA Lv2. SSA Lv1 maintains a database schema same as the data source system, while SSA Lv2 maintains a schema same as the data warehouse (SOR). The use of SSA Lv1 is the standard data warehousing practice, which is used as a temporary store to keep the data from source systems. In this chapter, the authors introduce the additional staging area, SSA Lv2, to lower the complexity of handling dynamic transaction data, and to support early/late-arriving data processing, as well as fast/slowly-changing data processing. The two staging areas can be different tables in the same database or in different databases, and the second staging area can even use main memory for temporarily storing data. The data in both staging areas will be removed at the end or at the beginning of a job iteration of ETL.

At the point of data extraction, an ETL process detects the changes in the data from a source operational system and assigns new operation codes to indicate the changes. As the source system is an operational system, the transaction records can be labeled with timestamps, which makes it possible for ETL to decide which data to be extracted. The job for data extraction typically is run during the non-peak period of an operational system, such as at midnight. The data in SSA Lv1 staging area can be re-used in case of job failures. The data from SSA Lv1 staging area are then transformed and loaded into the SSA Lv2 staging area according to user-defined transformation rules. At the same time, the necessary key validations are proceeded to validate the referencing relationship between tables. After the transformation and key validations, the data are saved in the SSA Lv2 tables, and ready for the loading into the SOR data warehouse. The design of using SSA Lv2 makes it possible to decouple the loading from the extraction and transformation processes, i.e., ET-L. The loading can be carried out at a later time when the decision support system is free. The SOR data warehouse maintains detailed transaction data and the changing history of dynamic data, such as customers' addresses, product shipping status. A common data warehousing practice usually builds OLAP cubes based on the SOR directly, but this may be time-consuming, due to the big size of the data in SOR. To rectify it, the authors introduce a dimensional data store (DDS) process in the tier-2 segmentation to populate the data from SOR into DDS, then build OLAP cubes based on a multidimensional data warehouse. This makes the cube building lightweight and fast as no further transformation or re-structuring is needed. During the DDS data process, a data pipeline area (DPA) is employed to temporarily save the aggregated results from the summarization process, then the results will be further combined and saved into DDS.

TWO-LEVEL DATA STAGING ETL PROCESS

Data Extraction

The data extraction process is introduced as the following. The authors use a timestamp-capturing approach to extract the data from an operational system. i.e., the records are extracted according to the latest transaction dates appended to them. The extraction logic is simply to select the records whose latest transaction date falls into the date ranging between two consecutive ETL jobs. For example, suppose that the date of an ETL job running on day 1 is January 1, 2014. If it is the first time to run the data exaction job, all the data in the source systems will be extracted. Therefore, the extraction begin date is set to an earlier date, e.g., 1900-01-01 (no records were generated earlier than this date), and the extraction end date is set to the current date, i.e., 2014-01-01. On day 2, January 2, 2014, the extraction begin date is set to the last extraction end date, i.e., 2014-01-01, and the end date is set to the current date, i.e., 2014-01-02. If an ETL job runs more frequently, e.g., several times in a day, the attributes of date and time both have to be used in order to determine which records to be extracted from a source system within a time slot.

Data Transformation

The data transformation mechanism is introduced in the following. A record is extracted from a source system to SSA Lv1 staging area and marked with the transaction (Tx) type code, "I", "U" or "D", representing Insert, Update or Delete operations occurred in the source system. Since the used method is scoped to handle the data from online transaction processing systems, the transaction type codes can be explicitly specified in the source tables, or can be determined by reading the transaction logs, which is out of the discussion of this paper. When a record is extracted, a new operation code is used to identify the transaction occurred in the source system and based on the new operation code to decide which operation should be taken to add the record into the SOR, i.e., update or insertion. The reasons for using new operation codes, instead of the transaction type codes, are as follows. First, a transaction type code only represents the type of the action performed on a source table, which is not fully applicable to the detailed records in the SOR table. For example, in the source system, the tables, T 1 and table T 2 (Figure 2), both have the transaction type code "I", and the same business key "BK1". If populating the data to T 3 is according to the transaction type code, the operations taken both are "insert". Then,

Figure 1. The overview of the 2-tiered segmentation ETL solution for transaction data

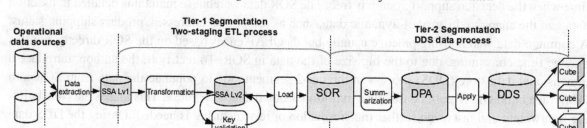

Figure 2. Many-to-one mapping

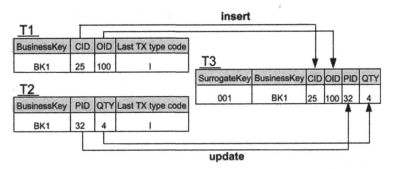

an exception will be raised. For the daily data extraction, the job runs at the end of the day to extract the data based on the last transaction action applied to a record. If multiple actions are applied on the same day, the extraction will skip all the previous actions. Suppose that a record is inserted then updated in the source system, and the corresponding transaction type codes are "I" and "U". If it is still based on the transaction type code to populate the data into an SOR table, the action will be "update", which is obviously wrong. Therefore, new operation codes are necessary to guide an ETL process on how to extract the data from a source table to a target table.

To handle the dynamic data from an operational processing system, different operation codes are needed to indicate what actions to be taken for transferring the data into an SOR table. Table 1 lists all the operation codes. Begin operation (B) means to add a new record into the SOR table by insertion, and to set the **B**egin date attribute to the current date. End begin operation (EB) means that there is a previous version of the record in the SOR table (with the same business key). The actions to be taken are: first mark the previous record as an old version by updating the **E**nd date attribute, and then add a new record with the new **B**egin date. End operation (E) means that there is a previous version in the SOR table, and it needs to be marked as "history" by setting its **E**nd date attribute to current date because the record was deleted in the source system. Augment operation (A) means to add a new **A**ugmented record into the SOR table. The augmented record is also a dummy record generated when handling early-arriving data, which only contains surrogate and business key values. Deactivate augment operation (DA) means that the values for the blank attributes of the augmented record are available for the update. The augment record in the SOR table will be **D**eactivated by turning off the augment flag.

Table 1. Operation codes

Operation Code	Description
B	Begin operation
EB	End begin operation
E	End operation
A	Augment operation
DA	Deactivate augment operation

Algorithm 1 describes the data transformation process. For each record from SSA Lv1, the algorithm first checks its existence by looking up the SOR table using its business key (BK) (see line 2). According to the result and the transaction type code, the algorithm then decides which operation code should be applied to the record (see line 4–11 and 13–19). If the record has already been labeled and added to the SSA Lv2 table, then the algorithm should update the record in SSA Lv2, instead of inserting a new record. This can be done by the following two approaches. The first approach is to look up the SSA Lv2 table, then to decide which action to be taken between insert and update. The second approach is to merge the two records, which is also called "upsert" in some ETL tools, such as Pentaho PDI (Pentaho, 2015). During the data transformation process, a new surrogate key is allocated to replace the natural primary key, which is simply done by assigning a sequence number to the record. If the extracted record has the last transaction type code "I" or "U", and cannot be found in the SOR table, it will be identified as a new record. The algorithm also needs to look up on the SSA Lv2 table to check its existence. If the record is also not found, the algorithm then assigns a new surrogate key, and inserts the record into the SSA Lv2 table (see line 14–19).

Figure 3 illustrates the transformation process using an example. In this example, the transformation process involves a source table, a lookup table and a target table. The example describes the change detection approach, and how to move records from SSA Lv1 to SSA Lv2 according to operation codes. Four representative data transformation scenarios are identified as follows. The first scenario is to handle

Algorithm 1. Transformation

```
Require: Data has been loaded into SSA Lv1
1:  row ← Read a record from SSA Lv1
2:   found ← Lookup the SOR table by row[BK]
3:  if found then
4:         if row[T xCode] = D then
5:             Transpose and merge SSA Lv2 with row[OP ] = E
6:         else          // row[T xCode] = U or I
7:             arg ← Is an argument record in the SOR table?
8:          if arg then
9:             Transpose and merge SSA Lv2 with row[OP ] = DA
10:        else
11:            Transpose and merge SSA Lv2 with row[OP ] = EB
12: else
13:         if row[T xCode] = U or I then
14:             found ← Look up SSA Lv2 by row[BK]
15:           if found then
16:               Transpose and merge SSA Lv2 with row[OP ] = B
17:         else
18:               row[SK] ← Get a new surrogate key
19:               Transpose and insert SSA Lv2 with row[OP ] = B
```

the records resulted by the update or insert operation from source systems. The previous versions of the records have already loaded into the SOR table, e.g., the records streamed from SSA Lv1 with the business key values, BK="BK1" and BK="BK2". Since the records with the same business key values are found in the SOR table, the end begin operation"EB" is identified for the transaction codes (TxCode), "I" and "U", which are added to the operation code field (OP) in the SSA Lv2 table. The surrogate key values from the SOR table are re-used and added to the SK field in the SSA Lv2 table. The new begin date (NEWBD) is set to the transaction date (TxDate), and the end date (ED) is set to one day before TxDate (recall that the ETL job runs at the daily time interval). The other attributes in the SSA Lv2 table, including CustomerID (CID) and OrderID (OID), are mapped from the corresponding attributes in the SSA Lv1 table directly. The second scenario is to handle late-arriving data from the source systems, e.g., the record with the business key value BK="BK3" and TxCode "U". Since an augmented record is found in the SOR table with SK="003" and augmentation flag value "yes" (AF=Y), the deactivate augmentation operation "DA" is identified. The attribute values from SSA Lv1 are added to the corresponding attributes in the SSA Lv2 table. The late-arriving values are used to update the blank attributes in the augmented record in the SOR table. The third scenario is to handle the deletions from the source systems, e.g., the record with BK = "BK4" and TxCode = "D". The transformation process looks up the SOR table using the business key value, and the record with the surrogate key value "004" is found. Hence, the end operation "E" is identified for this record, while the other attribute values do not have to be mapped from the SSA Lv1 table since it is the record of deletion. The fourth scenario is to handle newly inserted records from the source system, e.g., the record with BK = "BK5" and TxCode "I". Since the transformation process cannot find any previous version in the SOR table, the begin operation "B" is identified, representing that a new record will be added to the SOR table. Thus, a new surrogate key value is generated, and a new begin date (NEWBD) is set to the transaction date.

Figure 3. Data transformation

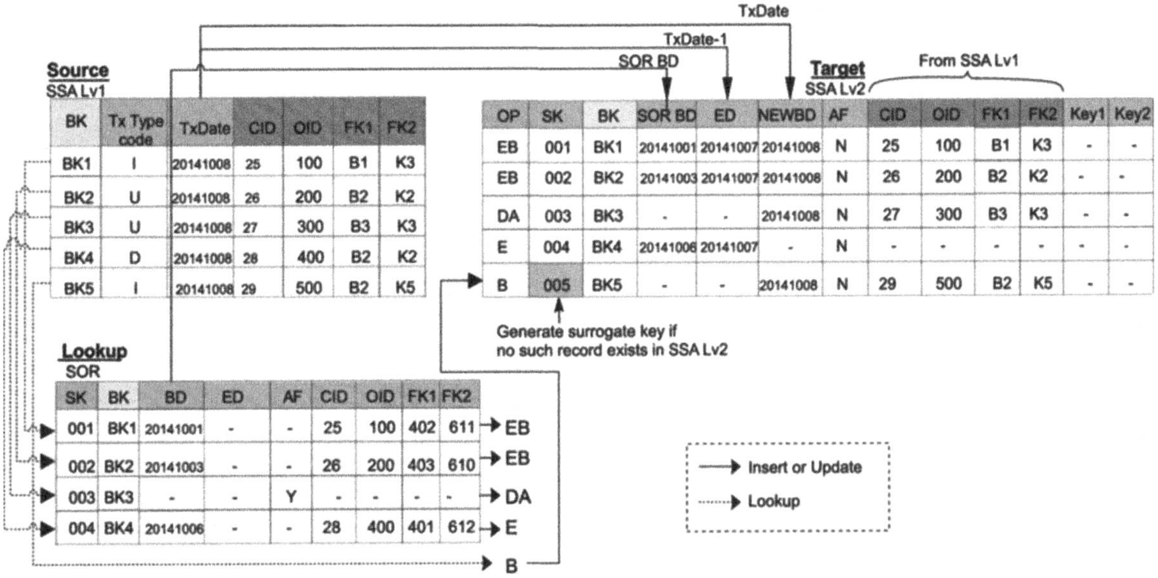

Key Validation

The key validation process is to ensure the referential integrity between tables. Recall that in the previous section, the foreign keys were mapped from the SSA Lv1 table to the SSA Lv2 table, but the foreign keys on the SOR table were not updated directly. The creation of foreign-key references is delayed to the stage of key validation. The purpose of doing this is to support handling early-arriving data in a timely manner, i.e., if the data from a child table (or referencing table) arrive, an ETL job can be run immediately without having to wait for the data to the parent tables (the tables referenced by the child table). Algorithm 2 describes the key validation process in detail. The algorithm first looks up the foreign-key value for a row in the tables both in SOR and SSA Lv2 using the business key value. If the foreign-key referenced row is found, the returned surrogate key value will be used to update the foreign-key attribute of the current row. The reason for looking up both SOR and SSA Lv2 tables is that the referenced rows might have already been loaded into the SOR table by the previous ETL job or loaded into the SSA Lv2 table in the current job. If the referenced row cannot be found both places, it means that the current row is early-arriving data. Then, the algorithm will create a blank record with only the new surrogate key value and the business key value and add the record into the referenced table (see line 10–11). This process is called *augmentation*. The blank values will be updated in the next key validation process later in the current ETL job or the next job. The augmentation process thus handles early- and late-arriving data without violating the referential integrity of the tables during the loading. Moreover, the augmentation process can improve the ETL efficiency. Let us take loading fact and dimension data as the example. If a record to a fact table arrives at 4:00 am, but the record to the dimension table arrives at 6:00 am, the loading of the fact data needs be halted to 6:00 am if the augmentation process is not used. Furthermore, the augmentation process makes parallel loading possible as there is no dependency.

Algorithm 2. Key validation

```
Require: Data has been loaded into the SSA Lv2 table
1: row ← Read a record from the SSA Lv2 table
2: found ← Look up the SOR referenced table to get the key value
3: if found then
4:          Update the row with the found key value
5: else
6:          found ← Look up the SSA Lv2 referenced table to get the key
value
7:      if found then
8:          Update the row with the found key value
9:      else
10:             sk ← Generate a new surrogate key
11:             Add an augmented record (with sk and OP=A) into the SSA Lv2
table
```

Figure 4 shows the key validation processes using two representative scenarios. The first scenario is to validate the foreign-key values from the referenced records that have already been loaded into the SOR table, while the second scenario is to validate the key through the augmentation process for the early-arriving data. Since SSA Lv2 table is used as the staging area for holding the data before loading, the key validation process in fact uses the SSA Lv2 table as the source and target tables for reading and writing the data, whereas the lookup tables may be in SOR and in SSA Lv2. In the first scenario, for the records with the surrogate key (SK) "001", "002" and "003", the key validation process finds the

Figure 4. Key validation

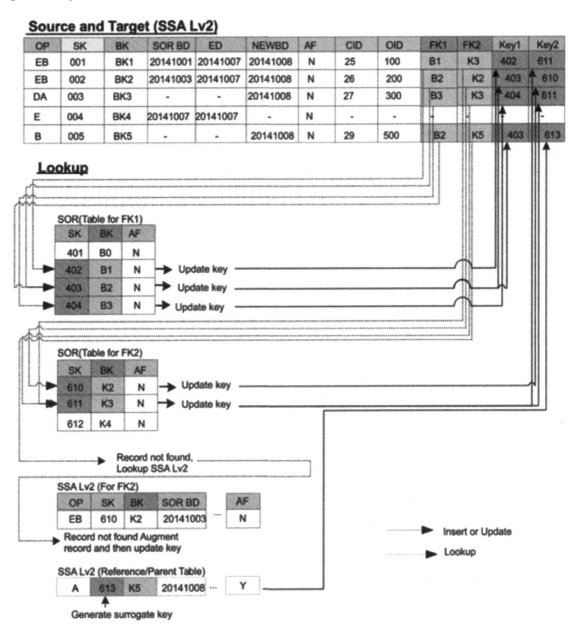

foreign key values (also the surrogate key values) in the SOR table, then updates the found values to the attributes, Key1 ("402", "403" and "404") and Key2 ("611", "610" and "611"), respectively. In the second scenario, for the record with SK="005", the foreign-key value is found in the SOR table using the business key value, "B2", but none is found for "K5" in FK2. The key validation process, thus, further looks up the foreign-key referenced table in the SSA Lv2 table but fails again. Then, an augmented record (dummy record) is created, with the business key value, "K5", and the new surrogate key value, "613". The new record is inserted into the SSA Lv2 table, and the augmentation flag (AF) is turned on, by setting its value as "Y". The blank values in the augmented record will be updated by the current or next running of the ETL job.

Data Loading

After data transformation and key validation, the data are saved temporarily in the SSA Lv2 table, and ready to be loaded into the SOR. Data loading process loads the data according to the operation code identified for each row. Before the loading step, no data is written into the data warehouse. Instead, the data is cached in the SSA Lv2 table, and the data are loaded into the data warehouse altogether by the loading step. This design can make the loading process simpler and more efficient (see the experimental results in Section 5). For standard data warehousing practices, writing data into a data warehouse lasts the whole ETL process. And, it is conducted usually under the condition that the business intelligence system is taken off-line to ensure data reading consistency from the system. In contrast, the proposed approach reduces data warehouse intervention time (or downtime) to the time of data loading. The data to be loaded into SOR tables are classified into two categories, *static data* and *dynamic data* (this classification is one of the common data warehousing practices). Static data is unlikely to be changed over time, such as name, birthday, gender in the customer information, while dynamic data is more likely to be changed, such as address and phone number. For static data, the loading process simply loads the data into a static SOR table, while for the dynamic data, a history table is used to track the change history of the data, with *begin* and *end* date attributes. Algorithm 3 describes how a row is loaded according to the operation codes.

The following lists four representative loading scenarios. The first one is of loading a new version of dynamic data, such as a slowly changing dimension record with the operation code, "EB" (see Figure 5). The static data in the row from SSA Lv2 table is directly updated to the static table in the SOR. For the dynamic data, the loading process first looks up the history table with SK="001", then updates the end date of the previous version, i.e., update the end date (ED) to "20141007". In the end, a new version of the dynamic data is created, and added to the history table, with the begin date (BD) set to "20141008", and end date set to "99991231", meaning that it is the latest record.

The second scenario is about loading late-arriving data (see Figure 6). The record from the SSA Lv2 table has an operation code of "DA", meaning that an augmented record exists in the SOR. The loading process, thus, locates the augmented record using the surrogate key, then updates the blank attributes with new values, and turns off the augmentation flag in the end. A new record is created, and added to the history table, with the same surrogate key "003", business key "BK3", begin date "20141008" and end date "9991231". The third scenario is of loading a new transaction record (see Figure 7). The record is labeled with the operation code, "B". There are two records generated, and added to the static

Algorithm 3. Data loading

Require: All the rows are in the SSA Lv2 table

1: *row* ← Read a record from the SSA Lv2 table

2: **if** *row[OP]* = B **then**

3:                    Insert into the static table

4:                    Insert into the history table

5: **else if** *row[OP]* = EB **then**

6:                    Update the static table if having changed values.

7:                    Update the end date of the previous version in the history table

8:                    Add a new record to the history table: with the same surrogate key as the previous version; with current date as the begin date; with "99991231" as the end date.

9: **else if** *row[OP]* = E **then**

10:                    Update the static table, and set the last Tx type code as "D".

11:                    Update the history table, and set the end date as the current date.

12: **else if** *row[OP]* = DA **then**

13:                    Update the static table with new static values and turn off the augmentation flag.

14:                    Add a new record to the history table: with the same surrogate key as the static table; with the current date as the begin date; with "9999-12-31" as the end date.

15: **else if** *row[OP]* = A **then**

16:                    Add a new record to the static table: with a new surrogate key; with the current date as the begin date; with "9999-12-31" as the end date; and with the augmentation flag on.

Figure 5. Load a new version of a dynamic record

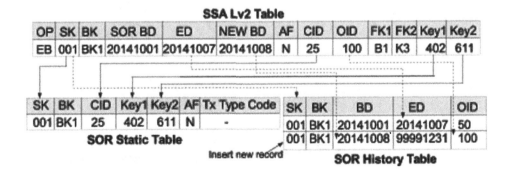

Figure 6. Load late-arriving data

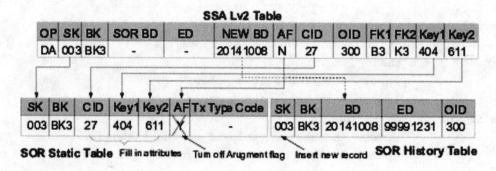

Figure 7. Load a new transaction record

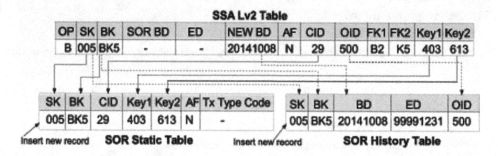

and dynamic tables, respectively. The two records maintain the same surrogate and business key. The last scenario is of loading an augmented record (see Figure 8). The record is labeled with the operation code, "A". The record was generated for handling early-arriving data during the key validation process. The record contains only surrogate key, business key, and the augmentation flag, while the other at-

Figure 8. Load an augmented record

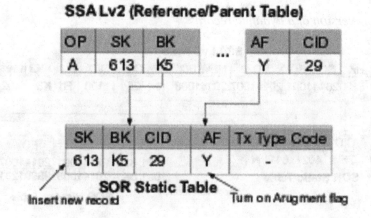

tributes are left to blank. The loading process simply adds the augmentation record to the static table. This augmented record will be deactivated (or updated) later in this iteration of an ETL job, or in the next iteration. The deactivation process is the second scenario above.

DDS DATA PROCESS

The DDS Data process summarizes and aggregates the SOR data into the DDS dimension and fact tables, and transforms data into MOLAP cubes. This process can be divided into the sub-processes including summarization, apply, and cube building, which are described in the following.

Summarization

Summarization is one of the DDS data processes in which data will be moved from SOR to DPA dimension and fact tables which have the similar schema as the tables in DDS. The rationale behind of moving data to DPA rather than directly to DDS tables is to absorb all the complicated process in this staging area such that the process of moving data to DDS will become simple. The summarization process uses a data extraction process to populate the data from SOR to DPA. The data staged in DPA can be processed and applied to DDS in the subsequent ETL process. In the following, the summarization processes for dimension and fact tables will be described, respectively.

Dimension Extraction

Algorithm 4 describes the dimension summarization process. The summarization process is run in the second phase which extracts the dimension data prepared by the two-staging ETL process described in Section 3. The data in SOR are the detailed records with the transaction date and type from the source systems. The dimension data in SOR are expressed in snowflaked or denormalized formats. The algorithm decides which records should be extracted to the DPA. That is, only the dimension records whose last transaction dates equal to or are greater than the current ETL starting date. If a record is not a slowly changing dimension and marked with "D" in its transaction type, it will not be extracted to DPA.

In fact, the dimension data extraction process is very similar to the two-staging ETL process described in Section 3. The tables in SOR also contain the last record transaction date and the transaction type. Based on the date and the transaction types, the dimension extraction process decides which extraction approach to be taken. Figure 9 uses a concrete example to illustrate this process. Assume that the dimension data have been loaded into the SOR table by the ETL process started at the "20141008" (see on the left of the figure). The extraction process will only retrieve the records with the Tx date equal or greater than the ETL starting date. The dimension data are extracted into the static DPA dimension table, and the SCD table, respectively (see on the right of the figure). The record marked with "D" is extracted to the SCD table for tracking changing history purpose.

Algorithm 4. Summarization for dimension tables

```
Require: Data are ready in SOR
1: t ← Select a table in SOR for extraction
2: if t is SCD table then
3:        if t is a snowflake and parent table then
4:                Extract all the records from t where last Tx date=current ETL
process date
5:                Extract the records from all the child tables that are refer-
ring the extracted records in parent table t
6:        else
7:                Extract all the records from t where last Tx date = ETL pro-
cess date
8: else
9:        Extract the records from t where last Tx date=ETL process date and
Tx type!=D
```

Figure 9. Dimension extraction from SOR to DPA

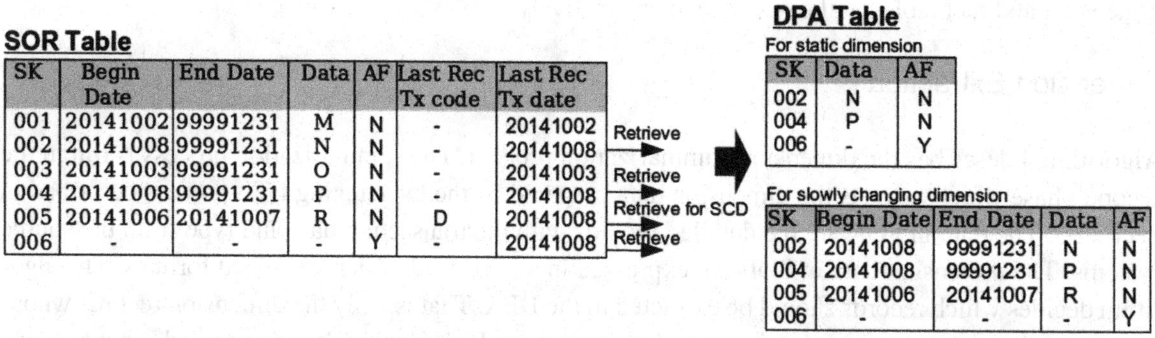

Fact Extraction

The fact extraction process is described in the following. Fact extraction is more complicated compared with the dimension extraction process. The purpose of fact extraction using DPA is to ensure the subsequent DDS Apply process to be simple, and the data in DDS will not be affected in case there is an error during the fact extraction process. In addition to the last record transaction date in SOR, the extraction process will also base on the actual affected date to determine records to be extracted. To identify which field in SOR is the actual affected date, it is required to examine what type of information the fact table is going to be stored. For example, to create a data warehouse with TPC-H star schema (Niel, 2007), the fact table lineorder holds the revenue, quantity, and supply cost measures. The actual affected date will be order date in the SOR table. For calculating the line order fact based on an actual affected date, the ETL process will select all the records in TPC-H tables in SOR with this affected date, process them and store in the DPA fact table. If the fact table in DPA contains the measures calculated previously, all the records in SOR table at or after the earliest affected date should be retrieved in order to rebuild the fact table. Figure 10 shows the example which the ETL process starts at "20140110", and the order date in this SOR table (orders) is the affected date. Suppose that now one of the customer keys was wrongly updated as 3 and must be corrected to 4. This will affect the aggregated amount in the lineorder fact table in the DPA. Then, the fact extraction process must retrieve all the SOR records with the affected date equal to "20140101", recalculates the measures for that date, and updates to the DPA.

Fact Measure Calculation

In the fact extraction process, the data retrieved from SOR tables are calculated before it can be inserted into the DPA fact table. For example, the quantity and supply cost of TPC-H are stored in SOR tables at the order level (or part level). As a customer might have multiple orders, in order to populate the data into the TPC-H with a star schema, the retrieved SOR records should be grouped by different customers, and the aggregated value is calculated and stored into the lineorder fact table.

Typically, there are several measures in a fact table, which are mapped from different SOR tables. An ETL job becomes complicated for handling the calculations for all measures together. Therefore, it would be easier to divide a calculation process into multiple small ETL processes. As shown in the lineorder fact table in Figure 11, there are eight measures total (the figure shows quantity and supply cost for the illustration). In this example, the ETL job 1 is responsible for calculating the item quantity found in the LineItem SOR table, and ETL job 2 is responsible for calculating the supply cost found in the PartSupp SOR table.

Figure 10. Fact extraction from SOR

SOR Table
OrderDate is the affected date

OrderKey	CustKey	OrderDate	...	TotalPrice	LastRecord TransactionDate
10	3	20140101	...	9.2	20140110

4

→ Retrieve all the records with affected date 20140101

Figure 11. Fact measure calculation by different ETL jobs

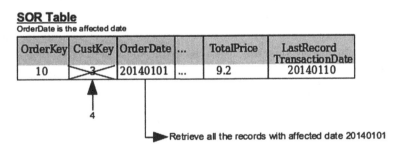

Fact Table
Lineorder

CustKey	SuppKey	PartKey	DateKey	Quantity	SupplyCost	...
10	3	1	1	10	120.2	...

Inserted by ETL job 1   Updated by ETL job 2

Since measures are calculated by different ETL jobs, the same fact record will be updated by different processes. There are two approaches for the DPA fact table to store the calculated measures from different jobs.

- **One Insert and Multiple Updates:** By this approach, the calculated measures for the same record from different ETL jobs are stored in the same record in DPA fact table. The first ETL job will insert the record into the DPA fact table with the measures for which it is responsible. The subsequent ETL jobs will update the same record for the other measures. It is shown in Figure 11 where ETL job 1 is responsible for inserting the record with the measure, *quantity,* while the subsequent jobs will do the update on the measures including supplyCost.
- **Multiple Inserts and Sum:** By this approach, the calculated measures for the same record from different ETL jobs are stored in different records in the DPA fact table. All the ETL jobs will insert the record with the measures for which it is responsible, together with dimension keys, into the DPA fact table. As shown in Figure 12, the Job 1 and 2 calculate the measures, quantity and supply cost, respectively, and insert as the separate rows with identical dimension key values into the lineorder fact table in DPA. These records will be merged into one record by the subsequent Apply process.

Apply

Apply is one of the DDS data process components in which data will be moved from DPA to DDS dimension and fact tables. For dimension table, the Apply process is described by Algorithm 5. Although the dimension extraction logic is nearly the same for static dimension and slowly changing dimension, the Apply process is quite different for them. In addition, the processing logic for slowly changing and snowflake dimension is more complicated. Suppose that the parent table in snowflake dimension is also an SCD table. In case there is a change in the attribute value in the parent dimension table, the current record will be ended by setting its end date, and a new record will be created in the parent table. In the child tables, all the records that are referring to the record in the parent table must be rebuilt (see line 8-11). Although DPA contains the latest record updated in SOR, it doesn't mean that the value changed in SOR is the field used in DDS. A Change Data Capture (CDC) process should be applied in order to detect the change in any attribute for the dimension table. If no change is found, no action has to be applied to the DDS.

Figure 12. DPA fact table for multiple inserts and sum approach

Fact Table
Lineorder

CustKey	SuppKey	PartKey	DateKey	Quantity	SupplyCost	
10	3	1	1	10		Inserted by ETL job 1
10	3	1	1		120.2	Inserted by ETL job 2

Measure calculated by ETL job 1   Measure calculated by ETL job 2

Algorithm 5. Apply process for dimension tables

```
1: Require: Dimension data are ready in DPA
2: t ← Select the dimension table t in DPA for Apply process
3:  row ← Read a record from the DPA dimension table
4: found ← Lookup DDS dimension table with the surrogate key, row[SK]
5: if found then
6:        if t is SCD table then
7:            if t is a snowflake table then
8:                Conduct CDC process. For change detected:
9:                    End the DDS record in the parent table, and insert
a new record with new SCD key
10:                   End all the records in the child table referring to
the parent table, and insert new records with
11:                   parent's new SCD key as the foreign key
12:           else
13:               Conduct CDC process.  For change detected:
14:                   End the DDS record and insert a new record with new
SCD key
15:      else
16:          Update the record found
17: else
18:       if t is SCD table then
19:           Insert a new record with a new SCD key
20:       else
21:            Insert a new record
```

Figure 13. The Apply process for slowly changing dimension table

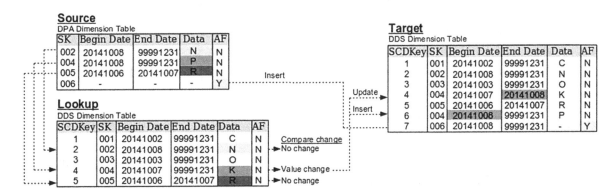

Algorithm 6. Apply process for fact tables

```
1: Require: Fact data are ready in DPA
2: t ← Select the fact table t in DPA for Apply process
3: Delete the records from DDS fact table with the same dimension key values
as t
4: Aggregate multiple fact records with the same dimension key (resulting from
Multiple insert and sum approach)
5: Insert the aggregated results into DDS fact table
```

For a static dimension table in SOR, its surrogate key can be reused when the data is extracted to DDS. However, it doesn't apply to a slowly changing dimension table since SOR adopts the same surrogate key plus the begin date and end date pair for different versions of a slowly changing dimension. A new surrogate key has to be generated for every slowly changing dimension in DDS, called Slowly Changing Dimension Key (SCD Key). SCD key is a sequence number generated by the ETL process, which is stored in a column of the fact table as the foreign key to the slowly changing dimension table. It is also shared across snowflake tables of the same dimension.

Figure 13 shows the example of the Apply process for slowly changing dimension table. The source is the DPA dimension table, while the target is the DDS dimension table. To populate new dimension records to the target table, the Apply process does the lookup operation on the target table based on the surrogate key and compare the required attribute to identify if there is change or not, e.g., on *Data* attribute in this example. In this example, no change is found for the records with SK="002" and "005". For the record with SK="004", a new value is detected, which results in updating the End date for the previous version in DDS table, and adding the new SCD dimension record. The End date of the previous version is updated as the current date of the ETL job. The last record with SK="006" is an argument record, and not found in the SCD table. A new record is inserted with the AF is on (AF=Y), and the Begin data is set to the current date of the ETL job.

The Apply process for fact tables is described in the following. It is much more simple compared with for dimension tables since all the complicated logic is handled in the Summarization process discussed in Section 4.3. Algorithm 6 describes the process.

As mentioned in Section 4.2.1, the Multiple Inserts and Sum approach is chosen for the fact extraction, by which DPA will store multiple records representing different measures for the same dimension key. In the Apply process, these records will be merged into a single record and populated to the DDS fact table (see Figure 14).

Cube Building

DDS is the multiple dimension data warehouse where the data are organized into a star schema, and snowflake schema. This data warehouse is to provide efficient OLAP analysis, which, for example, are further populated to a multidimensional OLAP (MOLAP) cube. Since DDS is already designed in dimensional modeling, the population from DDS to multi-dimensional cubes will not involve any business logic. All the necessary logics have been applied in Summarization and Apply described in the previ-

Figure 14. The Apply process for fact table

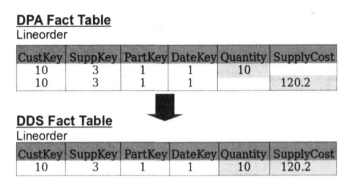

ous sections. This will greatly facilitate and accelerate the cube building process. There are many cube building tools available by the major Business Intelligence vendors, such as IBM, Microsoft, and Oracle. MOLAP cubes are typically deployed an OLAP engine to present the data from different dimensions.

EVALUATION

The evaluation was conducted on a DELL Latitude E7440 laptop (Intel i7-4600 quad-core processors 2.10GHz, 8GB RAM, and a 256GB SSD, running 64bit Fedora 21.0 with Linux 3.18.3 kernel). PostgreSQL 9.1 was used as the data warehouse system, with the following setting: *shared_buffers=1024MB, temp_buffers=512MB, work_mem=256MB, checkpoint_ segments=20* and default values for others. Pentaho Data Integration (PDI) (Pentaho, 2015) was used for the ETL.

TPC-H benchmark (TPC-H, 2015) was used for the evaluation of the two-staging ETL process, and TPC-H star schema benchmark (SSB) (Neil et. al., 2007) was for the DDS data process. The experimental data is generated using the TPC-H data generator, *dbgen*. For one scaling factor of dbgen, i.e., *SF = 1*, it can generate the following number of rows: 10,000 (supplier), 200,000 (part), 800,000 (partsupp), 150,000 (customer), 1,500,000 (order), 6,001,215 (lineitem).

The authors first create ETL jobs to load the data into the tables in SOR DW, in which each table is loaded by a separate job. The first scenario, *E1*, is a standard approach of loading data according to table dependencies (see Figure 15), while the second scenario, *E2*, uses the proposed approach (see Figure 16). E1 parallelizes loading the no-dependency tables (i.e., no foreign-key constraint between tables), while serializes loading the tables having dependency. The running of parallel and sequential jobs was achieved by the connected Pentaho job wrappers. That is, the jobs within the same job wrapper are run in parallel, while the jobs in different job wrappers are run sequentially. E2 uses the two-level staging ETL to handle the data arriving out of order, e.g., late/early-arriving data. The jobs, therefore, can be executed in parallel. For both scenarios, the authors lso measure the execution times when the pipeline parallelization is enabled, denoted by *E1'* and *E2'*. Figure 17 shows the execution times when the scale factor is increased from 1 to 4. As shown, the second scenario achieves about 26% (*E2*) and 30% (*E2'*) performance improvement. The proportion of the time in *E2* is shown in 17, including data transformation, key validation, and loading. In overall, loading uses less time than data transformation and key validation as there is no lookup operation, which is typically time-consuming. Now the downtimes of

Figure 15. Exec. with dependencies, E1

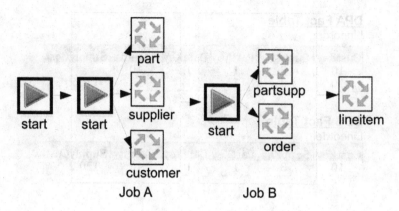

Job A   Job B

Figure 16. Exec. without dependencies, E2

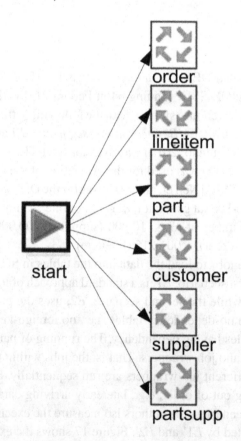

Figure 17. Execution time

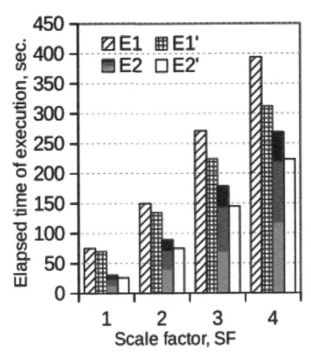

data warehousing system for *E*1 and *E*2 are compared (suppose that the system has to be taken off-line to refresh the data). The results in Figure 18 show that the standard approach needs to use much more time than the proposed solution because the records are added to the data warehouse individually by insertion. The system downtime in *E1, thus,* equals to the running time of the whole ETL job. In contrast, E2 first prepares the data into the SSA Lv2 tables, then loads to the data warehouse in bulk. Thus, the downtime is the bulk load time.

In the experiments shown in the figures, the authors considered loading the data generated by insertions. The authors now further consider populating the data with updates and deletions to the data warehouse, which simulate the update and delete operations in an operational system. The authors use the TPC-H benchmark data generator to generate update and deletion records for the *lineitem* and *order* tables. The authors set different update/delete percentage values in the command line options to produce the desired number of update and deletion records. The update and deletion records are saved into separate files; thus, the records can be labelled with a different transaction type code, *tx*, in the ETL program (Recall that different Tx type codes are used to identify record insertion, update or delete operations in an operational system). The data are generated by setting the scale factor, *SF*=1, but vary the update/delete percentage. Figure 19 shows the execution times, which indicate that the proposed solution is also more efficient if more updates and deletions are conducted. The reasons are twofold. One is that the proposed solution is able to handle out-of-order data in parallel and the other is that the solution prepares the data before the loading, e.g., some of the updates and deletions on the rows already have been done before the loading, thus, uses less time.

Figure 18. BI downtime/DW refreshing time

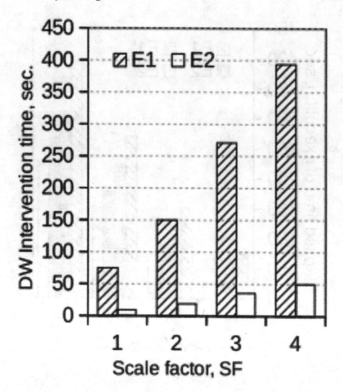

Figure 19. Execution time, SF=1

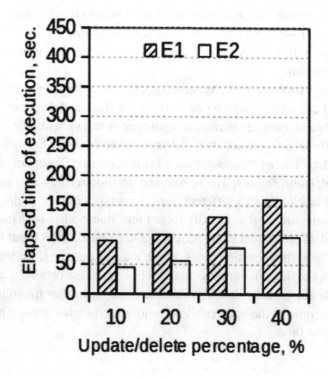

The DDS data process is evaluated in the following. The authors measure the time of processing the data from SOR to DDS, and the time of dimensional query on DDS tables, and the equivalent query on SOR tables. Tha authors use the SSB star-join queries between the fact and dimension tables on DDS, and the queries are rewritten for SOR. The purpose is to investigate how much performance gained after the being processed into the star schema. The results are shown in Figure 20. Obviously, the time on DDS is much less than on SOR for all the queries. The reason of Q3 using more time is due to placing the restrictions on the un-indexed attributes. The ETL time of DDS data process is 453 seconds, but this time is only paid for once, and the running is scheduled to the non-peak hours, which does not affect the business intelligence system.

The following studies the additional space needed for saving the data in SSA Lv2 tables in the two-staging ETL process and in DPA in the DSS data process. Table 2 shows the original data size generated with *SF*=1, and the size of SSA Lv2 tables. The authors measure the size of CSV files by exporting the data from SSA Lv2 tables to a hard driver. When the update/delete percentage is 0, it means that no updates or deletions are applied to the original records. The needed space size is almost the same as the size of the original data sets since no changes are applied to the data except for the additional columns for the surrogate keys whose size is negligible. But, when update/deletion percentage value is increased, an almost linearly growing number of records is deleted, corresponding to the decreased size of the SSA Lv2 tables. Then, the loading process will load a smaller size of the data into the SOR tables. As shown, the space used DPA is very limited as DPA has the star schema of SSB where some unnecessary attributes are eliminated, and the data are also aggregated.

Figure 20. Execution time of SSB queries on SOR and DDS, SF=1

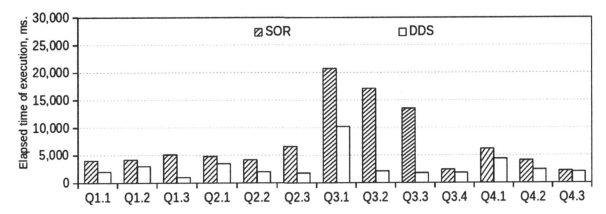

Table 2. Storage space needed by SSA Lv2 tables

Update/deletions (%)	0	10	20	30	40
Size of source data (GB)	1.00	1.07	1.14	1.21	1.28
Size of SSA Lv2 tables (GB)	1.00	0.91	0.83	0.76	0.67
Size of DPA tables (GB)	0.32	0.21	0.15	0.11	0.06

DISCUSSION

In this chapter, the authors proposed a two-tiered segmentation approach for transaction data warehousing. Some discussions are raised in the following.

First, the proposed method aims to handle transaction data from operational systems that generate dynamic data by insert, update or delete operations. Dynamic data changes are reflected and maintained in a data warehouse. Since the data come from operational systems, the operations are usually recorded or can be recognized; and are timestamped. Therefore, it is assumed that each record from an operational system can be marked by an operational code, I, D or U, which is often possible for banking systems, or online shopping stores. For other types of operational systems, such as website management systems, the timestamps and operations can be inferred from their system logs.

Second, the proposed method uses additional data area in the two-staging ETL process, and in the DDS data process to hold the data temporarily. They can be memory buffers or tables in a database system, depending on the size of the data. A common practice is to use tables in a database management system to hold large data sets, but this may compromise the performance, due to the temporary materialization. The advantage of the temporary staging area is that the load (L) can be decoupled, and can be executed later, for example, when the BI system is not busy, while the Data extraction (E) and Transformation (T) process can be scheduled to run whenever the source data is available.

Third, in the proposed method, the authors use an augmentation process to handle early/late-arriving data. This can decouple table dependencies for loading and make an ETL job to process the tables simultaneously, which is called *table parallelization* in this paper. This also means that the proposed approach can handle out-of-order data in the same ETL job, i.e., reading the data regardless of its dependencies as shown in Figure 10. Fourth, the time window size of late-arriving data for updating the augmented records can be less or greater than one time interval of ETL job iteration. If the window size is less than one time interval, the data cannot be counted as late-arriving as the data can be processed within the same job iteration, otherwise, the data is late-arriving, which will be processed by the argumentation process.

Last, the proposed method essentially uses the additional space, SSA Lv2 and DPA, to exchange better flexibility (i.e., the loading time), and performance (i.e., parallel loading and OLAP query). The trade-off, in this case, is reasonable and unlikely to be a problem, due to the cheap storage today.

RELATED WORK

ETL is typically implemented as a workflow process to process various tasks. ETL workflow optimization has received considerable attention. According to (Kimball & Caserta, 2004), 70% of the warehouse implementation and maintenance effort is spent on the ETL system. Simitsis et al. (2005, 2009) conduct the most extensive research on ETL workflow optimization and propose a logical optimization framework. The framework formalizes ETL state spaces into a directed acyclic graph (DAG), and then optimizes it by searching the best execution plan in terms of the time. The optimization framework, however, does not take into account data properties processed by the ETL workflow, such as out-of-order data and data dependencies. Li & Zhan (2005) analyze task dependencies in an ETL workflow and optimize an ETL workflow by applying parallelization upon the tasks without dependencies. The work, however, does not consider how to decouple the dependencies like the method proposed by this chapter. In this chapter, the authors make a further step to optimize ETL workflow through the decoupling of loading by introducing an additional staging area in the two-staging ETL process, such that the loading can proceed any time thereafter. Behrend and Jörg (2010), instead, use a rule-based approach to optimize ETL flows. The rule-based approach is more complicated than our approach as it requires the effort to define the rules according to data types and ETL operators. In contrast, the proposed method is very easy to implement by using most current ETL workflow designing tools, e.g., Pentaho and Informatica. The proposed ETL also emphasizes the consolidation of the ETLs for handling different types of the data, including fast/slowly-changing data, early/late-arriving data, dynamic and static data. The proposed method focuses on improvement of flexibility and performance by decoupling of job dependencies, and the load from extraction and transformation, which particularly suits for processing high dynamic data, e.g., transaction data.

Regarding handling early-arriving facts, Kimball (2015) provides a design tip. The idea is same to the solution proposed by Casters et al. (2010), and the latter also gives an example of processing facts using Pentaho Kettle. The idea is that if a fact record arrives earlier than the referenced dimension, an unknown record is first added into the dimension table with a reserved ID referenced by the early-arriving fact record. This method is known as the standard approach widely used. In this solution, the authors base on this method to develop the augmentation process, and introduce operational codes, which is to provide a one-stop uniform method for handling different types of data. Bliujute et al. (1998) studies slowly changing dimension processing and proposes a temporal star schema to handle slowly changing dimensions, however, the aim of the work is to compare the query performance and database size with a standard star schema. Moreover, Garcia-Molina et al. (1998) identify ETL transformation phase as a research challenge because transformation typically takes much more time than data extraction and data loading. The work also suggests ETL parallelization as an important research area, which was also emphasized by this chapter. The authors have further considered a comprehensive ETL scenario of handling transaction data in this chapter.

The latest trend of data warehousing is to support big data, and to offer real-time capability, e.g., (Cuzzocrea et al., 1998; Thomsen et al., 2008). The emerging technologies, such as MapReduce (Dean & Ghemawat, 2008), make it feasible for ETL to process large volumes of the data on many nodes. As the evidence, the open-source MapReduce-based systems, Pig (Olston et al., 2008), Hive (Thusoo et al., 2009), Spark (Meng et al., 2016) become increasingly popular in data warehousing, however, they were designed with big data analytics as the main purpose, thus only with limited ETL capabilities. To complement this, Liu et al. (2011, 2014) implement a MapReduce-based ETL tool, called *ETLMR,* by extending from the programming-based ETL framework (Thomsen & Pedersen, 2009). The implemented ETL program can be run on a cluster in parallel but maintains the simplicity as the programming-based framework, only a few code lines needed to implement a dimensional ETL, even for SCDs. Nevertheless, the authors see that there still exists a large market of using classical data warehousing solutions that handle "small" data. The proposed method is suitable for them to design or/and optimize ETLs. Furthermore, data warehousing technologies in big data are still evolving, and a lot of them can be learned from the traditional technologies. It is believed that the traditional approaches, such as the methods proposed in this chapter for handling slowly changing dimensions and early/late-arriving data, would be useful to the data warehousing for big data.

CONCLUSION

In data warehousing, it is a grand challenge to process frequently changing transaction data. In this chapter, the authors proposed a two-tiered segmentation ETL for this challenge. The proposed ETL method consists of a two-staging ETL process and a DDS data process. An additional data area is introduced to optimize the ETL processes for processing dynamic transaction data. The two-staging ETL identifies and maps the changes of the data into different operation codes, and transfers data from level-1 to level-2 staging area, in combination with doing necessary transformations and key validations. The proposed method decouples the loading from the whole ETL process in order to achieve better flexibility and performance. The proposed method provides an all-in-one solution for handling fast/slowly-changing, and early/late-arriving data, and unlock the loading dependencies by an augmentation process. The second segmentation uses the so-called DDS process to process detailed transaction records from SOR to the dimensional data warehouse, DDS, to improve performance for OLAP queries in the business intelligence system. The authors have evaluated the proposed data warehousing method and compared the standard ETL implementation. The results showed that the proposed ETL solution is efficient and less intrusive.

ACKNOWLEDGMENT

This research was supported by the CITIES project (NO.1035-00027B) funded by Danish Innovation Fund.

REFERENCES

Behrend, A., & Jörg, T. (2010). Optimized Incremental ETL Jobs for Maintaining Data Warehouses. *Proc. of IDEAS*, 1–9. 10.1145/1866480.1866511

Bliujute, R., Saltenis, S., Slivinskas, G., & Jensen, C. S. (1998). *Systematic Change Management in Dimensional Data Warehousing*. Time Center Technical Report TR-23.

Casters, M., Bouman, R., & Dongen, J. V. (2010). *Pentaho Kettle Solutions: Building Open Source ETL Solutions With Pentaho Data Integration*. John Wiley & Sons.

Cuzzocrea, A., Ferreira, N., & Furtado, P. (2014). Enhancing Traditional Data Warehousing Architectures with Real-Time Capabilities. *Proc. of ISMIS*, 456–465. 10.1007/978-3-319-08326-1_46

Dean, J., & Ghemawat, S. (2008). MapReduce: Simplified Data Processing on Large Clusters. *Communications of the ACM, 51*(1), 107–113. doi:10.1145/1327452.1327492

Design Tip #57: Early Arriving Facts. (n.d.). Retrieved from www.kimballgroup.com/2004/08/design-tip-57-early-arriving-facts

Garcia-Molina, H., Labio, W. J., Wiener, J. L., & Zhuge, Y. (1998). Distributed and Parallel Computing Issues in Data Warehousing (Invited Talk). *Proc. of SPAA/PODC*.

Inmon, W. H. (2002). *Building the Data Warehouse*. John Wiley and Sons.

Inmon, W. H. (2003). The System of Record in the Global Data Warehouse. *Information & Management*.

Kimball, R., & Caserta, J. (2004). *The Data Warehouse ETL Toolkit: Practical Techniques for Extracting, Cleaning, Conforming, and Delivering Data*. Wiley.

Li, H., & Zhan, D. (2005). Workflow Timed Critical Path Optimization. *Nature and Science*, *3*(2), 65–74.

Liu, X., Thomsen, C., & Pedersen, T. B. (2011). *ETLMR: A Highly Scalable Dimensional ETL Framework Based on MapReduce. Proc. of DaWak*.

Liu, X., Thomsen, C., & Pedersen, T. B. (2014). CloudETL: Scalable Dimensional ETL for Hive. *Proc. of the 18th International Database Engineering & Applications Symposium*, 195–206. 10.1145/2628194.2628249

March, S. T., & Hevner, A. R. (2007). Integrated Decision Support Systems: A Data Warehousing Perspective. *Decision Support Systems*, *43*(3), 1031–1043. doi:10.1016/j.dss.2005.05.029

Meng, X., Bradley, J., Yavuz, B., Sparks, E., Venkataraman, S., Liu, D., ... Xin, D. (2016). Mllib: Machine learning in Apache Spark. *Journal of Machine Learning Research*, *17*(1), 1235–1241.

Neil, P. O., Neil, E. O., & Chen, X. (2007). *The star schema benchmark*. Retrieved from http://www.cs.umb.edu/ ~poneil/StarSchemaB.pdf

Olston, C., Reed, B., Srivastava, U., Kumar, R., & Tomkins, A. (2008). Pig latin: a Not-so-foreign Language for Data Processing. *Proc. of SIGMOD*, 1099–1110. 10.1145/1376616.1376726

Pentaho. (2015). Retrieved from http://wiki.pentaho.com/display/EAI/eradata+TPT+Insert+Upsert+Bulk+Loader

Simitsis, A., Vassiliadis, P., & Sellis, T. (2005). State-space Optimization of ETL Workflows. *TKDE*, *17*(10), 1404–1419.

Simitsis, A., Vassiliadis, P., & Sellis, T. (2005) Optimizing ETL Processes in Data Warehouses. *Proc. of ICDE*, 564–575.

Simitsis, A., Wilkinson, K., Castellanos, M., & Dayal, U. (2009). QoX-driven ETL Design: Reducing the Cost of ETL Consulting Engagements. *Proc. of SIGMOD*, 953–960. 10.1145/1559845.1559954

Thomsen, C., & Pedersen, T. B. (2009). A Survey of Open Source Tools for Business Intelligence. *International Journal of Data Warehousing and Mining*, *5*(3), 56–75. doi:10.4018/jdwm.2009070103

Thomsen, C., & Pedersen, T. B. (2011). Easy and Effective Parallel Programmable ETL. *Proc. of DOLAP*, 37–44.

Thomsen, C., Pedersen, T. B., & Lehner, W. (2008). RiTE: Providing On-demand Data for Right-time Data Warehousing. *Proc. of ICDE*, 456–465. 10.1109/ICDE.2008.4497454

Thusoo, A. (2009). Hive: A Warehousing Solution Over a Map-Reduce Framework. *PVLDB*, *2*(2), 1626–1629.

TPC-H. (2015). Retrieved from http://tpc.org/tpch/

Chapter 2
Real–Time Big Data Warehousing

Francisca Vale Lima
University of Minho, Portugal

Carlos Costa
University of Minho, Portugal

Maribel Yasmina Santos
University of Minho, Portugal

ABSTRACT

The large volume of data that is constantly being generated leads to the need of extracting useful patterns, trends, or insights from this data, raising the interest in business intelligence and big data analytics. The volume, velocity, and variety of data highlight the need for concepts like real-time big data warehouses (RTBDWs). The lack of guidelines or methodological approaches for implementing these systems requires further research in this recent topic. This chapter presents the proposal of a RTBDW architecture that includes the main components and data flows needed to collect, process, store, and analyze the available data, integrating streaming with batch data and enabling real-time decision making. Using Twitter data, several technologies were evaluated to understand their performance. The obtained results were satisfactory and allowed the identification of a methodological approach that can be followed for the implementation of this type of system.

INTRODUCTION

The technological evolution of the last years has called the attention of organizations for the analysis of data, increasing the interest in Business Intelligence (BI). BI allows the understanding of the business needs and opportunities, and represents a competitive advantage (H. Chen, Chiang, & Storey, 2012). The technologies available for data analysis have been increasingly requested, with a special focus on ways of extracting information from large volumes of data and identifying patterns and trends that support decision-making (Di Tria, Lefons, & Tangorra, 2014b).

DOI: 10.4018/978-1-5225-5516-2.ch002

The volume, velocity and variety of data have imposed considerable challenges to traditional data storage and processing technologies, being almost impossible using them to extract useful information from data (Cuzzocrea, Song, & Davis, 2011). Traditional technologies fail to respond to requests on time and, therefore, solutions based on Big Data concepts were introduced (M. Chen, Mao, & Liu, 2014; Goss & Veeramuthu, 2013; Zikopoulos, Eaton, DeRoos, Deutsch, & Lapis, 2011), substituting traditional data storage and processing technologies with much more efficient ones (H. Chen et al., 2012).

Data Warehouses (DWs) in Big Data contexts, i.e., Big Data Warehouses (BDWs), allow the analysis of large volumes of data, extracting relevant information from them, in order to fulfill organizational analytical needs (Di Tria, Lefons, & Tangorra, 2014a). The use of BDWs increases the ability to question data faster than usual, also enhancing the access to real-time data. Having more updated data prepared for analysis is nowadays of upmost importance, creating the need for Real-Time Big Data Warehouses (RTBDWs), as traditional tools are not able to process large volumes of data in real-time.

This is even more relevant in a context where the advent of real-time technology (e.g., distributed message queueing systems and stream processing) makes faster data changes, requiring an up-to-date analysis of large amounts of data. The challenge lies in real-time data access with no processing delays and a reduced latency of processing operations (Li & Mao, 2015). Therefore, it is relevant to understand the real-time requirements for modeling and implementing BDWs, in order to obtain updated information in a faster way, enhancing business's competitive advantage.

In order to materialize the real-time requirements for BDWs, this work proposes a BDW architecture for real-time processing. Although some research contributions can be found in the literature (as can be seen in the next section), this work proposes an innovative approach that allows timely collection, processing, storage and analysis of real-time data.

This work explores and evaluates the role of each technology included in the proposed architecture, and summarizes a set of considerations for the implementation of BDWs in real-time. By analyzing the performance of the technologies in different scenarios, it is possible to understand and identify best practices regarding streaming data collection, processing and storage. For that, both real-time data repository and a historical data repository are used, allowing data to flow faster from the data source to the data analysis component. The logical architecture proposed in this work can be adopted by any organization, making available an analytical environment able to integrate historical data with streaming data.

The following sections, in outline, include: i) an overview of related work and the scientific contributions of this work; ii) the BDW architecture for real-time contexts; iii) the demonstration case describing data collection, processing and storage; iv) the results obtained from the several benchmarks, discussing the main findings; v) some remarks about the undertaken work and its future developments.

Big Data Warehousing

Nowadays, organizations are increasingly aware of BI and Business Analytics. However, as the volume of available data has been increasing at ever growing rates, its integration for analysis purposes becomes increasingly complex (M. Chen et al., 2014; Goss & Veeramuthu, 2013). The DW is the essential component of a BI infrastructure, integrating strategic indicators that bring analytical value to the decision-making process (Vaisman & Zimányi, 2012), which highlight relevant hidden patterns or insights in data (Di Tria et al., 2014a). Although a DW allows the collection, storage and management of data to support the decision-making process (Krishnan, 2013), it is constrained by the volume, velocity and variety of the data (Cuzzocrea et al., 2011), requiring the adoption of Big Data techniques and technologies (M. Chen et al., 2014; Goss & Veeramuthu, 2013; Zikopoulos et al., 2011).

The concept of BDW emerged with the aim of enhancing the traditional DW, taking into consideration new properties, features, and Big Data characteristics. This paradigm shift allows the collection, integration and storage of large volumes of data, from structured to unstructured data sources, being generated at high velocity, and having high complexity. The BDW can be distinguished from traditional solutions by being able to easily integrate new data sources. It can process all the available data sources in the organization, supporting the continuous and rapid evolution of the organizational analytical needs and providing sophisticated analyzes over the data (Di Tria et al., 2014a).

Moreover, with the evolution in technology, users start requiring real-time access to the data, an important functionality to react quickly to business changes, allowing the analysis of data and the extraction of value from it as soon as it is being generated (M. Chen et al., 2014; Goss & Veeramuthu, 2013; R. J. Santos, Bernardino, & Vieira, 2011). Although being an added value to any organization, each business needs to evaluate its real-time requirements, as they differ according to the business area.

In order to achieve real-time requirements in data processing, practitioners need to consider: the latency associated with query execution; the availability of the data to make decisions when it is needed; how quickly data should be stored for further analyzes; the transformation and cleansing needed to process the data; and, the inclusion of both historical and real-time data in analytical queries, providing up-to-date business information (Bruckner, List, & Schiefer, 2002; Mohamed & Al-Jaroodi, 2014).

Previous works made some contributions to the implementation of BDWs using more traditional approaches, as the works of Vaisman & Zimányi (2012), Freudenreich et al. (2013), R. J. Santos & Bernardino (2008), Li & Mao (2015), Golab & Johnson (2014), which are mainly solutions of real-time data flowing in a traditional DW. In a conceptual perspective, the work of Kimball & Ross (2013) presents a methodological approach for the implementation of a real-time DW, without any technological proposal or validation. Recently, with the relevance of Big Data, Marz & Warren (2015) and G. J. Chen et al. (2016) provide interesting contributions, proposing architectural solutions capable of dealing with historical and real-time data, without testing or evaluating technologies or systems to accomplish the proposed architecture.

The main difficulties, problems and challenges mentioned by these previous authors constitute a starting point for the architecture proposed in this work, which is an evolution of the Lambda Architecture (Marz & Warren, 2015) considering its three main layers allowing access to data in real-time, and also the real-time processing approach of Kimball & Ross (2013), suggesting that real-time data needs to flow as fast as possible. This work proposes and implements a RTBDW considering a small data processing latency wherein each query should run using less time as possible.

An Architecture for Real-Time Big Data Warehousing

The implementation of a real-time BDW requires the proper exploration of concepts and technologies to define data flows and logical components. Different scenarios are explored, meeting different application domains and contexts, all allowing the collection, storage, processing and analysis of data in real-time. To address a specific application domain, this work includes the requirements of the research project "Business Intelligence Platform for Data Integration" (M. Y. Santos, Oliveira e Sá, et al., 2017), a work in a partnership between the University of Minho and Bosch Braga. These requirements constrained some of the technological choices made for the implementation of the proposed architecture. Before describing the implementation, this section presents the data flows and logical components included in the architecture.

Data Flows

The RTBDW architecture here proposed integrates real-time data sources (streaming data) and historical data sources (batch data), which are collected, processed, prepared and stored as presented in Figure 1. The real-time data is stored in a repository that provides quick access to the data, fast read and write, in order to meet the real-time requirements. Periodically, the real-time data is moved to the historical data storage, where huge amounts of historical data are stored in a way that is optimized for large sequential reads.

The technologies for data collection, processing and storage must allow the data to be analyzed shortly after being generated, providing low latency for real-time analytics. The data analysis component can query real-time data and, if necessary, historical data, by joining the data in a single query. This is possible through the use of distributed query engines capable of simultaneously querying different data sources.

This architecture, and its data flows, gathers contributions from the various approaches mentioned previously, but distinguishes from them by being able to quickly collect, process and store data in such a way that the analysis can be made in a few seconds, including data from recent events.

Logical Components

Giving the fact that this work is part of a broader research project, the architecture and technological choices were constrained by Bosch's needs, and by the analysis of the current trends and state-of-the-art technologies in BDW for supporting real-time requirements. Figure 2 presents the architecture proposed in this work, which includes as main components data sources, ETL (Extraction, Transformation and Loading) process, data storage, data analysis, and security, administration and monitoring. The relationships between these components are highlighted in the figure, as well as the technologies used in its implementation.

Figure 1. Streaming and Batch Data Flows

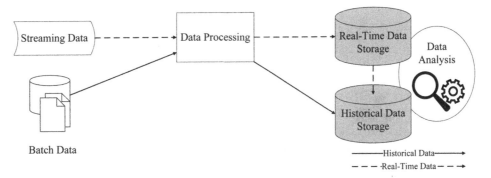

Figure 2. Architecture for a RTBDW. Adapted from M. Y. Santos et al. (2017)

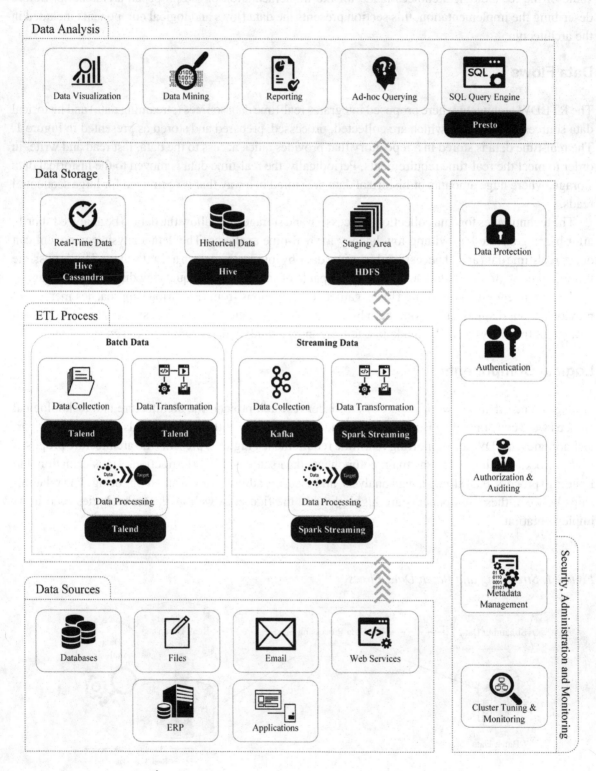

In this architecture (Figure 2), data sources include batch data (files and databases) and streaming data (from one or more real-time applications), besides other data sources available in the organization. The ETL process consists in extracting the data, transforming and storing it into the BDW, where real-time and historical data are stored in different data storage repositories. For data analysis, several mechanisms can be used, as long as queries are quickly executed. Security, administration and monitoring are not detailed in this chapter, although it is important to include in such an architecture.

In the instantiation of the proposed architecture, several technologies were selected to support the entire process from data collection to analysis. The streaming data collection is performed by Kafka, which allows the collection of data generated by multiple applications (Kafka producers). This data, once collected, is sent by Kafka to be processed by Spark Streaming (a Kafka consumer), which includes appropriate cleansing and transformation steps giving structure to data. Then, data flows to the technologies for real-time data storage (Hive or Cassandra). As several technologies can be used, this work proposes and evaluates two of them in the demonstration case, Hive and Cassandra, providing useful insights about the suitability of each one and the context where organizations benefit more from the use of one or another. While Hive stands out for its analytical capabilities, enabling the analysis and management of large amounts of data, Cassandra stands out for the low latency of data access. In both cases, for the proposed architecture, the real-time data is moved to the Hive historical data storage, as Cassandra is not suited for processing long batches of data.

The extraction and processing of batch data is made with Talend, a data integration tool, which allows the inclusion of cleansing and transformation tasks and the definition of the logical data model, with the attributes and corresponding data types. When this process is completed, data is stored in HDFS, acting as a staging area, and then moved to the historical data storage supported by Hive, for future data querying.

The distributed SQL (Structured Query Language) query engine can be assured by Presto, Spark, Drill, or any other similar technology capable of querying multiple Big Data sources (e.g., HDFS and NoSQL databases) in a single query. Based on the benchmark of M. Y. Santos, Costa, et al. (2017), where the performance of several querying technologies was evaluated, only Presto is considered in this work, as it was the technology with best execution times proving the required low latency. With Presto, queries can use both the real-time and historical data storage systems, either separately or simultaneously.

Technological Implementation

For the implementation of the proposed architecture, which will be evaluated with a demonstration case that will benchmark different scenarios, real-time data is collected from the Twitter social network. Each tweet is extracted, processed and stored in the real-time data storage for later analysis. Two scenarios of real-time storage are used, one with Hive and the other with Cassandra. In both cases, data is stored in a denormalized table, not requiring joins between different data tables. Moreover, data is stored at its raw level, allowing its detailed analysis. In the different scenarios, data organization strategies (e.g., data partitioning) are also evaluated and discussed, as well as the impact of data volume in the performance of these two technologies.

Furthermore, files with historical tweets are used as batch data, which are loaded, processed and stored directly in the historical data storage. As already mentioned, real-time data is moved to the historical data storage after a certain pre-determined periodicity.

The different testing scenarios are represented in Figure 3, aiming to evaluate the most appropriate technologies considering different data volumes and velocities, ensuring that the proposed architecture is adequate for a vast set of real-time applications. As can be seen in Figure 3, the testing scenarios include the possibility to use Hive or Cassandra as real-time data storage, while the historical data storage is always maintained in Hive. All the tasks and data flows are described afterwards.

Technological Infrastructure

The infrastructure used in this work consists of a Hadoop cluster (Hortonworks Data Platform – HDP 2.6.0) with 5 nodes, namely 1 HDFS NameNode (YARN ResourceManager) and 4 HDFS DataNodes (YARN NodeManagers). Each node includes the following hardware: Intel core i5, quad core, 3.1GHz-3.3GHz; 32GB of 1333MHz DDR3 Random Access Memory (RAM), with 24GB available for query processing; Samsung 850EVO 500GB Solid State Drive (SSD) with up to 540MB/s read speed and up to 520MB/s write speed; and 1 gigabit Ethernet. The operating system installed on each node is CentOS 7 with XFS file system. In addition, Cassandra is installed on the 4 HDFS DataNodes, as well as Presto's workers. The Presto coordinator is installed on the HDFS NameNode.

Experimental Component

The process from collecting data to storing it has two starting points, namely the data that is collected from Twitter via streaming mechanisms and the historical data that is loaded in batch from files with tweets. The data extracted from Twitter has a set of attributes about each of the tweets, collected through a Java application that is responsible for capturing the tweets that are posted. Each of the extracted Twitter messages is sent through a Kafka topic, as shown in Figure 4. The Kafka topic allows sending messages and then receiving them for processing in Spark Streaming, acting as a communication channel.

Figure 3. Testing Scenarios

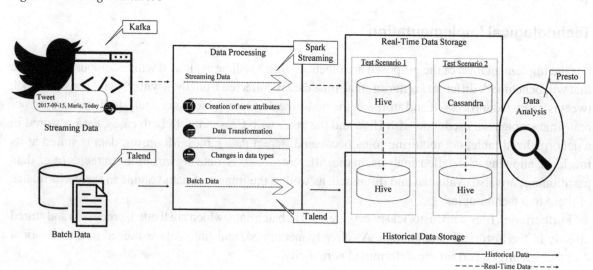

Figure 4. Twitter Data Collection

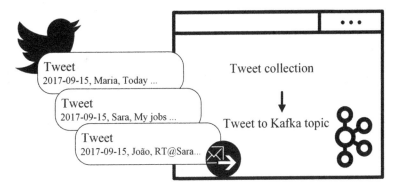

As the tweets are sent, they are received by the Spark Streaming consumer, to transform data by creating new attributes and changing data types, preparing it to be stored. In Spark Streaming, a micro-batch is created to receive each tweet, transform the data, and insert it later in a Cassandra or Hive table, as represented in Figure 5.

It should be noticed that the data, before its storage in Cassandra or Hive, could be stored in a staging area, namely HDFS, as a backup mechanism, for example. However, this possibility was tested and the results showed that this operation delays the insertion of the data in the real-time data storage and, therefore, it is not here considered.

For batch data, the data is loaded through files and processed so that new attributes are created, data types are changed, and data is prepared to be inserted into the Hive historical data storage, as shown in Figure 6. Before the data is inserted in a Hive table, it is loaded into a staging area in HDFS, and then moved to the respective table. This ETL process for batch data uses Talend as the integration tool, with no pre-defined periodicity, thus able to run when desired.

Figure 5. Streaming Data Processing and Storage

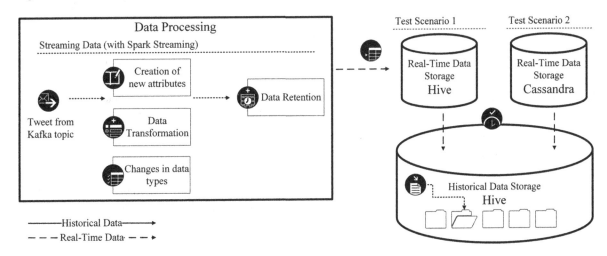

Figure 6. Batch Data Collection, Processing and Storage

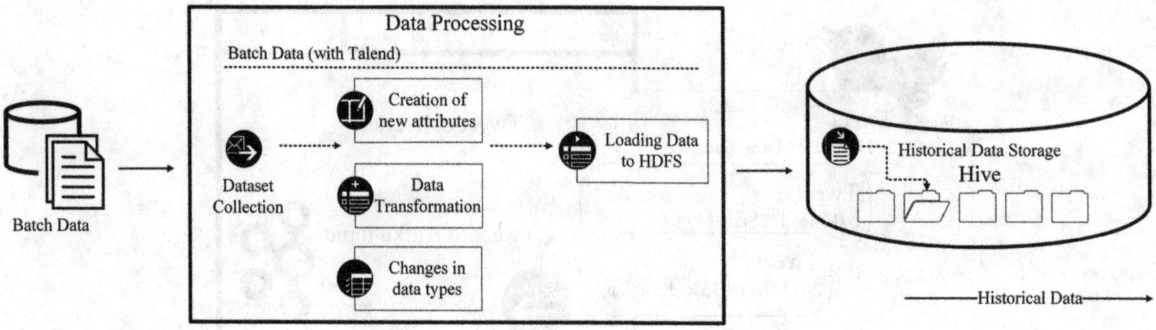

Despite the fact that the experimental architectural components consider streaming and batch data, the demonstration case only considers streaming data, since the focus is on testing real-time processing with timely responses to queries using recently updated data. Nevertheless, some tests are also performed over the historical data storage component to evaluate its performance.

Demonstration Case

In this area of research, several conceptual and technological issues arise, requiring the need for a careful evaluation that points for best practices and recommendations when implementing a RTBDW. This guides the development of this demonstration case, in which the focus is on evaluating the performance of each technology in different scenarios, namely Kafka for data collection, Spark Streaming for data processing, Cassandra for real-time data storage, Hive for real-time and historical data storage, and Presto for distributed SQL query processing.

Data Collection

Data is collected from Twitter, using a connector that produces a stream of tweets. This data source represents real data, with significant volume, velocity and variety. Each message collected from Twitter is sent from Kafka to Spark Streaming through a Kafka topic that acts as a communication channel for sending 1 500 to 2 500 messages each second. Taking into consideration the way Kafka and Spark Streaming are integrated, messages can be sent through a batch of multiple messages or through a streaming mechanism in which one message at a time is sent. Given the context of this work, what makes sense is sending messages as soon as they are available (streaming), in order to ensure that each message is sent by Kafka and received by Spark Streaming immediately after being collected.

In order to understand the performance of Kafka, this work tested the task of sending messages with different sizes. The main objective was to understand the influence of the message's size in the performance of Kafka, analyzing how many messages Kafka is able to send and how many messages Spark Streaming is able to receive per second. However, the application used for collecting data from Twitter limits by itself the amount of data that can be collected, independently of the size of the message.

Besides that, the performance of Kafka, after tuning certain Kafka properties, was also analyzed, in order to ensure that the messages are sent and received as quickly as possible. However, with the results here obtained, no significant improvements can be made. Nevertheless, in other implementation context, optimizing Kafka's performance is an open issue that needs further analysis attending to the several available properties.

Data Processing

Spark Streaming is responsible for processing data in real-time, so it is expected to perform its tasks as quickly as possible, not delaying the data flow from collection to storage. This technology allows the processing of data in micro-batches, accumulating a set of data to be processed by Spark Streaming in relatively small intervals (e.g., a few seconds). This micro-batch duration is defined when the application is created and it should be higher than the processing time needed to complete each micro-batch, having enough time to process the data without any delay.

In this work, a 5 second micro-batch was initially defined, since the defined processing tasks had a duration of around 3 seconds. In addition, with this 5 second micro-batch, about 1 500 to 2 500 messages per second are consumed, which implies a variation of 7 500 to 12 500 messages in 5 seconds, considering the tweets variations in a day.

In strict real-time contexts, a micro-batch of 1 second would be tempting, although this is not enough for data processing considering the infrastructure used in this work, leading to consequent delays. The focus of this work is not on achieving a 1 second micro-batch, but in observing if the data is processed on time and if the data is adequately prepared and enriched for further analyses. Therefore, in a specific application domain, the micro-batch duration must be defined considering the latency requirements as well as the technological infrastructure.

As already mentioned, the micro-batch duration should be higher than the processing time. When this does not happen, the execution of the tasks is compromised, accumulating tasks in a queue. For example, in this work, when the micro-batch is 5 seconds and the processing time needs 7 seconds to complete, the tasks are accumulated in a queue and, after a while, the data flow has a total delay of 22 minutes.

In addition, it must be remembered that Spark Streaming micro-batches can be typically processed in multi-tenant clusters with several concurrent tasks (e.g., multi-user queries against the data stored in Cassandra) and, therefore, the micro-batch duration should consider the overhead of executing tasks in such concurrent environments.

Data Storage

The data storage component, both for real-time and historical data, is based on denormalized tables supported by the respective technologies. Data is denormalized and in its raw format, without aggregations, in order avoid reducing the volume of data, since the goal is to store and process a large amount of data. Nevertheless, this does not invalidate the possibility of presenting other ways of modeling data, both for the real-time data storage and for the historical data storage. In many organizational contexts, the same granularity is not required for real-time and historical data, and aggregations can be performed, or even the use of star models, taking into consideration the cost of processing joins as mentioned by Costa,

Costa, & Santos (2017), Floratou, Minhas, & Özcan (2014), Golab & Johnson (2014), M. Y. Santos et al. (2017) and Ward & Barker (2013).

For real-time data storage on Hive and Cassandra, the data is queried by Presto every hour, in a period of 8 hours, with data arriving via streaming, representing an average of 1 500 to 2 500 records per second and a range of 7 500 to 12 500 records per 5 seconds, considering the variations of the data flow throughout the day. For the historical data storage, the data is moved from the real-time data storage, being the data queried with different volumes. The queries performed on both storages represent a sample of possible analytical workloads, and take into consideration the variety and complexity of SQL operators.

To evaluate the performance of each technology, some tests are performed to understand which one is the most suitable for certain real-time contexts, and the results are discussed below.

Hive Real-Time Data Storage

Hive mainly organizes data into tables, which can be further divided into partitions (multiple subfolders stored within the main folder of the table), thus creating smaller and more manageable parts to optimize the performance of specific queries. As referred by Costa, Costa, & Santos (2017), Rutherglen, Wampler, & Capriolo (2012), Thusoo et al. (2009, 2010) and White (2012), the organization of the data into partitions brings benefits related to a more efficient data access. Partitions are organized according to the partitioning attributes, in which each folder stores the corresponding records. In addition, inside tables or partitions, buckets can be created to organize the data. However, these are more appropriate for data sampling, as Rutherglen et al. (2012) mention, reason why they are not included in this work.

To evaluate the performance of Hive, the data is collected, processed and stored in real-time in two storage areas, one partitioned table (PT) and another non-partitioned table (NPT). The partitioning attribute is the hour of the tweet, and the real-time data storage only includes data from that day.

Given that partitions are favored when queries include the partitioning attribute in the "where" clause, queries with and without this clause are here used. In the partitioned table, when the "where" clause includes the partitioning attribute, there is no need to search through all the partitions, which is what happens in a non-partitioned table. Moreover, the tests are performed in external tables, not managed by Hive, and with dynamic partitioning, since it can help to reduce the time needed to insert the data (Rutherglen et al., 2012; White, 2012). The file format of the Hive tables is the ORC file, which is optimized for data analysis, being a suitable format to use in the context of this work (Floratou et al., 2014).

Figure 7 presents the results of query 1 (Q1), which counts the records in the table, being both PT and NPT tables fueled by the streaming mechanism discussed previously. Since this query does not include the "where" clause, all the records have to be searched.

In the first hours, the results of Q1 are similar and not equal, as the number of rows stored in the PT and NPT are not exactly the same, due to the variations that can be verified in the streaming data flow. After 5 to 6 hours, the NPT begins to have less records and, consequently, queries are faster, since it stores less volume of data and, therefore, there is less data to read. This situation is mainly related to the metadata operations needed to insert data in HDFS, as mentioned by White (2012), given the fact that when inserting new records, many small files are created, and before records are inserted, there is a set of metadata operations needed to check if the file already exists and if there is permission to create it. This difficulty causes severe delays in the NPT, because there are thousands of small files stored in a single folder that needs to be checked for metadata operations, in contrast with the PT, which is divided

Figure 7. Results of query 1 (Q1) for the partitioned table (PT) and the non-partitioned table (NPT)

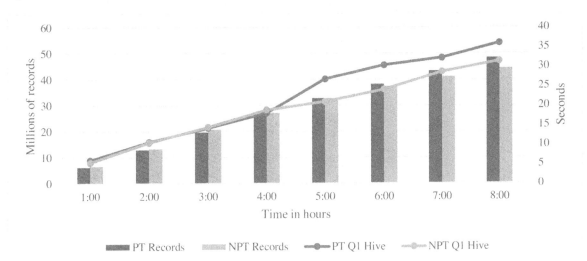

into several subfolders containing less small files in each one of them. One solution to this problem is to increase the micro-batch duration, allowing files to be larger. Another solution is to concatenate these files in larger ones using an operation executed with certain periodicity or before the insertion of new data. However, this solution causes delay in the stream processing, such as, after a few hours, some insertion tasks start being queued, because there are even more files to be verified. This raises the micro-batch processing time from around 3 to 10 seconds, surpassing the micro-batch duration, which inevitably causes an accumulation of tasks. According to the conducted tests, after a few hours, there may be a delay of roughly 2 hours along the streaming pipeline.

However, in an organizational context, many of the needed queries search in a specific time window using a temporal filter, where the partitioning strategy can show its potential. Figure 8 shows the results of query 2 (Q2), which counts the existing records in the last hour, and Figure 9 shows the results of query 3 (Q3), which checks the five most used languages in the last hour, both queries with the partitioning attribute in the "where" clause.

Regarding the results of Q2 and Q3, the performance of the PT is better than the NPT, given that only the folder of the last hour is read, instead of all records of the table. As the data volume increases, the results of the PT are maintained, as only the folder corresponding to a specific hour is being accessed. In contrast, the results of the NPT are getting worst, since it has to go through many more records to obtain the result, being a higher query response time. As also seen in Figure 7, after 5 to 6 hours, the number of records in the NPT starts to decrease.

Therefore, when the queries make use of partitions, the results of the PT are more satisfactory, but when the queries do not consider the partitioning attributes, the results of the NPT are more positive, although in this case the difference is not very significant. Moreover, when Hive is queried by Presto, it does not reveal any delay in the PT, which is not true for the NPT, since when inserting new data, some tasks are being accumulated and they are causing a slight delay in querying, for the reasons previously explained. Thus, the partitioned table is more suitable to use in these contexts, because although it is not necessarily the one that has the best performance in all queries, when the data is filtered according

Figure 8. Results of query 2 (Q2) for the partitioned table (PT) and the non-partitioned table (NPT)

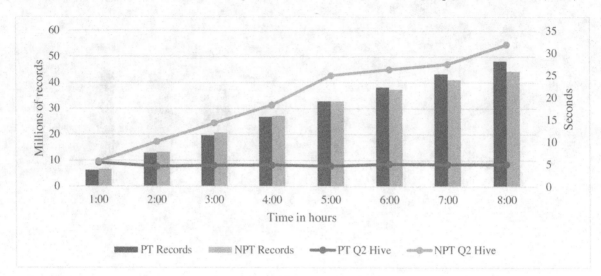

Figure 9. Results of query 3 (Q3) for the partitioned table (PT) and the non-partitioned table (NPT)

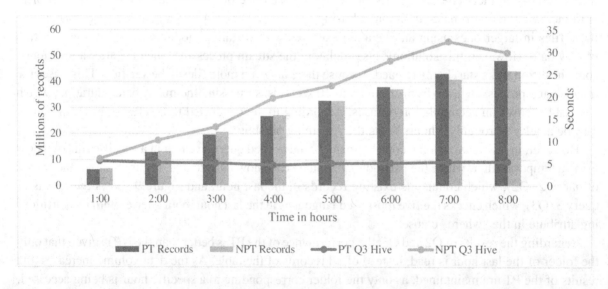

to the partitioning attributes, it has better performance, and when the data is not filtered, the difference can be considered negligible. Considering that typically the interest is in the analysis of the events that recently happened in the organization, partitioning tables on an hourly basis and analyzing the most recent hours make significant sense. In addition, the NPT after a few hours does not support the real-time needs of a BDW. Thus, depending on the business context, the table must be partitioned by one or more attributes, optimizing query performance.

Cassandra Real-Time Data Storage

Cassandra tables need a primary key, i.e., an identifier of each line that is composed by the partition key and the clustering key (Chebotko, Kashlev, & Lu, 2015; Hewitt & Carpenter, 2016). Since Cassandra is distributed across multiple nodes in the cluster, the partition key determines in which node the data is stored, and the clustering key (optional) determines the order in which the data is stored in each node. Thus, to evaluate the performance of Cassandra, one table is created only with the partition key (PKT), and another one with the partition and the clustering keys (PCKT). The partition key is the concatenation of a random number and the timestamp of the tweet's date, while the hour of the tweet is the clustering key. Figure 10 presents the results of Q1 requiring similar times in both tables, highlighting no benefit from using a clustering key. In fact, the small difference in the number of records of both tables and in their results is mainly related to the fact that the streaming data flow is not exactly the same, as previously highlighted.

To try to understand in which scenarios the PCKT could bring advantages, in Figure 11 and Figure 12, the results of Q2 and Q3 are presented, recalling that these queries search the data of the last hour, since the hour of the event is the clustering key.

Considering the results depicted in Figure 11 and Figure 12, it is possible to say that the results do not favor the table with the clustering key in any of the queries. The fact is that the clustering key will only show advantages when the query filters data through the partition key or the partition and the clustering keys. This phenomenon occurs in the Cassandra connector used by Presto 0.180. However, given the context of this demonstration case, analytical scenarios intended to process vast amounts of data in a query, it does not make sense to filter the partition key because this uniquely identifies a specific row. For the clustering key, the attribute has already been used as a filter, as Figure 11 and Figure 12 demonstrate, but these do not show any performance advantage, as performance advantages will only emerge

Figure 10. Results of query 1 (Q1) for the table with the partition key (PKT) and the table with the partition and the clustering keys (PCKT)

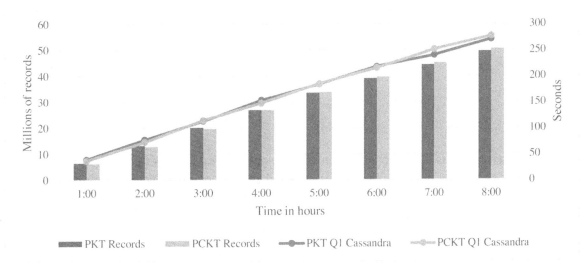

Figure 11. Results of query 2 (Q2) for the table with the partition key (PKT) and the table with the partition and the clustering keys (PCKT)

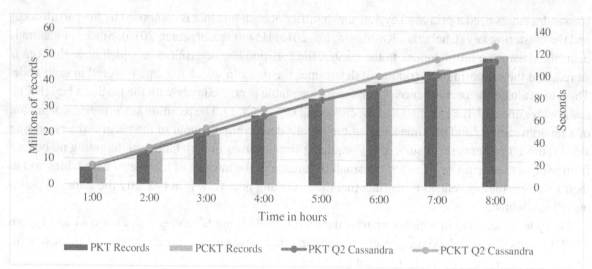

Figure 12. Results of query 3 (Q3) for the table with the partition key (PKT) and the table with the partition and the clustering keys (PCKT)

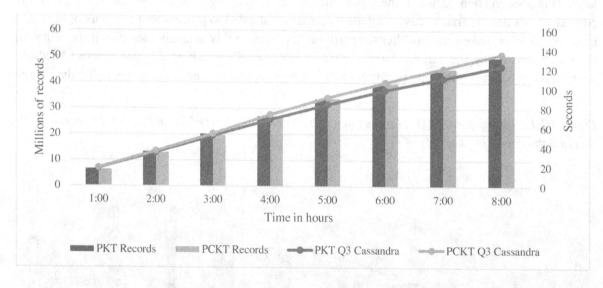

when the clustering key is used in conjunction with the partitioning key. As this type of queries is out of the scope of this work, it is possible to remark that there are no advantages in using the clustering key, as there is no improvement in the performance of the queries. Therefore, the use of tables with the partition key represents the most appropriate solution.

In addition, in Cassandra, unlike Hive, there is no delay when inserting data, but when the table is being queried by Presto, the writing operations reveal delays and the micro-batches processing time increases. However, this situation is eventually compensated in the following seconds, as the delay is mitigated and the processing time returns to its normal state. However, it is important to recall that during these delays some tasks are waiting to be processed.

Cassandra vs. Hive Real-Time Data Storage

Comparing Hive and Cassandra is relevant to understand which one best fits the needs of a real-time data storage system in this demonstration case. To evaluate this scenario, a partitioned Hive table and a Cassandra table with a partition key are considered, according to the previous results discussed in this work.

Figure 13 presents a comparison of the results obtained in Q1 in Hive and Cassandra. Hive performs significantly better than Cassandra, and by analyzing the results over time, it is possible to say that Hive has a better capacity to handle large volumes of data. With the increase in data volume, Cassandra presents increasingly slower response times, suggesting the migration of the data to another storage that allows a quicker analysis of the data. It should be noticed that the difference in the number of records between Cassandra and Hive is due to, as already mentioned, the variations of the data flow along the day.

The results of Q2 shown in Figure 14, demonstrate that the performance difference is even more clear. Compared to Figure 13, the performance of Hive is almost constant over time, due to the fact that this query checks the number of records in the last hour, reading only the data of the folder corresponding to the last hour, while Cassandra reads all the records. Although Cassandra's performance is worse in this scenario, it should be noticed that the maximum execution time for this Cassandra query is lower than the execution times presented in Figure 13, so it can be said that the queries that need to count all the records have more impact in Cassandra's workloads. The performance of Q3 is similar to the performance of Q2, reason why the results are not shown.

Figure 13. Results of query 1 (Q1) for Hive and Cassandra tables

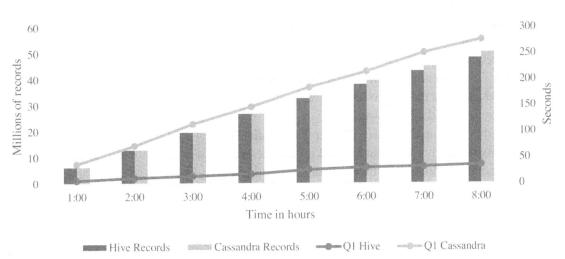

Figure 14. Results of query 2 (Q2) for Hive and Cassandra tables

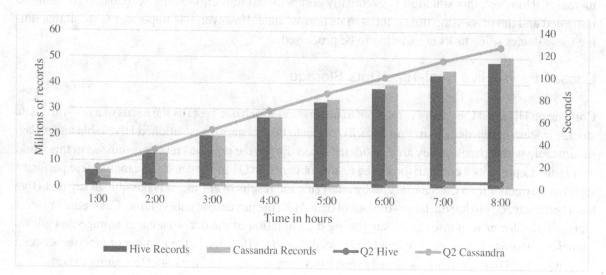

By comparing the performance of the real-time data storages, Hive stands out as the one with better performance. Due to Hive's fast sequential access capabilities, in this context, it presents a very satisfactory performance, standing out for its capacities in real-time data analysis. In addition, data stored in Cassandra would have to be moved more frequently to the historical data storage, because as the volume of data increases, the timeliness of the data analysis cannot be guaranteed, and the real-time requirements are compromised. However, these requirements will depend on each organization, according to the expected latencies. Other requirements like dealing with data updates may play a relevant role in the implementation of a RTBDW, and it is believed that Cassandra could perform better in these scenarios, since one of its key features is the fast random access to data needed for such workloads. In addition, by comparing the Spark Streaming micro-batch processing time of Cassandra with Hive, writing to Cassandra takes about 1 second while the same operation in Hive takes about 3 seconds, so in a context where a quick access to the most recent data needed, without having large amounts of stored data, Cassandra could be an adequate solution. Nevertheless, in this case, it must be considered that analytical queries will be slower. Consequently, depending on the business requirements, the ideal is a balance between what is required and what the technologies offer, or even the choice of various technologies for different contexts, integrating the data afterwards.

As previously mentioned, the size of the micro-batches impacts the performance of a system like the one here proposed. In order to understand this impact, next subsection presents the performance of Hive and Cassandra testing two different Spark Streaming micro-batch durations (5 and 20 seconds) and different data volumes.

Variation of Micro-Batch Duration

In order to analyze the performance with different micro-batch durations, a 20 seconds duration instead of 5 seconds is defined and the results for Q1, Q2 and Q3 are presented both in Figure 15 and Figure 16. Hive with a 20 seconds micro-batch duration (Figure 15) presents better query performance when

Figure 15. Hive's results with 20 seconds (20s) micro-batch duration

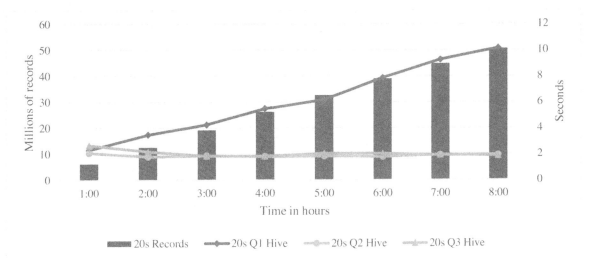

compared to a 5 seconds micro-batch duration (Figure 16). This difference in performance is because there is less overhead in writing operations when the micro-batch has a longer duration, i.e., a larger amount of data is inserted at once, representing a lower number of inserts and fewer small files created, which will inevitably speed up data querying. When the data is in the historical data storage, those files are concatenated allowing better query performance on large amounts of data.

Regarding Cassandra's results, its performance with a 20 seconds micro-batch duration is similar to its performance with a 5 seconds micro-batch duration, as presented in Figure 17 and Figure 18, respectively. Consequently, the duration of the micro-batch does not influence the performance of Cas-

Figure 16. Hive's results with 5 seconds (5s) micro-batch duration

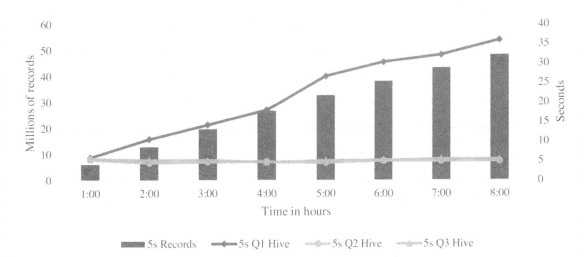

Figure 17. Cassandra's results with 20 seconds (20s) micro-batch duration

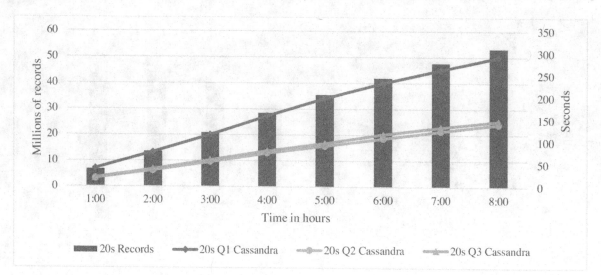

Figure 18. Cassandra's results with 5 seconds (5s) micro-batch duration

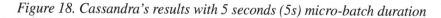

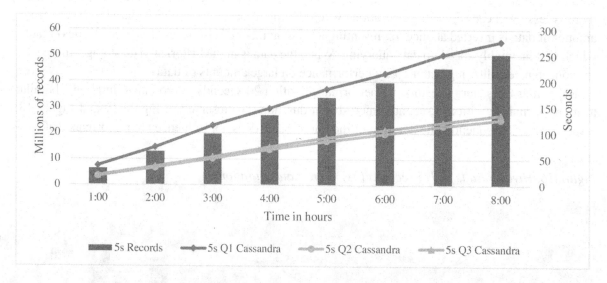

sandra. In the 20 seconds micro-batch, the delay in processing is also verified when the data is queried by Presto, phenomenon that was already highlighted in the 5 seconds micro-batch. Moreover, during this delay, the Spark Streaming processing time of the 20 seconds micro-batch is even higher than the one verified in the 5 seconds micro-batch.

As writing operations are not so demanding in the 20 seconds micro-batches, it was expected that in both technologies the 20 seconds micro-batch would provide better results. Although the performance of Hive is better when the micro-batch duration is higher, with Cassandra, the difference in the micro-batch duration does not have a significant impact.

Variation of Data Volume

In order to analyze the performance of the technologies with different data volumes, other scenarios were tested using twice the volume (V2) of the previous benchmarks (V1), i.e., about 3 000 messages flowing per second, and half the volume of V1 (corresponding to V3), namely about 800 messages flowing per second. Figure 19 and Figure 20 compare these different data volumes (V1, V2 and V3) using Hive, and Figure 21 and Figure 22 using Cassandra. Considering the context of this research work and the performance of Hive over Cassandra, it is possible to claim that Hive better meets the analytical requirements of a RTBDW.

Figure 19. Results of Q1 and Q2 for V1 and V2 in Hive

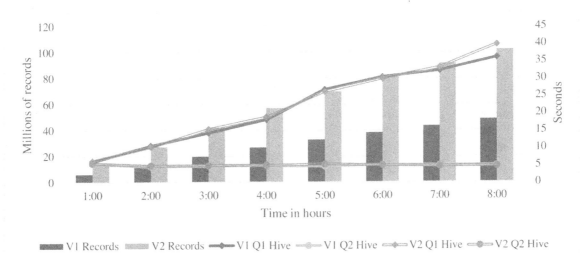

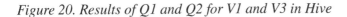

Figure 20. Results of Q1 and Q2 for V1 and V3 in Hive

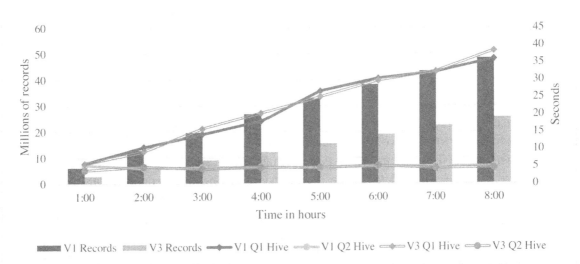

Figure 21. Results of Q1 and Q2 for V1 and V2 in Cassandra

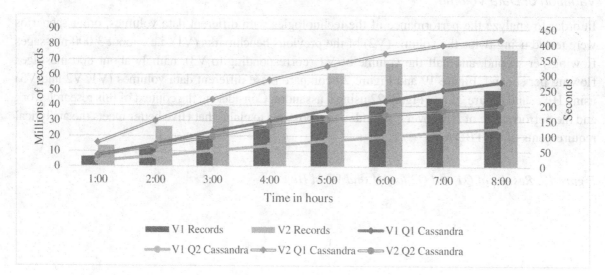

Figure 22. Results of Q1 and Q2 for V1 and V3 in Cassandra

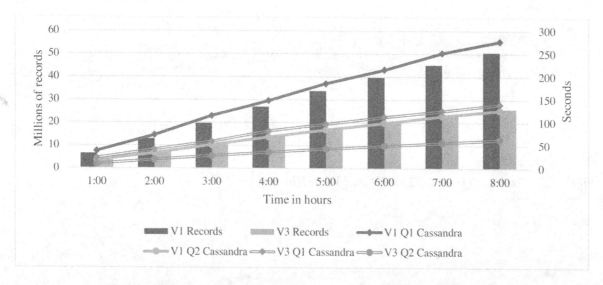

In the case of Hive, presented in Figure 19 and Figure 20, the time required to process the queries is roughly the same, even when the volume of data is higher. Thus, it is possible to verify Hive's ability to handle large volumes of data, as it maintains its performance with both large and small volumes of data. This is because, regardless of the data volume, the number of files being generated in real-time is similar, since it is related to the insert operations. However, in V2, Hive stores larger files with more records than in V1, and smaller files in V3. Thus, comparing the results of V1, V2 and V3, the query execution time is not only related with the volume of data that is arriving in streaming, but mainly constrained by the size of files created in Hive considering the different micro-batch durations. The improvement of these results involves increasing the micro-batch duration, in order to create a smaller number of files in the insertion of data, or periodically moving this data to another data storage technology.

In Figure 21 and Figure 22, Cassandra shows that with a larger volume of data the response time increases. The fact is that Cassandra is not able to scan large volumes of data, so after a few hours, the response time of Q1 in test V2, for example, is 300 seconds. During V2 testing, there was a higher delay in Cassandra response times comparing to V1, and a higher delay in processing time that is not compensated in the following seconds, increasing even more as time goes by. The processing time also increases because queries are being performed at the same time as the data is inserted. However, unlike test V2, with test V3, when Cassandra is queried while data is being stored, its processing time increases, as well as the delay for insertion of data. Despite this delay, after a few minutes, this returns to the usual processing time of less than 1 second and presenting practically no waiting time for the data insertion tasks. For this scenario, the Spark Streaming micro-batch duration could be adjusted, since the processing time of less than 1 second is substantially less than 5 seconds, due to Cassandra's concurrent writing capabilities.

Considering the context of this research work and the performance of Hive over Cassandra, it is possible to claim that Hive better meets the analytical requirements of a RTBDW.

Historical Data Storage

Regarding the historical data storage, Hive is used to allow the detailed analysis of historical information about the business. This repository can handle large amounts of data stored in large files, and represents a solution that can better satisfy the analytical needs of any organization.

As the volume of data in the real-time data storage increases, the technology begins to show a considerable performance degradation. When facing this problem, the main investment will be on hardware to scale-out, which is not always applicable in all scenarios. Consequently, the focus of this work is to reinforce the need of migrating data at some point, by periodically moving real-time data to the historical data storage. The latter represents a good option to store large amounts of data, since is not being fueled in real-time, being more efficient with less latency requirements, wherein the partitioning scheme is optimized for the most frequent analyses (e.g., day/week/month of the event). Nevertheless, depending on the business context, the partitioning scheme should be adequate for what the organization is looking for. For example, considering the analysis of the sales for the last three months, it makes sense to partition data by month. In addition, the amount of time that the data must remain in the real-time data storage before being moved to the historical repository should be studied according to each context, depending on the real-time requirements, as well as the volume of data.

Figure 23 illustrates Hive's performance as an historical data storage, considering different volumes of data. Q1, Q2 and Q3 are the same queries, defined previously. Query 4 (Q4) is a new query that counts the number of tweets with English as the writing language, and query 5 (Q5) is also a new query that counts the number of tweets published each minute for a given date. Comparing these results with some of the previous ones presented for Hive and Cassandra (Table 1), the historical data storage presents better performance considering different data volumes of 250, 500 and 1 000 million records. Comparing more specifically with the Hive real-time data storage partitioned by the hour of the event, even though the data is already organized into partitions, it can be seen that larger files bring considerable

Figure 23. Results of Hive as an historical data storage with three different volumes of data

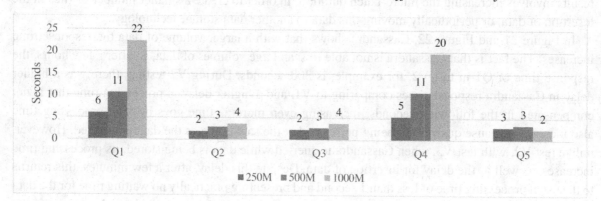

Table 1. Results of Hive and Cassandra for query Q1, Q2 and Q3

Time in hours	Hive Records	Q1 Hive (s)	Q2 Hive (s)	Q3 Hive (s)
4:00	27M	18,0	4,8	4,7
8:00	48M	35,9	4,9	5,4
Time in hours	Cassandra Records	Q1 Cassandra (s)	Q2 Cassandra (s)	Q3 Cassandra (s)
4:00	27M	147,9	68,3	73,8
8:00	51M	276,9	126,5	135,8

performance advantages. Even though there are more records in the historical data storage, its performance is comparatively better than the real-time data storage, reinforcing the idea of achieving better performance by periodically moving real-time data to the historical repository. This analysis comparing the real-time storage with the historical storage is important to know the limitations of each repository considering the volume of data and the expected real-time analysis, relevant to define the periodicity in which data must be moved.

Analyzing the results of Figure 23, even though most queries are not filtered by the partitioning attribute, they perform well. Q5 is the only one filtered by the partitioning attribute and shows the benefit of partitioning the table, Q2 and Q3 still have faster response times as they only look for data of the last hour. This last finding is very relevant as it shows that data in a partitioned table, when moved to another partitioned table, inherits the data from the both tables, namely its metadata. This allows the historical table partitioned by the date of the event to easily find where the data from a respective hour must be (which is the partitioning attribute of the real-time data storage), namely in which folder of the historical data storage the data must be. Thus, the historical data storage partitioned by the date of the event shows its specificities in the queries that are filtered by certain dates (namely Q5), but also in the queries that are filtered by the hour of the event (namely Q2 and Q3). Such phenomenon happens because there is a feature in Hive and Presto called predicate pushdown at the level of the ORC file, and several file statistics are used to understand if the same file contains data relevant to answer the query and, if not, Hive and Presto can skip the whole file. The fact that they are able to ignore some of the files becomes relevant to allow performance gains, as presented in the results of Q2 and Q3. Although Q3, compared with Q2, is not only counting records of that moment but also aggregating results in another way, its performance remains similar to Q2.

In order to reinforce the integration of the real-time data storage with the historical repository, as an example, some queries were performed integrating historical data with real-time data. The purpose of these queries was to validate the capabilities of the proposed architecture, so that, as already mentioned, queries can not only be put to the real-time data storage and historical data storage separately, but also to both repositories simultaneously. Considering the results obtained in those queries, it is possible to claim that these technologies also perform well when data is gathered from two different repositories. In addition, the higher the volume of real-time data, the worse the performance will be. In contrast, the historical data storage is not so sensitive to the increase in data volume, as it is optimized for fast sequential access.

Main Findings

To support BDWs in real-time, the technologies for data collection, processing and storage have to be the ones that present adequate performance, not compromising data analytics, which must occur as fast as possible.

The data collection process should start from a data source that offers the capability to stream a large amount of data per second, so Kafka represents a tool capable of handling data velocity and can be optimized for better performance.

Regarding the data processing technology, namely Spark Streaming, it is important that the defined micro-batch is appropriate to the business context, as well as the processing time and the volume of data flowing in real-time. The micro-batch adequate duration ensures that the most recent data is quickly processed, not delaying its storage and subsequent analysis.

Real-time storage technologies are able to guarantee the low latencies, however, under different conditions. Hive, with its ability to handle large volumes of data, performs well regardless of the amount of data that is extracted via streaming mechanisms. It reveals better performance when the specificities of partitioning are appropriate to the business context, as the queries that use filters by the partitioning attribute show benefits in performance. Moreover, when the micro-batch duration is bigger, less files are created and less writing operations are needed. The volume of data in each insertion does not influence query performance. However, in Hive, when several files are inserted at once, the insertion process is compromised. To avoid this, data should be moved to a historical storage where it is concatenated, creating larger files.

Cassandra, after a few hours of data collection, presents delays in the data insertion process, since analytical queries are performed at the same time as data is collected, processed and stored, so, given the increase in the volume of data, queries become slower. Nevertheless, in scenarios with a lower volume of data, its behavior is more appropriate, achieving a lower delay in the data insertion process while analytical queries are also being executed. The increase or decrease of the micro-batch duration does not influence its performance. Given the context of this work, analytical needs with large amounts of data, updating operations were not used nor queries with filters that use the partition and the clustering keys, situations where the benefits of Cassandra could be highlighted.

Considering all the evaluated scenarios and the obtained results, both data storage technologies are adequate and the choice of one or another must be constrained by the business context in which they need to perform. In both cases, it is important to recall, data will remain in the real-time storage component for a short period of time. Nevertheless, Hive with a partitioned table according to the hour of the event is the real-time data storage system suggested in this work, as it ensures that the data flows in real-time. In any case, there is the need to move real-time data to a historical data storage, a procedure that follows the best practices also used in traditional contexts Kimball & Ross (2013). The historical data repository is able to maintain an adequate performance even with large amounts of data.

CONCLUSION

Real-time analysis has become an advantage over competitors, increasing the search for these solutions that should be prepared for Big Data contexts. However, real-time represents a big challenge since most of the existing technologies can offer relatively high latencies. The search for new solutions and technologies motivates new research contributions that help organizations in their daily activities. There is the need of advancing the state-of-the-art in this area. This work analyzed existing related works and proposed an architecture for RTBDWs that is able to integrate streaming data with batch data for decision support. This architecture is an evolution of the Lambda Architecture by Marz & Warren (2015) and the real-time processing approach of Kimball & Ross (2013).

The proposed architecture was implemented and evaluated, exploring the performance of different solutions. The analysis of the obtained results show that it is able to collect, process and store data that arrives in real-time, and to perform analytical queries over the data in a timely fashion, not compromising the analytical needs of the organizations.

The presented benchmark was useful to understand the limitations of the analyzed technologies and their characteristics, namely where each one performs better. Different volumes of data were used testing the technologies' restrictions. With the used technological infrastructure and the different data volumes, the proposed architecture was able to properly handle real-time data, from collection to analysis, also ensuring timely processing and storage. For the different data storage technologies, their advantages and disadvantages were pointed out.

In summary, taking into consideration the proposed architecture, a RTBDW can be implemented, allowing streaming and batch data to flow, to be stored, to be processed and to be analyzed, integrating both time perspectives into the decision-making process. The fact that this work is not focused on a specific application domain, but rather on the design of a solution that can be adapted to any organization, allows its use in the implementation of a BDW that offers a fast response time to queries over fast data.

FUTURE RESEARCH DIRECTIONS

Within the research topic of this work, namely Big Data Warehouses with real-time requirements, several research challenges exist. Since not all of them were possible to address in this chapter, they are here named as future research.

Within the research project running at Bosch Braga, the architecture will be fully implemented in an industrial context, with real-time data being collected from the shop floor. The real-time requirements associated with this specific implementation need to be identified, as they will influence how the data needs to be processed, the data models that must be defined and, of course, the technologies that should be used for data storage.

Moreover, and as new technologies for data storage and processing are emerging, it is important to study those technologies and their advantages and disadvantages in specific implementation scenarios. One of these technologies is Kudu, a data storage technology that claims being able to integrate the features of Hive and Cassandra, i.e., fast sequential and random access to data.

In addition, it would also be interesting to analyze contexts where data needs to be updated, in order to evaluate the performance of Cassandra in more operational contexts that can be needed for refreshing a BDW. Moreover, supporting for ACID transactions could also be analyzed, as some processing technologies, like Presto, may support, in the near future, this kind of functionality.

Finally, different data modeling strategies can be analyzed for the storage of the historical data, like a multidimensional model based on a star schema, as some of these modeling strategies are extensively used in organizations.

ACKNOWLEDGMENT

This research was supported by COMPETE: POCI-01-0145- FEDER-007043 and FCT (*Fundação para a Ciência e Tecnologia*) within the Project Scope: UID/CEC/00319/2013, and by European Structural and Investment Funds in the FEDER component, through the Operational Competitiveness and Internationalization Programme (COMPETE 2020) [Project n° 002814; Funding Reference: POCI-01-0247-FEDER-002814]. Some of the figures in this chapter use icons made by Freepik, from www.flaticon.com.

REFERENCES

Bruckner, R. M., List, B., & Schiefer, J. (2002). Striving towards Near Real-Time Data Integration for Data Warehouses. In Y. Kambayashi, W. Winiwarter, & M. Arikawa (Eds.), *Data Warehousing and Knowledge Discovery* (pp. 317–326). Berlin: Springer Berlin Heidelberg; doi:10.1007/3-540-46145-0_31

Chebotko, A., Kashlev, A., & Lu, S. (2015). A Big Data Modeling Methodology for Apache Cassandra. In *Proceedings of the 2015 IEEE International Congress on Big Data* (pp. 238–245). Washington, DC: IEEE Computer Society. 10.1109/BigDataCongress.2015.41

Chen, G. J., Wiener, J. L., Iyer, S., Jaiswal, A., Lei, R., & Simha, N., ... Yilmaz, S. (2016). Realtime Data Processing at Facebook. In *Proceedings of the 2016 International Conference on Management of Data* (pp. 1087–1098). New York, NY: ACM. 10.1145/2882903.2904441

Chen, H., Chiang, R. H. L., & Storey, V. C. (2012). Business Intelligence and Analytics: From Big Data to Big Impact. *Management Information Systems Quarterly*, *36*(4), 1165–1188. doi:10.2307/41703503

Chen, M., Mao, S., & Liu, Y. (2014). Big Data: A Survey. *Mobile Networks and Applications*, *19*(2), 171–209. doi:10.100711036-013-0489-0

Costa, E., Costa, C., & Santos, M. Y. (2017). Efficient Big Data Modelling and Organization for Hadoop Hive-Based Data Warehouses. In M. Themistocleous & V. Morabito (Eds.), *Information Systems: 14th European, Mediterranean, and Middle Eastern Conference, EMCIS 2017, Coimbra, Portugal, September 7-8, 2017, Proceedings* (pp. 3–16). Cham: Springer International Publishing. 10.1007/978-3-319-65930-5_1

Cuzzocrea, A., Song, I.-Y., & Davis, K. C. (2011). Analytics over Large-Scale Multidimensional Data: The Big Data Revolution! *Proceedings of the ACM 14th International Workshop on Data Warehousing and OLAP*, 101–104. 10.1145/2064676.2064695

Di Tria, F., Lefons, E., & Tangorra, F. (2014a). Big Data Warehouse Automatic Design Methodology. In Big Data Management, Technologies, and Applications (pp. 115–149). IGI Global. doi:10.4018/978-1-4666-4699-5.ch006

Di Tria, F., Lefons, E., & Tangorra, F. (2014b). Design Process for Big Data Warehouses. *2014 International Conference on Data Science and Advanced Analytics (DSAA)*, 512–518. 10.1109/DSAA.2014.7058120

Floratou, A., Minhas, U. F., & Özcan, F. (2014). SQL-on-Hadoop: Full circle back to shared-nothing database architectures. *Proceedings of the VLDB Endowment International Conference on Very Large Data Bases*, *7*(12), 1295–1306. doi:10.14778/2732977.2733002

Freudenreich, T., Furtado, P., Koncilia, C., Thiele, M., Waas, F., & Wrembel, R. (2013). An On-Demand ELT Architecture for Real-Time BI. In M. Castellanos, U. Dayal, & E. A. Rundensteiner (Eds.), *Enabling Real-Time Business Intelligence* (pp. 50–59). Berlin: Springer Berlin Heidelberg; doi:10.1007/978-3-642-39872-8_4

Golab, L., & Johnson, T. (2014). Data Stream Warehousing. In *International Conference on Data Engineering* (pp. 1290–1293). IEEE Computer Society. 10.1109/ICDE.2014.6816763

Goss, R. G., & Veeramuthu, K. (2013). Heading Towards Big Data Building A Better Data Warehouse For More Data, More Speed, And More Users. In ASMC (Advanced Semiconductor Manufacturing Conference) (pp. 220–225). Academic Press. doi:10.1109/ASMC.2013.6552808

Hewitt, E., & Carpenter, J. (2016). *Cassandra: The Definitive Guide* (2nd ed.). O'Reilly Media, Inc.

Kimball, R., & Ross, M. (2013). *The Data Warehouse Toolkit: The Definitive Guide to Dimensional Modeling*. John Wiley & Sons.

Krishnan, K. (2013). *Data Warehousing in the Age of Big Data*. Elsevier Inc. doi:10.1016/B978-0-12-405891-0.00001-5

Li, X., & Mao, Y. (2015). Real-Time Data ETL Framework for Big Real-Time Data Analysis. In *2015 IEEE International Conference on Information and Automation* (pp. 1289–1294). Institute of Electrical and Electronics Engineers Inc. 10.1109/ICInfA.2015.7279485

Marz, N., & Warren, J. (2015). *Big Data: Principles and best practices of scalable real-time data systems* (1st ed.). Greenwich, CT: Manning Publications Co.

Mohamed, N., & Al-Jaroodi, J. (2014). Real-Time Big Data Analytics: Applications and Challenges. In *2014 International Conference on High Performance Computing Simulation (HPCS)* (pp. 305–310). Academic Press. 10.1109/HPCSim.2014.6903700

Rutherglen, J., Wampler, D., & Capriolo, E. (2012). *Programming Hive* (1st ed.). O'Reilly Media, Inc.

Santos, M. Y., Costa, C., Galvão, J., Andrade, C., Martinho, B. A., Vale Lima, F., & Costa, E. (2017). Evaluating SQL-on-Hadoop for Big Data Warehousing on Not-So-Good Hardware. In *Proceedings of the 21st International Database Engineering & Applications Symposium* (pp. 242–252). New York, NY: ACM. 10.1145/3105831.3105842

Santos, M. Y., Oliveira e Sá, J., Andrade, C., Vale Lima, F., Costa, E., Costa, C., … Galvão, J. (2017). A Big Data system supporting Bosch Braga Industry 4.0 strategy. *International Journal of Information Management*.

Santos, R. J., & Bernardino, J. (2008). Real-time Data Warehouse Loading Methodology. In *Proceedings of the 2008 International Symposium on Database Engineering & Applications* (pp. 49–58). New York, NY: ACM. 10.1145/1451940.1451949

Santos, R. J., Bernardino, J., & Vieira, M. (2011). 24/7 Real-Time Data Warehousing: A Tool for Continuous Actionable Knowledge. In *2011 IEEE 35th Annual Computer Software and Applications Conference* (pp. 279–288). IEEE. 10.1109/COMPSAC.2011.44

Thusoo, A., Sen Sarma, J., Jain, N., Shao, Z., Chakka, P., & Anthony, S., … Murthy, R. (2009). Hive - A Warehousing Solution Over a Map-Reduce Framework. In *Proceedings of the VLDB Endowment* (*Vol. 2*, pp. 1626–1629). Academic Press. 10.14778/1687553.1687609

Thusoo, A., Sen Sarma, J., Jain, N., Shao, Z., Chakka, P., & Zhang, N., … Murthy, R. (2010). Hive - A Petabyte Scale Data Warehouse Using Hadoop. In *International Conference on Data Engineering* (pp. 996–1005). Academic Press. 10.1109/ICDE.2010.5447738

Vaisman, A., & Zimányi, E. (2012). Data warehouses: Next Challenges. *Lecture Notes in Business Information Processing*, 1–26. doi:10.1007/978-3-642-27358-2_1

Ward, J. S., & Barker, A. (2013). Undefined By Data: A Survey of Big Data Definitions. *arXiv.org*, 2.

White, T. (2012). *Hadoop: The Definitive Guide* (4th ed.; Vol. 54). O'Reilly Media, Inc.;

Zikopoulos, P., Eaton, C., DeRoos, D., Deutsch, T., & Lapis, G. (2011). *Understanding Big Data: Analytics for Enterprise Class Hadoop and Streaming Data* (1st ed.). McGraw-Hill Osborne Media.

ADDITIONAL READING

Costa, E., Costa, C., & Santos, M. Y. (2017). Efficient Big Data Modelling and Organization for Hadoop Hive-Based Data Warehouses. In M. Themistocleous & V. Morabito (Eds.), *Information Systems: 14th European, Mediterranean, and Middle Eastern Conference, EMCIS 2017, Coimbra, Portugal, September 7-8, 2017, Proceedings* (pp. 3–16). Cham: Springer International Publishing. 10.1007/978-3-319-65930-5_1

Martinho, B., & Santos, M. Y. (2016). An Architecture for Data Warehousing in Big Data Environments. In A. M. Tjoa, L. Da Xu, M. Raffai, & N. M. Novak (Eds.), *Research and Practical Issues of Enterprise Information Systems: 10th IFIP WG 8.9 Working Conference, CONFENIS 2016, Vienna, Austria, December 13--14, 2016, Proceedings* (pp. 237–250). Cham: Springer International Publishing; doi:10.1007/978-3-319-49944-4_18

Marz, N., & Warren, J. (2015). *Big Data: Principles and best practices of scalable real-time data systems* (1st ed.). Greenwich, CT, USA: Manning Publications Co.

Santos, M. Y., & Costa, C. (2016). Data Models in NoSQL Databases for Big Data Contexts. In Y. Tan & Y. Shi (Eds.), *Data Mining and Big Data* (pp. 475–485). Cham: Springer International Publishing; doi:10.1007/978-3-319-40973-3_48

Santos, M. Y., Costa, C., Galvão, J., Andrade, C., Martinho, B. A., Vale Lima, F., & Costa, E. (2017). Evaluating SQL-on-Hadoop for Big Data Warehousing on Not-So-Good Hardware. In *Proceedings of the 21st International Database Engineering & Applications Symposium* (pp. 242–252). New York, NY, USA: ACM. 10.1145/3105831.3105842

Santos, M. Y., Martinho, B., & Costa, C. (2017). Modelling and implementing big data warehouses for decision support. *Journal of Management Analytics*, 4(2), 111–129. doi:10.1080/23270012.2017.1304292

Santos, M. Y., Oliveira e Sá, J., Andrade, C., Vale Lima, F., Costa, E., & Costa, C. … Galvão, J. (2017). A Big Data system supporting Bosch Braga Industry 4.0 strategy. *International Journal of Information Management*.

Santos, M. Y., Oliveira e Sá, J., Costa, C., Galvão, J., Andrade, C., & Martinho, B. … Costa, E. (2017). A Big Data Analytics Architecture for Industry 4.0. In *WorldCist'17 - 5th World Conference on Information Systems and Technologies*.

KEY TERMS AND DEFINITIONS

Batch Processing: A sequential processing mode in which the data is read from the data source, processed or stored, being performed in a non-iterative way, each task at a time.

Big Data: A concept mainly characterized by the volume, velocity and variety of data being generated.

Big Data Warehouse: A system capable of dealing with high volume, velocity and variety of data, integrating data from heterogeneous data sources and allowing the extraction of information relevant to the decision-making process. With state-of-art technologies, lower cost solutions can be implemented, overcoming some of the limitations of traditional solutions.

Business Analytics: A process of continuously exploration of hidden patterns and insights in data.

ETL Process: The process of extracting, transforming and loading the data, namely the extraction of data from its data sources to a staging area, the transformations to add structure or to clean the data and the act of loading it to its final destination.

Real-Time: The time in which the data is collected, processed and stored. Collected data must be processed as soon as it is received, providing an up-to-date availability and analysis of the data.

Stream Processing: A processing mode in which data is continuously collected and processed, as new events take place.

Chapter 3
Deductive Data Warehouses:
Analyzing Data Warehouses With Datalog (By Example)

Kornelije Rabuzin
University of Zagreb, Croatia

ABSTRACT

This chapter presents the concept of "deductive data warehouses." Deductive data warehouses rely on deductive databases but use a data warehouse in the background instead of a database. The authors show how Datalog, as a logic programming language, can be used to perform on-line analytical processing (OLAP) analysis on data. For that purpose, a small data warehouse has been implemented. Furthermore, they propose and briefly discuss "Datalog by example" as a visual front-end tool for posing Datalog queries to deductive data warehouses.

INTRODUCTION

Databases (DB) have been with us for a long time: relational databases for more than four decades, and hierarchical and network databases for even longer. Codd's papers of the 1960s and 1970s on the relational data model have greatly influenced research in past decades. The ability to store and efficiently manage large amounts of data is very important in the modern era, making relational databases quite popular. Some good database reference works include (Date, 2004; Garcia-Molina, Ullman & Widom, 2009; Paton, 1998; Date, 2012; Hernandez, 2013; Coronel & Morris, 2016; Hoffer, Ramesh, & Topi, 2015; Silberschatz, Korth, & Sudarshan, 2011; Elmasri & Navathe, 2003).

In order to build a database that end users (usually) perceive as a set of tables, various techniques may be used to build a data model for an application domain. One of the most famous such techniques is the ERA (Entity – Relationship – Attribute) diagram. This technique has been in use for almost four decades, making it one of the few ideas in the IT field that could perhaps be described as "old." The reason for its popularity is that it is simple to understand, even for non-technical users. When building a model, the main goal is to define entities (i.e., types of entities), relationships among them (i.e., types of relation-

DOI: 10.4018/978-1-5225-5516-2.ch003

ships) as well as attributes (i.e., those that belong to types of entities). Once an ERA diagram is drawn, it can easily be transformed into a set of tables. With a little experience, we can avoid some common pitfalls and end up with good database design. A good book on database design is (Hernandez, 2013).

Normalization is also relevant for database design. During normalization, the set of normal forms (1NF, 2NF, 3NF, BCNF, 4NF, 5NF, etc.) is used to reduce anomalies and to avoid potential inconsistencies, which also advances good database design. Although people that work with databases are not usually aware of normalization theory, logical database design is a very important component of good database design. Since a more detailed discussion of normalization is beyond the scope of this paper, please consult (Date, 2012) for more information on database design.

In order to work with relational databases, a database language must be used. The most popular of these languages is SQL (Structured Query Language), which is both standardized and supported by many relational database management system vendors. SQL consists of a set of statements that can be divided into several categories:

- DDL stands for Data Definition Language; DDL is used to define (create) objects in the database (i.e., tables, functions, sequences, etc.),
- DML stands for Data Manipulation Language; DML is used to manipulate data, i.e., to insert, update or delete data entries, and
- QL stands for Query Language with a SELECT statement used to query the data from the database.

In order to use certain statements, one has to be familiar with statement syntax. The most popular way to represent (define) the syntax of an SQL statement is to use BNF (Backus-Naur Form) notation. This notation uses several symbols (like [], {}, ...) whose meanings allow one to construct a valid SQL statement. For example, this is the syntax of an SELECT statement in the PostgreSQL 10 database management system (https://www.postgresql.org/docs/10/static/sql-select.html):

```
[ WITH [ RECURSIVE ] with_query [, ...] ]
SELECT [ ALL | DISTINCT [ ON (expression [, ...]) ] ]
    [ * | expression [ [ AS ] output_name ] [, ...] ]
    [ FROM from_item [, ...] ]
    [ WHERE condition ]
    [ GROUP BY grouping_element [, ...] ]
    [ HAVING condition [, ...] ]
    [ WINDOW window_name AS (window_definition) [, ...] ]
    [ { UNION | INTERSECT | EXCEPT } [ ALL | DISTINCT ] select ]
    [ ORDER BY expression [ ASC | DESC | USING operator ] [ NULLS { FIRST |
LAST } ] [, ...] ]
    [ LIMIT { count | ALL } ]
    [ OFFSET start [ ROW | ROWS ] ]
    [ FETCH { FIRST | NEXT } [ count ] { ROW | ROWS } ONLY ]
    [ FOR { UPDATE | NO KEY UPDATE | SHARE | KEY SHARE } [ OF table_name [,
...] ] [ NOWAIT | SKIP LOCKED ] [...] ]
```

Square brackets represent optional elements, | represents or, and ... means that something can be repeated more than once. However, over the years SQL has become quite complex and some statements (especially queries) have started to cause problems even for professionals (as well as for end users). More information on SQL can be found in (Beaulieu, 2009; Celko, 2005; Karwin, 2010; Lawrence, 2014; Rabuzin, Maleković, & Lovrenčić, 2007; Rith, Lehmayr, & Meyer-Wegener, 2014).

During the past two decades, however, one problem has arisen that continues to cause difficulties in many companies when making decisions. The problem is that over the years, many applications have been implemented within companies to support business processes, and these applications are incompatible and cannot work with each other (i.e., in the context of exchanging data). In other words, many different applications exist but they are implemented in different programming languages and they use different ways to store data. As a direct consequence, it is not possible to retrieve relevant data that could be used to make decisions. The problem with many heterogeneous applications (i.e., applications that use different programming languages and different ways to store data) is that each application supports one or more business processes, but to understand the big picture someone within the company has to be able to compare data from different applications. All data from different systems has to be integrated in order to make decisions. This is not an easy task, even if this data is in databases. When data is scattered across different systems and stored in different formats, the integration problem is even more obvious. The integration and cleaning of data subsumes complex queries used to extract, clean and conform the data in order to make it appropriate for decision-making (this is known as the ETL process, i.e., Extract Transform Load).

In order to resolve this problem of making decisions based on data, the concept of data warehousing has been introduced. A data warehouse is a special kind of a database that is organized according to different design principles then a standard database. Its purpose is to (physically) integrate data from different sources and provide a trusted place to store important pieces of information. Once a data warehouse is implemented, relevant reports should be available within seconds or minutes, offering different possibilities for reorganization (e.g., slicing, dicing, and drilling). Although it may at first seem simple to implement a data warehouse, it is in fact difficult to accomplish. Indeed, many data warehousing projects are not successful and fail because of the number of data issues that have to be resolved along the way. Once the process is completed, however, the integration of data from different sources produces a new source that contains integrated, de-duplicated, cleaned and transformed data from different applications, and such data can be used to make important decisions.

The problem of large amounts of heterogeneous data has become even more obvious over the past few years with extremely large amounts of data coming from different sources in different formats. The speed at which data is produced is also an important factor: in order to manage large amounts of data, we need real-time systems which operate much quicker than conventional relational database systems. We call such data "Big Data" as they cause the following problems to existing data processing systems:

- Volumes of data are measured in PB and EB, and existing data processing systems have problems with such large amounts of data,
- The formats of individual pieces of data are different and mostly unstructured, i.e., data is heterogeneous, possibly including pictures (people publish pictures in social networks), video clips, posts, messages, sensor data, etc.

- Data is produced really quickly; by the time you are finished with this paper, millions of new messages and pictures will have been published and exchanged.

In the Big Data era, we need to implement data lakes. A data lake contains large volumes of versatile data that are different in format and in size, and whose speed production is high. For this purpose, new data storage and processing tools are being developed. In particular, NoSQL databases and the Hadoop framework are the best-known solutions for Big Data.

When using data warehouses, SQL can be used for the relational data warehouse and MDX can be used when cubes are implemented. When using NoSQL databases, things become more complicated as languages are not yet standardized. When talking about NoSQL databases, we distinguish four main types:

1. Document oriented databases (for example, MongoDB)
2. Column oriented databases (for example, HBase)
3. Graph databases (for example, Neo4j)
4. Key value databases (for example, Redis)

Each NoSQL database type has many representative systems, and there are significant differences between these systems. For more information on NoSQL databases, consult (Redmond & Wilson, 2012; Robinson, Webber, & Eifrem, 2013). Predominantly, the languages that are used are quite different and not standardized. There were some attempts to build a universal language for different systems, as it is not easy to learn many new languages. Such papers as (Holanda & Souza, 2015), (Rabuzin, Maleković & Šestak, 2016), (Bach & Werner, 2014), (Wood, 2012), (Holzschuher & Peinl, 2013) and (He & Singh, 2008) discuss the problems of different query languages in NoSQL databases. However, in this paper we do not explore NoSQL databases. Instead, we focus on relational databases and relational data warehouses.

As noted above, one can use different query languages depending on the system that is being used. In this paper, we present the idea of deductive data warehouses. More specifically, we will use Datalog as a language to analyze data in a relational data warehouse and show how data can be analyzed by means of Datalog. When using data warehouses, different front-end tools are implemented and used that make it possible to analyze data and build queries without writing queries manually. We are also going to present a visual interface that could be used to pose Datalog queries graphically.

The paper is organized as follows: the next section defines deductive databases and proposes deductive data warehouses. Next, a small example is built and data is analyzed by means of advanced front-end tools and defined Datalog rules. Then a Datalog interface is proposed that could be used to pose Datalog queries graphically. Finally, the conclusion is presented.

This paper is an extended and improved version of one published in the *International Journal of Data Warehousing and Mining* (Rabuzin, 2014).

BACKGROUND

There are several important books on deductive databases. (Piattini and Diaz, 2000) represents an interesting source because it describes deductive databases as such in a precise and concise manner. More on the subject can be found in (Colomb, 2005).

On the subject of data warehouses, see (Han, 1997; Kimball & Caserta, 2004; Kimball and Ross, 2002; Kimball et al., 2008; Ponniah, 2001; Reinschmidt & Francoise, 1999; Silvers, 2008).

On Datalog, see the following papers: (Boulicaut, Marcel & Rigotti, 2001) use rules in a similar way to us, but they focus on knowledge discovery and their rules resemble those that we use in Datalog. (Neumayr, Anderlik & Schrefl, 2012) use Datalog-based reasoning over multidimensional ontologies. (Aligon, Marcel & Negre, 2013) explore how to summarize and query logs of OLAP queries. By focusing on a measurement of summarized data, (Tjioe & Taniar, 2005) show how association rules can be used in data warehouses. Regarding different query languages for relational and NoSQL databases, see (Holanda & Souza, 2015), (Rabuzin et al., 2016), (Bach & Werner, 2014), (Wood, 2012), (Holzschuher & Peinl, 2013) and (He & Singh, 2008).

There are some other papers that discuss the use of Datalog, but so far nobody has defined the term "deductive data warehouse." Furthermore, many front-end business intelligence tools can be used to query data warehouses visually. In the last part of this paper, an interface is proposed that should make it possible to build Datalog queries graphically. Therefore, "Datalog By Example" is presented in the last part of the paper.

DEDUCTIVE DATABASES AND DEDUCTIVE DATA WAREHOUSES

(Piattini and Diaz, 2000) provide a definition of deductive databases: "A deductive DB D is a triple D = (F, DR, IC), where F is a finite set of ground facts, DR a finite set of deductive rules, and IC a finite set of integrity constraints. The set F of facts is called the extensional part of the DB (EDB), and the sets DR and IC together form the so-called intensional part (IDB)". A good example comes from (Piattini and Diaz, 2000):

Facts
Father(John, Tony)
Mother(Mary, Bob)
Father(Peter, Mary)
Deductive Rules
Parent(x,y) ← Father(x,y)
Parent(x,y) ← Mother(x,y)
GrandMother(x,y) ← Mother(x,z) ∧ Parent(z,y)
Ancestor(x,y) ← Parent(x,y)
Ancestor(x,y) ← Parent(x,z) ∧ Ancestor(z,y)
Nondirect-anc(x,y) ← Ancestor(x,y) ∧ ¬Parent(x,y)
Integrity Constraints
IC1(x) ← Parent(x,x)
IC2(x) ← Father(x,y) ∧ Mother(x,z)

As we can see, there are three facts and several rules used to define different relationships (parent, grandmother, etc.); we have two integrity constraints, respectively preventing someone from being their own parent and preventing a person from being both a mother and a father at the same time. More information on deductive databases can be found in (Colomb, 2005; Piattini & Diaz, 2000).

Datalog is a logic programing language. Syntactically speaking, Datalog is a subset of Prolog. Here we do not explain the details, but more information on Datalog can be found in (Ajtai & Gurevich, 1994; Eiter & Gottlob, 1997; Green, 2012; Gurevich, 2012; Hellerstein, 2009; Huang, Green, & Loo, 2011; Levene & Loizou, 1999; Li & Mitchell, 2002).

A data warehouse is usually organized in the form of a star (or snowflake) schema. A star schema usually contains dimensions and facts; these are both tables, differing because dimension tables store attributes used to analyze data in fact tables, while the fact tables in turn contain measures (i.e., numbers) used to evaluate (measure) business processes (Figure 1).

This figure is easy to understand and end users can pose queries by themselves using OLAP tools that represent an intuitive way to analyze data. Furthermore, complex multi-table joins are avoided as the number of tables in the data warehouse is much smaller than the number of tables in the database. We will see some examples below.

Once again, a problem whose consequences are still visible is the direct consequence of bad planning, or of a "no planning at all" approach. Many companies have over the years implemented many applications and/or information systems; however, they were all implemented in different applications languages (different generations of application languages were used) and they used different data storage mechanisms (some applications used different types of files, some applications used databases, etc.). In recent years, even more data is coming from other unstructured sources (the Big Data paradigm). Today we know that one cannot focus on just one aspect of business; one must consider the whole picture. For example, one cannot focus on sales data without considering purchasing department results and global trends. Let us assume that incomes were reduced in the past quarter. Although this may seem bad, if we compare global trends and our competitors' (sales) results, we might conclude that we are in fact performing acceptably. By using different front- end OLAP tools, we should be able to analyze the data in the data warehouse.

A deductive data warehouse contains ground facts as well. Unlike databases where we avoid anomalies and redundancies, in data warehouses we use redundant data to reduce the number of tables to be joined as well as to reduce the complexity of the model. As a result, some queries (goals) in Datalog should be less complicated and more intuitive, although this usually results in redundant data in tables. Basically, the data warehouse should have a smaller number of tables which should in turn reduce the number of joins; however, dimension tables should have a few more attributes than tables in OLTP (On-Line Transaction Processing) systems, as several tables from OLTP systems are usually integrated into one dimension table with more attributes. Thus, ground facts can be found in both dimension and fact tables.

Figure 1. Star schema

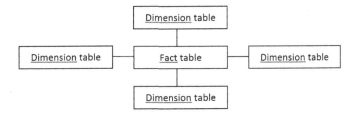

In deductive databases, rules are used to produce new pieces of information based on the facts that we have in the database. In deductive data warehouses, rules will be used in the same way (i.e. for the same reason) as in deductive databases; in particular, we define rules that simulate On-Line Analytical Processing (OLAP) capabilities supported by many different OLAP tools (slice, drill down, what-if, etc.). This is demonstrated in a later example.

We all agree that data warehouses are useful; however, to build a complex data warehouse is not an easy task. The ETL phase is crucial in the process. There is a saying that ETL makes or breaks the data warehouse, and this is pretty much true (Inmon, 2002). ETL consists of many simple and/or complex transformations which must ensure that, among other factors,

- All values are known (and logical)
- All values are properly formatted
- All business rules are obeyed
- Data is properly transformed and aggregated
- Conflicting names are resolved
- Inconsistent values are corrected.

Business rules in databases are usually implemented in the form of integrity constraints (NOT NULL, UNIQUE, PRIMARY KEY, CHECK, etc.), although some more complex business rules require triggers and/or stored procedures (NOT NULL would require that a value is entered, UNIQUE would ensure that a certain value is unique, etc.). More on business rules in databases can be found in (Ross, 2003; Date, 2000).

When talking about data warehouses, things look a little bit different. Once the data is loaded in the data warehouse, integrity constraints are not specified. The reason is quite simple: since ETL designers are responsible for data being correct, and should ensure that it is (all data is de-duplicated, cleaned etc.), integrity constraints are not used in the final data warehouse structure. Basically, constraints could be checked, but they are not specified within the database management system because the database system needs to check them and this process is time-consuming. Even if integrity constraints were specified, they would sometimes have to be disabled. Consequently, deductive data warehouses do not use integrity constraints because ETL designers are responsible for all values in the data warehouse being consistent and correct. We can thus say that specified constraints impose certain overhead and should be enforced at the ETL stage. Therefore, integrity constraints need not to be covered further here.

To conclude, the deductive data warehouse has a set of ground facts as well as a set of rules; it can have a set of constraints, but they have to be enforced at the ETL stage and not in the data warehouse itself. Now that data warehouses and deductive databases have been defined, let us consider what a deductive data warehouse would look like.

DEDUCTIVE DATA WAREHOUSE: AN EXAMPLE

Let's build a small data warehouse to be used to analyze log files; this was in fact a project that the author of this paper previously worked on (in a reduced form). The main purpose of the project was to analyze users and their actions, i.e., it was important to analyze their actions in order to increase the total number of users as well as the total number of activities on one specific developed web application.

Since scientific research should be repeatable, i.e., other people should be able to reproduce the same results based on the information presented in this paper, table definitions are given below. The PostgreSQL database management system (DBMS) is used and statements should be easy to follow:

```
CREATE TABLE actions (
id SERIAL PRIMARY KEY,
action VARCHAR (20),
points INT);
INSERT INTO actions (action, points) VALUES ('read', 3), ('write', 10);
INSERT INTO actions (action, points) VALUES ('modify', 5), ('delete', 2);
CREATE TABLE users (
id SERIAL PRIMARY KEY,
name VARCHAR(30));
INSERT INTO users (name) VALUES ('Smith Peter');
CREATE TABLE dates (
id SERIAL PRIMARY KEY,
date DATE,
year INT,
quarter INT,
month INT,
week INT);
INSERT INTO dates (date)
SELECT * FROM GENERATE_SERIES ('2012-01-01'::DATE, '2012-12-31', '1 day');
UPDATE dates SET year = EXTRACT (year FROM date),
quarter = EXTRACT (quarter FROM date),
month = EXTRACT (month FROM date),
week = EXTRACT (week FROM date);
CREATE TABLE log (
action_id INT REFERENCES actions,
date_id INT REFERENCES dates,
user_id INT REFERENCES users,
number_of_actions INT);
INSERT INTO log
SELECT actions.id, dates.id, users.id, CAST((RANDOM() * 10) AS INT)  FROM ac-
tions, users, dates;
```

The last INSERT statement is here to add some artificial data to the log table; although it is not used much and it usually means that somebody wrote the wrong query, in this statement a Cartesian product was used to generate data and add records to the table. Please keep in mind that if you implemented the statements above by yourself you would not get the exact same values in your own data warehouse, since the RANDOM() function is used to generate the data.

The data warehouse is implemented in PostgreSQL DBMS. In the following section, three front-end business intelligence tools are used, including Microsoft Power BI (desktop), QlikView and Business Objects XI. Datalog is used as a logic programming language (actually Datalog Educational System, i.e., DES). In order to work with PostgreSQL (from DES), an ODBC connection has to be specified, but this is not hard to do. Now let us look at some reports and queries expressed in the BI tools as well as in DES.

DATA ANALYSIS

In the following section, some reports (queries) are built in two ways: first, one business intelligence tool is used; next, DES is used to create adequate Datalog rules that produce the same results if or when invoked. Specifically, we show how advanced data analysis techniques (OLAP) can be implemented by means of Datalog rules. Some Datalog rules could be specified in a different way, but we do not discuss advantages and disadvantages in this paper.

Simple Queries

Although such queries are not common in data warehouses (it is much more common to aggregate values for a larger number of records), they can be posed. One query returns action names, and the other returns user names. In the BI tools, one can usually just select or drag attributes and such a report is created (Figure 2 and Figure 3):

Similarly, the list of users (containing just one user) is given below:

Let us define rules that return some basic data, like action names or user names. In DES we should use the following (simple) rules:

```
user(X):-users(_,X).
action(X):-actions(_,X,_).
Let us determine action and user names:
DES> user(X).
{
  user('Smith Peter')
}
Info: 1 tuple computed.
DES> action(X).
{
  action(delete),
  action(modify),
```

Figure 2. List of actions (QlikView)

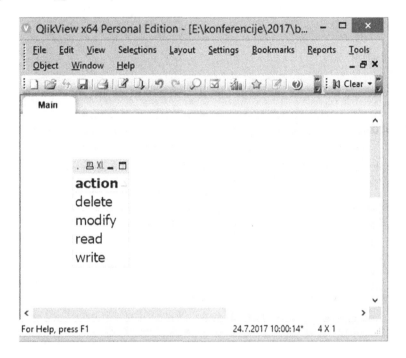

Figure 3. List of users (Microsoft Power BI)

```
   action(read),
   action(write)
}
Info: 4 tuples computed.
```

Since simple queries do not cause problems, let us move to more advanced queries.

Grouping Records

Let us move on and let us determine the total sum of actions in the data warehouse. In the Microsoft Power BI tool, there is no problem in calculating this value because all we need to do is to select this measure from the list of measures (Figure 4):

In DES, we add the following rule ("noa" stands for "number of actions"):

```
noa(R):-group_by(log(A,B,C,D), [], R=sum(D)).
```

When this rule is called, we get the same answer:

```
DES> noa(X).
{
  noa(7280)
}
Info: 1 tuple computed.
```

Figure 4. Total number of actions (Microsoft Power BI)

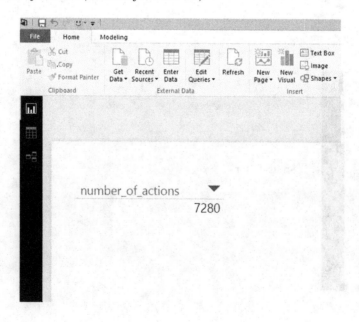

Now let us determine the number of actions per user (Figure 5):

In DES, the following rule must be added:

```
user_actions_noa(B,H,R):- group_by((users(A,B), log(C,D,A,F), actions(C,H,I)),
[B,H], R=sum(F)).
```

Let us see the result:

```
DES> user_actions_noa(X,Y,Z).
{
  user_actions_noa('Smith Peter', delete, 1746),
  user_actions_noa('Smith Peter', modify, 1717),
  user_actions_noa('Smith Peter', read, 1840),
  user_actions_noa('Smith Peter', write, 1977)
}
Info: 4 tuples computed.
```

We see that the results are the same.

Slice and Dice

One thing that is inherent to OLAP tools is the so-called "slice and dice" mode; a report be can easily reorganized (Figure 6):

While slice can be implemented in DES as well (by adding a certain condition), dice mode is more difficult. This is because DES is not per se a graphically oriented environment; therefore, dice is not covered in this paper.

Figure 5. Number of actions per user and action name (Microsoft Power BI)

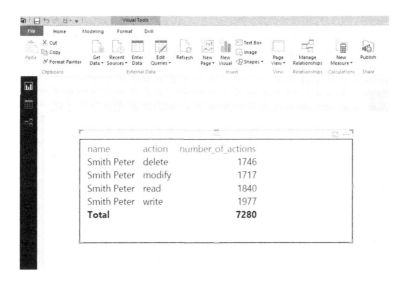

Figure 6. Slice and dice (Microsoft Power BI)

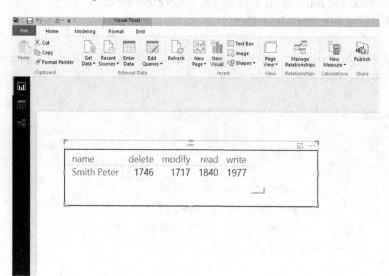

Hierarchies (Drill Down and Roll up)

Let us determine the total sum of actions for a user and a specified year (Figure 7):
    In DES, we should add the following rule:

```
user_year_noa(B,I,R):- group_by((users(A,B), log(C,D,A,F), dates(D,H,I,J,K,L)),
[B,I], R=sum(F)).
```

Figure 7. Drill down – number of actions per year (Microsoft Power BI)

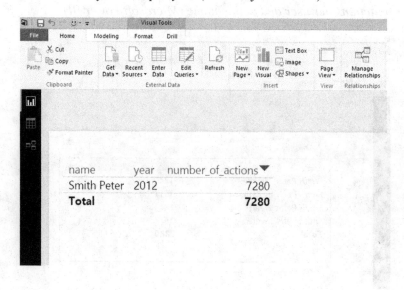

The answer is:

```
DES> user_year_noa(X,Y,Z).
{
  user_year_noa('Smith Peter', 2012, 7280)
}
Info: 1 tuple computed.
```

Furthermore, let us build a report that shows the same value, only per quarter for the specified year (Figure 8):

In DES, this would look quite similar to the previous example:

```
user_quarter_noa(B,J,R):- group_by((users(A,B), log(C,D,A,F),
dates(D,H,I,J,K,L)), [B,J], R=sum(F)).
```

The answer is:

```
DES> user_quarter_noa(X,Y,Z).
{
  user_quarter_noa('Smith Peter', 1, 1855),
  user_quarter_noa('Smith Peter', 2, 1831),
  user_quarter_noa('Smith Peter', 3, 1790),
  user_quarter_noa('Smith Peter', 4, 1804)
}
Info: 4 tuples computed.
```

Let us build the report that shows the same thing, only on a month level (Figure 9):

Of course, one would get the same result in DES with a slight modification of one of the previous two rules. What is interesting here is that this principle can be applied at further levels, leading us to

Figure 8. Number of actions per quarter (Microsoft Power BI)

name	quarter	number_of_actions ▼
Smith Peter	1	1855
Smith Peter	2	1831
Smith Peter	4	1804
Smith Peter	3	1790
Total		**7280**

Figure 9. Number of actions per month (Microsoft Power BI)

name	month ▲	number_of_actions
Smith Peter	1	645
Smith Peter	2	637
Smith Peter	3	573
Smith Peter	4	585
Smith Peter	5	642
Smith Peter	6	604
Smith Peter	7	645
Smith Peter	8	581
Smith Peter	9	564
Smith Peter	10	585
Smith Peter	11	626
Smith Peter	12	593
Total		**7280**

the concept of hierarchies. One year consists of four quarters; each quarter has three months; etc. In BI tools, one usually needs to specify a hierarchy to enable drill down/roll up analysis (Figure 10):

In some other BI tools, like Business Objects, drill mode has to be activated (menu Analysis -> Drill) when the report is built and opened. Once this has been done, mousing over the year value automatically offers drill down to the quarter level (Figure 11):

When we double-click the cell value, we get quarter values, and a double-click on a specified quarter leads us to the month level (Figure 12):

Now let us define rules in DES that behave as described.

```
drill_down(X,Y,H,R):- X=year, group_by((dates(B,F,Y,H,I,J), log(A,B,C,D)),
[H], R=sum(D)).
```

Let us see what the rule does. For a specified year (2012), we get quarter results (values 1 – 4) which, as we can see, are the same:

```
DES> drill_down(year,2012,A,B).
{
  drill_down(year, 2012, 1, 1855),
  drill_down(year, 2012, 2, 1831),
  drill_down(year, 2012, 3, 1790),
  drill_down(year, 2012, 4, 1804)
```

Figure 10. Specifying a hierarchy (Microsoft Power BI)

Figure 11. Drill down - year to quarter (Business Objects XI)

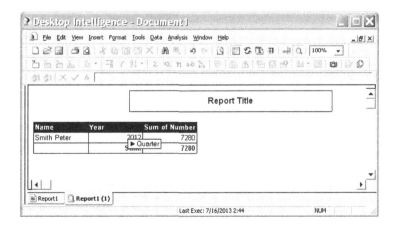

Figure 12. Drill down - quarter to month (Business Objects XI)

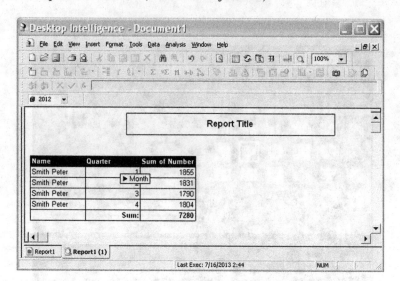

```
}
Info: 4 tuples computed.
```

To drill down to the quarter level, we could define a similar rule (if X = quarter go down to the month level):

```
drill_down(X,G,Y,I,R):- X=quarter, group_by((dates(B,F,G,Y,I,J), log(A,B,C,D)),
[I], R=sum(D)).
```

Let us check the rule; since we specified the third quarter, we get results for July, August and September (i.e. for 7, 8 and 9):

```
DES> drill_down(quarter,2012,3,A,B).
{
  drill_down(quarter, 2012, 3, 7, 645),
  drill_down(quarter, 2012, 3, 8, 581),
  drill_down(quarter, 2012, 3, 9, 564)
}
Info: 3 tuples computed.
```

The same analogy can be used to go to the month level and vice versa.

Calculations That Include Dimension Attributes

One day, a user came to our office with a request that we should determine the number of users according to action points. Since we used MOLAP (i.e. a cube), a complex MDX had to be written to produce such a report (in the next part we say a few words on calculations as well as where to put them; for now, we will just say that this is not a trivial question).

Since each user performs certain actions, and each action brings a certain amount of points, let us determine the number of points for each user. We have to define a calculation in the Desktop Intelligence tool (the last column is calculated, i.e., the two previous columns are multiplied):

This can be done more easily in Datalog, as it is easy to multiply dimension attributes and some measures from the fact table:

```
user_points(B,H,R,I,P):- group_by((users(A,B), log(C,D,A,F), actions(C,H,I)),
[B,H,I], R = sum(F)), P is R*I.
```

When called, the result is identical:

```
DES> user_points(X,Y,Z,W,T).
{
  user_points('Smith Peter', delete, 1746, 2, 3492),
  user_points('Smith Peter', modify, 1717, 5, 8585),
  user_points('Smith Peter', read, 1840, 3, 5520),
  user_points('Smith Peter', write, 1977, 10, 19770)
}
Info: 4 tuples computed.
```

What-If Analysis

What-if analysis is another interesting mechanism for analyzing data; for example, how much money would we have made yesterday if we had used today's prices? What would be the result if actions brought

Table 1. Calculations (Business Objects XI)

Name	Action	Points	Sum of Number Of Actions	Product
Smith Peter	delete	2	1746	3492
Smith Peter	modify	5	1717	8585
Smith Peter	read	3	1840	5520
Smith Peter	write	10	1977	19770

Table 2. What-if analysis (Business Objects XI)

Name	Action	Points	Sum of Number Of Actions	Product	What if Points	What if Results
Smith Peter	delete	2	1746	3492	4,00	6984,00
Smith Peter	modify	5	1717	8585	7,00	12019,00
Smith Peter	read	3	1840	5520	5,00	9200,00
Smith Peter	write	10	1977	19770	12,00	23724,00

+2 more points? When using Business Intelligence, there are generally several ways to calculate such numbers: it can be done in the data warehouse, it can be defined in the universe, or it can be determined as a calculation on a report. It is not always clear which choice is best. In this case, the calculation was performed on a report (we added 2 points for each action and determined the total number of points per actions and users):

In DES the following rule was defined:

```
what_if(B,H,R,Z,W):- user_points(B,H,R,I,P), A is I + Z, W is A * R.
```

The result would be:

```
DES> what_if(A1,A2,A3,2,A5).
{
  what_if('Smith Peter', delete, 1746, 2, 6984),
  what_if('Smith Peter', modify, 1717, 2, 12019),
  what_if('Smith Peter', read, 1840, 2, 9200),
  what_if('Smith Peter', write, 1977, 2, 23724)
}
Info: 4 tuples computed.
```

We see that the results are alike.

DATALOG BY EXAMPLE: A FRONT END QUERY TOOL FOR DATALOG

So far, we know that front-end BI tools, like Microsoft Power BI, QlikView, Tableau, can be used to pose queries graphically, i.e., one does not have to write complex SQL statements, as was the case with the Datalog queries above. The next thing to implement is an interface that would make it possible to build Datalog queries visually. In this way, one would be able to explore deductive data warehouses and deductive databases by means of the developed interface, and not need to write Datalog queries and rules manually.

Something else that would be interesting would be for this interface to look like something that users are already familiar with. For example, SQL is the dominant language for relational databases, but it is not the only one. Query By Example (QBE) is a language that can be used as well, and it is supported, for example, in Microsoft Access. QBE can help less experienced users work with databases and pose queries against them. Since it is a visual and intuitive language, end users with no database experience have no problems writing more complex queries that they would have difficulty writing manually.

Here we present "Datalog By Example", a prototype of a visual interface for building Datalog queries for deductive databases and deductive data warehouses in the same way as QBE is used to build visual queries for relational databases. This is still work in progress, but the idea is demonstrated in one example given below.

Let's determine and list all the actions that users could possibly take. As a reminder, this is a similar Datalog query to the one that we had to write above. Within the developed interface (Figure 13), we have to choose the table as well as the attributes that we want to include in the result. The "Add new table" and "Remove table" buttons are self-explanatory (we have to choose the table that we want to add or delete from the combo box). Once the table/tables is/are selected, the "Add attribute" button is used to add one or more attributes. Once we run the query (Run Query button), the result is presented in the white window (Figure 13) that starts in the middle of the screen (and continues below). The "Clear query" button clears the query.

We select the actions table and we add the action attribute in order to see the action names. In this way, we have created and posed the following Datalog query visually:

We see that Figure 13 contains the table in the middle with four rows and two columns; the first cell contains the word Table. This visible table structure resembles the one that is used in Microsoft Access when using QBE, and because of that this approach has been named "Datalog By Example". In QBE, one has to select the attribute and the table name, mark the Show row (optional), and specify the criteria. Here we have to do the same.

The bottom part of Figure 13 (the white window) contains the result. Here we see that actions are printed, i.e., the Datalog query was executed and the action names were returned and printed.

Overall, this is for now a functional prototype but it still needs some improvements. However, the results are interesting and promising.

CONCLUSIONS AND FUTURE STUDY

This paper proposes deductive data warehouses and shows how different (advanced) data analyzing capabilities can be implemented by means of Datalog rules. For the purpose of this paper, a small data warehouse was built that was used to analyze user activities within a web application in order to increase the time that users spent within the application. Instead of a database that contained facts, a data warehouse was used in the background. Datalog (i.e. DES) as such has proven to be an adequate tool for performing different kinds of analysis on data (simple queries, more complex queries, slice, drill down, what-if, etc.). This paper also describes how deductive data warehouses differ from deductive databases (the distinctions are small, but important).

Figure 13. Datalog By Example

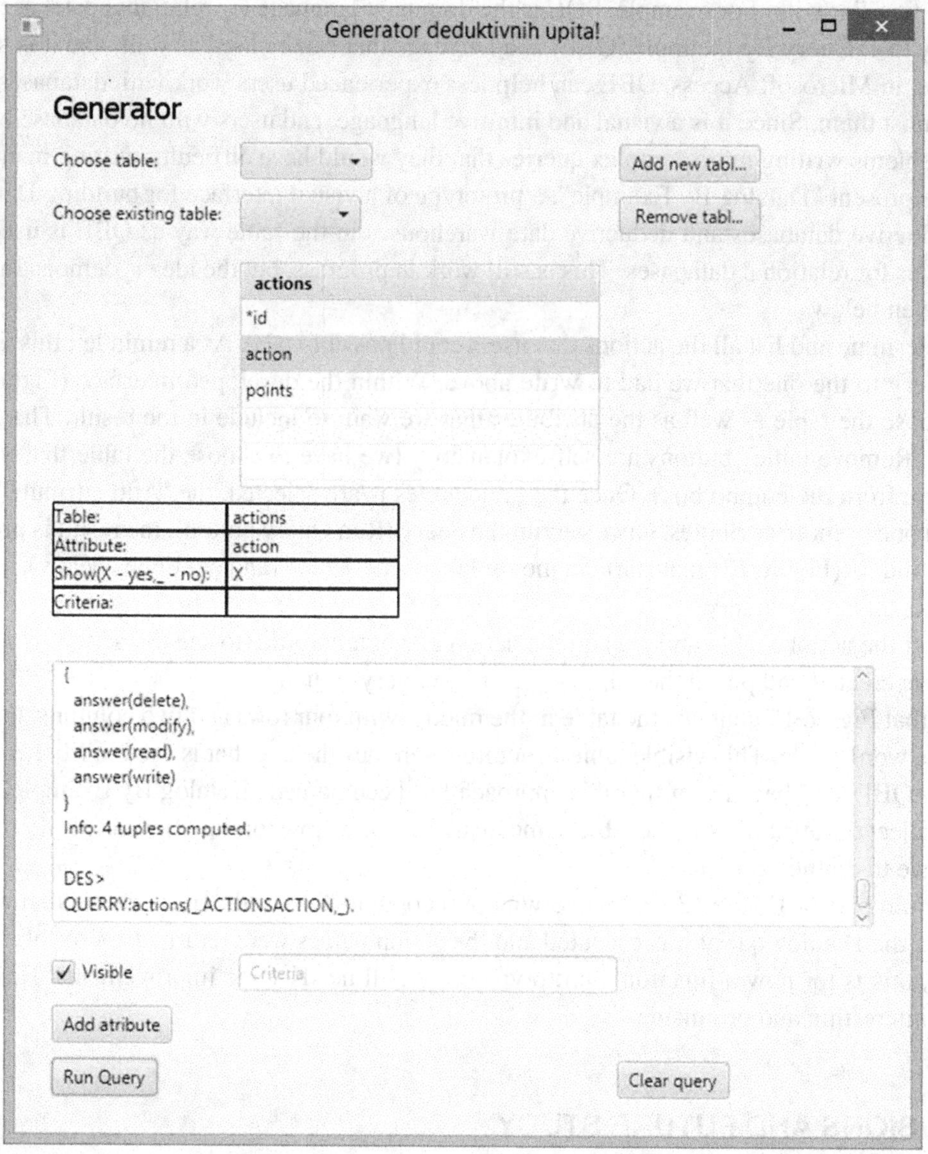

Although one can find papers where Datalog is used as a query language, this paper introduces a new term that has not been used earlier, to the best of author's knowledge. "Datalog By Example" is proposed as a visual interface for implementing Datalog queries on deductive databases and deductive data warehouses. Datalog By Example resembles Query By Example, and it is still a prototype that needs to be upgraded and improved. For now, however, the results are promising.

REFERENCES

Ajtai, M., & Gurevich, Y. (1994). Datalog vs first-order logic. *Journal of Computer and System Sciences*, *49*(3), 562–588. doi:10.1016/S0022-0000(05)80071-6

Aligon, J., Marcel, P., & Negre, E. (2013). Summarizing and Querying Logs of OLAP Queries. *Advances in Knowledge Discovery and Management. Studies in Computational Intelligence*, *471*, 99–124.

Bach, M., & Werner, A. (2014). Standardization of NoSQL database languages. In *International Conference: Beyond Databases, Architectures and Structures* (pp. 50–60). Academic Press.

Beaulieu, A. (2009). Learning SQL. *Database*. doi:10.1017/CBO9781107415324.004

Boulicaut, J. F., Marcel, P., & Rigotti, C. (2001). Query driven knowledge discovery via OLAP manipulations. *17èmes Journées Bases de Données Avancées (BDA 2001)*, 311 – 323. Retrieved June 13, 2013, from http://liris.cnrs.fr/~jboulica/bda01.pdf

Celko, J. (2005). *Joe Celko's SQL programming style*. Joe Celko's SQL Programming Style; doi:10.1016/B978-012088797-2/50000-5

Colomb, R. M. (2005). *Deductive databases and their applications*. London, UK: Taylor & Francis.

Coronel, C., & Morris, S. (2016). *Database systems: design, implementation, & management*. Cengage Learning.

Date, C. (2000). *What Not How: The Business Rules Approach to Application Development*. Reading, MA: Addison-Wesley.

Date, C. (2004). *An Introduction to Database Systems*. Boston, MA: Addison-Wesley.

Date, C. (2012). *Database Design and Relational Theory: Normal Forms and All That Jazz*. Sebastopol, CA: O'Reilly Media.

Eiter, T., Gottlob, G., & Mannila, H. (1997). Disjunctive Datalog. *ACM Transactions on Database Systems*, *22*(3), 364–418. doi:10.1145/261124.261126

Elmasri, R., & Navathe, S. B. (2003). Fundamentals of Database Systems. *Database*, *28*, 1029. doi:10.1016/S0026-2692(97)80960-3

Feuerstein, S., & Pribyl, B. (2015). *Oracle PL SQL Programming*, 867. Retrieved from http://www.amazon.com/s/ref=nb_sb_noss?url=search-alias%3Daps&field-keywords=9781449324452

Garcia-Molina, H., Ullman, J., & Widom, J. (2009). *Database Systems: The Complete Book*. London, UK: Pearson Education.

Green, T. J. (2012). Datalog and Recursive Query Processing. *Foundations and Trends® in Databases*, *5*(2), 105–195. doi:10.1561/1900000017

Gurevich, Y. (2012). Datalog: A perspective and the potential. Lecture Notes in Computer Science, 7494, 9–20. doi:10.1007/978-3-642-32925-8_2

Han, J. (1997). OLAP mining: An integration of OLAP with data mining. *Proceedings of the 7th IFIP*, 2, 1–9.

He, H., & Singh, A. K. (2008). Graphs-at-a-time: query language and access methods for graph databases. In *Proceedings of the 2008 ACM SIGMOD international conference on Management of data* (pp. 405–418). ACM. 10.1145/1376616.1376660

Hellerstein, J. M. (2009). Dedalus: Datalog in Time and Space. *Office*, (UCB/EECS-2009-173), 262–281. doi:10.1007/978-3-642-24206-9_16

Hernandez, M. J. (2013). *Database design for mere mortals: a hands-on guide to relational database design*. Pearson Education.

Hoffer, J. A., Ramesh, V., & Topi, H. (2015). *Modern Database Management*. Modern Database Management. doi:10.1017/CBO9781107415324.004

Holanda, M., & Souza, J. A. (2015). Query languages in nosql databases. Handbook of Research on Innovative Database Query Processing Techniques, 415.

Holzschuher, F., & Peinl, R. (2013). Performance of graph query languages: comparison of cypher, gremlin and native access in Neo4j. In *Proceedings of the Joint EDBT/ICDT 2013 Workshops* (pp. 195–204). Academic Press. 10.1145/2457317.2457351

Huang, S. S., Green, T. J., & Loo, B. T. (2011). Datalog and Emerging Applications: An Interactive Tutorial. In *Proceedings of the 2011 international conference on Management of data - SIGMOD '11* (p. 1213). ACM. 10.1145/1989323.1989456

Inmon, H. W. (2002). *Building the Data Warehouse*. New York: Wiley.

Kimball, R., & Caserta, J. (2004). *The Data Warehouse ETL Toolkit: Practical Techniques for Extracting, Cleaning, Conforming, and Delivering Data*. Indianapolis, IN: Wiley.

Kimball, R., & Ross, M. (2002). *The data warehouse toolkit: the complete guide to dimensional modeling*. New York: Wiley.

Kimball, R., Ross, M., Thornthwaite, W., Mundy, J., & Becker, B. (2008). *The Data Warehouse Lifecycle Toolkit*. Indianapolis, IN: Wiley.

Levene, M., & Loizou, G. (1999). *A guided tour of relational databases and beyond*. Springer. Retrieved from https://books.google.hr/books?id=CkYpI7QsLlQC&dq=datalog+is&hl=hr&source=gbs_navlinks_s

Li, N., & Mitchell, J. C. (2002). Datalog with Constraints: A Foundation for Trust Management Languages. PADL, 2562, 58–73. doi:10.1007/3-540-36388-2_6

Neumayr, B., Anderlik, S., & Schrefl, M. (2012). Towards ontology-based OLAP: datalog-based reasoning over multidimensional ontologies. In *DOLAP '12 Proceedings of the fifteenth international workshop on Data warehousing and OLAP* (pp. 41-48). New York: ACM.

Paton, N. W. (1998). *Active rules in database systems*. New York: Springer.

Piattini, M., & Diaz, O. (2000). *Advanced Database Technology and Design*. Boston: Artech House.

Ponniah, P. (2001). *Data Warehousing Fundamentals*. Chichester, UK: Wiley. doi:10.1002/0471221627

Rabuzin, K. (2014). Deductive Data Warehouses. *International Journal of Data Warehousing and Mining*, *10*(1), 16–31. doi:10.4018/ijdwm.2014010102

Rabuzin, K., Maleković, M., & Lovrenčić, A. (2007). The Theory of Active Databases vs. The SQL Standard. In *The Proceedings of 18th International Conference on Information and Intelligent Systems* (pp. 49–54). Academic Press.

Rabuzin, K., Maleković, M., & Šestak, M. (2016). Gremlin By Example. In H. R. Arabnia, F. G. Tinetti, & M. Yang (Eds.), *Proceedings of the 2016 International Conference on Advances in Big Data Analytics* (pp. 144–149). Las Vegas, NV: CSREA Press. Retrieved from http://www.worldcomp-proceedings.com/proc/proc2016/ABDA16_Final_Edition/ABDA16_Papers.pdf

Redmond, E., & Wilson, J. R. (2012). *Seven databases in seven weeks: a guide to modern databases and the NoSQL movement*. Dallas, TX: Pragmatic Bookshelf.

Reinschmidt, J., & Francoise, A. (1999). *Business Intelligence Certification Guide*. IBM International Technical Support Organization.

Robinson, J., Webber, J., & Eifrem, E. (2013). *Graph Databases*. Sebastopol, CA: O'Reilly.

Ross, R. G. (2003). *Principles of the business rule approach*. Boston: Addison Wesley.

Silberschatz, A., Korth, H. F., & Sudarshan, S. (2011). *Database System Concepts* (6th ed.; Vol. 4). Database; doi:10.1145/253671.253760

Silvers, F. (2008). *Building and Maintaining a Data Warehouse*. Boca Raton, FL: CRC Press. doi:10.1201/9781420064636

Stonebraker, M. (2010). SQL databases v. NoSQL databases. *Communications of the ACM*, *53*(4), 10. doi:10.1145/1721654.1721659

Tjioe, H. C., & Taniar, D. (2005). Mining Association Rules in Data Warehouses. *International Journal of Data Warehousing and Mining*, *1*(3), 28–62. doi:10.4018/jdwm.2005070103

W., K. M. (2010). SQL vs. NoSQL. *Linux Journal*.

Wood, P. T. (2012). Query languages for graph databases. *SIGMOD Record*, *41*(1), 50–60. doi:10.1145/2206869.2206879

KEY TERMS AND DEFINITIONS

Data Warehouse: A central data repository that contains cleaned and integrated data from different sources (databases, files, etc.).

Database: Collection of data usually perceived as a set of tables (relations).

Database Management System (DBMS): Software used to create, maintain, and use databases.

Datalog: A logic programming language used with deductive databases, as well as with deductive data warehouses.

Datalog by Example: Visual Datalog query language proposed in the paper.

ERA: Entity - relationship - attribute diagram is used to design the database (conceptual database model).

ETL: Extract - transform - load process used to integrate, clean, and load the data into the data warehouse.

SQL: Structured query language is a dominant query language for relational databases supported by many relational database management systems.

Chapter 4
A Trajectory Ontology Design Pattern for Semantic Trajectory Data Warehouses:
Behavior Analysis and Animal Tracking Case Studies

Marwa Manaa
University of Tunis, Tunisia

Thouraya Sakouhi
University of Tunis, Tunisia

Jalel Akaichi
University of Bisha, Saudi Arabia

ABSTRACT

Mobility data became an important paradigm for computing performed in various areas. Mobility data is considered as a core revealing the trace of mobile objects displacements. While each area presents a different optic of trajectory, they aim to support mobility data with domain knowledge. Semantic annotations may offer a common model for trajectories. Ontology design patterns seem to be promising solutions to define such trajectory related pattern. They appear more suitable for the annotation of multiperspective data than the only use of ontologies. The trajectory ontology design pattern will be used as a semantic layer for trajectory data warehouses for the sake of analyzing instantaneous behaviors conducted by mobile entities. In this chapter, the authors propose a semantic approach for the semantic modeling of trajectory and trajectory data warehouses based on a trajectory ontology design pattern. They validate the proposal through real case studies dealing with behavior analysis and animal tracking case studies.

DOI: 10.4018/978-1-5225-5516-2.ch004

INTRODUCTION

Advances in pervasive systems triggered by the incredible technical evolution of mobile devices and positioning technologies led to the eruption of disparate, dynamic, and geographically distributed mobility data. For a long while, location sensing devices and wireless networks started becoming widely untethered (Yan & Chakraborty., 2007). As a result, disparate mobility data revealing the details of instantaneous activities conducted by mobile entities can be collected and used for any mobile object trajectory reconstruction.

Note that, trajectory data, which is a record set of gathered mobility data, can be associated to different domain-specific information. Trajectories are naturally represented as *raw trajectory* denoting a sequence of temporally-indexed positions. For example, pedestrian displacement is described using a time-varying point which is a point whose position evolves over the time. In other cases, such as studying bird migration displacement, trajectories are defined by decision spatio-temporal points i.e., stops and moves according to predefined paths i.e., sub-trajectories. We will refer to the latter cases as *structured trajectory* (Spaccapietra et al., 2008). In other cases, *trajectory with Region Of Interest (ROI)* (Giannotti et al., 2007) represents trajectory data as a sequence of regions and time intervals. The phenomenon of adopt-ing raw trajectory referencing domain ontologies by organizations generates a new type of trajectory, called *semantic trajectory*. *Semantic trajectory* (Alvares et al., 2007), (Bogorny et al., 2009), (Yan & Chakraborty., 2007), (Richter et al.,2015) and *trajectory with Semantic ROI* (Yan., 2009) annotates decision points with con-textual information and enrich them by links with geographic and application domain concepts. In other cases, *space-time path* (Wannous et al., 2013) extends semantic trajec-tories with mobile object activity performed during the travel. An example of such trajectories occurs in Location-Based Social Networks (LBSN), where the raw trajectory are user check-ins to Points Of Interest (POI) and the contextual information includes names of POI and activities during the travel.

In a highly heterogeneous and dynamic environment, such as the Web, arriving at commonly agreed and stable domain ontologies is a prone-to-fail task and progress has been slow over the last years (Hu et al., 2013). Ontology design patterns have emerged as more flexible, reusable and manageable modeling solutions (Gangemi., 2005). It may provide common model for different representations of trajectory data where designers can pick the appropriate knowledge to define trajectories in view of share, exchange or integration. Alongside, data warehousing techniques are expected to analyze and extract valuable information from heterogeneous trajectory data sources.

In privious papers (Manaa & Akaichi., 2016) and (Manaa & Akaichi., 2017) authors presented repec-tively a trajectory ontology and a semantic approach for modelling trajtory data warehouses. In this paper we extend aforementioned papers and we set up (i) a Trajectory Ontology Design Pattern (TrODP) for Trajectory Data Warehouses (TrDW). We emphasize the geometric module in order to represent common structures encountered in trajectories associated with links to application and geographic modules in order to maintain semantic interoperability. More than that, the TrODP provides genericity as it covers most important trajectory data works and ensures consensuality because it is a deal on a consensual knowledge by a community. Furthermore, (ii) the TrODP serves to define the TrDW conceptual model. Our proposal permits to save too much designers efforts and time needed to acquire domain knowledge since the latter is extracted from the TrODP. The Semantic Trajectory Data Warehouse (STrDW) will mainly highlight the trajectory to be seen as a first class semantic concept, providing an ontology-based multidimensional model.

In the same research team, (Sakouhi et al., 2014) tried to solve the problem of trajectory data heterogeinity and sparsity using novel analytical techniques that can exploit the available rich mobility semantics and provide performance features at the same time. We tend to extend the traditional analytical techniques so as to take into consideration these limitations and handle efficiently raw trajectory data using the best of both Data Warehousing and Semantic Data Modeling worlds. Indicatively, a Trajectory Data Warehouse (TDW) is an efficient tool for analyzing and extracting valuable information from raw mobility data. For that we proposed in a first level, a multidimensional model presented by a TDW design, namely a Semantic Trajectory Data Warehouse (STrDW) conceptual model, inspired from an existing ontology model. On the one side, this emphased the trajectory to be seen as a first class semantic concept, not only a spatio-temporal path, providing then a semantic multidimensional model which is meant to be more than a spatio-temporal data repository for storing and querying raw movement. Indeed, the design of a Data Warehouse (a TDW as well) is a complex task that forces designers to acquire wide knowledge of the domain. Our solution permited, on the other side, to save too much designers efforts and time needed to acquire domain knowledge, as the latter is extracted from the ontology semantics. Then, in a second level, we applied the inference over the proposed model to see if we can enhance it and make the complexity of this mechanism manageable due to the increased performance of the DW technology. We exemplified our work using a scenario from the marine mammals tracking application. The main objective behind is analyzing the behavior of the seal animals during their travel.

The outline of this paper is structured as follows. In section 2, we present notions and related work required for the understanding of our trajectory design pattern. Section 3 introduces basic foundations for the pattern. In section 4, we define the formalization of the pattern using Description Logics (DL). Section 5 exemplifies the pattern with case studies dealing with human trajectories and animal tracking. Section 6 concludes the paper and suggests some future issues.

BACKGROUND AND RELATED WORK

In this section, we provide background materials and related research required for facilitating the understanding of our TrODP.

Heterogeneous Trajectories

Broadly, trajectory data is a record of the evolution of the position (perceived as a point) of an object that is moving in space during a given time interval in order to achieve a given goal (Spaccapietra et al., 2008). These points are often represented as $\{x_i, y_i, t_i\}$ (with x_i, y_i denoting a sequence of geometric location in 2D space, and t_i representing the time point) or $\{x_i, y_i, z_i, t_i\}$ (with z_i denoting the elevation information in 3D space).

Such sequence of spatio-temporal points called raw trajectory does not provide information about the displacement of mobile objects. Structured trajectory organizes raw trajectory in sub-trajectories including decision points such begin, end, stops and moves concepts (with begin, end, stop and move denoting spatio-temporal points) (Spaccapietra et al., 2008). Trajectory with Region of Interest (ROI) (Giannotti et al., 2007) represents trajectory data as sequence of regions and time intervals represented as $\{region_i,$

interval$_i$} (with interval denoting a starting and ending time points {s$_i$,e$_i$}, and region representing a set of consecutive line segments).

With such domain knowledge, trajectory applications may allow a more semantic interpretation for trajectory data to understand instantaneous behaviors and activities accomplished by the moving object. Semantic trajectories fill this gap by enriching spatio-temporal concepts with geographic and application do-main knowledge. Semantic trajectories (Alvares et al., 2007), (Bogorny et al., 2009), (Yan & Chakraborty., 2007), (Richter et al.,2015) and trajectory with Semantic ROI (Yan., 2009) facilitates the discovery of different views of novel knowledge for under-standing object movements and behavior. Yet, semantic trajectory and trajectory with semantic ROI lack information about moving object activity performed during the travel. Space-time path (Wannous et al., 2013) extends semantic trajectories with mobile object activity. Pedestrian trajectories are best understood when spatio-temporal points can be annotated with activities performed at these spatio-temporal concepts associated with points of interest such as coffee or labs.

Ontology Design Patterns

Ontology design patterns are modeling solutions to solve recurrent ontology development problems that can be solved by means of a set of rules and shared guidelines that are packaged in the form of patterns. Ontology design patterns can be of different types, such as content (conceptual), logical, architectural, and so on. Content ontology patterns refer to small fragments of ontology conceptual models and are used to represent domain knowledge where more complicated and abstract ontologies may be difficult to apply (Gangemi., 2005). The participation pattern is a good example given by (Gangemi., 2005) which can be observed in different domains i.e., soft-ware management [17] and fishery information systems (Gangemi et al., 2004). Ontology design patterns have become popular also in the geospatial semantics community (Compton et al., 2012) (Carral et al., 2013). Recently, ontology design patterns attracted trajectory semantics community aimed at supporting trajectory-based applications with geo-ontology design pat-terns (Hu et al., 2013). In this context, the domain and geographic TrODP proposed in this work is a content (conceptual) ontology pattern addressing the heterogeneity of the trajectory geometric faces and the extent of concepts and properties found commonly in domain specific knowledge.

Trajectory Ontologies

The decision making process, obviously appeals the raw captured data, although it needs to be enhanced with additional information. This information is mainly domain or thematic. Also, the space-time nature of the data implies to draw up spatio-temporal relationships and requires geographic information about the environment where the data are captured (Malki et al., 2012). The latest years a big interest has been shown to the integration of domain-related concepts on the spatio-temporal data models, as it is difficult to use and manage raw trajectory data. Many researches has focused on enhancing it with semantic information, proposing then semantic trajectory models. Working on semantic modeling of trajectories is a recent matter, and it returns to the recency of applications and devices offering moving object data. Also, this can be explained by the lack of maturity of standards, languages and tools in the domain of semantic web.

Semantic models proposed in the literature are in many cases ontology-based as in the works of (Wannous et al., 2012), (Wannous et al., 2013) and (Malki et al., 2012). In these works, authors proposed some queries related to the domain of analyzing and understanding the marine mammals behavior, and bring out 3 main components of the ontology model: thematic (domain-related), spatial and temporal. This led to enriching the raw trajectory data with these semantic components to transform the former to a semantic trajectory and make it useful for reaching the application purpose. To efficiently exploit the semantic trajectories domain rules were implemented too. Therefore, the three ontological components (spatial, temporal and domain ontologies) are aimed to be integrated together to permit reasoning in a unified ontology model looking at responding to the asked queries. However, the implementation of the ontology presents some difficulties related to the reasoning task performed in a big amount of data considering the spatial, temporal and domain rules. In (Wannous et al., 2012) authors propose an onto-logical approach for modeling trajectories to represent the movement of seals while they are traveling, foraging or resting. This ontology is composed of two parts: spatial and domain ontologies, represent-ing the declarative part. In addition, they propose a set of rules applied to the relations and concepts of the ontology to make inference over them, this, representing the imperative part of the ontology. The authors in this paper used the OGC spatial model as the spatial part of the ontology. The main concept of this model is "Geometry". An integration between the domain and the spatial ontologies is proposed to get a unified model and give sense to the results of inference applied over it. Although, an inference complexity problem appears on the global ontology, to overcome it, authors proposed two refinement algorithms to minimize time and space taken by the inference: the area of interest and pass refinements. Yet, the inference is still time and space consuming. In (Wannous et al., 2013), authors did the same but with temporal ontology and rules. They used the OWLTime ontology developed by the W3C (World Wide Web Consortium) as a temporal ontology. Also they suggested a method for the integration of the two ontologies. As the inference mechanism over the amount of data considering all relations and rules takes a lot of time and storage space, a refinement algorithm is proposed, it is called Temporal Neighbor Inference and it consider only close trajectories to make inference over them. Whereas there are still difficulties in finding the best candidates for the refinement. Due to these difficulties, these propositions found problems on implementing a unified model containing domain, spatial and temporal ontologies to execute on it all the rules as the inference is already time and space consuming either with the temporal or the spatial ontology.

The exploitation of trajectories with additional semantic informations is a recent but active field. The main idea was at first introduced by (Spaccapietra et al., 2008). In this work authors proposed two conceptual modeling approaches to associate a semantic layer to trajectories: one based on design pat-tern and the other on dedicated data types. Authors provided also an evaluation of the two approaches. Those models consider simple trajectories (one continuous travel) and complex ones (separate sub-travel periods). Also they handled two types of semantic information, whether with trajectory attributes or using links between trajectory and other objects. Those considerations make the trajectory a first class concept of the conceptual model which is not the case for the existing spatio-temporal models. The model proposed in this work introduced the trajectory as a general semantic object. The latter is proposed because the notion of semantic trajectory makes it deeply depending on the application's domain. It is that the trajectory concept is semantically segmented into the main following components which are:

- **Stop:** Time subinterval where the moving object's position is fixed.
- **Move:** Time subinterval where the moving object's position changes.
- **Begin and End:** The time instants where the trajectory starts and ends.

In this conceptual model, trajectory is a sequence of moves going from one stop to another, starting at a start position instant and ending at an end position instant. Nonetheless, identifying stops (and then moves) is an application dependent task. This model is formalized after deeply analyzing the requirements of the dedicated application of stork's migration (long birds). The storks are equipped with transmitters sending mobile data to be collected and analyzed. Researchers record the storks' movement data during their migration presented by time stamped locations and decomposed into moves and stops. Additional environmental conditions information is provided too.

As ontology design patterns reflect a common conceptualization of a domain's knowledge in the matter of a modeling problem, it is important to analyze the existing trajectory ontologies in order to ensure consistency. A semantic trajectory ontology has been proposed by Baglioni et al. [3] who decompose trajectories in sub-trajectories including a series of stops and moves. This representation has been adopted in several other trajectory ontologies, and the stops and moves concepts are often associated to geographic and application domain information to improve understanding domain facts (Yan et al., 2014), (Vandecasteele, et al., 2014), (Willems et al., 2010). Trajectory with ROI has been also proposed to enrich trajectory data with geo-data i.e., POI and ROI (Yan., 2009). Space-time path extends semantic trajectories with mobile object activity. Trajectories are best understood when decision points can be annotated with activities associated with POI (Wannous et al., 2013). The majority of these approaches deal with ontology as a storage repository and not as a domain ontology, where designers can pick concepts and properties to represent their trajectories.

Analyzing relationships between application objects is important especially when adding spatial and temporal dimensions. To this end, in this paper (Mathew, 2008), a framework for analyzing thematic, spatial and temporal relationships between entities is presented using an RDF (Resource Description Framework) data model. The latter makes querying and analyzing relationships between entities very natural. Query operators using graph patters are also defined. Differently, the research work done in (Yan et al., 2008) presents a semantics-oriented framework that structure, model and query trajectory data in a semantic manner. For this, domain-dependent and domain-independent ontologies were defined to consider the semantic perspective of the application. The framework was finally applied on a traffic management application. Authors also proposed a detailed requirements analysis for the modeling of semantics-oriented trajectories. Therefore, three main components are needed: geometric component (trajectory path with stops and moves), also geographical and application domain components (concerning the moving object itself or other application objects) of the trajectory which are domain dependent modules. Then these components are gathered as ontological modules in an all-encompassing ontology by setting up roles between them. The purpose from making a modular structure is the easiness of design, maintenance, understandability as well as query optimization and re-usability. The geometric trajectory module is a generic application-independent ontology that describes the spatio-temporal features of a trajectory. It's tightly interrelated to the geographical module. It's also overlapping with the application domain module. The former itself (the geometry module) may be composed of several ontologies: Temporal ontology, spatial ontology, spatio-temporal ontology and trajectory ontology. The geometric trajectory ontology is the same as the aforementioned in (Spaccapietra et al., 2008) including the Stop, Move, Begin and End concepts.

Trajectory Data Warehouses

There are other ways for efficiently analyzing mobile data. Warehousing and mining techniques are ones among many others supporting the extraction of valuable information from raw moving object data.

In data warehousing area, furthermore, decision makers may need to analyze the spatial and time aspects of data at the same time. An example query is "how many people crossed this street at a given time". Pointing out the big mass of spatio-temporal data generated from mobile devices and applications manipulating them, the need to extract patterns from it is being a subject of interest for the research community. Spatio-temporal data warehousing is a global field including trajectory data warehousing. The components of the former are essential bases for sustaining the latter. While SDW involves GIS data and OLAP techniques, STDW involve additionally the temporal aspect of analysis.

A trajectory is defined as a line described by an object (a point) during its movement resulting from the change of its spatial location in time. Indeed, trajectory data is a special case of spatio-temporal data. Then, a TDW is obviously a special case of STDW. Authors in (Marketos, 2009) proposed a complete framework designed to transform raw trajectories to valuable information that can be used for decision making purposes. It is that they enhanced the traditional aggregation techniques to make use of summarized trajectory information and provide OLAP analyses. In fact, the system contains all necessary processes, to get eventually the needed information, from trajectory reconstruction to visual OLAP analysis. Typical ubiquitous applications that are using TDWs are: location-based services, traffic control management, transportation management, etc.

A TrDW is the application of data warehousing techniques on trajectory data (Leonardi et al., 2014), Wagner et al., 2013). Before getting to the TrDW, research communities were interested in analyzing spatio-temporal data in Spatio-Temporal Data Warehousing (STDW). There have been various proposals of multidimensional models for STDW (Zimányi, 2012) aiming at the integration of various data sources containing spatio-temporal data. Trajectory data is a particular case of spatio-temporal data characterizing objects mobility. Then, a TrDW is obviously a particular case of STDW where trajectory is the fact (Leonardi et al., 2014, Braz., 2007). However, obtaining an implementation of the DW is a complex task that often forces designers to acquire wide knowledge of the domain, thus requiring a high level of expertise and becoming it a prone-to-fail task. The first attempt to set a Semantic Spatio-temporal Data Warehouse is given by authors in (Diamantini & Potena., 2008) who annotate the datacube elements with domain ontologies as well as mathematical ontology.

Recently ontology building attracted researches aimed at supporting TrDWs with semantic models (Sakouhi et al., 2014) (Manaa & Akaichi., 2016). The multidimensional model presented by a STrDW conceptual model, inspired from an existing ontology model. This will emphasis the trajectory to be seen as a first class semantic concept, not only a spatio-temporal path. Thus, the semantic multidimensional model is meant to be more than a spatio-temporal data repository for storing raw mobility data.

PROBLEM STATEMENT

In order to create an ontology design pattern, we need to define: (i) a Generic Use Case (GUC), i.e., a generalization of use cases that can be provided as examples for recurring issues of domain modeling. (ii) Competency questions to discover and refine the generic use case in a domain of interest i.e., a typical query that a domain expert might want to submit to a knowledge base to achieve a particular task. (iii) A rigorous ontology design pattern that should define only the con-ceptualizations that are necessary to answer competency questions requested by domain experts (Hu et al., 2013). The hereinafter TrODP is motivated by the scenario related to pedestrians trajectories, without restricting the pattern to this case study. The TrODP should answer the following recurrent questions that arise in the trajectory data modeling domain such as these:

Question 1 *"Analyze pedestrian activities in a given time interval in a spe-cific point of interest"*

Question 2 *"Analyze pedestrian activities in a given time interval in a specific point of interest according to pedestrian age"*

Question 3 *"When do the pedestrian stop during the trip (temporal zones)"*

Question 4 *"What are the spatial zones where the activity of the pedestrian phone call is the highest"*

Question 5 *"Where do the pedestrian stop during the trip"*

In this context, we hold a different point of view for unifying the modeling and the analysis of trajectory data. The innovation of our work consists of of-fering a TrODP that describes heterogeneous trajectory data models and covers most important existing formalisms and representations of trajectory data i.e "conceptual modeling" used for designing database schema and "ontology". This ontology design pattern serves as semantic layer for the STrDW allowing the integration and the analysis of heterogeneous trajectory data sources.

THE PATTERN

This section presents the TrODP by discussing the more interesting classes, properties and axioms. DL notation has been used to present the axioms as we believe this improves the readability. To encode the pattern, we use the formal Ontology Web Language (OWL-DL). We choose OWL-DL since it has a great expressive power. A schematic view of the pattern is shown in (Figure 1). The TrODP holds the following modules:

- *The geometric module* contains generic concepts and properties relevant to the description of trajectory geometric facet including common structures encountered in trajectories.
- *The geographic module* contains resources relevant to the geographical space in which the mobile object moves.
- *The application domain module* contains resources relevant to the domain of interest i.e., traffic management ontologies, bird migration ontologies and transportation ontologies.

Figure 1. A schematic view of the trajectory ontology design pattern

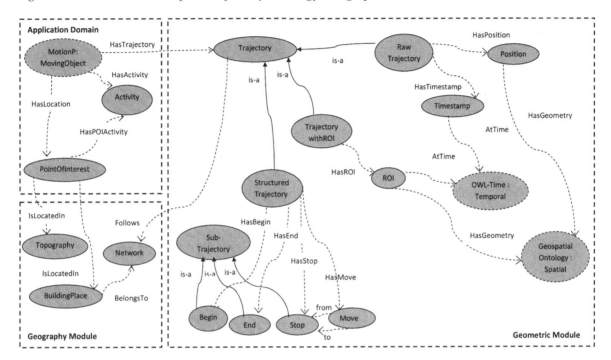

Geometric Module

The geometric module holds resources to describe how moving objects movement can be understood and trajectories can be represented. This module reuses exist-ing ontology design patterns and holds different geometric facets of trajectories. In the following we define most important resources.

OWL-Time. We reuse OWL-Time ontology [1] to express the temporal infor-mation. OWL-Time is part of the W3C Semantic Web Activity and has been used in many applications before, e.g., (Wannous et al., 2012). It can express rich temporal in-formation using relations and classes based on Allen temporal relationships (Allen., 1983). Embedding OWL-Time ontology in the TrODP makes the pattern more reusable for those familiar with W3C ontologies.

Geospatial Ontology. We reuse Geospatial ontology [2] to represent the spa-tial information. Geo ontology developed likely by the W3C standard and has been used in many applications, e.g., (Wannous et al., 2013). Embedding Geospatial ontologies in the TrODP makes the pattern more reusable for those familiar with this ontology.

Raw Trajectory. Raw trajectory defined by a sequence of spatio-temporal po-sition recording the trace of a moving object i.e., $\{(x_0, y_0, t_0), ..., (x_n, y_n, t_n))\}$, *where* $x_i, y_i, t_i <$ for i=0, ..., N and $t_0 < t_n$. By Axioms 1-2-3, a raw trajectory is enforced to have a timestamps and a position and to belong to a raw trajectory.

$$\text{Raw Trajectory} \equiv \text{Position} \cap \text{Timestamp} \qquad (1)$$

Position $\subseteq$ Point (2)

Timestamp $\subseteq$ Instant (3)

Structured Trajectory. Structured trajectory defined by a set of sub-trajectories according to pre-defined paths. A sub-trajectory includes strictly one Begin and one End. It includes also at least one Stop. Moves are used to connect stops to other elements i.e., $\{(\text{Sub-trajectory}_1, ..., \text{Sub-trajectory}_n),$ Sub-trajectory=$\{\text{Begin}, \text{Move}_1, ..., \text{Stop}_{n-1}, \text{Move}_n, \text{End}\}$, Begin=$\{x_0, y_0, t_0\}$, $\text{Stop}_{n-1}=\{x_{n-1}, y_{n-1}, t_{n-1}\}$, End=$\{x_n, y_n, t_n\}\}$ *where* $x_i, y_i, t_i <$ for i = 0, ..., N and $t_0<t_{n-1}< t_n$. By Axioms 4-5, a structured trajectory holds sub-trajectories. A sub-trajectory is enforced to have strictly one begin and one end and to have moves between stops and other concepts. Axioms 6-7-8-9 defines Begin, End, Stop and Move by a time-varying geometry.

Structured Trajectory $\equiv \exists$ hasBegin.Begin $\cap$ =1 hasBegin $\cap$ (4)

$\exists$ hasEnd.End $\cap$ =1 hasEnd $\cap$ $\exists$ hasMove.Move $\cap$ $\exists$ hasStop.Stop

Sub-trajectory $\equiv$ Begin $\cup$ End $\cup$ Stop (5)

Begin $\subseteq$ Point $\cap$ Instant (6)

End $\subseteq$ Point $\cap$ Instant (7)

Stop $\subseteq$ Point $\cap$ Interval (8)

Move $\subseteq$ Line $\cap$ Interval (9)

Trajectory with ROI. Trajectory with ROI defined by a sequence of regions associated with time intervals. A region is a set of consecutive line segments i.e., $\{(\text{ROI}_1, ..., \text{ROI}_n), \text{ROI}_i=(\text{Region}_i, \text{Interval}_i)\}$ *where* $i <$ for i= 1, ..., N and Interval_1 *before* Interval_N. By axioms 10-11, a Trajectory with ROI is enforced to have a region and a time interval.

Trajectory with ROI $\equiv$ ROI (10)

ROI $\subseteq$ Region $\cap$ Interval (11)

Semantic Trajectory. Semantic trajectory defined by a set of semantic sub-trajectories which extend decision points Begin, Stop, Move and End by links with Points of interest i.e., Semantic Trajectory=$\{(\text{SemanticSub-trajectory}_1,..., \text{SemanticSub-trajectory}_n)$, SemanticSub-trajectory=$\{\text{SemanticBegin}, \text{SemanticMove}_1,$

..., SemanticStop$_{n-1}$, SemanticMove$_n$, SemanticEnd}, SemanticBegin= {x_0, y_0, t_0, Point of Interest}, SemanticStop$_{n-1}$= {x_{n-1}, y_{n-1}, t_{n-1}, PointofInterest}, SemanticEnd= {x_n, y_n, t_n, PointofInterest}} *where* x_i, y_i, t_i < for i=0, ...,N, t_0<t_{n-1}<t_n, and PointOfInterest is located into a geographical place. With axioms 12-13, a semantic trajectory is enforced to have semantic sub-trajectory. Each sub-trajectory should contain semantic (Begin, End, Stop and Move). By axioms 14-15-16-17, we define previous concepts linked to point of interest.

$$\text{Semantic Trajectory} \equiv \exists \text{hasSemanticBegin.SemanticBegin} \cap \tag{12}$$

$$=1 \text{ hasSemanticBegin} \cap \exists \text{hasSemanticEnd.SemanticEnd} \cap$$

$$=1 \text{ hasSemanticEnd} \cap \exists \text{hasSemanticMove.SemanticMove} \cap$$

$$\exists \text{hasStop.Stop (} \tag{13}$$

$$\text{SemanticSub-trajectory} \equiv \text{SemanticBegin} \cup \text{SemanticEnd} \cup$$

$$\text{SemanticStop} \tag{14}$$

$$\text{SemanticBegin} \subseteq \text{Begin.IsLocatedIn PointOfInterest}$$

$$\text{SemanticEnd} \subseteq \text{End.IsLocatedIn PointOfInterest} \tag{15}$$

$$\text{SemanticStop} \subseteq \text{Stop.IsLocatedIn PointOfInterest} \tag{16}$$

$$\text{SemanticMove} \subseteq \cup \exists \text{fromStop} \cup \exists \text{toStop} \tag{17}$$

Semantic ROI. Trajectory with Semantic ROI defined by a sequence of ROI linked to points of interest i.e., trajectory with Semantic ROI={(SemanticROI$_1$, ..., SemanticROI$_n$), SemanticROI$_i$=(Region$_i$, Interval$_i$, Pointof Interest)} *where i* ∈ < for i=0, ...,N, Interval$_1$ *before* Interval$_N$, and PointofInterest is a geo-graphical place. By Axioms 18-19, a trajectory with Semantic ROI is defined by a semantic ROI linked to a point of interest.

$$\text{Trajectory with SemanticROI} \equiv \text{SemanticROI} \tag{18}$$

$$\text{SemanticROI} \subseteq \text{ROI.IsLocatedIn PointOfInterest} \tag{19}$$

Space-Time Path. Space-time path defined by a sequence of semantic stops associated with information about the moving object activity performed dur-ing the stop i.e., space-time path={(Space-time$_1$, Activity$_1$), ..., (Space-time$_n$, Activity$_n$), Space-time$_i$={x_i, y_i, t_i, PointofInterest}} *where i* ∈ < for i=0, ..., N. PointofInterest is a geographical place, and activity is a contextual information about moving object activity. By axioms 20-21, a space-time path is defined by a semantic stop annotated with moving object activity.

$$\text{SpaceTime path} \equiv \text{Spacetime} \cap \text{Activity} \tag{20}$$

Spacetime

$$\subseteq \text{SemanticStop} \tag{21}$$

Application Domain Module

Application domain module should hold the wide range of concepts that make up the universe of discourse for a set of applications in the same field such as application domain related to traffic management or bird migration domain. In a given sphere, we should usually define the moving object i.e., pedestrian or animal, the activity fulfilled while moving i.e., walking or eating, and relevant points of interest i.e., home or work. We reuse MotionP: MovingObject class from the Motion Pattern developed in a Geo-Vocabulary Camp (Carral et al., 2013). An encoded formalization for concepts and relationships is given respectively by Table 1 and Axioms 22-23-24-25.

$$\text{HasActivity} \subseteq \text{MovingObject} \circ \text{Activity} \tag{22}$$

$$\text{HasLocation} \subseteq \text{MovingObject} \circ \text{PointOfInterest} \tag{23}$$

$$\text{HasTrajectory} \subseteq \text{MovingObject} \circ \text{Trajectory} \tag{24}$$

$$\text{HasPOIActivity} \subseteq \text{PointOfInterest} \circ \text{Activity} \tag{25}$$

Table 1. Application domain module dictionary

Concept	Description	Logical Form
Moving Object	represents the mobile object eg.person or animal	MobileObjecti= $< A, P >$
Activity	represents mobile object activities e.g. sending mail, meeting, walking and eating	$A= \{a_1, a_2, a_3, ..., a_n\}$
Point Of Interest	represents application domain places e.g. home, work and office	$P= \{p_1, p_2, p_3, ..., p_n\}$

Geographic Module

Geographic module contains concepts about the geographic environment in which mobile objects involved. Concepts are likely to include those describing the to-pography of the land (e.g. mountain, lake), networks (e.g. road network, railway network), building places (e.g. home, work, supermarket) and anything else that is of interest to the application. This module is closely related to the geometric trajectory module, as each trajectory concept that has a spatial implication is to be linked to a type of geography that is used by the application to specify the corresponding spatial measure. The module is also related with the application domain module as its concepts may also have a thematic description providing application information beyond geographic and geometric facet. For example, concepts about building places may include standard schemes defined in the ge-ographic module in addition to other features specific to the application domain. An encoded formalization for the concepts and relationships is given respectively by Table 2 and Axiom 26-27-28-29.

$$\text{IsLocatedInT} \subseteq \text{PointOfInterest} \circ \text{Topography} \tag{26}$$

$$\text{IsLocatedInB} \subseteq \text{PointOfInterest} \circ \text{BuildingPlace} \tag{27}$$

$$\text{BelongsTo} \subseteq \text{BuildingPlace} \circ \text{Network} \tag{28}$$

$$\text{Follows} \subseteq \text{Trajectory} \circ \text{Network} \tag{29}$$

Table 2. Geographic module dictionary

Concepts	Description	Logical Form
Building place	represents places where mobile	$B = \{b1, b2, b3, ..., bn\}$
	object moves such home or work.	
Topography	represents natural topography such	$T = \{t1, t2, t3, ..., tn\}$
	as mountain or lake.	
Network	represents road network that	$S = \{s1, s2, s3, ..., sn\}$
	follows mobile object while moving.	

APPLICATIONS TO TRAJECTORY DATA

A rigorous ontology design pattern should have the usability that allows it to be instantiated to a wide range of datasets, solving problems of discovery and integration (Hu et al., 2013). In the following sub-sections, we apply our trajectory ontology design pattern to case studies dealing with human trajectories and animal tracking.

Application to Human Trajectories

Studying human trajectories is expected to extract useful and novel knowledge about the moving object and facilitate then the understanding of their instanta-neous behavior and accomplished activities according to domain' specific knowl-edge. In the following, we apply our proposal to pedestrians walking through the Informatics Forum of the School of Informatics at the University of Edinburgh (Majecka., 2009). Pedestrians' trajectories are time-stamped locations collected by using a vertical camera fixed overhead.

Figure 2 shows part of pedestrian's trajectory annotation, that instantiates the trajectory design pattern, for his displacement in the Informatics forum, inte-grating trajectory data representation type space-time

Figure 2. Graphic representation for part of a pedestrian's trajectory annotation (blue rectangles represent instances and orange circles represent concepts)

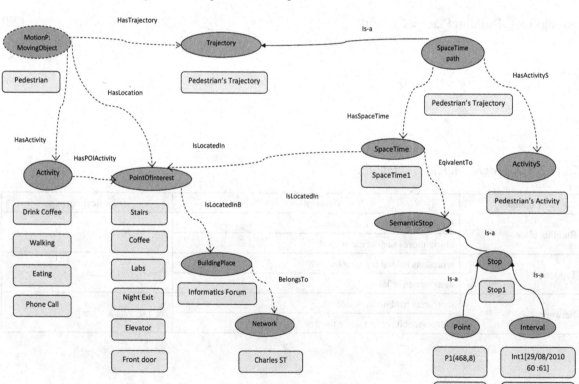

path, application domain concepts including visited points of interest i.e., front door, stairs, elevator and performed activities i.e., walking, eating, drink coffee and geographic concepts i.e., buildings located in streets. The STrDW model is derived from this ontology including geometric, geographic, application-domain, spatial and temporal on-tologies. The projection of resources allows then the extraction of a sub-ontology from the TrODP. This step is of paramount importance because it will permit, later, the definition of the STrDW conceptual model based on ontological con-cepts that express as much as possible effective user's requirements (trajectory representation type). In addition, user's requirements are also used for the anno-tation of the extracted sub-ontology by multidimensional concepts such as fact, dimension, measures and dimension attributes, to result on the STrDW concep-tual model. A first possible design model for the application scenario represented using MultiDimER notation from (Ma-linowski., 2005) is given in (Figure 3).

Here is a statement that incorporates a competency question *"Analyze pedes-trian activities in a given time interval in a specific point of interest"*. The re-sult to analyze is the rate of different pedestrian activities in specific place and time. The STrDW design model is given in (Figure 3) appeals numeric measures (Stop_duration and Time_allocation) and 3 dimensions. Temporal dimension organized fol-lowing the hierarchy: second, minute, hour, day, month and year. Spatial dimension organized following the hierarchy: space-time, position. Pedes-trian dimension represented by the pedestrian' attributes: identifier, name, gen-der and age.

Figure 3. Proposed model of the STrDW related to humans trajectories case study

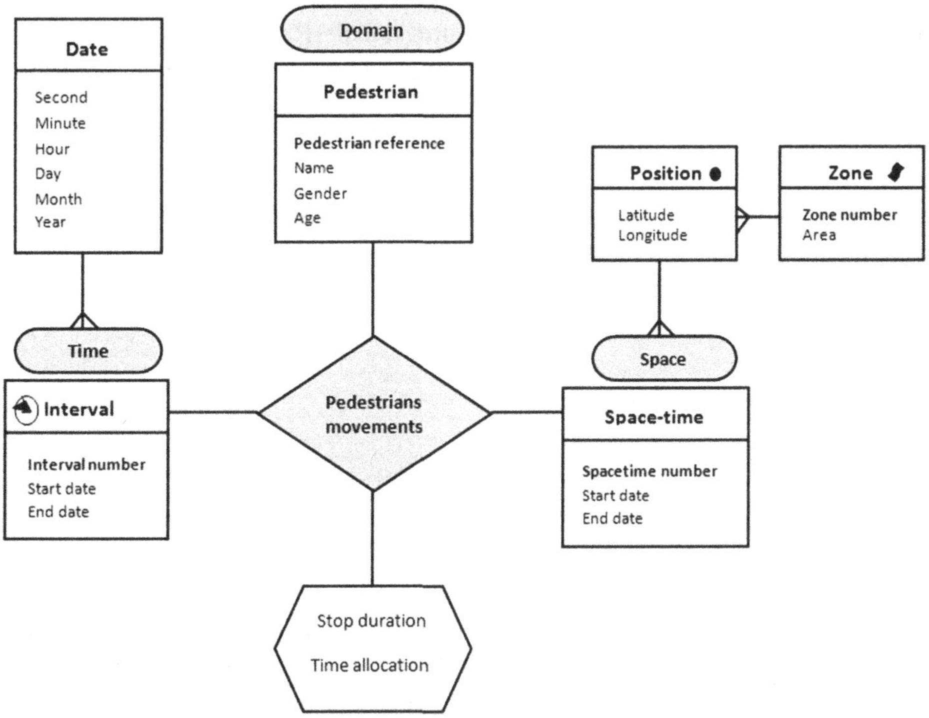

Figure 4. Graphic representation of a part of the seal's trajectory annotation (blue rectangles represent instances and orange circles represent concepts)

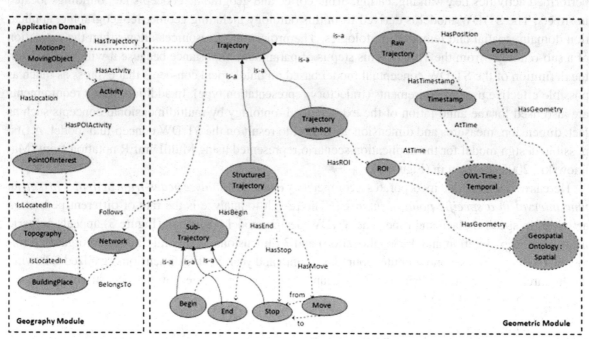

The aggregation function applied against the measure Activity-Rate is ac-tually the rate of pedestrian activities (phone call/drink coffee/walking/eating) calculated using the following formula:

Activity – rate = Walking – sum ÷ All – activities - sum

The fact table is composed of dimensions keys at their lower level that form the sym-bolic coordinates for the value of the measure. In this model, activities are the subject of the multidimensional analysis, so the designer can analyze the activity of the pedestrian during a special period of time and location in the forum.

Application to Animal Tracking

Now we look at another case study to exemplify our model. To do so, we applied it to the application scenario from the marine mammals tracking application domain, related to the biology research filed, regarding especially the seal animals' trajectories. Trajectory datasets are time-stamped locations col-lected from the GPS devices tied to a selected list under test of seals of the English Channel who are distributed in many islands of the Brittany Coast and tripping until the Britannic islands in 2011. The embedded system continuously captures data and maintains a model of three states: Haul-out, Cruise and Dive. Researchers are more interested on the seal's activities conducted during dives. According to the experts, this comes to four main activities: *resting*, *traveling*, *foraging* and the joint activity *traveling-foraging*. The seal's activity is determined based on the dive duration, surface duration, and maximum depth and TAD, which are parameters describing the dive state of the seal and included in the datasets.

As in the previous scenario, we used the *space-time path* representation for the instantiation of the TrODP to allow activity analysis, as shown in (Figure 4). To get finally then the STrDW model shown in (Figure 5), represented using *MultiDimER* notation from (Malinowski., 2005).

Here is a competency question related to an informational requirement of biologists in our application scenario *"Analyze seal activity (foraging, resting, traveling, traveling-foraging) rate during dives in a given time interval in a specific area according to seal Age, Gender and Type (gray or harbor seal)"*. The information to analyze (seal activity) is quantified by numeric measures which are in this case: *Dive duration, Surface duration, Maximum depth* and *TAD*. The *Criteria* influencing it are the time, the space and the seal characteristics (Genre, Age and Type). A first possible design model to fit in the application scenario is given figure 5. It uses numeric measures (Dive duration, Surface dura-tion, Maximum depth, TAD) and 3 dimensions. *Sequence*, the time dimension, organized according to the hierarchy: *Sequence, Date. GeoSequence*, the space dimension, with the hierarchy: *GeoSequence, Position, Zone. Seal*, the domain-related dimension, with the attributes: *type, gender and age*.

Figure 5. The STrDW model related to the seals tracking case study

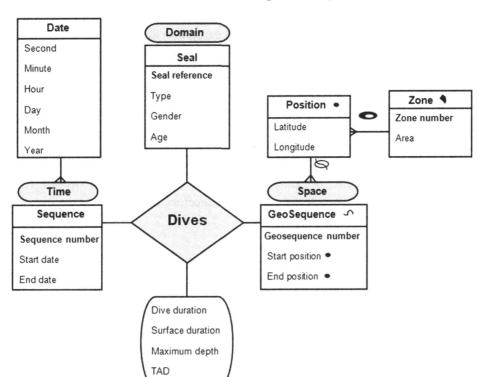

Finally, to analyze the seal's activity rate the aggregation function *Activity Rate* is calculated. The latter represents the rate of seal activities (foraging/ resting/ traveling/ traveling-foraging) calculated based on the aforementioned measures using the following formula:

Activity – rate = Activity – sum ÷ All – activities - sum

So *for the Foraging* activity for example, this formula will be as follows:

Foraging – rate = Foraging – sum ÷ All – activities - sum

Foraging-sum is the sum of dives number where the activity is *Foraging. All –Activities –Sum* is the sum of dives number with any other activity.

CONCLUSION

In this paper, we proposed a domain and geographic ontology design pattern for trajectories. In this approach we defined a high level formalism for representing trajectory related information allowing interoperability, reusability, and mainte-nance between applications supporting trajectory data. As future work, we will adopt an ontological approach to integrate different trajectory data sources in a trajectory data warehouse by using the trajectory pattern. This integration will support trajectory-oriented applications dealing with mobility data, enhance the decision making process and allow querying mobility data on the semantic level, revealing then information about the mobile objects' activity and behavior.

ACKNOWLEDGMENT

The authors would like to thank the creator of the pedestrians trajectory dataset Barbara Majecka as part of her MSc projects (University of Edinburgh) (Majecka., 2009) and the AMARE research team (University of La Rochelle), that provided as with seals trajectory dataset.

REFERENCES

Allen, J. F. (1983). Maintaining knowledge about temporal intervals. *Communications of the ACM*, *26*(11), 832–843. doi:10.1145/182.358434

Alvares, L. O., Bogorny, V., Kuijpers, B., de Macedo, J. A. F., Moelans, B., & Vaisman, A. (2007). A model for enriching trajectories with semantic geographical information. *Proceedings of the 15th Annual ACM International Symposium on Advances in Geographic Information Systems GIS*, 22:1–22:8. 10.1145/1341012.1341041

Baglioni, M., de Macêdo, J. A. F., Renso, C., & Wachowicz, M. (2008). An ontology-based approach for the semantic modelling and reasoning on trajectories. Academic Press. doi:10.1007/978-3-540-87991-6_41

Bogorny, V., Kuijpers, B., & Alvares, L. O. (2009). ST-DMQL: A Semantic Trajectory Data Mining Query Language. *International Journal of Geographical Information Science*, *23*(10), 1245–1276. doi:10.1080/13658810802231449

Braz, F. J. (2007). *Trajectory data warehouses: Proposal of design and application to exploit data*. GeoInfo.

Carral, D., Scheider, S., Janowicz, K., Vardeman, C., Krisnadhi, A. A., & Hitzler, P. (2013). An ontology design pattern for cartographic map scaling. *The Semantic Web: Semantics and Big Data, 10th International Conference, ESWC*. 10.1007/978-3-642-38288-8_6

Compton, M., Barnaghi, P. M., Bermudez, L., Garcia-Castro, R., Corcho, Ó., Cox, S. J. D., ... Taylor, K. (2012). The SSN ontology of the W3C semantic sensor network incubator group. *Journal of Web Semantics*, *17*, 25–32. doi:10.1016/j.websem.2012.05.003

Diamantini, C., & Potena, D. (2008). Semantic enrichment of strategic datacubes. *ACM 11th International Workshop on Data Warehousing and OLAP, DOLAP*. 10.1145/1458432.1458447

Gangemi, A. (2005). Ontology design patterns for semantic web content. *Proceedings of the 4th International Semantic Web Conference, ISWC*. 10.1007/11574620_21

Gangemi, A., Fisseha, F., Keizer, J., Lehmann, J., Liang, A., Pettman, I., ... Taconet, M. (2004). A core ontology of fishery and its use in the fos project. *Proceedings of the EKAW Workshop on Core Ontologies in Ontology Engineering*.

Giannotti, F., Nanni, M., Pinelli, F., & Pedreschi, D. (2007). Trajectory pattern mining. In *13th ACM SIGKDD International Conference on Knowledge Discovery and Data Mining* (pp. 330–339). ACM.

Hu, Y., Janowicz, K., Carral, D., Scheider, S., Kuhn, W., Berg-Cross, G., . . . Kolas, D. (2013). A geo-ontology design pattern for semantic trajectories. *Spatial Information Theory - 11th International Conference, COSIT*, 438–456. 10.1007/978-3-319-01790-7_24

Leonardi, L., Orlando, S., Raffaetà, A., Roncato, A., Silvestri, C., Andrienko, G., & Andrienko, N. (2014). A general framework for trajectory data warehousing and visual olap. *GeoInformatica*, *18*(2), 273–312. doi:10.100710707-013-0181-3

Majecka, B. (2009). *Statistical models of pedestrian behaviour in the forum* (Master's thesis). University of Edinburgh.

Malinowski, E., & Zimányi, E. (2005). Spatial hierarchies and topological relationships in the spatial multidimer model. *Database: Enterprise, Skills and Innovation, 22nd British National Conference on Databases, BNCOD*. 10.1007/11511854_2

Malki, J., Bouju, A., & Mefteh, W. (2012). *An ontological approach for modeling and reasoning on trajectories taking into account thematic, temporal and spatial rules*. Technique et Science Informatiques.

Manaa, M., & Akaichi, J. (2017). Ontology-based modeling and querying of trajectory data. *Data & Knowledge Engineering, 111*, 58–72. doi:10.1016/j.datak.2017.06.005

Manaa, M., & Akaichi, J. (2016). Ontology-based trajectory data warehouse conceptual model. *Big Data Analytics and Knowledge Discovery - 18th International Conference, DAWAK*. 10.1007/978-3-319-43946-4_22

Mapelsden, D., Hosking, J., & Grundy, J. (2002). Design pattern modelling and instantiation using dpml. *Proceedings of the Fortieth International Conference on Tools Pacific: Objects for Internet, Mobile and Embedded Applications*.

Marketos, G. D. (2009). *Data Warehousing and Mining Techniques for Moving Object Databases* (PhD thesis). University of Piraeus.

Matthew, P. (2008). *A Framework to Support Spatial, Temporal and Thematic Analytics over Semantic Web Data* (PhD thesis). Wright State University.

Richter, K.F., Schmid, F., & Laube, P. (2015). Semantic trajectory compression: Representing urban movement in a nutshell. *Journal of Spatial Information Science*, (4), 3–30.

Sakouhi, T., Akaichi, J., Malki, J., Bouju, A., & Wannous, R. (2014). Inference on semantic trajectory data warehouse using an ontological approach. *Foundations of Intelligent Systems - 21st International Symposium, ISMIS*. 10.1007/978-3-319-08326-1_47

Spaccapietra, S., Parent, C., Damiani, M. L., de Macedo, J. A., Porto, F., & Vangenot, C. (2008). A conceptual view on trajectories. *Data & Knowledge Engineering, 65*(1), 126–146. doi:10.1016/j.datak.2007.10.008

Vandecasteele, A., Devillers, R., & Napoli, A. (2014). From movement data to objects behavior using semantic trajectory and semantic events. *Marine Geodesy, 37*(2), 126–144. doi:10.1080/01490419.2014.902885

Wagner, R., de Macêdo, J. A. F., Raffaetà, A., Renso, C., Roncato, A., & Trasarti, R. (2013). Mob-warehouse: A semantic approach for mobility analysis with a trajectory data warehouse. Advances in Conceptual Modeling - ER 2013 Workshops.

Wannous, R., Malki, J., Bouju, A., & Vincent, C. (2013). Modelling Mobile Object Activities Based on Trajectory Ontology Rules Considering Spatial Relationship Rules. *Studies in Computational Intelligence, 488*, 249–258.

Wannous, R., Malki, J., Bouju, A., & Vincent, C. (2012). Time integration in semantic trajectories using an ontological modelling approach. *New Trends in Databases and Information Systems, Workshop Proceedings of the 16th East European Conference, ADBIS.*

Willems, N., van Hage, W. R., de Vries, G., Janssens, J. H. M., & Malaise, V. (2010). An integrated approach for visual analysis of a multisource moving objects knowledge base. *International Journal of Geographical Information Science, 24*(10), 1543–1558. doi:10.1080/13658816.2010.515029

Yan, Z. (2009). Towards semantic trajectory data analysis: A conceptual and computational approach. *Proceedings of the VLDB PhD Workshop. Co-located with the 35th International Conference on Very Large Data Bases.*

Yan, Z., & Chakraborty, D. (2014). *Semantics in mobile sensing.* Morgan & Claypool Publishers. doi:10.2200/S00577ED1V01Y201404WBE008

Yan, Z., Macedo, J., Parent, C., & Spaccapietra, S. (2008). Trajectory ontologies and queries. *Transactions in GIS, 12*, s1. doi:10.1111/j.1467-9671.2008.01137.x

Zimányi, E. (2012). Spatio-temporal data warehouses and mobility data: Current status and research issues. *19th International Symposium on Temporal Representation and Reasoning*, 6–9.

KEY TERMS AND DEFINITIONS

Conceptual Model: A high-level description for a system. It allows us understanding and interpreting information related to a field. The later formalize information using a language in order to construct a system. The conceptual model includes a graphical representation of model concepts and represents relations between these elements.

Mobile Object: It is an identifiable geometries real word element that moves. Geometries may be points, lines, areas, or volumes, changing over the time like person, car, or natural phenomenon.

Model: An abstraction of a system designed as a set of facts constructed in a particular intention. It must be used to answer questions about the system under study. In the field of trajectory data, models are used to formalize and analyze trajectories of mobile objects.

Ontology: Ontology is a cognitive artefact allowing the shared design and operation for knowledge. Ontology is composed from concepts related to a domain of interest linked with relations.

Ontology Design Pattern: Is a modelling solution to solve recurrent ontology development problems that can be solved by means of a set of rules and shared guidelines that are packaged in the form of pattern.

Reasoning Mechanism: Reasoning mechanisms allow deriving new facts from existing concepts and roles that are not expressed in the initial ontology.

Trajectory: Trajectory is the record of a time-varying spatial phenomenon. Trajectory consists in the description of the movement of some moving objects at specific moment's time. In reality, trajectory has to be built from a set of sample points which correspond to moving object positions.

ENDNOTES

[1]   http://www.w3.org/TR/owl-time/

[2]   http://www.w3.org/2005/Incubator/geo/XGR-geo-ont-20071023/

Chapter 5
Personalized Spatio–Temporal OLAP Queries Suggestion Based on User Behavior and a New Similarity Measure

Olfa Layouni
ISG Tunis, Tunisia

Jalel Akaichi
University of Bisha, Saudi Arabia

ABSTRACT

Spatio-temporal data warehouses store enormous amount of data. They are usually exploited by spatio-temporal OLAP systems to extract relevant information. For extracting interesting information, the current user launches spatio-temporal OLAP (ST-OLAP) queries to navigate within a geographic data cube (Geo-cube). Very often choosing which part of the Geo-cube to navigate further, and thus designing the forthcoming ST-OLAP query, is a difficult task. So, to help the current user refine his queries after launching in the geo-cube his current query, we need a ST-OLAP queries suggestion by exploiting a Geo-cube. However, models that focus on adapting to a specific user can help to improve the probability of the user being satisfied. In this chapter, first, the authors focus on assessing the similarity between spatio-temporal OLAP queries in term of their GeoMDX queries. Then, they propose a personalized query suggestion model based on users' search behavior, where they inject relevance between queries in the current session and current user' search behavior into a basic probabilistic model.

INTRODUCTION

Spatio-Temporal data warehouse has recently become an active research area. This is due to the explosive growth in the use of the recent ubiquitous location technologies devices (Vaisman et al., 2014) such as GPS, smart phones, PDA, etc. The concept of a spatio-temporal data warehouse appeared in order to

DOI: 10.4018/978-1-5225-5516-2.ch005

store moving data objects and temporal data information. Moving objects are geometries that change their position and shape continuously over the time; the time could be an instant or a set of time intervals. In order to support spatio-temporal data, a data model and associated query language is needed for supporting moving objects.

Spatio-Temporal data warehouse stores large volumes of consolidation and historized multidimensional data, to be explored and analyzed by various users in order to make the best decision. In order to analyze and explore a spatio-temporal data warehouse, users need a Spatio-Temporal OLAP (ST-OLAP) system to help them to make the best decisions. The ST-OLAP system is realized in order to analyze and explore spatio-temporal data warehouse. A ST-OLAP explores a spatio-temporal data warehouse, which we find a moving data type for the movement of an object in the time. It's obtained after the combination of Geographic Information Systems (GIS) with OLAP tools and operations. A ST-OLAP system is the enhancement for an OLAP system to consider moving objects, so it takes into account the spatial objects which evolve over time. For the exploration of a data cube, the user should have operations and a manipulation language. Bardar (Badard, 2011) defined that the language used for a spatial data warehouse and a spatio-temporal data warehouse is the MDX (Multi-dimensional eXpressions) with spatial functions language, called also GeoMDX. In this case, a query can contain spatial, no spatial and temporal data types. The GeoMDX language represents the evolution of MDX language to support spatial relationships: topological, direction and metric distance relationships and temporal data. Users interactively navigate a spatio-temporal data cube (Geo-cube) by launching sequences of ST-OLAP queries over a spatio-temporal data warehouse. The problem appeared when the current user may have no idea of what the forthcoming ST-OLAP queries should be and if it's relevant for him or not. Adding to that, spatio-temporal data cubes store a big amount of data that have become increasingly complex to be explored and analyzed. The notion of similarity has been considered as an important component for the development of recommendation and personalization systems. Personalization has been mentioned for many years in various domains such as information retrieval, web search, e-commerce, query suggestions in databases and data warehouses. In these domains, personalization usually consists of exploiting user preferences to provide pertinent answers to users. In our chapter, we focus on providing users with queries suggestion based on the exploration of a spatio-temporal data warehouse in order to obtain pertinent set of ST-OLAP queries results to address their information needs. Queries suggestion help users refine their queries after they input an initial query. Previous work mainly concentrated on similarity-based and context-based query suggestion approaches. However, models that focus on adapting to a specific user can help to improve the probability of the user being satisfied. In this chapter, we propose a personalized ST-OLAP queries suggestion model based on users' search behavior (UB model), where we inject relevance between queries and users' search behavior into a basic probabilistic model. For that purpose and as a solution for helping the current user in his navigation and his exploration, in this chapter, we propose a behavior-based model for ST-OLAP queries suggestion personalization that incorporates the current user's short-term search context in his current session to detect search interests. But before, we need a similarity measure to compare between ST-OLAP queries. In our context, similarity measures are used to identify the degree of similarity between two ST-OLAP queries. To the best of our knowledge, there is no proposed similarity measure between ST-OLAP queries (GeoMDX queries (Tranchant, 2011)) and no proposed approach for ST-OLAP queries suggestion personalization. So, in this chapter, we aim at filling this gap.

The remainder of this chapter is structured as follows. Section 2 present the related works for the personalization query suggestion methods. Section 3 briefly reviews related work; this section presents the different similarity assessment models proposed in the literature for comparing between queries and the proposed approaches for personalization. Section 4 presents the basic definitions in the context of spatio-temporal data warehouses and ST OLAP systems. Section 5 presents our proposal of the new spatio-temporal similarity measure. The details of the personalized ST-OLAP query suggestion based on user behavior model are described in Section 6. Section 7 presents the performance evaluation. Finally, Section 8 concludes this chapter.

PERSONAMIZED QUERIES SUGGESTION BASED ON USER BEHAVIOR AND ON THE EXPLORATION OF DATA CUBES

First, we interest on researches that resolve the problem of the personalization query suggestion. Query suggestion is a way to interact with the user and help him to improve the quality of the queries launched by users (Cao et al., 2008; Liu et al., 2009). In recent years, a significant amount of work has gone into methods for query suggestion (Chen et al., 2018; Verberne et al., 2015; Kharitonov et al., 2013; Kruschwitz et al., 2013). In those method (Verberne et al., 2015; Kharitonov et al., 2013) we find that personalized query suggestion acquire knowledge based on a user's search history in order to guess his search intent, in this case, we note that those approach are based on the long-term search behavior. Also, we find that the work proposed by (Kruschwitz et al., 2013) aims to personalize query suggestions based on the current query and the data explored from the search context in their current session. The proposed method by (Jiang et al., 2014) build the user profiling model to personalize a ranking list of the query suggestion to a user according to the user's preference. The method proposed by (Chen et al., 2018) build a personalized query suggestion model based on user behavior, which integrate a user's short-term (the current session) and long-term search (search history) behavior to deal with the personalized query suggestion task and also examine different impact factors for query suggestion personalization.

Then, we interest on query personalization methods based on the exploration of data cubes. In the literature, we find little number of works that trait only the problem of OLAP query personalization based on the exploration of OLAP data cubes. The approach proposed by Bellatreche et al. in (Bellatreche et al., 2005, 2006) treats the problem of OLAP query personalization and recommendation. In this method, the authors took into account of three particularities of OLAP queries. The first particularity is to know if a query is related to various levels of aggregations. The second particularity is to know if the user profile is apt for the type of the proposed query and if it is possible to calculate automatically the preferred facts for a given user. The third particularity allows the possibility to access into the fact table in order to personalize queries. The proposed approach gives the possibility to secure two principal objectives. The first objective is to compute the utility of query and the second one is to display the best query to a user by taken into account his preferences according to his profile and his visualization constraints. More precisely, the authors proposed a framework for personalization MDX queries. This framework takes as input an instance of the data warehouse, a query, constraints and a user profile. The profile is defined by the user preferences and his visualization constraints. The proposed framework is composed in three different steps. The first step consists on using the user profile. In this step, authors proposed two functions Perso and MaxSubset which were used to compute the best subsets of references from the current query and to satisfy the proposed constraint. This step was realized for computing structures that give the possibility to visualize the different subsets and also for integrating predicates in the initial query. The second step consists in searching elements, firstly by comparing between the stored preferences and a given query, secondly by selecting an order set of references for a specific query. The third step, the authors proposed to build a personalization query by using the best references, sorted and recommended them in an ascending order. Besides, this step is realized by affecting for each reference a predicate that should be inserting into the initial query. We deduce that this method is based on the content. In fact, this approach doesn't take into consideration the previous queries launched by users in the data cube and the sequencing of queries launched by the current user. It takes into account only a given query proposed according to the profile of the current user.

The approach proposed by Jerbi in (Jerbi, 2012) treats the problem of OLAP analysis personalization within data warehouses. In fact, the user must launch several queries over an OLAP data cube in order to obtain a result that is can be similar or close to his preferences. An OLAP system doesn't assure the adaptation of the results obtained of these queries to the specific needs of each user. Those needs may be different according to the interests and objectives of analysis for each user. The proposed approach gives the possibility to improve the current query by using the preferences of the current user, and recommends the best query for him by guiding him in his exploration of data. Firstly, in this approach, the author proposed a model to analyze OLAP data cube through a graph where nodes represent the analysis contexts and edges represent the user operations for moving from one context to another. The analysis context regroups the user query and the query result. In fact, it is described by a specific tree structure. This tree is independent on the visualization structures of data and the query languages. Secondly, the author proposed to build a model for user preferences on the multidimensional schema and values. In this step, each preference is associated with a specific analysis context. Finally, the author proposed a generic framework including two personalization processes. The first process denoting an OLAP query personalization. This process aims to enhance a query according to the user preferences in order to produce a new one. Indeed, in this process, two phases must be performed: the selection and the integration of preferences. The second process is recommendation queries. In this process, two types of personalization have to be performed: a personalization of an explicit or a dynamic type. Moreover, the proposed recommendation framework supports recommendation scenarios: assisting the user in a query composition by proposing elements of the query and suggesting the forthcoming and alternative queries. The system recommends a set of queries by comparing the user preferences and alternative queries. Concerning the algorithm of the proposed recommendation system, is takes as inputs the analysis context, a schema, an instance of the data warehouse, the current session and the user profile. Also, it's takes as output a set of sorting of queries that basing on the current user preferences. Consequently, we find that his framework is based on the content method. Also, this method resolves many problems but it doesn't take into consideration the sequencing of queries launched by the current user; it takes only the last launched query and the current session.

COMPARING QUERIES

Comparing queries has attracted a lot of attention in different areas like information retrievals (Marcel et al., 2012; Sapia, 2000; Jerbi, 2012; Sarawagi, 2000; Aligon et al., 2014), bio-informatics (Moreau et al., 2008), etc. We note that the most proposed approach focused on assessing the similarity between queries. This section reviews the literature for similarity functions that could possibly be used to compare ST-OLAP queries. We note that a ST-OLAP query can contain one or more spatial relations. So, in this section we begin by presenting some methods for comparing queries. Then, we present some methods proposed for comparing queries based on spatial relations.

Comparing OLAP Queries

In the literature, we find two different motivations that could be used for comparing queries. The first one is query optimization (Sapia, 2000). This motivation is based on comparing a query q to another q' in order to find a better way to evaluate the query q. The second motivation is the most interesting for us because it is used to compare a query q to another q' in order to help the user explore and analyze data, by recommending him queries, without focusing on the query evaluation (Jerbi, 2012; Sarawagi, 2000; Sarawagi, 1999; Aligon et al., 2014; Giacometti et al., 2011; Aufaure et al., 2013).

From a technical point of view, we find in the literature that the existing approaches could be classified in three different ways:

- **According to the Query Models**

Query models can be presented as a set of tuples resulting from the query evaluation (Sarawagi, 2000; Sarawagi, 1999). Also, query can be modeled as sets of parts which each part represents a particular part of the query, such as attributes required in select or from clauses or such as levels or references used in the query (Sapia, 2000; Sarawagi, 2000; Sarawagi,1999; Giacometti et al., 2011; Aufaure et al., 2013; Bellatreche et al., 2005). Besides, queries can be modeled as graphs, following the schema of data warehouse like in (Giacometti et al., 2011; Jerbi, 2012).

- **According to the Query Expression**

The proposed approaches, in this category, can be based on the select, from and group by clauses and also it takes into account attributes, levels, references, etc. for comparing queries (Sathe & Sarawagi, 2001; Sarawagi, 1999; Sarawagi, 2000; Sapia 1999; Sapia, 2000; Sapia et al., 2001; Giacometti et al., 2011). We find that this category also includes approaches for measuring similarity between data cubes and sub-cubes (Sathe & Sarawagi, 2001; Sarawagi, 1999; Sarawagi, 2000). Moreover, the query expression category can be related to a probabilistic model such as the Markov Model (Sapia, 1999; Sapia, 2000; Sapia et al., 2001; Aufaure et al., 2013) and the maximum entropy theory (Sathe & Sarawagi, 2001; Sarawagi, 1999; Sarawagi, 2000; Marcel et al., 2012).

- **According to the Distance Functions Used for Computing Similarity**

We distinguish that the most popular functions used for measuring similarity, can be classified in two different categories, the first one is based on the query corpus measures (Sarawagi, 1999; Sarawagi, 2000; Aligon et al., 2014; Giacometti et al., 2011) and the second is based on the query representation model (Layouni & Akaichi, 2014; Aligon et al., 2014).

We conclude that those methods don't take into account spatial relations and temporal data in the same time, essentially Spatio-temporal OLAP queries.

Comparing Queries Based on Spatial Relations

In order to measure the similarity between ST-OLAP queries, we need to compare between spatial objects and scenes invoked in ST-OLAP queries, by taking into account spatial relations. However, topological relation, distance relation and direction relation are the most three types of spatial relations considered in the literature for the assessment of the spatial similarity. Besides, to measure the spatial distance between queries, we need to measure the topological distance, the metric distance and the direction distance between spatial objects and scenes invoked in queries (Li & Fonseca, 2006; Glorio et al., 2012; Aissi et al., 2014).

In the literature, we distinguish five main approaches that are adopted to compare spatial relations. Those approaches are: the conceptual neighborhood approach, the projection-based approach, the combination of the conceptual neighborhood approach with the projection-based approach, the spatial relations-oriented model (the TDD model) and the spatial semantic-oriented models/measures (Egenhofer, 2002; Frank, 1996; Goyal & Egenhofer, 2001; Li & Fonseca, 2006).

We note that the TDD model (Li & Fonseca, 2006) is the best approach that could be used in our case because it's applicable in queries expressions and by using it, we could compare between their spatial relations and spatial attributes launched in different queries without any transformations.

BASIC FORMAL DEFINITIONS

We give, in this section the formal definitions of the basic concepts used in our proposal.

Definition 1: Spatio-Temporal Dimensions and Hierarchies:

A dimension, in our case can be: a spatial dimension (*SDim*), a temporal dimension (*TDim*) and a classical dimension (*Dim*).

$$STDim = \{SDim_1, ..., SDim_n, Dim_{n+1}, ..., Dim_{m-1}, TDim_m\}$$

STDim represents a set of dimensions.

A dimension has different levels of members, so these members are arranged into a spatio-temporal hierarchy *ST_H*.

$$ST\_H = \{ST\_h_1, ST\_h_2, ..., ST\_h_n\}$$

$ST\_h_i \in T\_H$ is the level *Lev* of a hierarchy for a dimension $SDim_i$, $l \in .ev\ (ST\_h_i)$, $\forall$. $\in .[1,n]$, l represents a level that belongs to the sets of levels for a dimension hierarchy.

$$Allmeb\{STDim_i\} = \{meb_0, ..., meb_n\}$$

For *each j* $\in .[0, n]$, j represents the level of a member meb_j.

Definition 2: Spatio-Temporal Cube (Geo-cube):

A spatio-temporal cube is:

$$ST\_C = \{STDim, ST\_F\}$$

$$ST\_C = \{SDim_1, ..., SDim_n, Dim_{n+1}, ..., Dim_{m-1}, TDimm, ST\_F\}$$

STDim represents the set of dimensions and *ST_F* represents the fact table.

$$ST\_F = \{SPK_1, ..., SPK_n, SM_1, ..., SM_n\}$$

For each $i \in .1, n]$, SPK_i represents the primary key of the dimension $STDim_i$ and SM_i represents the different values and measures.

Definition 4: ST-OLAP sessions of queries:

A ST-OLAP session is an ordered sequence of ST-OLAP queries formulated by a user.

We consider a geo-cube ST_C, a ST-OLAP session $S_i = <q_{i1}, ..., q_{in}>$ is a sequences of ST-OLAP queries.

SPATIO-TEMPORAL OLAP QUERY SIMILARITY

In the literature, we distinguish the gaps of the similarity measures between ST-OLAP queries. So, we propose a similarity measure between ST-OLAP queries by taking into account not only the spatial data with specific characteristics such as topological, directional and metric distances, but also temporal data. We define the similarity function used in our approach to compare ST-OLAP queries. In fact, this function must consider the peculiarities of the multidimensional spatio-temporal data model and be calculable based on query expression only, GeoMDX query expression. In order to compare similarity of ST-OLAP queries, we propose three new similarity measures: spatial similarity measure to compute spatial distance between ST-OLAP queries, temporal similarity measure to compute temporal distance between ST-OLAP queries, and spatio-temporal similarity measure to compute spatio-temporal aspects of the ST-OLAP queries. Furthermore, the spatio-temporal similarity measure is a combination of three components: one related to *measure* sets, one to the set *selection* and one to the *where* set.

Similarity Between Spatial Relations

In a ST-OLAP queries, we find the use of the three main categories of spatial relations, which are defined in the literature as follows: topological relation, direction relation and metric distance relation (Li & Fonseca, 2006; Glorio et al., 2012; Aissi et al., 2014). So, to compare between two ST-OLAP queries, we need to measure the similarity between the topological relation, direction relation and metric distance relation, invoked in each query. We note that a spatial object can be a point, a line or a polygon.

Topological Distance

A spatial scene could be a topological relation between spatial objects (Clementini & Felice, 1995; M. J. Egenhofer, 1991).

Given two spatial topological relations $TR(a,b)$ invoked by a ST-OLAP query q and $TR'(a',b')$ invoked by a ST-OLAP query q'. The topological distance between two ST-OLAP queries $Dist_{Top}(q,q')$ is calculated as follows:

$$Dist_{Top}(q,q') = Dist_{top}(TR(a,b),TR'(a',b'))$$

With:

- TR and TR' represent the topological relationships with TR and $TR' \in$ *.disjoin, meet, overlap, coveredBy, equal, covers, contains, inside}.*
- a, a', b and b' are spatial objects invoked in each query q and q'.

If $a \neq .a'$ and $b \neq .b'$ then we measure the similarity distance between TR and TR', and the similarity distance between objects a, a', b and b' invoked in each query q and q', respectively. In this case, to measure the topological distance, we use the distance proposed by (Egenhofer & Al-Taha, 1992), in order to measure the similarity between TR and TR'. So, the $Dist_{top}(TR,TR')$ represents this similarity and takes a value by comparing between TR and TR' lake as indicated in table and represented in (Figure 1).

Figure 1. Topological distance (Egenhofer & Al-Taha,1992)

	disjoint	meet	equal	inside	coveredBy	contains	covers	overlap
disjoint	0	1	6	4	5	4	5	4
meet	1	0	5	5	4	5	4	3
equal	6	5	0	4	3	4	3	6
inside	4	5	4	0	1	6	7	4
coveredBy	5	4	3	1	0	7	6	3
contains	4	5	4	6	7	0	1	4
covers	5	4	3	7	6	1	0	3
overlap	4	3	6	4	3	4	3	0

To compare between objects, we need to compute the similarity between references. The distance between ref_1 and ref_2 is:

$$Dist_{ref}(ref_1, ref_2) = \sum_{i=1}^{n} Dist_{meb}\left(ref_1, ref_2\right).$$

So, the topological distance is computed as follows:

$$Dist_{top}(TR(a,b), TR'(a',b')) = Dist_{topR}(TR,TR') + Dist_{ref}(ref_1, ref_2)$$

If $a = a'$ and $b = b'$ then we measure the similarity distance between *TR* and *TR'* which represents the topological relationships invoked in each query q and q', respectively. In this case, the topological distance is computed as follows:

$$Dist_{top}(TR(a, b), TR'(a', b')) = Dist_{topR}(TR,TR')$$

Direction Distance

To compute the direction distance between two spatial direction scenes invoked in ST-OLAP queries q and q'. We propose to adopt the direction distance proposed by (Li & Fonseca, 2006); which is based on the 9-direction system {north, northwest, west, southwest, south, southeast, east, northeast, and equal} to represent directions (Li & Fonseca, 2006; Egenhofer & Al-Taha, 1992). This distance measure represents the transformation cost from any direction to any other, each transformation is equal to 2 as shown in (Figure 2).

The direction distance between two ST-OLAP queries $Dist_{Dir}(q,q')$ with two spatial scenes invoked in q and q', respectively, is calculated as follows:

$$Dist_{Dir}(q, q') = \sum_{i=1}^{n} Cost\left(TOR(a,b), TOR'(a',b')\right). \text{With:}$$

- *TOR(a,b)* represents a direction, invoked in q.
- *TOR'(a', b')* represents a direction, invoked in q'.
- *Cost* is the transformation cost.
- $\forall$. [1,n] with $n = 2$, in our case, because we have two spatial scenes based on direction relation *TOR(a,b)* and *TOR'(a', b')*.

Figure 2. Direction distance

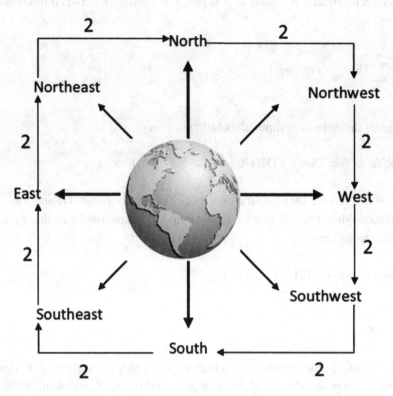

Distance in Term of the Metric Distance

To compute the metric distance between two spatial metric distance scenes invoked in ST-OLAP queries q and q'. We propose to adopt the distance proposed by (Li & Fonseca, 2006); which is based on the traditional 4-granularity metric distance {equal, near, medium, far} (Li & Fonseca, 2006; Egenhofer & Al-Taha, 1992). This distance measure represents the cost of transitions from one granularity to another, each transformation is equal to 1 as shown in (Figure 3).

Figure 3. Metric distance

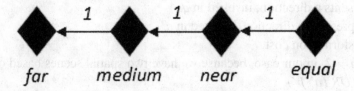

The metric distance between two ST-OLAP queries $Dist_{MetD}$ (q, q') with two spatial scenes based on the metric distance TD (a, b) and $TD'(a', b')$ invoked in q and q', respectively, is calculated as follows:

$$Dist_{MetD}(q, q') = Dist_{MetD}(TD(a,b), TD'(a',b')) = \sum_{i=1}^{n}\sum_{j=1}^{m} a_{ij}.$$

With:

- a, b, a' and b' are spatial objects invoked in each query q and q'.
- $\forall$. [1, n] with n equals to the number of objects invoked in q, in our case $n=2$, because we have two objects a and b.
- $\forall$. [1, m] with m equals to the number of objects invoked in q', in our case $m=2$, because we have two objects a' and b'.
- $a_{ij} = \begin{cases} 0 \, if \, i \, is \, equal \, to \, j \\ 1 \, if \, i \, is \, near \, to \, j \\ 2 \, if \, i \, is \, medium \, to \, j \\ 3 \, if \, i \, is \, far \, to \, j \end{cases}$.

Spatial Distance

ST-OLAP queries launched by users in the geo-cube have spatial scenes. Each scene represents a spatial representation of one or more spatial objects. This scene could be a topological relation, direction relation and distance relation between them (Glorio et al., 2012; Li & Fonseca, 2006; Clementini & Felice, 1995; M. J. Egenhofer, 1991). Given two ST-OLAP queries q and q' the spatial distance measure between them $Dist_{SpatialR}(q,q')$ is modeled as follows:

$$Dist_{SpatialR}(q,q') = Dist_{Top}(q,q') + Dist_{Dir}(q,q') + Dist_{MetD}(q,q')$$

A ST-OLAP query launched by the user can invoke one or more spatial scenes at the *Measure* clause or \and *Select* clause.

Spatial Similarity Measure

The similarity is inversely proportional to the distance, the higher is the distance, the lower is the similarity and vice versa. Thus, we define the spatial similarity based on the spatial distance between queries as follows: Given two GeoMDX queries q and q'. The spatial similarity between q and q' denoted $Sim_{spatial}(q,q')$ is computed as follows:

$$Sim_{spatial}(q,q') = 1/(1 + Dist_{SpatialR}(q,q'))$$

Similarity Between Measure Sets

Our definition of measure sets similarity takes into account both the spatial calculated measures and measures that are represented in the schema of the spatio-temporal data warehouse. So, to define the measure similarity that is represented in the schema, we use the Jaccard index (Bank & Cole, 2008) and for the spatial calculated measures similarity we propose a $Dist_{SCMeas}$ distance that takes into account spatial relations.

- Distance between Spatial Calculated Measures:

Given two ST-OLAP queries q and q' *with* spatial calculated measure *CMeas* and *CMeas'*, respectively. The spatial calculated measure distance between q and q' is:

$$Dist_{SCMeas}(q,q') = Dist_{SpatialR}(CMeas, CMeas')$$

- Distance between Measure Sets:

Given two ST-OLAP queries q and q' with measure sets *MeasSM* and *MeasSM'*, respectively. The measure sets similarity between q and q' is:

$$Dist_{Meas}(q,q') = [|MeasSM \cap .easSM'|/|MeasSM \cup .MeasSM'|] + Dist_{SCMeas}(q,q')$$

Similarity Between Selection Sets

Our definition of measure similarity between selection sets is based on comparing between two sets of members and spatial scenes. We first introduce the notion of distance between members. Given a dimension $STDim_i \in STDim$ with its hierarchy ST_H, the distance between two members meb_1 and meb_2 in this dimension is the shortest path (Dijkstra, 1959) from meb_1 and meb_2 in ST_H is noted as $Dist_{meb}(meb_1, meb_2)$. Given two ST-OLAP queries q and q' with selection sets *Sel* and *Sel'*, respectively. The selection sets similarity between q and q' is:

$$Dist_{Sel}(q,q') = Dist_{Sel}(Sel, Sel') = Dist_{meb}(meb_1, meb_2) + Sim_{spatial}(q,q')$$

Similarity Between Where Sets

Our definition of measure similarity between the where sets is based on the temporal similarity between ST-OLAP queries. In our contribution, we define the temporal similarity between two ST-OLAP queries in term of a temporal distance which is the time difference between time values of two queries. We adopt the temporal similarity defined in (Chang et al., 2007). So, we need to compute the time range distance, the day distance and the week distance between two queries q and q' by comparing between the time values t invoked in q and t' invoked in q'.

The temporal distance $Dist_{Temp}$ between two queries q and q' is:

$$Dist_{Temp}(q,q') = \alpha .Dist_{TRng}(t,t') + \beta .Dist_{TDay}(t,t') + \gamma .Dist_{TWeek}(t,t')$$

With:

- $Dist_{TRng}$, $Dist_{TDay}$ and $Dist_{TWeek}$ stand for time range distance, day distance and week distance, respectively.
- α. β.and γ.are temporal weights. The near optimal values of α. β.and γ.are: 60, 20 and 1, respectively.

Similarity Measures Between ST-OLAP Queries

To measure the similarity between two ST-OLAP queries q and q' we need to calculate the distance between them. Thus, we define the similarity function between two STOLAP queries q and q' as follows:

Given two ST-OLAP queries q and q'. The distance between q and q' is:

$$Dist_{STq}(q,q') = \alpha .Dist_{Meas}(q,q') + \beta .Dist_{Sel}(q, q') + \gamma .Dist_{Temp}(q,q')$$

With α. β.and γ.are normalized to 1.
So, the similarity between q and q' is:

$$Sim_{STq} = 1/(1+Dist_{STq}(q,q'))$$

PERSONALIZED ST-OLAP QUERIES SUGGESTION BASED ON USER BEHAVIOR

In order to help the user to go forward in his exploration of the geographic data cube and to find relevant information, we propose a behavior-based model for ST-OLAP queries suggestion personalization approach. It incorporates a user's short-term search context based on the current session, so, it uses the sequences of ST-OLAP queries of the current session which are formerly launched on the Geo-cube. The aim of our approach is to return for the current user a reordered set of candidates ST-OLAP queries based on the current session, in order to find relevant information.

We propose a personalization ST-OLAP queries suggestion model based on the current user behavior (UB model) after exploring the geographic data cube. For that purpose, we inject relevance between ST-OLAP queries and user searches behavior into a basic probabilistic model.

The main notation we used in this chapter is presented in Table 1.

First, we propose to compute the similarity measure between each ST-OLAP query in the current session with the current query. Then, we propose to rank the set of those ST-OLAP queries according to the similarity measure results by applying the Quick Sort method because it has the fast average run time

Table 1. Main notations used in our approach

Notation	Description
U_c	The current user
$S_c = <q_1, ..., q_n>$	The current session.
$S'_c = <q_{c1}, ..., q_{cn}>$	An initial ranked set of ST-OLAP queries suggestions candidates
q_0	The current query.
q_{ci}	An ST-OLAP query suggestion candidate.
N	Number of queries in the current session
S'_r	A reordered set of ST-OLAP queries suggestions candidates returned to the current user.
M	Number of queries in S'_r with $M<=N$.
Sim_{STq}	The similarity measure between two ST-OLAP queries.

and has the best complexity by applying it in our case, it is equals to O (n Log n) (Sedgewick, 1978) with n represents the number of candidates ST-OLAP queries in the current session and this set is stored in S'_c.

Then, we propose to use a probabilistic graphic model to indicate the relationship between the current user U_c, the current ST-OLAP query q_0 and the candidate ST-OLAP query q_{ci}. The figure 4 illustrates the probabilistic graphic model.

Figure 4. Probabilistic graphic model indicating the relationship between the current user U_c, the current ST-OLAP query q_0 and the candidate ST-OLAP query q_{ci}.

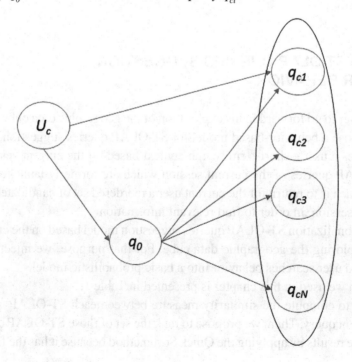

From the graphic model shown in Figure 4, we proposed the joint probability $P(U_c, q_0, q_{ci})$, with $q_{ci} \in S'_c$, q_{ci} represent each ST-OLAP query in the set of candidates ST-OLAP queries and $i \in .[1, M]$ with $M=$ the number of queries in S'_c. The joint probability is calculated as follows:

$P(U_c, q_0, q_{ci})=P(U_c).P(q_0|U_c). P(q_{ci}|U_c, q_0)$

We begin by estimating the relevance of a candidate ST-OLAP query according to the current ST-OLAP query for the current query by computing $P(q_{ci}|U_c, q_0)$, it's based on the Bayes rules (Vidakovic, 1998).

$P(q_{ci}|U_c, q_0)= P(U_c, q_0, q_{ci})/(P(U_c).P(q_0|U_c))$

$P(q_{ci}|U_c, q_0)= P(q_0, U_c |q_{ci}).P(q_{ci})/(P(U_c).P(q_0|U_c))$

With $P(U_c)=1$ and $P(q_0|U_c)=1$.

$P(q_{ci}|U_c, q_0) \leftarrow .(q_0, U_c |q_{ci}).P(q_{ci})$

In this step, we proposed to estimate the probability of $P(q_0, U_c |q_{ci})$ by using a trade-off parameter Λ_1 for controlling the contribution of the current query and the behavioral information, with $\Lambda_1 \in [0, 1]$ (Vidakovic,1998).

$P(q_0, U_c |q_{ci})=(1- \Lambda_1). P(q_0| q_{ci})+ \Lambda_1 . P(U_c |q_{ci})$

So, $P(q_{ci}|U_c, q_0)$ become as follows:

$P(q_{ci}|U_c, q_0)=(1- \Lambda_1). P(q_0| q_{ci}) .P(q_{ci})+ \Lambda_1 . P(U_c |q_{ci}).P(q_{ci})$

With:

- $P(q_0| q_{ci})$: describe the relevance between a ST-OLAP query suggestion q_{ci} and the current query q_0.
- $P(U_c |q_{ci})$: means the current user's preference for a given ST-OLAP query suggestion q_{ci}.

By applying the Bayes rules, it can be rewritten as follows:

$P(q_{ci}|U_c, q_0)=(1- \Lambda_1). P(q_{ci}| q_0) .P(q_0)+ \Lambda_1 . P(q_{ci}|U_c).P(U_c)$

We estimate that the probability of $P(q_0)= P(U_c)=1$.

$P(q_{ci}|U_c, q_0)=(1- \Lambda_1). P(q_{ci}| q_0)+ \Lambda_1 . P(q_{ci}|U_c)$

In this step we need to compute $P(q_{ci}| q_0)$ and $P(q_{ci}|U_c)$.

$P(q_{ci}|q_0)$ present the probability that a given ST-OLAP query suggestion q_{ci} is relevant to the current query q_0. It estimated by using our similarity measure Sim_{STq} between q_0 and q_{ci}. $P(q_{ci}|q_0)$ is calculated as follows:

$P(q_{ci}|q_0)= Sim_{STq} =1/(1+Dist_{STq}(q_{ci}|q_0))$

$P(q_{ci}|U_c)$ present the prediction of the user's current preference for a given ST-OLAP query suggestion q_{ci} according to his behavior in the ranked current session S_c. For that purpose, we prose to apply the Bayesian probabilistic matrix factorization (BPMF) proposed by (Chen et al., 2018). We consider user's short-term search behavior to generate $P(q_{ci}|U_c)$. For computing this probability, we prose to use a trade-off parameter for controlling the contribution of the current user's short-term behavior for individual preference Λ_2, we note that $\Lambda_2 \in [0, 1]$. It's calculated as follows:

$P(q_{ci}|U_c)=(1- \Lambda_2). P(q_{ci}|U_c)$

The user short-term reflects the current user search intent in the ranked current session. Based on the assumption of query independence (Chen et al., 2018), we estimate $P(q_{ci}|U_c)$ as follows:

$$P(q_{ci}|U_c)= \sum_{qb\in S'c}^{M} \alpha.\beta.\ P(qb\,|\,Uc).$$

Where:

α .is a normalized decay factor brought by the temporal interval between qb and q_{ci}, as we consider that temporally close queries in a ranked search session, if $qb = q_{ci+1}$ query it is the position of the most similar to the corresponding query q_c. So we calculate α .as follows:

$$\alpha = 1 / \left(Position\left(qb\right) +1 \right)$$

With *Position(qb)+1* refers to the position interval between qb and last query in the ranked session S'_c.

For β, we get it as follows: $\beta= \sum_{qj,qci\in S'c}^{M} 1.\ Dist_{STq}(qj, q_{ci}).$

β is a normalization factor where we calculate the distance between two queries q_{ci} and qj $Dist_{STq}(qj, q_{ci})$.

After that, our UB model $P(q_{ci}|U_c, q_0)$ become as follows:

$P(q_{ci}|U_c, q_0)=(1- \Lambda_1). Sim_{STq}+ \Lambda_1 .((1- \Lambda_2). P(q_{ci}|U_c))$

The main process of our UB model is described in the algorithm 1. First, we calculate the score for every query in the ranked candidates ST-OLAP queries suggestion session S'_c with our UB model. Then, we iteratively choose the ST-OLAP query suggestion with the maximum score to fill the reordered set of ST-OLAP queries candidates S'_r and removed it from S'_c, till the number of queries in S'_r is equals to N (M=N). Finally, we return the reordered set of candidates ST-OLAP queries suggestion S'_r to the current user.

Algorithm 1: UB_model

```
1: Inputs:
q₀: the current ST-OLAP query.
Uc: The current user
S'c: An initial ranked set of ST-OLAP queries suggestions candidates
N: Number of queries in the current session
P(qci |Uc): Preference of the current user
2: Output: S'r: A reordered set of ST-OLAP queries suggestions candidates re-
turned to the current user.
3: S'r ← ∅
4: M ← 0
5: While M <= N Do
6:   For each ST-OLAP query qci ∈ S'c DO
7:     UB_M(q0, qci) ← (1- λ1) . Sim_STq(q0, qci) + λ1 . ((1- λ2) . P(qci |Uc))
8: End for
9: M ← M+1
10: S'r ← S'r ∪ {arg_max(UB_M(q0, qci))}
11: S'c ← S'c \{arg_max(UB_M(q0, qci))}
12: End While
13: return S'r
```

EXPERIMENTATION

In the experimental evaluation, we present the results of the experiment that we have conducted to assess the capabilities of our personalized system.

First, we have developed the *ST-OLAPSIM* system using *Java* language. *ST-OLAPSIM* system implements our proposal of the spatio-temporal similarity measure. It identifies the references of two given ST-OLAP queries (GeoMDX queries) and computes the spatio-temporal distance between them. For more explanation, we illustrate an example of a spatio-temporal similarity measure computed between two ST-OLAP queries using *ST-OLAPSIM*. In this example, the spatio-temporal data warehouse used has been elaborated by (Hasanah & Trisminingsih, 2016). It contains the hotspots data generated by forest fires in Indonesia from year 2006 to 2015. The collected data is obtained by satellite imagery that captures the form of hotspots, indicating the existence of forest fires based on location and time. The spatio-temporal data warehouse model is represented in (Figure 5). The star schema composed of one fact table and six dimensions: Satellite, Geo_Hotspot, District, Province, Island and Time.

Figure 5. Star schema of the spatio-temporal data warehouse: Forest Fire

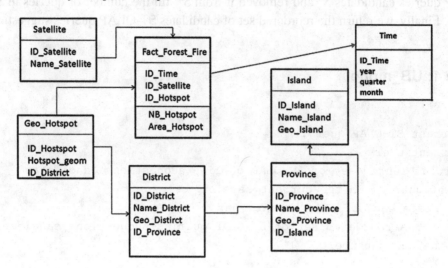

Our system *ST-OLAPSIM* computes the spatio-temporal similarity measure between two ST-OLAP queries launched in the forest fire geographic data cube. In the example presented in Figure 5, we have two ST-OLAP queries *q* and *q'*. The GeoMDX formulation of each query is as follows:

- *q: with member [Measures].[Geom_Union] as 'ST_UnionAgg([Hotspot_geom].[All Hotspot_ geom]. CurrentMember .Children, "geom")' select {[Measures].[NB_Hotspot], {[Measures]. [Area_Hotspot], [Measures]. [Geom_Union]} on columns {[Satelit].[All Satelit} on rows from [Forest_fire] where [Time].[2000]*

- *q': with member [Measures].[Geom_area_in_km2] as 'ST_Area (ST_Transform(ST_ UnionAgg([geohotspot].[All geohotspot].CurrentMember.Children, "geom"),4326,2991)) /1E6' select {[Measures].[NB_Hotspot], [Measures].[Geom_area_in_km2]} on columns, { Filter ({[Location].[Hotspot_geom].member}ST_Within([Location].CurrentMember. Properties("Hotspot_geom"), ST_GeomFromText("Point ((136.16 – 3.27} on rows from [Forest_ fire] where [Time].[2000]*

So, after launching those two GeoMDX queries in our system *ST-OLAPSIM*, we find out that the similarity measure between ST-OLAP queries $Dist_{STq}(q,q')$ is equal to summing the distance between measure set $Dist_{Meas}(q,q')$; and the distance between the selection sets and where sets are equal to zero because it is the same between *q* and *q'*. In the selection sets we find the use of spatial data: the topological relationships in each query. Moreover, in the measure sets we find a spatial calculated measure in each query: the calculated measure in *q* is *[Measures].[Geom_Union]* and the calculated measure in *q'* is *[Measures].[Geom_area_in_km2]*. This example is presented in (Figure 5).

Secondly, we present the architecture used to evaluate and compare the prediction performance of the proposed system. The ST-OLAP queries personalization system implements all phases of the proposed approach to provide user with useful and relevant GeoMDX queries. First, to navigate in the geo-cube, the current user launch a sequence of ST-OLAP queries by using the ST-OLAP server GeoMondrian[1] over a spatiotemporal data warehouse *"forest fires"* stored in the PstgreSQL[2] integrating PostGIS[3] in order to take into account spatial and temporal data types. Second, the set of queries in the current session proposed to ranked then by applying the proposed similarity measure and our *ST-OLAPSIM System*. After that, we proposed to apply our UB model in order to obtain finally a reorder set of candidates' ST-OLAP (GeoMDX) queries to the current user. The architecture of the system is presented in the figure 7.

Our experiment evaluates the efficiency of our approach proposed to personalize ST-OLAP queries according to the current user behavior. The efficiency of our system assesses the time taken to generate a reordered set of ST-OLAP queries for various current session sizes according to the number of queries. It's important because ST-OLAP queries should be resolved in a short time to enable an interactive analysis.

The performance is presented in Figure 8 according to various current session sizes. These sizes are obtained by playing with the parameter that change over the time: the maximum number of queries that could be launched for the current session, it ranges from 3 to 20. Note that what is measured is the execution time taken by the steps proposed: computing similarity, ranking the set of ST-OLAP queries in the current session, applying our UB model and reordering the candidates ST-OLAP queries. The goal of our experimentation is to measure the execution time taken by applying our proposed approach.

Figure 8 shows the evolution of the average computation time by applying our system. The goal of our experimentation is to measure the execution time taken by applying our proposed approach. So, we conclude that the time taken to suggest a set of ST-OLAP queries according to the user behavior and based only in the short-temp research increases linearly with the current session size as shown in figure 8. As can be seen from figure 8, it is obvious that the trend of execution time is upwards with the session size.

Figure 6. ST-OLAPSIM System

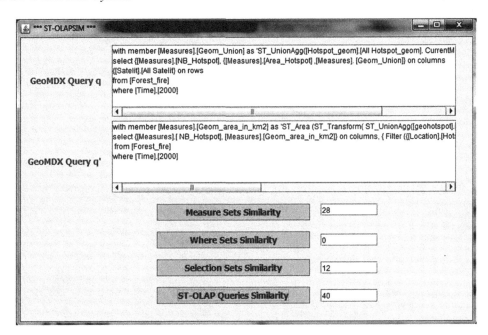

Figure 7. The architecture of ST-OLAP queries suggestion system

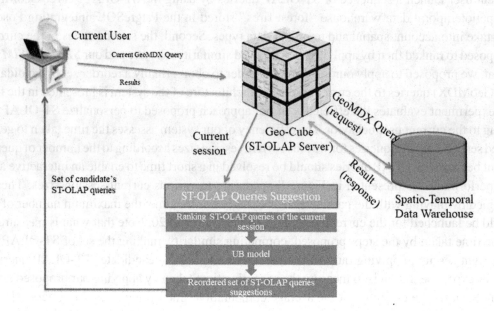

Figure 8. Performance analysis: Average computation time for obtaining a set of candidates' ST-OLAP queries

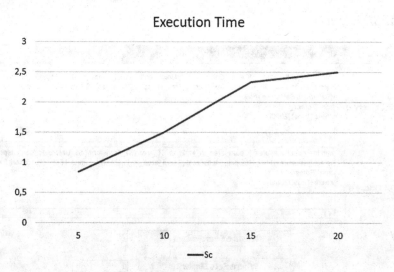

CONCLUSION

In summary, in this chapter, we have provided an overview of the evolution methods for comparing queries. So, we have proposed a spatio-temporal similarity measure in order to compute the similarity between Spatio-Temporal OLAP queries (GeoMDX queries). However, there is a little evidence that researchers have approached the issue of comparing between Spatio-Temporal OLAP queries. To the best of our knowledge, our proposal is the first work proposing a spatio-temporal similarity measure between ST-OLAP queries. We have built a personalized query suggestion model based on user behavior (UB), based on the user's short term search behavior to deal with the personalized query suggestion task. To address it, we build the UB model based on a probabilistic approach with Bayes's rule and incorporates the information from the current query, also by computing the similarity measures between Spatio-Temporal OLAP queries. The proposed measure takes into account not only the spatial data with specific characteristics such as topological, orientation and distance, but also the temporal data. Furthermore, our approach is validated by an implementation of the spatio-temporal similarity system *ST-OLAPSIM* system and our proposed approach ST-OLAP queries suggestion. Adding to that, to validate our proposed approach, we evaluated the efficiency and the effectiveness of our proposal.

REFERENCES

Aissi, S., Gouider, M., Sboui, T., & Bensaid, L. (2014). *Enhancing spatial datacube exploitation: A spatio-semantic similarity perspective*. Academic Press.

Aligon, J., Golfarelli, M., Marcel, P., Rizzi, S., & Turricchia, E. (2014). Similarity measures for olap sessions. *Knowledge and Information Systems, 39*(2), 463–489. doi:10.100710115-013-0614-1

Aufaure, M., Kuchmann-Beauger, N., Marcel, P., Rizzi, S., & Vanrompay, Y. (2013). Predicting your next OLAP query based on recent analytical sessions. *Data Warehousing and Knowledge Discovery - 15th International Conference, Proceedings*, 134-145. 10.1007/978-3-642-40131-2_12

Badard, T. (2011). *L'open source au service du géospatial et de l'intelligence D'affaires*. Geomatics Sciences Department.

Bank, J., & Cole, B. (2008). *Calculating the jaccard similarity coefficient with map reduce for entity pairs in Wikipedia*. Academic Press.

Bellatreche, L., Giacometti, A., Marcel, P., Mouloudi, H., & Laurent, D. (2005). A personalization framework for OLAP queries. *DOLAP 2005, ACM 8th International Workshop on Data Warehousing and OLAP Proceedings*, 9-18. 10.1145/1097002.1097005

Bellatreche, L., Mouloudi, H., Giacometti, A., & Marcel, P. (2006). Personalizationof MDX queries. 22_emes Journées Bases de Données Avancées, BDA2006, Lille, 17-20 octobre 2006, Actes (Informal Proceedings).

Cao, H., Jiang, D., Pei, J., He, Q., Liao, Z., Chen, E., & Li, H. (2008, August). Context-aware query suggestion by mining click-through and session data. In *Proceedings of the 14th ACM SIGKDD international conference on Knowledge discovery and data mining* (pp. 875-883). ACM. 10.1145/1401890.1401995

Chang, J.-W., Bista, R., Kim, Y.-C., & Kim, Y.-K. (2007). Spatio-temporal similarity measure algorithm for moving objects on spatial networks. In *Proceedings of the 2007 International Conference on Computational Science and Its Applications - Volume Part III, ICCSA'07* (pp. 1165-1178). Berlin, Germany: Springer-Verlag. 10.1007/978-3-540-74484-9_102

Chen, W., Hao, Z., Shao, T., & Chen, H. (2018). Personalized query suggestion based on user behavior. *International Journal of Modern Physics C, 29*(04), 1850036. doi:10.1142/S0129183118500365

Clementini, E., & Felice, P. D. (1995). A comparison of methods for representing topological relationships. *Information Sciences - Applications, 3*(3), 149-178.

Dijkstra, E. W. (1959). A note on two problems in connexion with graphs. *Numerische Mathematik, 1*(1), 269–271. doi:10.1007/BF01386390

Egenhofer, M. J. (2002). Toward the semantic geospatial web. In *Proceedings of the 10th ACM International Symposium on Advances in Geographic Information Systems, GIS '02* (pp. 1-4). New York, NY: ACM.

Egenhofer, M. J., & Al-Taha, K. K. (1992). Reasoning about gradual changes of topological relationships. In *Theories and Methods of Spatio-Temporal Reasoning in Geographic Space: Proc. of the International Conference GIS,* (pp. 196-219). Springer. 10.1007/3-540-55966-3_12

Egenhofer, M. J., & Franzosa, R. D. (1991). Point-set topological spatial relations. *International Journal of Geographical Information Systems, 2*(5), 161–174. doi:10.1080/02693799108927841

Frank, A. U. (1996). *Qualitative spatial reasoning: Cardinal directions as an example.* Academic Press.

Giacometti, A., Marcel, P., Negre, E., & Soulet, A. (2011). Query recommendations for OLAP discovery-driven analysis. *International Journal of Data Warehousing and Mining, 7*(2), 1–25. doi:10.4018/jdwm.2011040101

Glorio, O., Mazon, J.-N., Garrigos, I., & Trujillo, J. (2012). A personalization process for spatial data warehouse development. *Decision Support Systems, 52*(4), 884–898. doi:10.1016/j.dss.2011.11.010

Goyal, R., & Egenhofer, M. (2001). Similarity of cardinal directions. *Lecture Notes in Computer Science, 2121,* 36-55. doi:10.1007/3-540-47724-1_3

Hasanah, G. U., & Trisminingsih, R. (2016). Multidimensional analysis and location intelligence application for spatial data warehouse hotspot in indonesia using spagobi. *IOP Conference Series: Earth and Environmental Science, 31*(1). 10.1088/1755-1315/31/1/012011

Jerbi, H. (2012). *Personnalisation d'analyses décisionnelles sur des donnes multidimensionnelles* (PhD thesis). Institut de Recherche en Informatique de Toulouse UMR 5505, France.

Jiang, D., Leung, K. W. T., Vosecky, J., & Ng, W. (2014, March). Personalized query suggestion with diversity awareness. In *Data Engineering (ICDE), 2014 IEEE 30th International Conference on* (pp. 400-411). IEEE. 10.1109/ICDE.2014.6816668

Kharitonov, E., Macdonald, C., Serdyukov, P., & Ounis, I. (2013, October). Intent models for contextualising and diversifying query suggestions. In *Proceedings of the 22nd ACM international conference on Conference on information & knowledge management* (pp. 2303-2308). ACM. 10.1145/2505515.2505661

Kruschwitz, U., Lungley, D., Albakour, M. D., & Song, D. (2013). Deriving query suggestions for site search. *Journal of the American Society for Information Science and Technology, 64*(10), 1975–1994. doi:10.1002/asi.22901

Layouni, O., & Akaichi, J. (2014). A novel approach for a collaborative exploration of a spatial data cube. IJCCE. *International Journal of Computer and Communication Engineering, 3*(1), 63–68. doi:10.7763/IJCCE.2014.V3.293

Li, B., & Fonseca, F. (2006). Tdd: A comprehensive model for qualitative spatial similarity assessment. *Spatial Cognition and Computation, 6*(1), 31–62. doi:10.120715427633scc0601_2

Liu, J. G., Zhou, T., Wang, B. H., Zhang, Y. C., & Guo, Q. (2009). Effects of user's tastes on personalized recommendation. *International Journal of Modern Physics C, 20*(12), 1925–1932. doi:10.1142/S0129183109014825

Marcel, P., Missaoui, R., & Rizzi, S. (2012). Towards intensional answers to OLAP queries for analytical sessions. *DOLAP 2012, ACM 15th International Workshop on Data Warehousing and OLAP Proceedings*, 49-56. 10.1145/2390045.2390054

Moreau, E., Yvon, F., & Cappé, O. (2008). Robust similarity measures for named entities matching. In *Proceedings of the 22Nd International Conference on Computational Linguistics - Volume 1, COLING '08*, (pp. 593-600). Stroudsburg, PA: Association for Computational Linguistics. 10.3115/1599081.1599156

Rivest, S., Bdard, Y., Proulx, M., Nadeau, M., Hubert, F., & Pastor, J. (2005). Solap technology: Merging business intelligence with geospatial technology for interactive spatio-temporal exploration and analysis of data. *ISPRS Journal of Photogrammetry and Remote Sensing, 60*(1), 17–33. doi:10.1016/j.isprsjprs.2005.10.002

Sapia, C. (1999). On modeling and predicting query behavior in olap systems. Proc. Intl Workshop on Design and Management of Data Warehouses (DMDW 99), 1-10.

Sapia, C. (2000). Promise: Predicting query behavior to enable predictive caching strategies for olap systems. Lecture Notes in Computer Science, 1874, 224-233.

Sapia, C., Alexander, F., & Erlangen-nrnberg, U. (2001). *Promise: Modeling and predicting user behavior for online analytical processing applications* (PhD thesis). Technische Universitt Mnchen.

Sarawagi, S. (1999). Explaining differences in multidimensional aggregates. In *Proceedings of the 25th International Conference on Very Large Data Bases, VLDB '99*, (pp. 42-53). San Francisco, CA: Morgan Kaufmann Publishers Inc.

Sarawagi, S. (2000). User-adaptive exploration of multidimensional data. In *VLDB* (pp. 307–316). Morgan Kaufmann.

Sathe, G., & Sarawagi, S. (2001). Intelligent rollups in multidimensional olap data. In *Proceedings of the 27th International Conference on Very Large Data Bases, VLDB '01*, (pp. 531-540). San Francisco, CA: Morgan Kaufmann Publishers Inc.

Sedgewick, R. (1978). Implementing quicksort programs. *Communications of the ACM, 21*(10), 847–857. doi:10.1145/359619.359631

Tranchant, M. (2011). *Capacités des outils solap en termes de requêtes spatiales, temporelles et spatio-temporelles. Technical report*. Conservatoire National Des Arts Et Metiers Centre Regional Rhone- Alpes Centre Denseignement De Grenoble.

Vaisman, A., & Zimányi, E. (2014). *Data Warehouse Systems: Design and Implementation*. Heidelberg, Germany: Springer. doi:10.1007/978-3-642-54655-6

Verberne, S., Sappelli, M., Järvelin, K., & Kraaij, W. (2015, March). User simulations for interactive search: Evaluating personalized query suggestion. In *European Conference on Information Retrieval* (pp. 678-690). Springer. 10.1007/978-3-319-16354-3_75

Vidakovic, B. (1998). Nonlinear wavelet shrinkage with Bayes rules and Bayes factors. *Journal of the American Statistical Association, 93*(441), 173–179. doi:10.1080/01621459.1998.10474099

ENDNOTES

[1]   www.spatialytics.org/fr/projelts/geomondrian/
[2]   https://www.postgresql.org/
[3]   postgis.net/

Chapter 6
Building OLAP Cubes From Columnar NoSQL Data Warehouses

Khaled Dehdouh
Cherchell Military Academy, Algeria

ABSTRACT

In the big data warehouses context, a column-oriented NoSQL database system is considered as the storage model which is highly adapted to data warehouses and online analysis. Indeed, the use of NoSQL models allows data scalability easily and the columnar store is suitable for storing and managing massive data, especially for decisional queries. However, the column-oriented NoSQL DBMS do not offer online analysis operators (OLAP). To build OLAP cubes corresponding to the analysis contexts, the most common way is to integrate other software such as HIVE or Kylin which has a CUBE operator to build data cubes. By using that, the cube is built according to the row-oriented approach and does not allow to fully obtain the benefits of a column-oriented approach. In this chapter, the main contribution is to define a cube operator called MC-CUBE (MapReduce Columnar CUBE), which allows building columnar NoSQL cubes according to the columnar approach by taking into account the non-relational and distributed aspects when data warehouses are stored.

INTRODUCTION

The data warehouse is a database for online analytical processing (OLAP) to aid decision-making. It is designed according to a dimensional modelling which has for objective to observe facts through measures, also called indicators, according to the dimensions that represent the analysis axes (Inmon, 1992). It is often implemented in the relational database management system (RDBMS) (Imho, Geiger, & Galemmo, 2003). Thanks to the OLAP (On-Line Analytical Processing), the users can create multidimensional representations related to the particular analysis contexts in compliance with the specific needs, according to the criteria which they define, called hypercubes or OLAP cubes (Chaudhuri &

DOI: 10.4018/978-1-5225-5516-2.ch006

Dayal, 1997). Cube computation produces aggregations that are beyond the limits of the Group by (Gray et al., 1997). For example, in the case of calculation of the sum, it computes in a multidimensional way and returns sub-totals and totals for all possible combinations. This involves performance of all aggregations according to all levels of hierarchies of all dimensions. For a cube with three dimensions A, B and C, the performed aggregations relate to the following combinations: (A, B, C), (A, B, ALL), (A, ALL, C), (ALL, B, C), (A, ALL, ALL), (ALL, B, ALL), (ALL, ALL, C), (ALL, ALL, ALL). The (A, B, C) combination corresponds as the lowest (least) aggregate level of the cube, and the rest are considered as the high aggregate levels. The advent of the big data has created new opportunities for researchers to achieve high relevance and impact amid changes and transformations in how we study several science phenomena. Companies like Google and Microsoft are analyzing large volumes of data for business analysis and decisions, which impact the existing and the future technologies (Gandomi & Haider, 2015).

However, unusual volumes of data become an issue when faced with the limited capacities of traditional systems, especially when data storage is in a distributed environment which requires the use of parallel treatment as MapReduce paradigm (Dean & Ghemawat, 2004). To solve a part of this issue, other models have appeared such as the column oriented NoSQL (Not Only SQL) which gives a data structure more adequate to the massive data warehouses (Bhogal & Choksi, 2015). In the big data warehouses context, a column-oriented NoSQL database system is considered as the storage model which is highly adapted to data warehouses and online analysis (Rabuzin & Modruan, 2014). Indeed, the storage of data column by column allows values belonging to the same column to be shared in the same disk space which improves the column access time enormously when the aggregate operations are performed. Furthermore, the non-relational aspect that characterizes the NoSQL model when data are stored allows to deploy data easily in a distributed environment (Jerzy, 2012).

To build OLAP cubes corresponding to the analysis contexts, the most common way is to integrate other softwares such as HIVE which has a CUBE operator to build data cubes. By using that, the cube is built according to the row-oriented approach and does not allow to fully obtaining the benefits of a column-oriented approach. To solve this problem, we propose an aggregation operator, called MC-CUBE (MapReduce Columnar CUBE) which allows OLAP cubes to be computed according to the columnar approach from big data warehouses implemented by using column-oriented NoSQL model. MC-CUBE implements the invisible join, used by the columnar RDBMS (Abadi, Madden, & Hachem, 2008), in order to compute aggregation from several tables and extend it to take into account all possible aggregations at different levels of granularity of the cube. To deal with very large data, MC-CUBE uses the MapReduce paradigm when handling data stored in a distributed environment.

Given that the join performing is costly in the context of big data when dimensions and fact are stored in different tables, we propose the use of star join index (SJI) and we called it Columnar Star Join Index (C-SJI) once adapted to columnar NoSQL model. Using it allows to optimize the performing of the OLAP cubes.

We have evaluated the performance of MC-CUBE operator on star schema benchmark (SSB) (O'Neil, O'Neil, & Chen, 2007), implemented within the column-oriented NoSQL DBMS HBase1[1] using Hadoop2[2]. The HBase DBMS and the Hadoop platform were chosen because of their distributed context which was necessary for storing and analyzing big data.

The rest of this paper is organized as follows. Section 2 presents the fundamental concepts related to this research study. Section 3 gives a related work. Section 4 explains the columnar approach that we propose for building a data cube. Section 5 introduces the MC-CUBE operator and shows the execution phases through an example. Section 6 addresses a functional aspect of the use of the star join index in order to optimize performing columnar OLAP cubes. Section 7 shows performance results and exemplifies of MC-CUBE operator when OLAP cubes are performed. Finally Section 8 concludes the paper and suggests some possible directions for future research work.

KEY CONCEPTS

The main purpose of this section is to briefly introduce the key concepts and terms related to our research work.

Columnar NoSQL Data Warehouse

In the case of data warehouse implementation by using the columnar NoSQL model, both the dimensions and the fact are stored by column-wise. Each data is stored in the form of a "key/value" pair. When the data belongs to the dimension, the key part is represented by the key of this dimension. By cons, if the data belongs to the fact table, the part key is represented by the key of the fact table. As the dimensions and fact are stored in different tables, the link between them is ensured by the join attributes, where the key contains the key of the fact table and in the value part contains the key of dimension.

Formalization: Given the columnar NoSQL star data warehouse DW which is composed by the fact table F and dimensions tables $D = \{d_1, d_2, ..., d_n\}$. Each dimension table d_j, with $j \in [1, n]$ is composed by a^i_j attributes with $i \in [1, k]$, such as $d_j = \{a^1_j, a^2_j, ..., a^k_j\}$, where k varies from dimension to another. Each dimension attribute value is stored in the form of a "key/value" pair. The key part contains the dimension identifier $d_j.RowKey$ and the value part contains $a^i_j.value$. The fact table, on the other hand, groups together a number of attributes which represent the measures to aggregate $M = \{m_1, m_2, ..., m_t\}$. Each measure m_q, with $q \in [1, t]$, is identified by the fact table key (F.RowKey, m_q.value). Furthermore, F contains the join attributes $F.d_j$, where each one is composed by the fact table identifier and the identifier of dimension table that represent (F.RowKey, d_j.RowKey). Columnar NoSQL star data warehouse composed of one fact table F and two dimension tables' d_1, d_2 is depicted in figure 1.

MapReduce Paradigm: In order to face large data, developers have produced large amounts of complex code to deal with issues such as data partitioning, parallel/distributed processing, failure management, etc. As a reaction to this situation, Google has designed a new abstraction of parallel/distributed processing called "MapReduce" (MR) (Dean & Ghemawat, 2004) which hides the complex details of parallelization, fault tolerance, data distribution and load balancing in a library.

In the MR model, any computation can be expressed as two functions, map() and reduce(), which are defined as generic primitives on the MR library and are supplied (written) by the programmer. The function map() takes an input pair and produces a set of intermediate key/value pairs, where each mapper provide partial results in its local area. The MR library groups all intermediate values associated with the same intermediate key and passes them to the reduce() function. The function reduce() consolidates the map outputs and provides the final results (output files)

Figure 1. Columnar NoSQL Data Warehouse

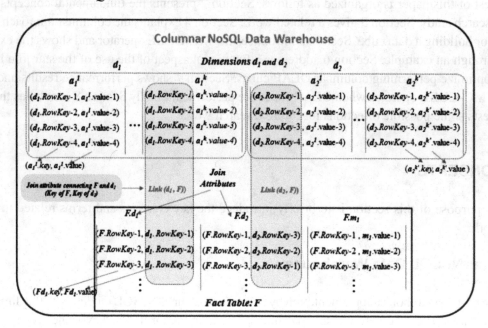

RELATED WORK

Big data have lead data warehouses towards to distributed environments to store and to analyze the large amount of data. Since the column storage has outperformed the row storage, several research projects based on the columnar relational model have been commercialized such as InfoBright (Lezak & Eastwood, 2009), Brighthouse (Lezak, Wrblewski, Eastwood, & Synak, 2008), Vectorwise (Zukowski, van de Wiel, & Boncz, 2012), MonetDB (Idreos et al., 2012), SAP HANA (Farber et al., 2012), Blink (Barber et al., 2012), and Vertica (Lamb et al., 2012). These systems have led legacy RDBMS vendors to add columnar storage options to their existing engines (Larson, Hanson, & Price, 2012). However, the relational model that is often used for storing data warehouses has shown its limits. Indeed, the use of distributed solutions based on the relational model is as costly as the implementation of the referential integrity constraints (RIC) that ensures the validity of relation between tables in the RDBMS, because the system must continuously ensure that the associated data are stored in the same node. Furthermore, it is very difficult to respect the ACID (Atomicity, Consistency, Isolation and Durability) properties that characterize the transactional systems with correct consistency when data are stored in distributed environment (Cattell, 2011). Moreover, the variety aspect of data cannot be supported by the relational model. Thus, for analytical purposes, Google developed a massively scalable infrastructure that includes a distributed system, a column-oriented storage system, a distributed coordination system and parallel execution algorithm based on the paradigm of MapReduce, and opened them to the community in 2004 and 2006, respectively (Chang et al., 2008).

Regarding the implementation of the big data warehouses within the column-oriented NoSQL model, two approaches are defined (Dehdouh, Bentayeb, Boussaid, & Kabachi, 2015). The first one (normalized approach) uses different tables for storing fact and dimension at physical level which requires to achieve the join between tables when aggregation is performed. The second approach (denormalized approach) stores the fact and dimensions into one table, which allows to avoid performing join between tables.

For building OLAP cubes, we would name four relevant works: (Abello, Ferrarons, & Romero, 2011), (Dehdouh, Bentayeb, Boussaid, & Kabachi, 2014), (Chevalier, Malki, Kopliku, Teste, & Tournier, 2015), and (Chavan & Phursule, 2014). Firstly, (Abello, Ferrarons, & Romero, 2011) outlines the possibility of having data in a cloud by using columnar NoSQL DBMS to store data and MapReduce as an agile mechanism to build cubes. However, the cube is built at one level of granularity (least level) and from data warehouse implemented according the denormalized approach. Thus, the authors do not give any indications regarding the computing of the aggregates when the others levels of granularities that compose the cube are performed. A similar proposal to build cubes using MapReduce can be found in (Dehdouh, Bentayeb, Boussaid, & Kabachi, 2014), but in this case the authors just perform the cube at different level of granularity and do not provide a solution for performing join between tables (fact and dimensions) when data warehouses are implemented according the normalized approach. In (Chevalier, Malki, Kopliku, Teste, & Tournier, 2015), the different level of granularity that compose the OLAP cube can be computed using the naive method, using a combination of group-by queries and gathering the outputs via the UNION operator. This solution is not suitable for big data warehouses. Indeed, for D dimensions, the execution of 2^D sub-queries to perform the various aggregations, which considerably increase the number of times when the data warehouse is accessed. Consequently, the naive method reduces DBMS performance, particularly when scaling-up. Finally, (Chavan & Phursule, 2014) gives a solution to perform join between tables and performing aggregates from data warehouses implemented according the normalized approach. It consists to integrate software and tools such as Hive and Kylin in the ecosystem used for implementing the data warehouse, and use their cube building operators. However, the use of these tools is limited; because they are row-oriented, and once integrated into column-oriented NoSQL DBMS, they do not allow to take a full effective of the columnar NoSQL DBMS when data are handled.

BUILDING COLUMNAR OLAP CUBES

To generate an OLAP cube compound aggregates of several levels of granularity, it is necessary to firstly identify data which satisfy all the predicates (filters) from the data warehouse. To carry out this phase, query predicates are applied separately to the respective dimensions to obtain the primary keys of dimensions that will be involved in the join with the fact table. Since the keys are foreign keys at the level of the fact table, they are used to identify the related fact table key. The result of this phase allows then to calculate the different levels of granularity that compose the cube. Indeed, to optimize the data cube calculating, it is better to perform from the data warehouse the calculation of aggregates of the lowest level, and then uses it to compute the other levels of aggregation that compose the data cube. This allows to avoid returning to data warehouse and performs more join between tables when higher level aggregates are performed. We present here in after the general way for computing aggregates of several levels of granularity of the OLAP cube obtained according to the row-oriented approach, versus, our proposition for building the cube according the column-oriented approach.

Row-Oriented Approach

The storage of data is row-oriented; each table (dimension or facts) stores data by row (record). Each record stores the column (attribute) values which is a row of the table. Once the column value belonging to a record is accessed, the other values of columns that compose this record do the same. Therefore, to optimize the computation of aggregates when the cube is built, and after the identification of data that compose the cube, it would be more adequate to compute the most aggregate level from the least one, and to be used for computing the one after as it contains fewer attributes (Beyer & Ramakrishnan, 1999).

For instance, for a cube with three dimensions A, B, C, the computing of aggregates is defined according to four levels of granularity (LG1, LG2, LG3, LG4) where LG1 represents the least aggregate level (A, B, C) and LG2 represents aggregation level corresponding to dimensions' combinations and LG3 represents aggregation level corresponding to each dimension and LG4 represents the most aggregate level.

To optimize building OLAP cube, the LG1 which represents the least aggregate level (A, B, C) is performed first; then, it is used to compute aggregates of others levels of granularity (LG2, LG3, LG4). The transition from one level of granularity to another is carried out sequentially with a downward direction (LG2 → LG3 → LG4). Thus, the second level of granularity LG2: (A, B, ALL), (A, ALL, C), (ALL, B, C) allows to compute the third LG3: (A, ALL, ALL), (ALL, B, ALL), (ALL, ALL, C), that can be used to compute the next level LG4: (ALL, ALL, ALL) (figure 2).

Thus, according to the row-oriented approach, the fourth level of granularity can be obtained only if the third level of granularity has already been performed. This approach (used by the traditional DBMS), based on the exploitation of least aggregate levels of granularity to perform the most aggregate levels, is effective when the storage environment is row-oriented.

Figure 2. Row-oriented approach for building the cube

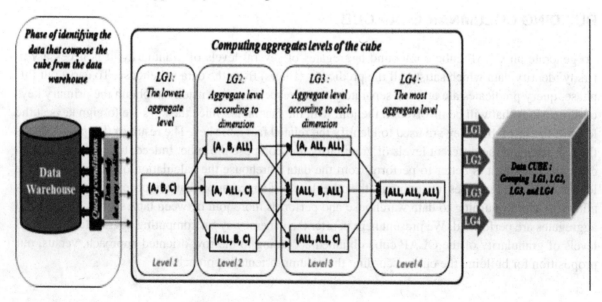

Column-Oriented Approach

When data warehouse is stored according to column-oriented approach, the data is stored column by column. Therefore, the computing of aggregates requires access only to the values of columns (dimensions or measures) involved in the decisional query. For building the OLAP cube, and after identifying the data that compose the cube, it is not necessary to seek for reducing the number of attributes in order to compute a cube's aggregates at different levels of granularity. The aggregations of the second, the third, and the fourth levels can be performed from the first level. Also, the transition from levels 2 to 4 does not need to be sequential, and can be achieved at the same time in a parallel way. Thus, we propose this new approach for optimizing the computing of the cube where the aggregates granularity levels are all performed from one single level, which is the least aggregated one (figure 3).

We are positioning in this approach to provide MC-CUBE an aggregation operator to generate OLAP cubes from column-oriented data warehouses.

MC-CUBE OPERATOR

Traditionally, building OLAP cubes tools have been focused on the row-by row data layout, since it performs better on the most common application for database systems (transactional data processing). However, in the context of the data warehouses storage, where the column by column data layout offers a better opportunity than row by row, these cube building tools have been integrated through connectors as Kylin and Hive tools. To perform aggregates of the cube, the data which are stored column by column are used according to the row-oriented approach because these tools build the cube according to row-oriented approach and lead consequently to the loss of the column-by-column data layout opportunity.

Figure 3. Column-oriented approach for building the cube

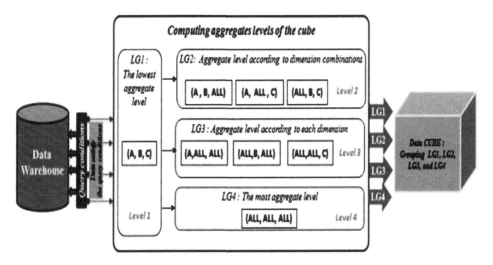

As a solution to this problem, the MC-CUBE operator extends the use of the column-oriented approach beyond data storage in order to achieve data processing and building OLAP cubes. MC-CUBE allows the following:

- To avoid the use of additional algorithms which are used by the row-oriented approach in order to better organize the steps of the aggregates computing based on exploiting of the intermediate results to obtain a level of granularity from the smaller results of another level of granularity;
- To perform aggregates processing of the higher levels independently (simultaneously) since each of these levels of granularity is calculated from the same finest level;
- To optimize the time needed to perform aggregates corresponding to the different granularity levels (lowest to highest);
- To reduce the build time of the cube.

Operating Principle

In this section, we present MC-CUBE operator for building OLAP cubes according to NoSQL columnar-wise approach. The MC-CUBE uses the MapReduce paradigm to optimize the processing of massive data. MC-CUBE operator allows to perform a cube in five phases. In the first phase, the MC-CUBE identifies the data which satisfy all the predicates (filters) from the columnar data warehouse and allows the aggregation according to all columns representing dimensions to be produced. Since, the fact and dimensions are stored in different tables, the MC-CUBE operator implements in distribute environment the invisible join, which is used by the relational column-oriented to perform the join between tables (fact and dimensions) and achieve the aggregation computing. It is worth to mention, the invisible join improves substantially join performance in the case of column stores, especially on the types of schemas found in data warehouses. The result of the first phase corresponds to the first level of granularity of the cube which allows then to perform the different levels of granularity that compose the cube. In the second phase, the first level of granularity (output of the first phase) is used to perform the aggregations of the granularity level according to each dimension separately. The third phase uses the output of the first one to produce aggregations of the dimension combinations. The fourth phase uses the output of the first one to computes the highest levels of granularity. The last phase groups together the outputs of the previous four phases in order to produce the cube.

Execution Phases of MC-CUBE Operator

To deal with massive data processing, MC-CUBE operator uses paradigm MapReduce model for processing large volumes of data and optimizes the calculation of OLAP cubes. Indeed, with MapReduce programming model, MapReduce job specifies a "Map" function that processes a "key/value" pair to generate a set of intermediate "key/value" pairs, as well as a "Reduce" function that merges all intermediate values associated with the same intermediate key. The five phases for building OLAP cube by MC-CUBE are achieved by executing MapReduce jobs.

The First Phase

This phase involves using the data warehouse to identify data which satisfy all the predicates (filters) and allows to produce the lowest level of granularity of the cube. Firstly, the query predicates are applied on dimensions tables to identify the pairs of dimensions keys that will be involved in the join with the fact table. The outputs are used to perform the join with the fact table in order to give the values of the primary key of the fact table which satisfy all query predicates. As soon as the join results identify the data that compose the cube, the aggregations of the lowest level of granularity of the cube are performed. The MapReduce jobs that perform the first phase are achieved as follows:

Job 1 (MRJ-1): The "key/value" pairs of dimensions which will be use to perform the join with the fact table are identified when this job is performed (algorithm 1 and 2). At the Map function, the treatments are parallelized in order to apply the query predicates to the respective dimensions (algo1: line2). The result is output to the Reduce function which gathered the partial results and provides a set of pairs "key/value" representing the dimension values involved in the join with the fact table. The key part of "key/value" pair contains the value of the dimension (algo2: line1) and the other part contains the dimension identifier corresponding (algo2: line3).

Figure 4. Job 1 pseudo-code

Algorithm 1: MC-CUBE - *Job 1 of phase1* - **Fonction Map()**

Input : $(d_j.RowKey, a_j^i.value)$: (key,value) pair of dimension.
         C : query condition.
Output: (key_{tmp}, val_{tmp})

/* Identify (key, value) of dimensions that verify condition query.   */

1   **foreach** $a_j^i \in d_j$ **do**
2   **if** $a_j^i.value$ *verify* C **then**
3         $key_{tmp} \leftarrow a_j^i.value$
4         $val_{tmp} \leftarrow d_j.RowKey$
5   **end**
6   Emit (key_{tmp}, val_{tmp})
7 **end**

Algorithm 2: MC-CUBE - *Job 1 of phase1* - **Fonction Reduce()**

Input : (key_{tmp}, val_{tmp}): output of Map function.
Output: (key_{out}, val_{out}): (key, value) pairs that verify condition query

/* Set dimensions identifiers to join with the fact table   */

1 $key_{out} \leftarrow key_{tmp}$
2 **foreach** $v \in val_{tmp}$ **do**
3     $val_{out} \leftarrow concat(v)$ // Concatenate dimension identifiers verifying the query condition C
4 **end**
5 Emit $(key_{out-Job1}, val_{out-Job1})$

Job 2 (MRJ-2): This job (algorithm 3 and 4), uses the result of the first, and identifies at the map function level, the values of the primary key of the fact table corresponding to the dimensions' primary keys which satisfied the query predicates. This allows building a list of "key/value", where the key part contains the primary key of the fact table, and the value part contains a boolean value (0 or 1). This latter shows if the query predicate is satisfied (1) (algo3: line4) or not (0) (algo3: line7). For optimization reasons, only the first join attribute at the fact table is scanned, the others are scanned by using the keys that are obtained from the first scan. Indeed, the first scan allows to have the values of the primary key of the fact table that satisfied the predicate's dimension (boolean value corresponding to 1). Thus, from this set of keys that the others join attributes will be checked. This avoids to scan the values of the primary key unnecessary of the fact table and reduces the treatment of the number of "key/value" pairs. The result of the Map function is used by the Reduce function which apply the logical AND on the boolean value belonging to the same key (algo4: line4). The set of keys that keeping their boolean value to 1, represents the values of the primary key of the fact table which satisfy all query predicates.

Job 3 (MRJ-3): The granularity level according to all columns representing dimensions that corresponds to the lowest (least) aggregation of the cube, that we call it R1, is achieved when this job is performed (algorithm 5 and 6). Indeed, the Map function uses the result of the job 2 to identify the keys of dimensions (algorithm 5: line3) and the values of measure corresponding (algorithm 5: line4), and

Figure 5. Job 2 pseudo-code

Algorithm 3: MC-CUBE - *Job 2 of phase1* - **Fonction Map()**

Input : $(F.RowKey, d_j.RowKey)$: (key,value) pair of fact table.
$\quad\quad\quad (key_{out-Job1}, val_{out-Job1})$: output of Job1
Output: (key_{tmp}, val_{tmp})

/* Identify the keys of fact table that verify condition query. */
1 foreach $v \in val_{out-Job1}$ do
2 $\quad$ if $d_j.RowKey = v$ then
3 $\quad\quad$ $key_{tmp} \leftarrow F.RowKey$
4 $\quad\quad$ $val_{tmp} \leftarrow 1$
5 $\quad$ else
6 $\quad\quad$ $key_{tmp} \leftarrow F.RowKey$
7 $\quad\quad$ $val_{tmp} \leftarrow 0$
8 $\quad$ end
9 $\quad$ Emit (key_{tmp}, val_{tmp})
10 end

Algorithm 4: MC-CUBE - *Job 2 of phase1* - **Fonction Reduce()**

Input : (key_{tmp}, val_{tmp}): Output of Map function.
Output: $(key_{out-Job2}, val_{out-Job2})$: keys of fact tables that verified queries conditions

/* Set keys of fact table that verified queries conditions. */
1 $key_{out-Job2} \leftarrow key_{tmp}$
2 $val_{out-Job2} \leftarrow 1$
3 foreach $v \in val_3$ do
4 $\quad$ $val_{out-Job2} \leftarrow val_{out-Job2}$ & v
5 $\quad$ if $val_{out-Job2} = 1$ then
6 $\quad\quad$ Emit $(key_{out-Job2}, val_{out-Job2})$
7 $\quad$ end
8 end

Figure 6. Job 3 pseudo-code

Algorithm 5: MC-CUBE - *Job 3 of phase1* - **Fonction Map()**

Input : $((key_{out-Job2}, val_{out-Job2})$: output of *job 2*.
$(F.RowKey, d_j.RowKey)$: (key,value) pair of fact table (join attribute $F.d_j$).
$(F.RowKey, m_q.value)$: (key,value) of fact table corresponding to measure attribute m_q.

Output: (key_{tmp}, val_{tmp})

/* Identify the keys of dimensions and the values of measure corresponding.   */
1 foreach $v \in key_{out-Job2}$ do
2   if $F.RowKey = v$ then
3          $key_{tmp} \leftarrow concat(d_j.RowKey)$ //Concatinate dimensions' keys having the same fact table key
4          $val_{tmp} \leftarrow m_q.value$
5   end
6   Emit (key_{tmp}, val_{tmp})
7 end

Algorithm 6: MC-CUBE - *Job 3 of phase1* - **Fonction Reduce()**

Input : (key_{tmp}, val_{tmp}): Output of Map function.
Output: $(key_{out-R1}, val_{out-R1})$: (key, value) pairs that compose the cube R_1

/* Produce the least aggregate level of the cube (R1).   */
1 $key_{out-R1} \leftarrow key_{tmp}$
2 foreach $v \in val_{tmp}$ do
3      $val_{out-R1} = Aggregate(v)$ // Apply the aggregate function
4   Emit $(key_{out-R1}, val_{out-R1})$
5 end

---

sends it to the Reduce function in the form of "key/value" pairs (algorithm 5: line 6). The key part contains dimensions and the value part of pair contains the measure corresponding. At the second stage, the values of measure are aggregated according dimensions when the Reduce function is performed (algorithm 6: line1&3) and the least aggregate level of the cube (R1) is produced.

The Second Phase

This phase allows, from the result obtained by job 3 of the first phase, to perform the aggregations according to each dimension separately. It is achieved by executing one MapReduce job as follows.

Job (MRJ): To achieve the aggregation level corresponding to each dimension that we call it R2, the result of the job 3 (R1) is used. Recall that the part key of pairs composed the R1 contains the dimensions identifiers, and the part value contains the corresponding measure. Thus, at the Map function level, each identifier of dimension is extracted (algorithm 7: line2) with the corresponding measure (algorithm 7: line3) which produces a pair of "key/value". The key part contains an identifier of dimension, and the part value contains the corresponding measure. For each same dimension identifier (key), the measures (value) are aggregated (algorithm 8: line3) when the Reduce function is performed.

Figure 7. Job pseudo-code of second phase

Algorithm 7: MC-CUBE - *Job of phase2* - **Fonction Map()**

Input : $(key_{out-R1}, val_{out-R1})$: output of *job 3*
Output: (key_{tmp}, val_{tmp})

/* Getting each identiier of dimension with measure corresponding.   */
1 foreach $v \in key_{out-R1}$ do
2 | $key_{tmp} \leftarrow d_j.RowKey$ // Getting each dimension separately
3 | $val_{tmp} \leftarrow m_q$
4 | Emit (key_{tmp}, val_{tmp})
5 end

Algorithm 8: MC-CUBE - *Job of phase2* - **Fonction Reduce()**

Input : (key_{tmp}, val_{tmp}): Output of Map function
Output: $(key_{out-Job}, val_{out-Job})$: (key, value) pairs that compose the cube R_2

/* Produce the aggregations according to each dimension separately (R_2).   */
1 $key_{out-R2} \leftarrow key_{tmp}$
2 foreach $v \in val_{tmp}$ do
3 | $val_{out-R2} = Aggregate(v)$ // Applying the aggregate function
4 end
5 Emit $(key_{out-R2}, val_{out-R2})$

The Third Phase

It involves using the result obtained by job 3 of the first phase, to perform the aggregations according to dimension combinations. It is achieved by executing one MapReduce job, and we call the result of this operation R3.

Job (MRJ): The result of the job 3 of the first phase (R1) is used when the aggregation corresponding to the combinations of the dimensions is achieved. Thus, at the Map function level, the identifiers of dimension with different combinations are extracted with the corresponding measure (algorithm 9: line2&3) which produces in each case a pair of "key/value". The key part contains a combination of dimension identifiers, and the part value contains the corresponding measure. For each same combination of dimensions identifiers (key), the measures (value) are aggregated (algorithm 10: line3) when the Reduce function is performed.

The Fourth Phase

It involves using the result obtained by job 3 of the first phase, to perform the aggregations according to dimension combinations. It is achieved by executing one MapReduce job, and we call the result of this operation R3.

Figure 8. Job pseudo-code of third phase

Algorithm 9: MC-CUBE - *Job of phase3* - Fonction Map()

Input : $(key_{out-R1}, val_{out-R1})$: Output of *job 3*
Output: (key_{tmp}, val_{tmp})

/* Getting combinations of the dimensions' identifiers with measure corresponding. */
1 foreach $v \in key_{out-R1}$ do
2     $key_{tmp} \leftarrow$ combinat$(d_j.RowKey)$ // Getting combinations of the dimensions' identifiers
3     $val_{tmp} \leftarrow m_q$
4   Emit (key_{tmp}, val_{tmp}) // Emitting combinations of the dimensions' identifiers with measure corresponding
5 end

Algorithm 10: MC-CUBE - *Job of phase 3* - Fonction Reduce()

Input : (key_{tmp}, val_{tmp}) : Output of Map function
Output: $(key_{out-R3}, val_{out-R3})$: (key, value) pairs that compose the cube R_3

/* Produce the aggregations according to combinations of the dimensions (R_3). */
1 $key_{out-R3} \leftarrow key_{tmp}$
2 foreach $v \in val_{tmp}$ do
3     $val_{out-R3} = Aggregate\ (v)$ // Applying the aggregate function
4 end
5 Emit $(key_{out-R3}, val_{out-R3})$

Job (MRJ): The granularity level corresponding to the total aggregation, that we call it R4, is achieved when this job is performed. Thus, the Map function uses the result of job 3 of the first phase (R1) in order to extract the measure values and aggregate it when Reduce function is performed. This allows the most aggregate level of the cube (R4) to be produced.

The Fifth Phase

Since the aggregates are performed with dimensions identifiers, this phase replacing these identifiers with the dimensions attributes cited in the query, and gathered it to provide the cube. It is achieved by executing one MapReduce job.

Job (MRJ): This job allows to adapt the results obtained in the previous phases to the query context. Indeed, at the Map function the identifiers of dimensions belonging to the R1, R2, and R3 are changed by the values of dimensions cited in the query (algorithm 13: line2). The results of this function are gathered when Reduce function is performed which produce the cube.

In order to set out the jobs that defined the MC-CUBE execution phases, we use in the next section an example.

Figure 9. Job pseudo-code of fourth phase

Algorithm 11: MC-CUBE - *Job of phase 4* - Fonction Map()

Input : $(key_{out-R1}, val_{out-R1})$: Output of *job 3*
Output: (key_{tmp}, val_{tmp})

/* Getting the measure corresponding to the total aggregations. */
1 foreach $v \in key_{out-R1}$ do
2 | $key_{tmp} \leftarrow ALL$ // Refers to the total aggregate
3 | $val_{tmp} \leftarrow val_{out-R1}$
4 end
5 Emit (key_{tmp}, val_{tmp})

Algorithm 12: MC-CUBE - *Job of phase 4* - Fonction Reduce()

Input : (key_{tmp}, val_{tmp}) : Output of Map function.
Output: $(key_{out-R4}, val_{out-R4})$: (key, value) pairs that compose the cube R_4

/* Produce the total aggregations. */
1 $key_{out-R4} \leftarrow key_{tmp}$ foreach $v \in val_{tmp}$ do
2 | $val_{out-R4} = Aggregate\ (v)$ // Applying the aggregate function Emit $(key_{out-R4}, val_{out-R4})$
3 end

Figure 10. Job pseudo-code of fifth phase

Algorithm 13: MC-CUBE - *Job of phase 5* - Fonction Map()

Input : $(d_j.RowKey, a_j^i.value)$: (Key, value) of an attribute belonging to the dimension
            $(key_{out-R1}, val_{out-R1})$: Output of phase 1 (R_1)
            $(key_{out-R2}, val_{out-R2})$: Output of phase 2 (R_2)
            $(key_{out-R3}, val_{out-R3})$: Output of phase 3 (R_3)
            $(key_{out-R4}, val_{out-R4})$: Output of phase 4 (R_4)
Output: (key_{tmp}, val_{tmp})

/* Adapting results of previous phases to the context of query. */
1 foreach $v \in key_{out-R1}$ ou key_{out-R2} ou key_{out-R3} ou key_{out-R4} do
2 | $key_{tmp} \leftarrow a_j^i.value$ // changed identifier by the values of dimensions cited in the query.
3 | $val_{tmp} \leftarrow m_q$
4 end
5 Emit (key_{tmp}, val_{tmp})

Algorithm 14: MC-CUBE - *Job of phase 5* - Fonction Reduce()

Input : (key_{tmp}, val_{tmp}): Output of Map function
Output: (key_R, val_R): (key, value) pairs corresponding to the cube R

/* Produce the cube. */
1 foreach $v \in key_{tmp}$ do
2 | $key_R \leftarrow key_{tmp}$
3 | $val_R \leftarrow val_{tmp}$
4 end
5 Emit (key_R, val_R)

Figure 11. Building of (key, value) pairs that satisfy the dimension conditions

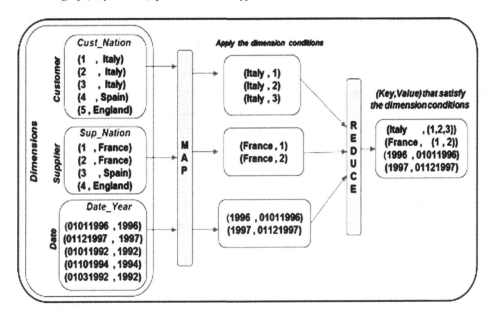

Deployment of Building a Cube by Using MC-CUBE

We use the Star Schema Benchmark as a data warehouse example in order to set out the different jobs required to perform the compute phases of the cube by using MC-CUBE operator from columnar NoSQL data warehouse. Recall that SSB is a data warehouse which manages line orders according to dimensions, PART, SUPPLIER, CUSTOMER and DATE. It consists of a single fact table called LINEORDER made up of seventeen columns to give the information about order, with a composite primary key consisting of the Orderkey and Linenumber attributes, and foreign keys that refer to the dimension tables.

In order to provide more detail on MC-CUBE execution phases, we illustrate our explanation with an example. This example computes the sales revenue from products delivered by FRENCH suppliers and for which orders were placed by ITALIAN customers in the years 1996 and 1997. According to the example, the four phases are performed as follows.

The First Phase

MJR-1: The Map function applies query predicates Customer.nation = Italy and Supplier.nation = France and Date.year 1996 and Date.year 1997, to the appropriate dimension table respectively Customer, Supplier, and Date in order to identify the primary keys of dimensions that satisfied the query conditions. The Reduce function grouped dimension keys corresponding to the Italy, France, 1996, and 1997. The result is a set of the keys of FRENCH suppliers, ITALIAN customers, and 1996 and 1997 years that will be used in the join with the fact table Lineorder (figure 11).

MRJ-2: Performs the join between dimensions and the fact table, and allows to identify the key of Lineorder (fact table) that satisfy all the query conditions at once. Thus, in Map function, for each dimension key found in fact table, the mapper associate to the Lineorder key a boolean value "1", otherwise "0". For example, for Lineorder key = 6, the Map function produces three pairs (6, 1), (6, 1), and (6, 0) corresponding respectively to the scan of the join attributes Custkey, Suppkey, and Orderdate. It means that when the Lineorder key = 6, it satisfies the predicates of CUSTOMER and SUPPLIER dimensions but does not satisfy the predicate of DATE dimension. The Reduce function uses the "logical AND" to associate the boolean values of to the same key which excludes Lineorder key = 6 from the list of Lineorder key that satisfy all query conditions (1 and 1 and 0 = 0). The result is a Lineorder key (1, 2, 3, 5) that keeps the boolean value equal "1" represents the one which satisfies all join predicates (figure 12).

MRJ-3: In Map function, the value of measure (Revenue) corresponding to the Lineorder key (1, 2, 3, 5) are extracted and will be aggregated in Reduce function according Custkey, Suppkey, Orderdate. The result is the granularity level corresponding to ((Custkey, Suppkey, Orderdate), Revenue); ((2, 1, 01011996), 600), ((3, 2, 01011996), 200), and ((1, 1, 01121997), 300) (figure 13).

Figure 12. Building a list of fact table key that satisfy all query conditions

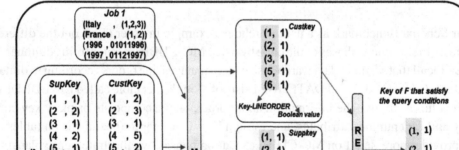

Figure 13. Building the lowest aggregate level of the cube

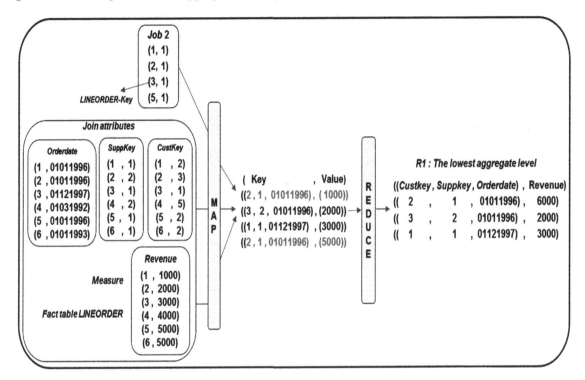

The Second Phase

This phase performs the aggregations according to each dimension separately which correspond in our case to (Custkey, ALL, ALL), (ALL, Suppkey, ALL) and (ALL, ALL, Orderdate).

MRJ: In Map function, each dimension key is extracted with their measure corresponding. For example, (2, 600), (3, 2000), (1, 3000) that correspond to (Custkey, Revenue). The Reduce function aggregates the values of measure (revenue) when the dimension key is the same. For example, for (Suppkey, Revenue), the (1, 6000), (2, 2000), (1, 3000) will be aggregate to (1, (6000+3000)), (2, 2000) (figure 14).

Figure 14. Building the aggregate level according to each dimension

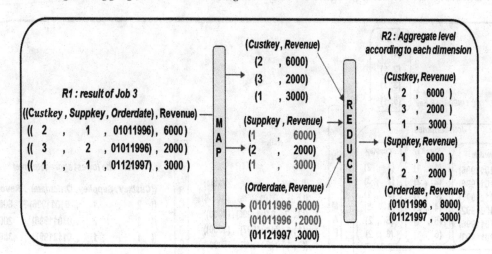

The Third Phase

It performs the aggregations corresponding to (Custkey, Suppkey, ALL), (Custkey, ALL, Orderdate), and (ALL, Suppkey, Orderdate).

MRJ: Produces the aggregations according to the different dimensions combinations remaining to compose the cube. The Map function extracts for each dimension keys combinations with their measure corresponding. For example the ((2, 1), 6000), ((3, 2), 2000), ((1, 1), 3000) that correspond to (Custkey, Suppkey, Revenue). The Reduce function aggregates the values of measure (revenue) when the dimension key combination is the same (figure 15).

Figure 15. Building the aggregate level according to dimension combinations

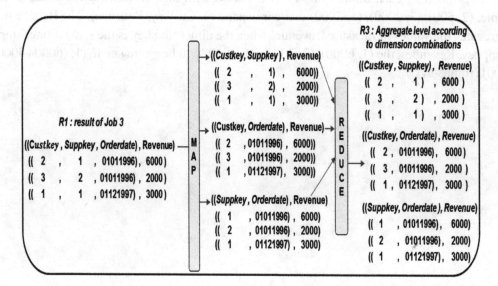

Figure 16. Building the most aggregate level of the cube

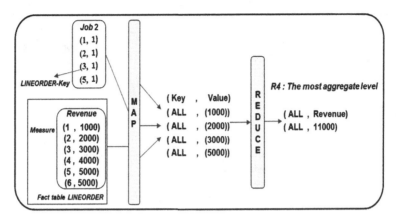

The Fourth Phase

This phase performs the highest (total) aggregation of the cube corresponding to (ALL, Sum (Revenue)).

MJR: In Map function, the value of measure (Revenue) corresponding to the Lineorder key (1, 2, 3, 5) are extracted and aggregated (Revenue: 1000 + 2000 + 3000 + 5000) in Reduce function (figure 16).

The Fifth Phase

It gathers the outputs of previous phases and produces the OLAP cube which corresponds to (c.city, s.city, d.year), (c.city, s.city, ALL), (c.city, ALL, d.year), (ALL, s.city, d.year), (c.city, ALL, ALL), (ALL, s.city, ALL), (ALL, ALL, d.year), and (ALL, ALL, ALL).

MRJ: The Map function changes the identifiers of dimensions that are used with the dimensions attributes cited in the query, and gathered it in Reduce function to provide the cube. According to our example, at the Map function, the keys (2, 3, 1) of the Custkey, the keys (1, 2) of the Suppkey, and the keys (01011996, 01121997) are replaced respectively by (Rome, Naples, Milan) of the SUPPLIER dimension, (Lyon, Paris) of the CUSTOMER dimension, and finally (1996,1997) of the DATE dimension. The output is gathered to produce the OLAP cube when the Reduce function is performed (figure 17).

OPTIMIZATION OF OLAP CUBES COMPUTING

To increase the performance of columnar NoSQL data warehouse and speed-up the join queries, the use of the star join index is a solution to achieve joining between tables (fact and dimensions) especially in the context of big data. Indeed, this kind of index is often used in relational star data warehouses to

Figure 17. Gathering the aggregate levels and producing the cube

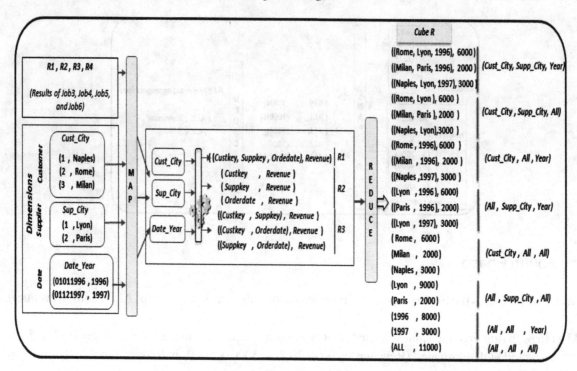

Figure 18. Job pseudo-code of building the C-SJI

Algorithm 15: MC-CUBE - *Job of index building -* **Fonction Map()**

Input : $(F.Rowkey , d_j.Rowkey)$: Join attributes J of fact table
$(F.Rowkey , d_s.Rowkey)$: Join attributes S of fact table

Output: (key_{tmp}, val_{tmp})

```
/* scanning the join attributes of fact table                              */
1 value_tmp ← F.Rowkey
2 foreach v ∈ value_tmp do
3 |   key_tmp ← concat(d_j.Rowkey , d_s.Rowkey) // concatenate the dimension identifiers having the same F.Rowkey
4 end
5 Emit (key_tmp, val_tmp)
```

Algorithm 16: MC-CUBE - *Job of index building -* **Fonction Reduce()**

Input : (key_{tmp}, val_{tmp}): Output of Map function

Output: $(key_{out}, value_{out})$: Columnar Star join index *C-SJI*

```
/* Produce the index                                                       */
1 key_out ← key_tmp
2 foreach v ∈ value_tmp do
3 |   value_out ← concat(v) ;
4 end
5 Emit (key_out, value_out)
```

---

optimize the join when decisional queries are performed. Once adapted and implemented to the column-oriented NoSQL data model, we have called it C-SJI (Columnar Star Join Index), and we have used it to pre-calculate the join between dimensions tables and fact table.

Data Model of C-SJI

The Columnar Star Join Index allows to perform the join between columns in a single column where each data is stored in the form of "key/value". The key contains the dimension identifiers combination and the value part contains the fact identifier. We can formalize it as C-SJI = (d_1.Rowkey, d_2.Rowkey, ..., d_n.Rowkey), F.Rowkey).

When the Columnar Star Join Index is built according to the MapReduce paradigm, the Map function scans the join attributes of fact table (algorithm 15: line1). For each fact table identifier, the dimension identifiers corresponding are combined and kept as the part key of result (algorithm 15: line3). On the other hand, the value of map function result contains the fact table identifier. For each same combination of dimensions' identifiers (key), the fact table identifiers (value) are combined (algorithm 16: line3) when the Reduce function is performed.

Thus, three steps are involved in the cost calculation: (1) data processing cost at the Map() step. This includes reading the source data (input) and applying the necessary processing to produce the "key/value" set corresponding to the Map results. (2) Cost of shuffle() which corresponds to the cost of sorting and moving the Map() results to reducers. (3) Finally, the cost of data processing at the reduce() step which corresponds to the cost of reading and processing data during the Reducer step.

Using the C-SJI by MC-CUBE

The use of C-SJI when the MC-CUBE operator builds the cube is beneficial at the second job which is going to scan the index (C-SJI) instead of scanning several join attributes in order to retrieve the fact table identifiers that satisfy join between the tables of dimensions and the fact table.

Once the index is built, the second job of MC-CUBE operator uses both the index and the output of job1 as input in order to identify the fact table key which satisfies the query predicates, when the cube is performed. Thus, in Map function, for each dimension' keys (result of job1) found in the index (key part of the index), the mapper associate to the fact table key (value part of the index) a boolean value "1", otherwise "0". The Reduce function keeps only the set of keys which have a boolean value equal "1". This result represents the values of the fact table key that satisfy all query conditions.

According the example, the index is built on CustKey, SuppKey, and Orderdate of the fact table which represent the join attributes and it is performed by execution a MapReduce job. We called it C-SJI-LCSD (LCSD: LINEORDER, CUSTOMER, SUPPLIER et DATE). Thus, for building it, the Map function scans CustKey, SuppKey, and Orderdate (the join attributes of fact table). For each LINEORDER identifier, the corresponding dimension identifiers are combined and kept as the result in the part key. On the other hand, the value of map function result contains the fact table identifier. For each same combination of dimensions' identifiers (key), the fact table identifiers (value) are combined when the Reduce function is performed (figure 19).

Figure 19. Building the C-SJI-LCSD

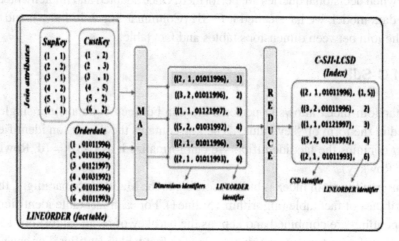

Once the index is built, the second job of MC-CUBE operator uses both the index and the output of job1 as input in order to identify the LINEORDER key, which satisfies the query predicates, when the cube is performed. Thus, the Map function scans the C-SJI-CSD index to find the dimension' keys obtained by job1 which correspond to (1, 2, and 3), (1, and 2), and (01011996, and 01121997) respectively for Customer, Supplier, and Date dimensions.

If the part key of the index contains the combination of dimension' keys of job1 (1,or 2, or 3), and (1, or 2), and (01011996, or 01121997), the mapper associates with the part value of index that corresponds to the Lineorder key a boolean value "1", otherwise "0". This scan produces six pairs (1, 1), (5, 1), (2, 1), (3, 1), (4, 0), and (6, 0). The Reduce function keeps only the keys that have boolean value corresponding to 1. In this case, only the (1, 1), (5, 1), (2, 1), (3, 1) will be taken. This result represents the Lineorder key (1, 2, 3, 5) that satisfies all join predicates (figure 20).

IMPLEMENTATION AND TESTING

In order to show the feasibility of our approach and the opportunity to extend the advantage of the columnar approach (beyond the data storage) to build OLAP cubes, we have implemented the MC-CUBE operator in a columnar NoSQL environment using MapReduce, and put in place a non-relational distributed storage and processing environment. This environment is produced by using the Hadoop-2.6.0 and HBase-0.98.8 DBMS (the most popular column-oriented NoSQL system).

- **Dataset:** We used the warehouse benchmark SSB described in section 5.2 which is popular for generating data for decision support systems, and we have populated it with data samples by using the data generator (SSB-dbgen) (Sundstrom, 2010). This SSB-dbgen allows to generate data sets with different sizes by specifying the scalability factor (SF: Scale Factor). Thus, we have populated the data warehouse by a sample of data comprising 6×10^7 records (SF = 1).
- **Queries set:** Query configuration has been decided on criteria of selectivity. The selectivity is a degree of filtering of the data when the conditions of a query are applied (low (L), average (A), high (H), very high (VH)).

Figure 20. Building a list of fact table key that satisfies the query conditions by using the C-SJI

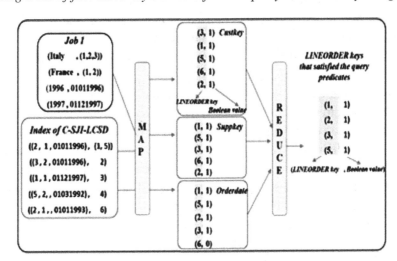

Experiment 1

In this experiment, we have exposed the MC-CUBE operator to scaling-up which is the raison of advent of NoSQL data models to store and manage massive data. Thus, we have generated 1 TB of data samples and involved building OLAP cubes with the queries set of previous experiment by using this time a cluster made up of 15 machines (nodes). Each machine has an intel-Core TMi3-3220 CPU@3.30 GHZ processor with 4GB RAM. These machines operate with the operating system Ubuntu-14.04 and are interconnected by a switched Ethernet 1 GBps in a local area network. One of these machines is con-

Table 1. Queries set

Query	Selectivity	Dimension: Attribute	Predicate	Measure
Query 1	L: $1,9 * 10^{-2}$ (116.883 rows)	Customer: Nation Supplier: Nation Date: Year	Date: Year = 1993 Lineorder: Discount between1 and 3 Lineorder: Quantity < 25	Sum (revenue)
Query 2	A: $2 * 10^{-4}$ (1200 rows)		Part: Brand1 = 'MFGR#2221' Supplier: Region = 'EUROPE'	
Query 3	H: $9.1 * 10^{-5}$ (549 rows)		Customer: Region = 'AMERICA' Supplier: Nation = 'UNITED STATES' Date: Year = (1997 or 1998) Part: Category = 'MFGR#14'	
Query 4	VH: $7.6*10^{-7}$ (5 rows)		Customer: City=('UNITED KI1' or 'UNITED KI5') Supplier:City= ('UNITED KI1' or 'UNITED KI5') Date: Yearmonth = 'Dec1997'	

figured to perform the role of Namenode in the HDFS system, the master and the Zookeper[3] of HBase. However, the other machines are configured to be HDFS DataNodes and the HBase RegionServers.

Figure 21 reports the time needed to compute the OLAP cubes and we compared between MC-CUBE and the CUBE operators of Hive and Kylin (often used to build OLAP cubes from big data warehouses (see section 2).

Experiment Results: This experiment allowed to evaluate OLAP cubes building times with the MC-CUBE and compared it to CUBE operators of Hive and Kylin in a distributed environment which is represented by cluster made up to 15 nodes. Overall, we observed that MC-CUBE achieves a better performance than CUBE of Hive and Kylin when the cubes are built. Indeed, Hive and Kylin build the cube according to the row-oriented approach which consists to use the aggregates of the lower level of granularity having the fewest attributes when the aggregates of the above level of granularity are performed. By cons, MC-CUBE benefits from the column store, and performs the aggregates of the above levels of granularity, from the one level which is the least aggregated. This allows the MC-CUBE to generate the cube quickly in terms of execution times.

From the results obtained, we find that the MC-CUBE operator allows optimizing the time when the OLAP cubes are performed.

Experiment 2

In this experiment, we have used the columnar star join index C-SJI when the cubes are performed. Thus, we created a columnar Star join index to materialize the join between dimensions (CUSTOMER, SUPPLIER, PART and DATE) and the fact table (LINEORDER) and we have called it CSPD-C-SJI (Customer Supplier Part Date Columnar-Star-join-Index). The key part of the index contains the identifiers of the four dimensions. However, the value part contains the fact table identifier.

Figure 21. OLAP cubes computation

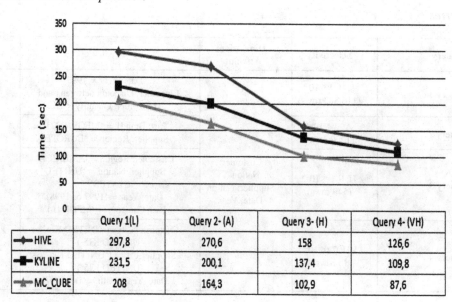

	Query 1(L)	Query 2- (A)	Query 3- (H)	Query 4- (VH)
HIVE	297,8	270,6	158	126,6
KYLINE	231,5	200,1	137,4	109,8
MC_CUBE	208	164,3	102,9	87,6

The queries show better execution time when the index is used, regardless the selectivity query. However, the execution time varies for each query. Indeed, the use of index allows to improve the performance mainly when the query returns a little number of tuples from the fact table (low selectivity). By contrast, when the index is not used, the query is disadvantaged by the materialization of the joins between dimensions and fact tables which decrease significantly the execution time to compute the aggregation corresponding to the lowest level of granularity of the cube. Therefore, we find that the use of indexes can improve on average up to two times the execution time when the query has a high selectivity.

CONCLUSION

This paper aims at building OLAP cubes from big data warehouses. Indeed, as big data continues down its path of growth, a major challenge of the decisional information systems has become how to deal with the explosion of data and its analysis when the data warehouses are implemented and the OLAP cubes are built. Consequently, the implementations of data warehouses are oriented towards the new technologies in order to allow more scalability and flexibility for storing and handling data. The solutions that meet with the needs of big data must take into account the distributed storage of data and the parallelized process of data treatment. For such data intensive database management systems, the NoSQL databases infrastructure that is based on "key/value" model is very well adapted to the heavy demands of big data.

Fortunately, this work is focalized on the implementation of big data warehouses by using the columnar NoSQL model and proposed the MC-CUBE that is an aggregate operator which allows to generate OLAP cubes according to the column-wise approach. MC-CUBE benefits from column-oriented storage

Figure 22. OLAP cube computations by using columnar star join index

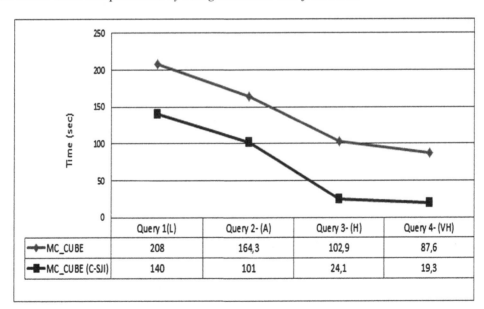

	Query 1(L)	Query 2- (A)	Query 3- (H)	Query 4- (VH)
MC_CUBE	208	164,3	102,9	87,6
MC_CUBE (C-SJI)	140	101	24,1	19,3

of data when aggregates are performed. In order to take into account the distributed environment for storing data, MC-CUBE uses the MapReduce paradigm to parallelize handling of data and performs the aggregates of different level of granularity that compose the OLAP cube. Contrary to the row-oriented approach where the higher levels of aggregations (2, 3, and 4) are obtained sequentially, the column-wise approach allows to the MC-CUBE operator to obtain the higher levels of aggregations in a parallel way; as a consequence, the time corresponding to the OLAP cube building is considerably reduced.

In order to optimize the OLAP cube building by using the MC-CUBE operator, this work has addressed a functional aspect of the use of the star join index to speed-up the join queries and shown the possibility and the way to implement it in a columnar non-relational environment. Since that optimization is a key issue, as a next step, we plan ongoing work more detailed about the optimization area (including the use of star join index) of the columnar NoSQL data warehouses and the cost models corresponding to each solution proposed with more experiments.

In the coming extended work, we look ahead to use spark instead of MapReduce in order to give more performance when the cubes are performed. The reason is that Spark uses memory instead of disk to relocate the processed data between the two steps of "Map" and "Reduce".

The results of this work are intended to show the feasibility of our approach and the opportunity to extend the advantage of the columnar approach, beyond the data storage to create analysis contexts (OLAP cubes) when the NoSQL model is chosen to store and analyze the big data. However, we also plan to continue this work by extending further the column-based approach in the study of OLAP manipulation operators and create in a short term, as perspective, some operators such as drill-down & roll-up which allow exploring the cube and navigating in it in accordance with the characteristics of columnar NoSQL model.

Surely, the use of NoSQL technologies for implementing OLAP systems is a promising direction. Hence, we think that building the OLAP cubes from big data warehouses implemented via documents-oriented or graph-oriented models will be an interesting research issue which is worth to be pursued of we want to reach the expected benefits of big data.

REFERENCES

Abadi, D., Madden, S., & Hachem, N. (2008). Column stores vs. row stores: how different are they really? *Proceedings of the 2008 Special Interest Group on Management of Data international conference*, 967-980. 10.1145/1376616.1376712

Abello, A., Ferrarons, F., & Romero, O. (2011). Building cubes with MapReduce. *14th international workshop on Data Warehousing and OLAP*, 17-24.

Barber, R., Bendel, P., Czech, M., Draese, O., Ho, F., Hrle, N., ... Lee, J. (2012). Business analytics in (a) blink. *A Quarterly Bulletin of the Computer Society of the IEEE Technical Committee on Data Engineering*, *35*(1), 9–14.

Beyer, K., & Ramakrishnan, R. (1999). Bottom up computation of sparse and iceberg cube. In *International Conference on Management Of Data* (vol. 28, pp.359-370). Philadelphia, PA: Academic Press. 10.1145/304182.304214

Bhogal, J., & Choksi, I. (2015). Handling big data using NoSQL. *29th International Conference on Advanced Information Networking and Applications Workshops*, 393-398.

Cattell, R. (2011). Scalable SQL and NoSQL data stores. *Special Interest Group on Management of Data Record Journal.*, *39*(4), 12–27.

Chang, F., Dean, S., Ghemawat, W. C., Hsieh, D., Wallach, M., Burrows, T., ... Gruber, R. (2008). Bigtable: A distributed storage system for structured data. *ACM Transactions on Computer Systems Journal*, *26*(2), 4–26.

Chaudhuri, S., & Dayal, U. (1997). An overview of data warehousing and olap technology. *Special Interest Group on Management of Data Record Journal*, *26*(2), 65–74.

Chavan, V., & Phursule, R. (2014). Survey paper on big data. *International Journal of Computer Science and Information Technologies*, *5*(6), 7932–7939.

Chevalier, R., Malki, M., Kopliku, A., Teste, O., & Tournier, R. (2015). Implementation of multidimensional databases in column-oriented NoSQL systems. In *Conference on Advances in Databases and Information Systems* (*vol. 9282*, pp. 79-91). Academic Press. 10.1007/978-3-319-23135-8_6

Dean, J., & Ghemawat, S. (2004). Mapreduce: simplified data processing on large clusters. In *Proceedings of the 6th conference on Symposium on Opearting Systems Design & Implementation* (vol. 6, pp. 137-149). USENIX Association.

Dehdouh, K., Bentayeb, F., Boussaid, O., & Kabachi, N. (2014). Columnar NoSQL cube: Agregation operator for columnar NoSQL data warehouse. In *IEEE International Conference on Systems, Man, and Cybernetics* (pp. 3828-3833). San Diego, CA: IEEE. 10.1109/SMC.2014.6974527

Dehdouh, K., Bentayeb, F., Boussaid, O., & Kabachi, N. (2015). Using the column oriented NoSQL model for implementing big data warehouses. *The 21st International Conference on Parallel and Distributed Processing Techniques and Applications*, 469-475.

Farber, F., Cha, S., Primsch, J., Bornhovd, C., Sigg, S., & Lehner, W. (2012). SAP HANA database: Data management for modern business applications. *Special Interest Group on Management of Data Record Journal, 40*(4), 45–51.

Gandomi, A., & Haider, M. (2015). Beyond the hype: Big data concepts, methods, and analytics. *International Journal of Information Management, 35*(2), 137–144. doi:10.1016/j.ijinfomgt.2014.10.007

Gray, J., Chaudhuri, S., Bosworth, A., Layman, A., Reichart, D., Venkatrao, M., ... Pirahesh, H. (1997). Data cube: A relational aggregation operator generalizing group by, crosstab, and sub-totals. *Data Mining and Knowledge Discovery, 1*(1), 29–53. doi:10.1023/A:1009726021843

Idreos, S., Groen, F., Nes, N., Manegold, S., Mullender, S., & Kersten, M. (2012). Monetdb: Two decades of research in column-oriented database architectures. *A Quarterly Bulletin of the Computer Society of the IEEE Technical Committee on Data Engineering, 35*(1), 40–45.

Imho, C., Geiger, J., & Galemmo, N. (2003). *Relational Modeling and Data Warehouse Design*. New York: John Wiley & Sons.

Inmon, W. (1992). *Building the data warehouse*. New York: John Wiley & Sons.

Jerzy, D. (2012). Business intelligence and NoSQL databases. *Information Systems Management, 1*(1), 25–37.

Lamb, A., Fuller, M., Varadarajan, R., Tran, N., Vandiver, B., & Doshi, L. (2012). The vertica analytic database: C-store 7 years later. *Proceedings of the Very Large Database Endowment, 5*(12), 1790–1801.

Larson, A., Hanson, E., & Price, S. (2012). Columnar storage in SQL server. *A Quarterly Bulletin of the Computer Society of the IEEE Technical Committee on Data Engineering, 35*, 15–20.

Lezak, D., & Eastwood, V. (2009). Data warehouse technology by infobright. *Special Interest Group on Management of Data international conference*, 841-846.

Lezak, D., Wrblewski, J., Eastwood, V., & Synak, P. (2008). Brighthouse: an analytic data warehouse for adhoc queries. *Proceedings of the Very Large Database Endowment, 1*(2), 1337-1345.

O'Neil, P., O'Neil, B., & Chen, X. (2007). *The star schema benchmark (SSB)*. Retrieved from http://www.cs.umb.edu/~poneil/StarSchemaB.PDF

Rabuzin, K., & Modruan, N. (2014). Business intelligence and column-oriented databases. *Central European Conference on Information and Intelligent Systems*, 12-16.

Sundstrom, D. (2010). *Star schema benchmark dbgen*. Retrieved from https://github.com/electrum/ssb-dbgen

Zukowski, M., & van de Wiel, M., & Boncz, P. A. (2012). Vectorwise: A vectorized analytical dbms. *28th International Conference on Data Engineering*, 1349-1350.

ENDNOTES

[1]   https://hbase.apache.org/

[2]   http://hadoop.apache.org/

[3]   http://hbase.apache.org/0.94/book/zookeeper.html

Chapter 7
Commercial and Open Source Business Intelligence Platforms for Big Data Warehousing

Jorge Bernardino
ⓘ https://orcid.org/0000-0001-9660-2011
Polytechnic of Coimbra, Portugal

Joaquim Lapa
Polytechnic of Porto, Portugal

Ana Almeida
Polytechnic of Porto, Portugal

ABSTRACT

A big data warehouse enables the analysis of large amounts of information that typically comes from the organization's transactional systems (OLTP). However, today's data warehouse systems do not have the capacity to handle the massive amount of data that is currently produced. Business intelligence (BI) is a collection of decision support technologies that enable executives, managers, and analysts to make better and faster decisions. Organizations must make good use of business intelligence platforms to quickly acquire desirable information from the huge volume of data to reduce the time and increase the efficiency of decision-making processes. In this chapter, the authors present a comparative analysis of commercial and open source BI tools capabilities, in order to aid organizations in the selection process of the most suitable BI platform. They also evaluated and compared six major open source BI platforms: Actuate, Jaspersoft, Jedox/Palo, Pentaho, SpagoBI, and Vanilla; and six major commercial BI platforms: IBM Cognos, Microsoft BI, MicroStrategy, Oracle BI, SAP BI, and SAS BI & Analytics.

DOI: 10.4018/978-1-5225-5516-2.ch007

INTRODUCTION

Business Intelligence (BI) is a collection of decision support technologies for enterprises aimed at enabling knowledge workers such as executives, managers, and analysts to make better and faster decisions. Business Intelligence can be defined as a system that *"combine data gathering, data storage, and knowledge management with analytical tools to present complex and competitive information to planners and decision makers"* (Negash & Gray, 2003). It can also be described as the mechanism that *"provides actionable information delivered at the right time, at the right location, and in the right form to assist decision makers"* (Langseth & Vivatrat, 2003).

The concept of BI appeared around 1989 by Howard Dresner. Initially, this concept was associated with organizational management more than the technological area and referred to the set of models and methods that promoted decision making, using support systems sustained on data (Information Week, 2006; Lim et al., 2012).

The currently organizational contexts require rigorous planning, uniformity of procedures and optimization of the overall existing resources. These assumptions require access, in constant and regular basis, to up to date and relevant data and, enabling decision making in order to sustainability and growth of organizations.

BI platforms allow companies to measure and improve the metrics that matter most to their businesses, such as sales revenue, customer loyalty and retention, order status, units per transaction, operating productivity, monthly profit or loss, overhead costs, inventory size and so on (Marinheiro & Bernardino, 2015; King, 2009).

Consequently, the implementation of BI platforms for decision support in enterprises emerges as pressing needs, resulting from competitive dynamics experienced by business organizations. This requires enterprises to make efforts in order to put in the market products and services at competitive prices.

Business Intelligence points to a set of management methodologies, implemented through software tools, whose function is to provide profitability and leadership in decision-making and administration of organizations. Thus, at the highest level of management, decision-makers must have, in a given place and time, analytics tools which provide, as a group, important information and data. Organizations should combine tools and techniques, which go beyond simply data management. BI is an important contribution to the production and management of knowledge and, consequently, promotes the improvement of organizational performance.

As a result of the use of BI tools, all these data acquire structure and arrangements, providing essential and fundamental strategic information to decision-making. This is supported on the evidence generated by these platforms, such as tables, graphs, dashboards, KPIs (Key Performance Indicators), multidimensional OLAP (On-line Analytical Processing) and Data Mining, among others. By applying analytics throughout the decision life cycle, decision makers can answer operational requests quickly and confidently, predict and deduce trends, patterns or nonconformities in the respective business area. This will promote the establishment of strategic planning in organizations, as well as proper management of contractual relationships with different partners, resulting in effective business progress. Likewise, this evolution cannot ignore the dynamics of social networks as a source of information about behaviors and associations in markets and their agents. The conversion of such information into organizational knowledge, through the integration of collaborative technologies in BI turns out to be, in our opinion, essential to the sustainability of organizations.

Choosing the right BI platform for Big Data Warehousing is a critical aspect to ensure the success of its implementation. The failure rate of BI projects development is between 70 and 80% (Meehan, 2011; Yeoh & Koronios, 2010). Three groups were identified as key factors to the success of BI projects implementation: the Organizational dimension, the Process dimension and the Technological dimension. In this work, we analyze the Technological dimension, seen as the *"Business-driven, scalable and flexible technical framework; and Sustainable data quality and integrity"* (Adamala, & Cidrin, 2011).

This chapter aims to make a comparative analysis of existing functionalities in Commercial and Open Source BI platforms for Big Data Warehousing. We also intend to highlight the fact that the universe of Small and Medium Enterprises (SMEs) reveals a lack of knowledge about these tools and their potential to business development. We believe it is essential to promote adequate information about BI platforms, with special focus on the associated benefits. In this aspect, the academic context, through its various agents, can play along SMEs an active role. Many SMEs do not develop defined strategies in the IT area, presenting an incipient reality, with low professionalization and reduced profitability. There are several reasons for this lack of information: financial unavailability and/or insignificant innovative management processes. It is in this context that there is inexperience of BI potential and the competitive advantages for the positioning of companies in the market (Bernardino, 2013).

We want to help organizations choosing the right BI platform, assuming that finding all the BI tools in one environment it's a critical advantage. This can reduce the end-user training time, which is an important aspect for the development of such projects.

In a previous work, we only compare Commercial Business Intelligence platforms (Lapa, Bernardino, & Figueiredo, 2015). In this chapter, we improve and complement the former by adding and evaluating six more Open Source BI platforms, extending the tools evaluation criteria and providing more up to date and thorough information, updating each section with new and relevant information.

The remainder of this chapter is organized as follows. Section 2 presents some background on BI and reviews the literature. Section 3 presents the six open source BI platforms and Section 4 the six commercial BI platforms. Section 5 describes research methodology and the evaluation criteria used in the comparison of BI platforms. Section 6 presents the results of functionalities comparative analysis for each open source and commercial BI platform. Finally, Section 7 presents the conclusions and point out some future work.

BACKGROUND AND LITERATURE REVIEW

BI systems combine data collection, storage and knowledge management with analysis tools that allow to extract useful information. Therefore, the key concepts associated with BI are: Extract, Transform and Load (ETL), Data Warehousing (DW), On-Line Analytical Processing (OLAP) and Data Mining (Reddy et al., 2010).

The data collection is a critical process in BI projects, because without a correct loading of data in the database, it is not possible to use the potential of BI tools. This process is carried out with the use of extraction, transform, and load tools - ETL. The ETL extracts data from one or more Operational Database (On-line Transaction Processing - OLTP), and modify and transform the data, inserting it in the Data Warehouse (DW).

The term Data Warehouse appeared around 1992 (Intel, n.d.), considered a working base for all BI tools. Kimball & Ross (2013) defines the following objectives and characteristics of a Data Warehouse:

- Making the organization information readily accessible, understandable and navigable;
- Making the organization information consistent and comparable among different organizational units;
- Provide a source of information adaptable and reliable;
- Ensure secure access to information;
- Establish the foundation of decision-making processes.

Already, Inmon (2005) defines data warehousing as a set of data-oriented subject, integrated, time-cataloged and non-volatile, which supports managers in the decision-making process.

The Data Warehouse is maintained regardless of the operating database; nevertheless these two types of databases have different objectives. While a data warehouse keeps data in multiple years labeled temporally to enable the end user to perform analyzes, and complex issues. The operational database aims register daily data of the organization.

Following the definition of Inmon (2005), which characterized the data warehouse as a set of data-driven subject, the concept of a data mart emerges, this being a subset of data delimited at a particular department or business area. However, Ralph Kimball considered one of the most influential gurus of Business Intelligence disagrees with this definition and argues that the data marts should not be departmental, but oriented to data or data sources (Kimball & Ross, 2013).

Inmon uses data marts as physical separation from enterprise data warehouse, building them for departmental use. While in Kimball's architecture, it is unnecessary to separate the data marts from the dimensional data warehouse. Ralph Kimball recommends to build data warehouse that follows bottom up approach. Kimball's philosophy starts first with mission critical data marts that serve analytic needs of business processes that can work for several departments. Then these data marts are integrated for data consistency through a so called bus architecture, making use of dimensional model to address the needs of departments in various areas within enterprise. Kimball advocates the theory that the most viable solution for companies is to develop several data marts that can be integrated to each other and thus get the Enterprise DW. In its assessment, companies should build data marts oriented to business topics. At the end, they have a number of connection points between them, which would be the Fact and Dimension tables. Therefore, information between different data marts could be properly generated in a full and safely way. Kimball named this concept of Data Warehouse Bus Architecture.

However, this model is questioned by Bill Inmon, which proposes precisely the opposite. In its assessment, we must first build a data warehouse, shaping up the entire company to reach a single corporate model, starting later for data marts built by subjects or departments. Inmon defends the idea that the starting point would be the CIF - Corporate Information Factory - an ideal infrastructure to accommodate company data.

Some organizations implement a hybrid solution, combining the best of both models. First, they implement a standard data warehouse using the CIF method, followed later to the creation of Data Marts defended by Kimball.

The design of data warehouses is based on the dimensional modeling. Dimensional modeling aims to design a database easy to perceive, understand and use, optimizing performance processing issues and simplifying the reads, as opposed to optimizing the updates and processing of operational databases. In dimensional model are present two kinds of tables: Fact and Dimension tables. The Fact tables present numerical attributes (metrics or measures) corresponding to measurements of the business or records events (the facts) including also a set of foreign keys that link the table to the related business dimensions. These tables allow to store business events for decision support analysis and the facts can be assessed using for example OLAP cube tools.

A dimension table contains attributes used to constrain, group, or browse the fact data. There are two primary advantages of using a dimensional model in data warehouse environments. First, a dimensional model provides a multidimensional analytical space in relational database environments. Second, a typical denormalized dimensional model has a simple schema structure, which simplifies end-user query processing and improves performance.

The dimension tables contain a large number of attributes, reflecting the details of the business processes. Browsing is a user activity that explores the relationships between attributes in a dimension table. The attributes will serve as row headers and constraints for these views. It is common to have more than one hundred attributes in a real world application. Dimension tables are considered wide for this reason. Denormalization of dimension tables is an acceptable practice in data warehousing and any attempts to normalize a dimension table into a series of tables could reduce the browsing capabilities of the user, resulting in more complex queries and increased response time. The experiences with real-world data warehouse development shows that browsing and group-by queries are the two salient issues that drive the design of data warehouses.

The dimension tables allow answer the questions posed by the end user. The most common questions are: who, when, where, why, and how. As previously stated the dimensional database is read-only, the inclusion of changes is accomplished through a process known as Slowly Changing Dimensions (SCD). There are several ways to circumvent the dimensions data changes (Reddy et al., 2010), the main ones are called: overwrite (SCD type 1), insert a new record (SCD type 2) and adding a new column (SCD type 3).

The dimensional model can be implemented in one of the three following schemas:

- **Star:** Star schema is widely accepted as the most viable data representation for dimensional analysis, which maintains one-to-many relationships between dimensions and the fact table. A star schema is diagramed by surrounding each fact table with its associated dimensions, and the resulting diagram resembles a star.
- **Snowflake:** A dimensional model with highly normalized dimension structure is called a snowflake schema (Kimball & Ross, 2013). The normalization process of dimensions, makes the scheme more complex, but avoids excessive data redundancy. A disadvantage of this schema is the lowest performance in responding to issues due to such normalization.
- **Constellation:** A fact constellation schema consists of a set of star schemas with hierarchically linked fact tables. The links between the various fact tables provide the ability to "drill-down" between levels of detail as explained next.

The most common tool for exploring the dimensional databases is the OLAP cube, which allows explore the data cube from various perspectives (dimensions). The OLAP data cubes have three main operations:

- Drill-down is the leading form of data mining used by users, which lets explore different levels of detail in the information (Kimball & Ross, 2013). For example, using the Time dimension it is possible to drill-down analyzing the results annually or daily, if we increased the level of data detail (granularity).
- Roll-up is the reverse operation of Drill-down. Using the previously example, we can start with the daily details and making successive aggregations by Week, Month, Quarter, Year, etc.
- Slice and Dice is a major feature of an OLAP tool. Slice permits to select a subset of cube data, by restricting a certain dimension. The Dice allows to define a subset of restriction through more than one dimension (Kimball et al., 2008).

The architecture of BI projects includes also the Data Staging Area. The Data Staging Area is a temporary is temporary location where data from source systems is copied, and where the necessary changes to data are done before it is loaded into data warehouse. The changes made to the data are carried out by the ETL tools.

These are the most important concepts associated with Business Intelligence topic. In the next sections, we will describe the BI platforms.

OPEN SOURCE BI PLATFORMS

Open source tools are distributed using several licenses, where each license type defines the "openness" of the software tools, defining the rules by which the source code may be amended, modified and then distributed. Open source licenses allow unrestricted and costless access to software previously developed (Ghapanchi & Aurum, 2011; Wurst, Postner, & Jackson, 2014). Usually open source tools have a dynamic community that contribute to adapt, reconfigure, improve, and publish the software with unrestricted use.

In this section, we present the following six open source BI platforms: Actuate, Jaspersoft, Jedox/Palo, Pentaho, SpagoBI, and Vanilla.

Actuate (www.actuate.com)

Actuate provides software to developers and manufacturers allowing to built scalable and secure solutions that save time improving brand experience by delivering personalized analytics and insights of their customers, partners and employees. Actuate founded and supports the Eclipse BIRT project (Business Intelligence and Reporting Tools) – the open source IDE – and develop specific software for public institutions in partnership with the Eclipse Foundation[1]. Recently, in January 2015 the OpenText successfully completed its acquisition of Actuate Corporation, so this platform will be deeply integrated into OpenText Products.

This platform is available in two versions, the Open Source version BIRT and the commercial version Actuate ONE. Figure 1 illustrates the set of resources for the design and implementation of projects that BIRT open source contemplates and offers. BIRT Interactive Viewer lets users modify and personalize their report views. BIRT Studio is a web-based development tool deployed through the platform and accessed from a web browser with no client software to install. BIRT Spreadsheet Designer retrieves data directly from a data source. BIRT Page Security and BIRT Smartsheet Security provide the security at the platform. Eclipse BIRT Designers and Engine is responsible for creating and modifying report designs. BIRT iServer and BIRT iServer Express deploys, manages, schedules, secures, runs and shares BIRT and eSpreadsheet Reports. BIRT Mobile provides several mobile options for deployment based on project size and requirements. BIRT Performance Scorecard was developed specifically to address real life Performance Management situations. BIRT OnPerformance delivers a performance management system. The e.Reports is a very powerful tool for creating data driven content.

Actuate includes Reports, Dashboards, Microsoft Office Integration, OLAP, Mobile BI, Scorecards (KPI). Actuate platform also offers increased business process efficiencies, greater brand experience and personalized insight for better and faster decisions via analytics and visualization.

Figure 1. BIRT Product Line (Source: http://infodecisionnel.com/)

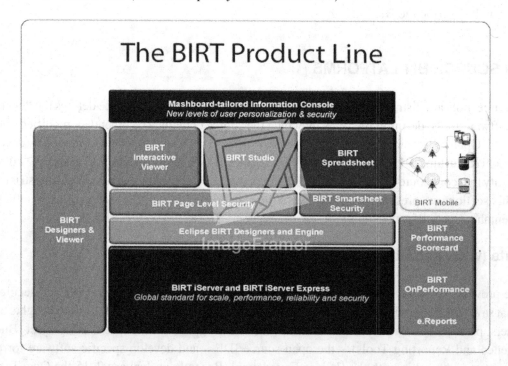

Jaspersoft (www.jaspersoft.com)

The Jaspersoft BI platform delivers reporting, dashboards, analysis, and data integration services for both stand-alone and embedded BI requirements, providing OLAP and in-memory data exploration.

The Jaspersoft platform is a SaaS (Software-as-a-Service), allowing fast transformation of data, reports and static graphics into interactive elements, with potential for immediate and automatic sharing by the entire company structure where it is implemented.

The final user can easily produce interactive reports, dashboards, analysis and exploitation of data, without the intervention of IT professionals. It also allows integration with iOS and Android mobile devices.

This platform is available under two types of licenses, the free GPL (Jaspersoft BI Community) and the commercial (Jaspersoft BI Express, for AWS, Professional and Enterprise).

Figure 2 illustrates the Jaspersoft BI platform architecture. At the top we can see the end user tools: Advanced Reporting, Production Reporting, End-User Ad-Hoc Query & Reporting, Dashboards, OLAP Analysis and Data Exploration. At the center of figure are the main components of platform: Jasper Reports (Java Reporting Library for developers); iReport Designer (Graphical Report Designer for developers and power-users); JasperReports Server (Interactive Report Server for business users); and Jaspersoft Analysis (Interactive Data Analysis/OLAP for business users). Jaspersoft BI uses Talend for the ETL process and WEKA for data mining.

Figure 2. Architecture Jaspersoft BI (Source: http://www.columnit.com)

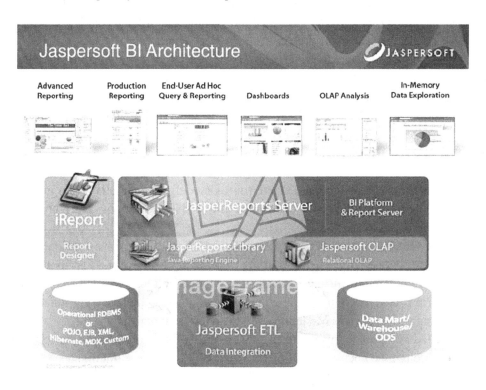

JasperReports Server provides reporting and analytics that can be embedded into a web or mobile applications. Correspondingly it can operate as a central information hub for the enterprise, by delivering mission critical information on real-time or a scheduled basis to the browser, mobile device, printer, or email inbox in a variety of file formats.

Jedox/Palo (www.palo.net)

Palo is a tool developed by the Jedox AG company, founded in 2002 and has a GNU license. The premium edition of the software has been renamed from Palo to Jedox with release 3.3. Jedox OLAP Server continues to be offered free-of-charge as commercial open-source software under the name of PALO. There is also an open-source integration with OpenOffice named PalOOCa (Palo for OpenOffice.org Calc).

The Jedox Suite provides cloud-ready, high-performance, in-memory planning, simulation, analysis and reporting capabilities. It can handle very large volumes of data and provides near-real-time performance via the browser or mobile devices, such as the iPad and iPhone, or Android-based mobile phones and tablets.

The Jedox/Palo platform combines the core components of a next-generation In-Memory OLAP database, with spreadsheet, web and mobile frontends to allow users and administrators to work seamlessly across all environments. Also at the core of the Jedox Suite is the Jedox Integrator, a sophisticated ETL module to read/write data from almost any data source.

Figure 3 gives an overview of Jedox/Palo architecture and shows the interaction of multiple data sources with the ETL tool. Optional components (shown in light blue) include the award-winning GPU OLAP accelerator designed to help manage extremely large datasets and provide lightning-fast report response times, and an ODBO XMLA module for integration into 3rd party tools and environments, as well as the SAP connector to read/write data from SAP environments. The Jedox platform provides a complete, integrated environment which can be used to address almost any planning or analytics-related business needs.

Jedox/Palo is unique in that its in-memory online analytical processing (OLAP) database engine uses graphics processing units (GPUs) for high-speed planning and reporting purposes.

Pentaho (www.pentaho.com)

Pentaho platform follows the commercial Open Source model of development. Its implementation is controlled by Pentaho Corporation and is distributed in two distinct editions: The Community Edition, and the Enterprise Edition.

The Community Edition is the open source version while the Enterprise Edition is a commercial product that includes not only all the features of the Community Edition, but also some more advanced tools to help the development of Business Intelligence Models and Reports, and a contract support.

Pentaho platform is developed in Java language, which includes the following functionalities: ETL, OLAP, Data Mining and Predictive Modeling, Reports and Dashboards.

As is exemplified in Figure 4, this platform consists of the following components: Data & Application Integration (through the open-source for ETL Kettle tool), Business Intelligence Platform (provide Administration, Security, Business Logic and Repository), the layer of Reporting with, Analysis (also

Figure 3. Jedox/Palo BI platform (Source: http://www.grid-dynamics.com)

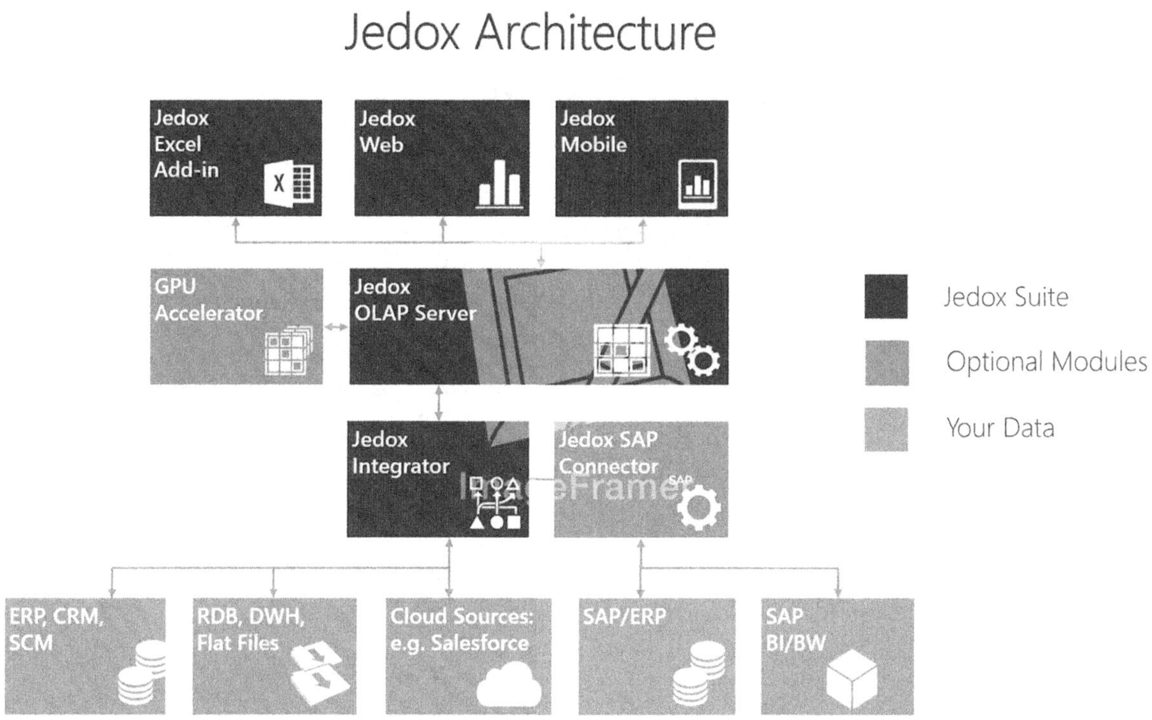

through an open source tool - Mondrian OLAP server and Pentaho Data Mining using the Weka software), Dashboards and Process Management. The Presentation layer includes Browser, Portal, Office, Web Services and E-mail.

The Pentaho platform provides the architecture and infrastructure required to build solutions to business intelligence problems. This framework provides core services including authentication, logging, auditing, web services, and rules engines.

SpagoBI (www.spagoworld.org)

SpagoBI is an application developed by SpagoWorld, an organization founded in 2006 with the support of an open source community.

The SpagoBI tool has a GNU LGPL license (Lesser General Public License), which allows users to use all the functionalities. SpagoBI platform is 100% open source, adopting the pure open source model and is released as only one stable version. It is an alternative to the "dual-licensing" or "open core" model, which also includes a parallel proprietary software released as an enterprise or professional version. The SpagoBI is developed in Java and available only on a completely free version.

The SpagoBI tool contains a variety of functionalities such as the creation and export of reports, *ad-hoc* reporting, charts, ETL (Talend), OLAP, Data Mining, KPIs, mobile, location intelligence, cockpits, free inquiry, office, external process, collaboration, master data management application server, login service, dashboards, task schedule, and Web server.

Figure 4. Pentaho Open BI Suite (Source: https://www.spec-india.com/)

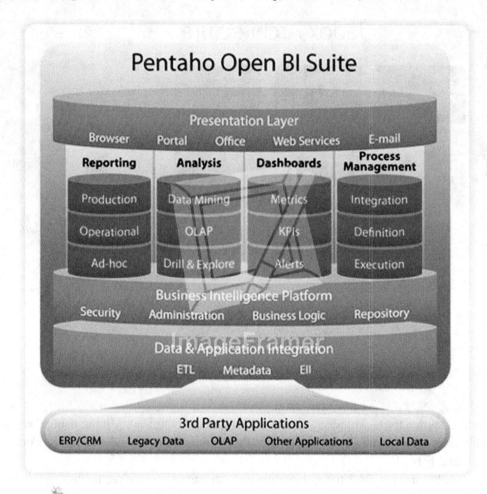

SpagoBI Architecture is composed of five main modules (see Figure 5): Server (offers all the core and analytical functionalities), Studio (integrated development environment), Meta (metadata environment), SDK (integration layer allowing to use SpagoBI with external tools) and Applications (collection of vertical analytical models developed using SpagoBI).

SpagoBI is a complete BI platform, robust, secure, and scalable. SpagoBI has unique solutions, not only usual reporting and charting tools but also with the following functionalities: Geo, Query by Example (QbE), KPIs, Interactive Dashboards, and Real-time BI.

Vanilla (www.bpm-conseil.com)

The French enterprise BPM-Conseil founded in 2004, is the leader of Open Source BI in France and responsible for the developing of Vanilla platform. Vanilla is 100% Open Source and has a MPL License (Mozilla Public License). It is developed in Java and the Web Portal in GWT (Google Web Toolkit) technology.

Figure 5. SpagoBI Architecture (Source: http://www.stratebi.com)

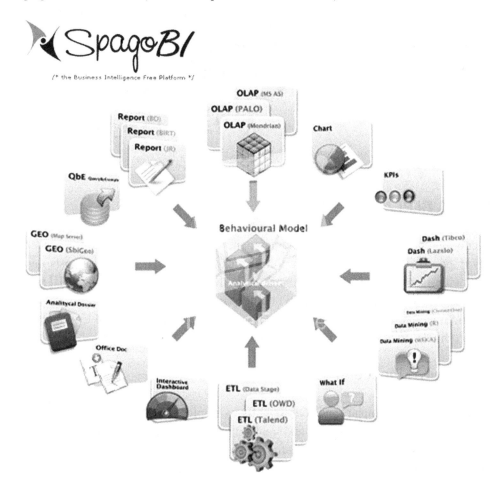

Vanilla platform includes all the necessary tools to manage data from applicative software to the end user visualization. The last version is Vanilla 5 which is composed of several components: Vanilla Gateway, Vanilla Workflow, Vanilla Metadata, Vanilla plugins for Birt, Vanilla Dashboard, Vanilla Analysis Designer, Vanilla Portal, Vanilla KPI, Vanilla Analysis, Vanilla WebReport, Enterprise Services and Hypervision.

Vanilla offers support for the latest database version from leading editors such as MySQL, MariaDB, Oracle, PostgreSQL and Microsoft SQLServer.

In Figure 6 are shown the different features and characteristics of the platform such as integrations with ETL (BiGateway), Data Warehouse, OLAP Cubes, Dashboards, Reports, KPI and Data Mining.

Figure 6. Vanilla Functional Schema (Source: http://www.bpm-conseil.com)

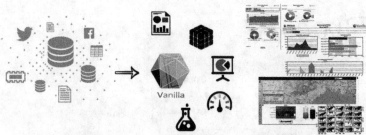

COMMERCIAL BI PLATFORMS

The use of commercial platforms requires the payment of expensive licenses to the holders. This fact immediately imposes a limitation and restriction on access, considering the high costs involved. Only organizations with major financial capacity can acquire them. However, commercial BI platforms have usually more capabilities than open source BI counterparts.

In this section, we present the following six commercial BI platforms: IBM Cognos, Microsoft BI, MicroStrategy, Oracle BI, SAP BI, and SAS Business Intelligence & Analytics.

IBM Cognos (www.ibm.com)

IBM acquired the Cognos Company and consequently its BI platform. The IBM Cognos family includes three suites: Cognos Insight for individuals and small businesses; Cognos Express for midsize businesses, departments and workgroups; and Cognos Enterprise for big organizations.

IBM Business Analytics offers five solutions: business intelligence, enterprise performance management, prescriptive analytics, predictive analytics and risk analytics. The BI solutions include reports, analysis (what-if scenarios), *ad-hoc* queries, scorecards, dashboards, mobile, real-time monitoring, collaboration, data visualization and self-service (see Figure 7).

This platform allows to proceed in real time to import and export data, to perform monitoring and to obtain statistics, forecasts and budgets, extending BI and making it more collaborative, which improves teamwork and decision making.

IBM Cognos also provide a version for mobile devices. This version is supported by: Apple iPhone and iPad, Android tablets and smartphones.

The ETL process is delivered to InfoSphere DataStage v9.1.

Figure 7. IBM Cognos (Source: http://pmsquare.com)

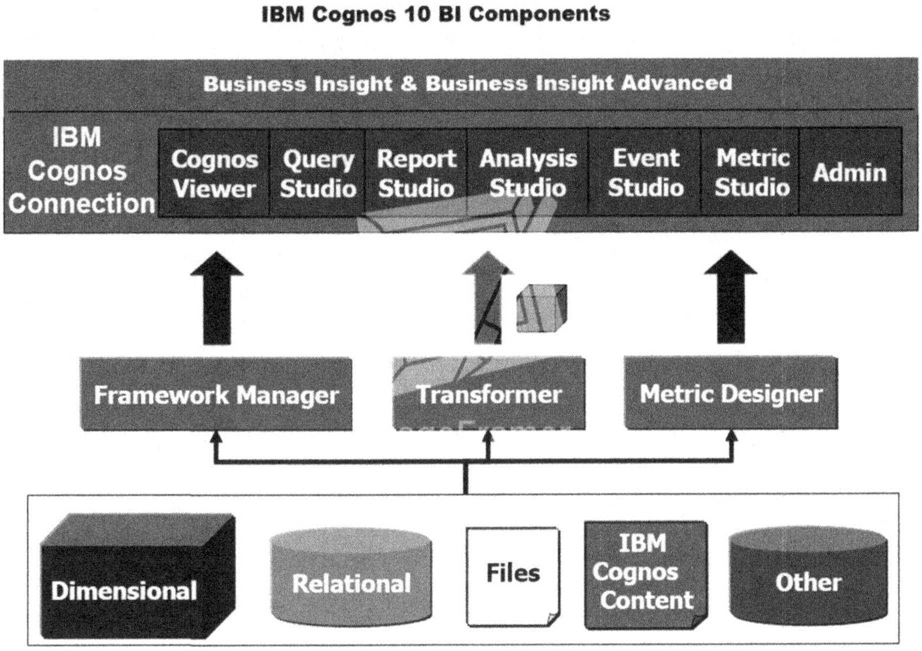

Microsoft BI (www.microsoft.com)

Microsoft offers three proposals to BI: Microsoft SQL Server, Microsoft Office and SharePoint. The ETL process is made from SQL Integration Services. Data analysis and reporting is possible using SQL Reporting Services from SQL Analysis Services.

The Microsoft BI platform shown in Figure 8 also enables queries, data integration, synchronization, research, cloud storage, import/export data, dashboards and scorecards, as well as access to this information from mobile devices.

Collaborative technologies are provided through SharePoint Server. The Microsoft platform is divided into three major groups: BI Platform (RDBMS, ETL, OLAP, Reporting), End User Tools & Performance Management APPS and, finally, Delivery.

In the last version are also presented new features, such as self-service and predictive analytics.

MicroStrategy (www.microstrategy.com)

MicroStrategy was founded in 1989 and provides integrated BI tools that allows, interactive visualizations through scorecards, dashboards, reporting, *ad-hoc* queries, thresholds and alerts, integration with Microsoft Office, mobile devices and self-service. In Figure 9 are represented all modules included in MicroStrategy Reporting Suite. For developers the Desktop Analyst & Designer and Architect (Centralized metadata builder) modules are offered. For Deploy / Manage it is available the Intelligence Server

Figure 8. Microsoft BI Stack (Source: https://www.microsoft.com)

Figure 9. MicroStrategy 9 (Source: https://www.microstrategy.com)

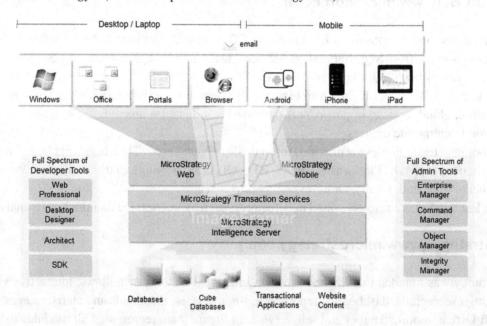

and for report the Web Report. The following additional products are also presented: Web Analyst & Professional, Office, Mobile, Report Services, Distribution Services, OLAP Services, Integrity Manager, Enterprise Manager, Object Manager, Command Manager, SDK and MultiSource Option.

MicroStrategy improved the utilization through the introduction of a new feature Visual Insight, which allows users to explore data and identify trends, minimizing the need to request IT professionals.

In response to market needs, MicroStrategy has developed applications compatible with social software, like Facebook. The availability of Social Intelligence MicroStrategy is divided into two categories: Enterprise Social Intelligence and Consumer Social Intelligence. The MicroStrategy platform does not include an ETL tool, in this way, the ETL process is carried out using an external tool.

Oracle BI (www.oracle.com)

Oracle BI is commercially available under the name Oracle Business Intelligence Foundation Suite. This includes the following capabilities: Enterprise BI Platform (OBIEE), OLAP Analytics, Scorecard and Strategy Management, Mobile BI, and Enterprise Reporting.

For small and medium enterprises, the Oracle offers the Oracle BI Suite Standard Edition One, this solution integrated reporting, dashboards, *ad-hoc* analysis, data modeling and database. The Enterprise BI (OBIEE) offers a range of solutions that allows to create and view reports, *ad-hoc* queries and analysis, and to develop, from the data, a whole set of management tools such as reports, dashboards, scorecards, graphics, collaboration, alerts, etc.

As can be seen in Figure 10, Oracle Business Intelligence Foundation, the tool for large enterprises, allows generating structured and concrete reports, *ad-hoc* exploration, interactive dashboards, scorecards, integration with mobile devices, what-if scenario modeling, geospatial visualization and Microsoft office integration.

The ETL process is based on the following two tools: Oracle Warehouse Builder (OWB) and Oracle Data Integrator (ODI).

Figure 10. Oracle Business Intelligence Foundation (Source: https://obibb.wordpress.com)

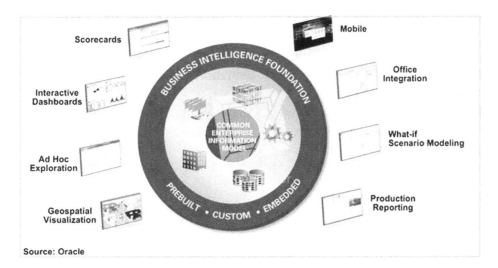

SAP BI (www.sap.com)

The SAP is an acronym of German language description, *Systemanalyse und Programmentwicklung*, which means System Analysis and Program Development. In 1972, the SAP was founded by five former IBM employees. Currently, SAP is strongly positioned in the enterprise software market, taking the leadership. Their solutions for promoting a more effective and efficient management are intended for all sizes and fields of business organizations.

From the beginning, SAP focuses on innovation and development, resulting in its presence in over 50 countries, and accordingly to its website a portfolio exceeding 250,000 customers. The available solutions allow organizations to increase cost efficiency and a permanent and sustainable adaptation to markets variation.

SAP offers a wide range of functionalities: reports, dashboards, *ad-hoc* queries, integration with Microsoft Office, Mobile BI, OLAP, interactive visualization, Predictive Modeling and Data Mining, KPIs and Cloud Computing. In spite of all the referred functionalities it doesn't yet integrates collaborative technologies.

Figure 11 shows the sub-areas and functions that are integrated into SAP Architecture: Data Warehousing, BI Platform, BI Suite (Business Explorer) and development tools (BI Java SDK, Open Analysis Interfaces and Web Design API).

For ETL the platform uses Business Objects Data Integration/Data Services.

SAS BI and Analytics (www.sas.com)

SAS (once stood for Statistical Analysis System) began at North Carolina State University as a project to analyze agricultural research. The demand for such software capabilities began to grow, and SAS was founded in 1976 to help customers in all sorts of industries – from pharmaceutical companies and banks to academic and governmental entities. Actually, SAS provide easy-to-use, self-service BI capabilities and the deployment of real-time analytics directly to mobile devices and Microsoft applications.

Data visualization, geolocation analysis, easy analytics, graphics, dashboards, KPI's, OLAP, data mining, collaboration, self-service BI, mobile BI, predictive analytics, and reporting are features provided by SAS Enterprise BI Server, SAS Analytics Pro, SAS Enterprise Guide, SAS Enterprise Miner, SAS Office Analytics, SAS Visual Analytics and SAS Visual Statistics. SAS Data Management provides the ETL process. Therefore every decision maker – wherever they are – can monitor key metrics and make informed decisions. And features like governance, centralized metadata and scalability make it suitable for enterprise IT.

Figure 12 demonstrates the main components of SAS framework: Data Management, High-performance Analytics, Business Intelligence and Analytics.

Figure 11. Architecture SAP BI (Source: https://www.sap.com)

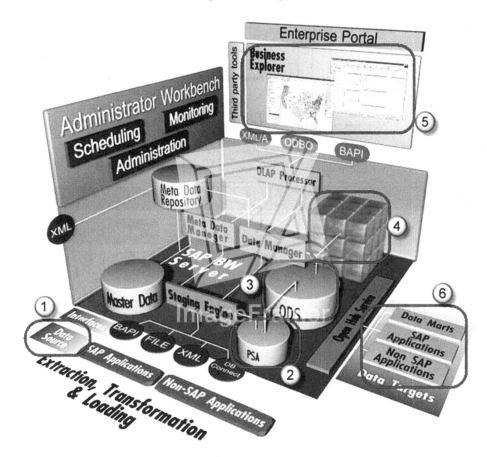

RESEARCH DESIGN AND METHODOLOGY

In this work, we adopted the evaluation criteria of BI platforms used in Gartner (2014). These criteria are grouped into three broad and fundamental categories: Information Delivery, Analysis and Integration.

In Gartner's perspective those criteria are functionalities which, once attached to BI platforms, enable organizations with clear systems of classification and measurement in order to give support to decision making and improve performance. Consequently, organizations may enhance their performance, efficiency and profitability levels, developing a clear vision of different business dimensions like customers, employees and products. BI and analytic platforms enable companies to measure and improve the metrics that matter most to their businesses, such as sales revenue, customer loyalty and retention, order status, units per transaction, operating productivity, monthly profit or loss, overhead costs, inventory size and so on.

According to the previously stated Gartner (2014) report, we selected the following 9 established criteria: Reporting, Dashboards, *Ad-hoc* queries, Microsoft Office integration, Mobile BI, OLAP, Interactive Visualization, Predictive Modeling/Data Mining, and Scorecards (KPI). The selection of these criteria was based on the fact that it is possible to measure the respective functionalities. The remain-

Figure 12. SAS Business Solutions framework (Source: https://www.sas.com)

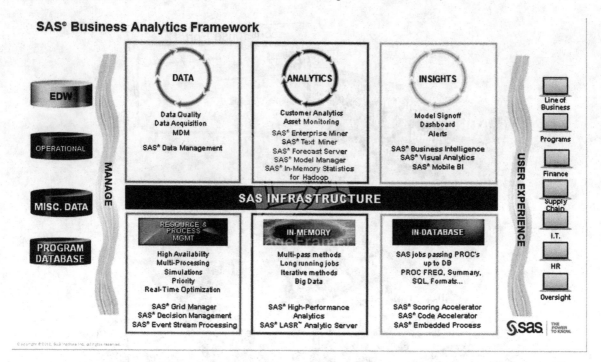

ing criteria show some commercial constraints of access and verification. We will therefore succinctly expose, what functionalities each chosen criteria entails.

1. **Reporting** criterion refers to the ability to generate formatted and interactive reports, with or without parameters, with highly scalable distribution and possibility of scheduling capabilities.
2. **Dashboards** consist of the publication of reports through intuitive, interactive dashboards that allow the evaluation and comparison of relevant information to achieve one or more business objectives. They allow an overview and an easier tracking of business indicators. The use of these panels is increasingly common to promote strategic, financial and operational data in real time.
3. **Ad-hoc queries** allow users to make their own data queries, without relying on IT to create a report. In particular, the tools must have a robust semantic layer to enable users to navigate through available data sources.
4. **Microsoft Office integration** criterion is based on the fact that Microsoft Office, particularly Excel, is often used in reports and analysis. In this context, it is essential to ensure that these tools enable integration with Microsoft Office.
5. **Mobile BI** enables organizations to develop and deliver content to mobile devices in a publishing and/or interactive mode, and takes advantage of mobile devices' native capabilities, such as touchscreen, camera, location awareness and natural-language query. Regardless of customers, employees or supplier's location, continuously updated information is available. On the other hand, and from a commercial point of view, the fact of organizations awareness of customers location,

via mobile devices, can be determinant in designing management strategies in order to a increase competitiveness.

6. **On-Line Analytical Processing** (OLAP) is another capability relevant for enhancing competitive strategies that enables users to analyze data with fast query and calculation performance, enabling "slicing and dicing". This capability could span a variety of data architectures (such as relational, multidimensional or hybrid) and storage architectures (such as disk-based or in-memory). There are different business dimensions such as sales figures, budgets, sold quantities, etc., so data at several levels, can be obtained with more or less detail depending on the needs of the user.

7. **Interactive Visualization** criterion enables the exploration of data via the manipulation of chart images, with the color, brightness, size, shape and motion of visual objects representing aspects of the dataset under analysis. This includes an array of visualization options that go beyond those of pie, bar and line charts, including heat and tree maps, geographic maps, scatter plots and other special-purpose visuals. These tools enable users to analyze the data by interacting directly with a visual representation of it.

8. **Predictive Modeling/Data Mining** enables organizations to classify variables into categories, to estimate continuous variables and identify patterns that establish predictive models of events and scenarios using mathematical algorithms.

9. **Scorecards (KPIs)** consist of measurable performance indicator elements. Depending on the organization's strategic objectives, it becomes essential to select and prioritize key performance indicators (KPIs). These arise as measures from which it is possible to analyze the evolution of business and quantify levels of efficiency and satisfaction in order to enhance the business objectives.

Currently new trends are emerging because of social technologies. Analyzing the results of a survey of 2300 CIOs (E2 WebCast, 2013), on its technological priorities, it can be observed that Collaborative Technologies emerged as a crucial issue for businesses. According to this survey, Collaborative Technologies climb from 11th place in 2010 to 4th place in 2012, shortly after Business Intelligence, Mobile Technologies and Cloud (Software as a Service - SaaS, Infrastructure as a Service - IaaS, Platform as a Service - PaaS), which emphasize that these three are already part of the BI platforms.

It is a fact that BI platforms are constantly and rapidly evolving, integrating new criteria corresponding to new technologies and market trends. It is illustrative of this, as can be seen in afore mentioned CIOs survey, the ability to access BI on Mobile Devices (Android, iPhone, Windows Mobile) and Collaborative Technologies. These functionalities that were not part of the criteria of the majority of BI platforms in 2011 became, after two years, available on most of all platforms.

As examples of this constant evolution, is the emergence of the Cloud Deployment criterion, the changing definition of Collaborative Technologies, with inclusion of integration of data from different social networks and finally the trend of self-service BI. Therefore, we add two new criteria to Gartner proposal: *Cloud Computing* and *Collaborative Technologies*.

10. **Cloud Computing** refers to the use of processing power, storage and memory existing in the Internet. *"Cloud computing is a model for enabling ubiquitous, convenient, on-demand network access to a shared pool of configurable computing resources (e.g., networks, servers, storage, applications, and services)"*(Mell & Grance, 2011). Thus, applications, data and services are available on the Internet and no longer confined to computers and servers of organizations. Despite the several as-

sociated advantages noticed (reduced equipment costs and operations, etc.) some questions remain as security and privacy guarantees.

11. **Collaborative Technologies** are assuming a significant and growing importance for decision makers in organizations, because they enable the integration of data from social networks. They represent an invaluable and unlimited source of information to organizations about behavior, preferences, trends, expectations and needs, from the most different points of the planet. These data, once processed, can be decisive in strategic planning and business management.

The above criteria are the 11 capabilities that enable organizations to support decision-making and improve performance. These are the criteria that were tested on the 6 open source BI and the 6 commercial BI platforms described in the previous sections 3 and 4.

RESULTS AND DISCUSSION

Based on the technical specifications of BI platforms available in the market and analyzed in this work according to the previously referred criteria, it was drawn up a comparative analysis on the availability of respective capabilities, taking into account their characteristics.

This analysis is intended to be useful to decision makers for the selection process of the most suitable BI platform to an organization. Table 1 shows the functionalities of the 12 platforms divided in two main groups: Open Source and Commercial.

Table 1. Comparison of BI Platforms Functionalities

Functionalities / Criteria	Business Intelligence Platforms											
	Open Source						Commercial					
	Actuate	Jaspersoft	Jedox/Palo	Pentaho	SpagoBI	Vanilla	IBM Cognos	Microsoft BI	MicroStrategy	Oracle BI	SAP BI	SAS BI
Reports	✓	✓	✓	✓	✓	✓	✓	✓	✓	✓	✓	✓
Dashboards	✓	✓	✓	✓	✓	✓	✓	✓	✓	✓	✓	✓
Ad-hoc Queries			✓	✓	✓	✓	✓	✓	✓	✓	✓	✓
Microsoft Office Integration	✓	✓	✓	✓	✓	✓	✓		✓	✓	✓	✓
Mobile BI	✓	✓		✓	✓	✓	✓	✓	✓	✓	✓	✓
OLAP	✓	✓	✓	✓	✓	✓	✓	✓	✓	✓	✓	✓
Interactive Visualization		✓	✓	✓	✓	✓	✓	✓	✓	✓	✓	✓
Predictive Modelling/Data Mining		✓		✓	✓	✓	✓	✓	✓	✓	✓	✓
Scorecards (KPIs)	✓			✓	✓	✓	✓	✓	✓	✓	✓	✓
Cloud Computing		✓	✓	✓	✓	✓	✓	✓	✓	✓	✓	✓
Collaborative Technologies					✓		✓	✓	✓	✓		✓

It wasn't the purpose of this work to evaluate the usability of the tools functionalities. That would require an individualized and case to case analysis, with the selection of only a few BI tools, according to any particular organizational context. Therefore, we are not making any judgment on the tools performance, but revealing what each is able to do showing the functionalities. Thus, in a logic of cost reduction, it may be implemented the BI tool most appropriate to the business, hence the one which can provide data with impact on organizational development.

The comparative analysis of the functionalities presented in BI tools emphasizes the fact that the commercial platforms cover a broader range of functionalities (see Table 1). This was expected, as there is strong commitment to its development. This development is sustained by the revenue generated by the sale of the platform and the constant investment converting into more and higher returns.

The platforms with full functionalities validated are SpagoBI, IBM Cognos, Microsoft BI, MicroStrategy, Oracle BI, and SAS BI & Analytics, followed by Pentaho, Vanilla and SAP BI, which validated 10 on the 11 functionalities analyzed.

Some of the open source platforms have also commercial versions with a bigger number of functionalities, while the respective open source versions exhibit a reduced amount of functionalities. This is the case of Jaspersoft that validates 8 of the 11 criteria in the open source version and in the commercial version (enterprise edition) almost all of the criteria are validated.

Analyzing only open source versions (community), SpagoBI validates 100% of the 11 criteria and Pentaho and Vanilla platforms present a validation of 91% supporting 10 of the 11 criteria evaluated. Therefore, there are three competitive platforms when compared with commercial ones, that maybe an effective alternative to these ones. From these three platforms, SpagoBI and Vanilla are "pure" open source with just a community version. However, this study does not focus on the comparative analysis of the platform functionalities effectiveness. So, we cannot present results of their performance, based on criteria such as speed, usability, reliability, robustness, etc.

All the platforms include the criteria Reporting, Dashboards, Microsoft Office Integration and OLAP. The presence of these criteria is justified by the fact that they are the management tools most used in organizations.

Contrary to these functionalities, collaborative technologies are only present in one open source platform, the SpagoBI and in five commercial platforms. This is due to the fact that it is a relatively recent requirement of organization's decision-makers and executives.

CONCLUSION AND FUTURE WORK

Business Intelligence gathers two essential capabilities to organizations enabling cost reduction and increasing revenue. Therefore, BI tools can be a vital support to management strategies and decisions. This happens because they provide analysis and interrelation of important data that can help to create, improve or redefine products, services and/or processes of marketing and trading. This way, any organization or company, regardless of size, business area or position in domestic and international markets, can benefit from BI implementation and consequently decision makers can do better informed and strategic decisions.

The selection process of the best BI tools suited to an organization will depend on many factors like the existing financial, human and material resources, but essentially on the vision of growth that the executive and/or entrepreneur has to the organization.

The selection and implementation of BI will have to start from a correct diagnosis of the organizational context; a survey of the conditions, resources, weaknesses and capabilities should be made. Next, there's the planning and scheduling of all phases to develop the tools implementation, their operationalization and the monitoring of the results and, if necessary, make adjustments.

It is essential that companies understand the investment in BI as a synonymous of new business opportunities. The use of several tools from different BI platforms leads to a difficulty in the configuration, usage and sharing data. As we see, the best decision is to choose a single BI platform, with a unique environment that integrates the necessary tools. This allows an easier and optimized process learning and better operationalization.

From our comparison, we concluded that the more effective BI platforms are SpagoBI, IBM Cognos, Microsoft BI, MicroStrategy, Oracle BI and SAS BI & Analytics. Both had a full validation of all functionalities analyzed. It is important to mention that from this list, only SpagoBI is a free and open source platform.

The analysis performed showed that almost all platforms integrate self-service BI technologies. It must also be noticed that MicroStrategy is the only commercial platform that does not include an ETL tool, which is an important feature in the Business Intelligence world.

As future work, we plan to perform a comparative analysis of the functionalities effectiveness and performance of these BI platforms in a real enterprise environment using a Big Data Warehouse.

REFERENCES

Adamala, S., & Cidrin, L. (2011). Key Success Factors in Business Intelligence. *Journal of Intelligence Studies in Business*, *1*(1), 107–127.

Bernardino, J. (2013). Open Business Intelligence for Better Decision-Making. *International Journal of Information Communication Technologies and Human Development*, *5*(2), 20–36. doi:10.4018/jic-thd.2013040102

E2 WebCast. (2013). *Building on Early Successes in UBM's Social Business Strategy*. Retrieved from http://event.on24.com

Gartner. (2014). *Magic Quadrant for Business Intelligence and Analytics Platforms*. Author.

Ghapanchi, A. H., & Aurum, A. (2011). The impact of project license and operating system on the effectiveness of the defect-fixing process in open source software projects. *IJBIS*, *8*(4), 413–424. doi:10.1504/IJBIS.2011.042398

Information Week. (2006). *Connecting the Business Technology Community. "Q&A: BI Visionary Howard Dresner"*. Author.

Inmon, W. (2005). *Building the Data Warehouse*. Wiley Publishing, Inc.

Intel. (n.d.). *Business Intelligence*. Intel - Diálogo TI - Next Generation Center.

Kimball, R., & Ross, M. (2013). *The Data Warehouse Toolkit, The Definitive Guide to Dimensional Modeling* (3rd ed.). John Wiley & Sons, Inc.

Kimball, R., Ross, M., Thornthwaite, W., Mundy, J., & Becker, B. (2008). *The Data Warehouse Lifecycle Toolkit* (2nd ed.). Wiley Technology Publishing.

King, W. R. (2009). Knowledge Management and Organizational Learning. *Annals of Information Systems, 4*. doi:10.1007/978-1-4419-0011-1_1

Langseth, J., & Vivatrat, N. (2003). Why Proactive Business Intelligence is a Hallmark of the Real-Time Enterprise: Outward Bound. *Intelligent Enterprise, 5*(18), 34–41.

Lapa, J., Bernardino, J., & Figueiredo, A. (2015). Commercial Business Intelligence Suites Comparison. In *WorldCIST'15 - 3rd World Conference on Information Systems and Technologies*. Ponta Delgada, Portugal: Springer. 10.1007/978-3-319-16486-1_24

Lim, E.-P., Chen, H., & Chen, G. (2012). Business intelligence and analytics: Research directions. ACM Trans. Manage. Inf. Syst., 3(4).

Marinheiro, A. & Bernardino, J. (2015). Experimental Evaluation of Open Source Business Intelligence Suites using OpenBRR. *IEEE Latin America Transactions, 13*(3), 810-817. doi:10.1109/TLA.2015.7069109

Meehan, P. (2011). *Gartner Business Intelligence Summit 2011*. Retrieved from http://link.brightcove.com/services/player/bcpid1156010110?bctid=741282639001

Mell, P. & Grance, T. (2011). *The NIST Definition of Cloud Computing*. National Institute of Standards and Technology Special Publication 800-145.

Negash, S., & Gray, P. (2003). Business Intelligence. *Ninth Americas Conference on Information Systems*.

Reddy, G., Srinivasu, R., Rao, M., & Rikkula, S. (2010). Data Warehousing, Data Mining, OLAP and OLTP Technologies are Essential Elements to Support Decision-Making Process in Industries. *International Journal on Computer Science and Engineering, 2*(9), 88–93.

Wurst, K., Postner, L., & Jackson, S. (2014). Teaching open source (software). In *Proceedings of the 45th ACM technical symposium on Computer science education*. ACM. 10.1145/2538862.2544248

Yeoh, W., & Koronios, A. (2010). Critical Success Factors for Business Intelligence Systems. *Journal of Computer Information Systems, 50*(3), 23–32.

ENDNOTE

[1]   The Eclipse Foundation is a nonprofit foundation that supports, develops and promotes open source software.

Chapter 8
Index Structures for Data Warehousing and Big Data Analytics

Veit Köppen
Otto von Guericke University Magdeburg, Germany

Martin Schäler
Karlsruhe Institute of Technology, Germany

David Broneske
Otto von Guericke University Magdeburg, Germany

ABSTRACT

With the ongoing increasing amount of data, these data have to be processed to gain new insights. Data mining techniques and user-driven OLAP are used to identify patterns or rules. Typical OLAP queries require database operations such as selections on ranges or projections. Similarly, data mining techniques require efficient support of these operations. One particularly challenging, yet important property, that an efficient data access has to support is multi-dimensionality. New techniques have been developed taking advantage of novel hardware environments including SIMD or main-memory usage. This includes sequential data access methods such SIMD, BitWeaving, or Column Imprints. New data structures have been also developed, including Sorted Projections or Elf, to address the features of modern hardware and multi-dimensional data access. In the context of multidimensional data access, the influence of modern hardware, including main-memory data access and SIMD instructions lead to new data access techniques. This chapter gives an overview on existing techniques and open potentials.

SCOPE OF THIS ARTICLE

With the ongoing increasing amount of data, these data have to be processed to gain new insights. Therefore, a solution is necessary to store and query multidimensional data efficiently. In relational databases, index structures like the B-tree (Bayer et al, 1972) have improved the data access drastically. In

DOI: 10.4018/978-1-5225-5516-2.ch008

a multidimensional domain, which is common for data warehouses as well as big data applications, these index structures have either a limitation to support a specialized scenario or cannot scale sufficiently. Additionally, the authors in (Berchtold et al, 1998) address the problem, called curse of dimensionality, which is an important insight for multidimensional data access. As a result many approaches and most present-day database systems rely on optimized sequential scans taking advantage of the capability of modern hardware. Moreover, this leads to the optimization of sequential scans for multidimensional data to support OLAP (Online Analytical Processing) analyses.

Predicate evaluation is a challenging task in the OLAP domain (Johnson et al, 2008) required amongst others for slice operations on the data cube. More generally, to extract important data for further analysis, fact and dimension tables are passed through several selection predicates involving several dimension attributes. Shrinking the processed data amount as soon as possible has become an important task, when all data have to fit into main memory. So, the I/O bottleneck is eliminated and a full table scan becomes less expensive. Therefore, we focus on how all approaches support this operation.

In case all data sets are available in main memory (e.g., in a main-memory database system (Boncz et al, 2008; Kemper et al, 2001; Plattner, 2009), the selectivity threshold for using an index structure instead of an optimized full table scan is even smaller than for disk-based database systems. In a recent study (Dasa et al, 2015), the authors propose to use an index structure for very low selectivities only, such as values below 2%. Hence, most OLAP queries would never use an index structure to evaluate the selection predicates. However, an interesting fact neglected by this approach is that the accumulated selectivity of several selection predicates is favored if this exploits the relation between all selection predicates of the query. Consequently, when considering multi-dimensional queries, we achieve the selectivity required to use an index structure instead of an accelerated scan.

Another fact for indexes that completely fit into the main memory is, that the structures should consider two aspects carefully: an optimization according to the restrictions of CPU caches and the opportunity of multi-core parallelism (Faeber et al, 2016). New main memory database systems, such as C-Store, HyPer, and SAP HANA, do not use a page-based indirection, but use the provided storage efficiently. Additionally, a pointer directly addresses the record and therefore, identifiers are omitted. Consequently, we illustrate how all approaches make efficient use of present-day hardware.

Altogether, there is a wide range of different approaches, each having their own advantages and limitations. In this paper, we aim at giving an overview on how such approaches work and how they are related to each other. This paper particularly addresses readers that start getting into contact with the domain of efficient data access methods on modern hardware. To this end, we introduce different approaches in the next section using one example data set to illustrate differences between the approaches. After that, we show how an exemplary evaluation of different approaches looks like and we also give a first indication of strengths and weaknesses of either approach.

TECHNIQUES FOR MULTIDIMENSIONAL DATA ACCESS

In principle, there are three groups of approaches. The first group follows a direct sequential access pattern, most database systems rely on. Therefore, this can be considered as industry standard. The second group consists of state-of-the-art approaches usually aiming at highly compressing the data set and making use of modern CPU capabilities, such as SIMD, to process multiple data items in one step.

However, they still process entire columns and one column after another. The final group is conceptually different as it aims at exploiting the combined selectivity of multiple columns to prune large parts of the data, i.e., aims at scanning at the least amount of data as possible.

RUNNING EXAMPLE DATA SET AND PREDICATES ON CUBES

For a suitable comparison of the presented structures, we use an ongoing example, as depicted in Figure 1. Note, we use only some tuples and three attributes (dimensions) to illustrate the upcoming storage and index structures briefly. Furthermore, only one fact is included, which is summable, although the structures could also be applied to other data types. Nevertheless, this example can be generalized without restrictions.

In our example, the first dimension consists of two distinct values, the second dimension value domain has three values, and the third dimension consists again of only two different values. Note, we use a dense value domain for each dimension. This could be easily obtained from any data set by applying an order-preserving dictionary encoding, see for further details (Antoshenkov, 1997).

Data Cube. Besides computation of aggregates on the fly, a precomputation is possible in case sufficient storage is available. In the data warehouse, the corresponding data structure is called cube, which is a materialization of the cube operator (Gray et al, 1997) In Figure 2, we indicate the result of the example relation for the cube operator. Note, all intermediate aggregations are stored and we use the ALL representation in our depiction in case a dimension is summarized to the top-node.

The data cube C is defined as: $C = \{ DS, M \} = \{\{ D^1, ..., D^n\}, \{M^1, ... M^m\}\}$ where the set of dimension schemas DS and the set of facts M build the n-dimensional analysis space consisting of m different facts. A dimension schema is a partially ordered set of dimension elements and each dimension set consists of an element TOP_D that can be derived from each dimension level. A fact schema in

Figure 1. Example relation

Table

	Dim_1	Dim_2	Dim_3	Fact
T_1	0	1	1	1
T_2	0	2	0	1
T_3	1	0	1	2
T_4	1	2	0	3

Figure 2. Data cube

Cube

Dim$_1$	Dim$_2$	Dim$_3$	SUM(Fact)
0	1	1	1
0	2	0	1
1	0	1	2
1	2	0	3
ALL	1	1	1
ALL	2	0	4
ALL	0	1	2

⋮

0	ALL	ALL	2
1	ALL	ALL	5
ALL	ALL	ALL	7

M requires information of the granularity G, the fact which is defined by the dimension attributes, the aggregation function f (), as well as the summation type, either flow, stock, or value-per-unit. For an easy use and interpretation of the data cube data, it is assumed that dimensions are orthogonally structured. This means, there is no functional dependency between different dimensions and their levels. To this end, after materialization of the cube, any desired report can be generated by predicate evaluation. However, efficient predicate evaluation is even more important than on the normalized schema, because dimensionality as well as data volume is by far higher.

Group 1: Sequential Access Pattern as Industry Standard

In our first consideration, we present access methods that are widely applied in systems. We briefly present the pros and cons for these access patterns. Whereas the first architecture decision is based on the storage layout, the second focuses on modern hardware.

Sequential Scans: Row-Wise vs. Column-Wise

Traditional database access is realized in a row store manner, which means that the data is organized tuple-wise. However, in the domain of OLAP this is not the best storage layout, because aggregations are only computed on some selected attributes of the data set, but theses aggregations require the complete column. Boncz & Kersten (1999) suggest a column-oriented storage to achieve a performance advantage for OLAP queries. This led to different systems, like C-Store (Stonebreaker et al, 2005) or MonetDB (Bonzc, 2005), for an overview see for instance (Abadi et al, 2012) and for a comparison (Abadi et al, 2008).

Note, both storage concepts can be used for the same data. In the context of data warehousing the column stores seem more efficiently due to the fact that on the one side per column a compression technique can be applied which reduces the storage cost and on the other hand data is stored in the way it is usually accessed. Nevertheless, the disadvantage of column stores is the necessity to reconstruct tuples in case they are required. The operator Scan, Predicate, Construct (SPC) is introduced by Abadi (2007) that deals with this reconstruction. Therefore, for a decision on the underlying architecture, the query or analysis workload should be considered (Lubcke et al, 2012). Both architectures are suitable for multidimensional data analysis, but aggregate computation is performed on-the-fly. With the available main memory this challenge seems decreasing over time.

Figure 3. Table storage layout: row and column

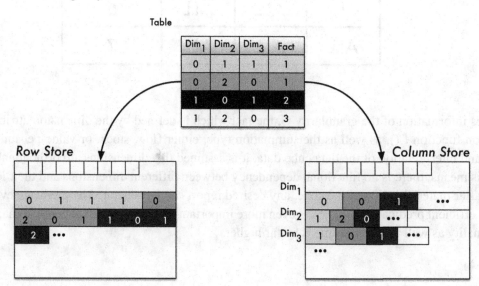

SIMD-Sequential Scan

Current trends in main-memory databases show that optimized full-table scans are able to compete with specialized index structures. The reason for this is the fast access in main memory compared to traditional disk-based approaches. Moreover, the sequential access pattern leads to cache consciousness.

With the rise of single instruction multiple data (SIMD) on modern processors, its usage became inevitable for full-table scans. Hence, instead of comparing one data item per clock cycle, several data items can now be filtered at one clock cycle simultaneously. Therefore, using SIMD to accelerate database operations has gained much attention. In particular, accelerating selection conditions using SIMD scans resulted in significant performance increases (Polychroniou et al, 2014; Sidirougos et al, 2013; Willhalm et al, 2013; Zhou et al, 2002)

In Figure 4, we show the general workflow of a SIMD-accelerated scan. First, the search value v_1 is broadcasted to a SIMD register. Then, in each iteration, a number of values (e.g., 4 integer values for 128-bit SSE 4.2 registers) from the column are loaded and compared with the broadcasted search values. The result of this comparison is a SIMD register with each value being either 0x0000 (false) or 0xFFFF (true), which essentially represents a bit mask of matching entries. The resulting bit masks of several such scans can be easily combined using logical operators (i.e., AND or OR). However, outputting a list of matching values (i.e., TIDs) without touching every bit again is hardly possible and creates an overhead to this processing style.

Figure 4. SIMD-accelerated scan

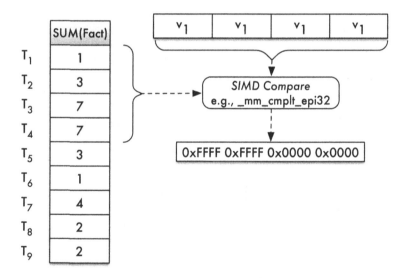

Group 2: State-of-the-Art Optimized Sequential Scans

In this group, we consider two approaches. The first one is BitWeaving and the second one Column Imprints, which are implemented inside MonetDB as alternative to aforementioned sequential columnar-access pattern.

BitWeaving

BitWeaving is a bit-packing technique proposed by Li and Patel (2013) The idea of BitWeaving is to store the necessary bits w.r.t. the given value range of several values into one processor word (with a typical size of 64 bit). With this, BitWeaving adapts the idea of SIMD even for scalar registers to exploit data parallelism in computation. BitWeaving offers two different methods to pack values into processor words: BitWeaving/H and BitWeaving/V. However, as the results of (Li et al, 2013) and the experiments of (Broneske et al, 2017; Schaler et al, 2013) suggest, BitWeaving/V is the superior approach. Thus, we focus on this layout and refer to it in the remainder only as BitWeaving.

The vertical bit-parallel storage layout partitions one value across several processor words. For illustration, the binary representation can be seen as a set of columns of a table, which are then stored in a column store (Li et al, 2013). Consequently, the ith bits of w values are stored consecutively in a processor word of length w (e.g., the most significant bits of eight values in one word in Figure 5). So, we construct k words that can be independently processed. Although, packing and unpacking of values for this storage layout is expensive (Polychroniou et al, 2015), scanning values in a vertical bit-parallel storage layout offers several benefits. It is possible to do an early pruning of the search. Since we start

Figure 5. BitWeaving approach

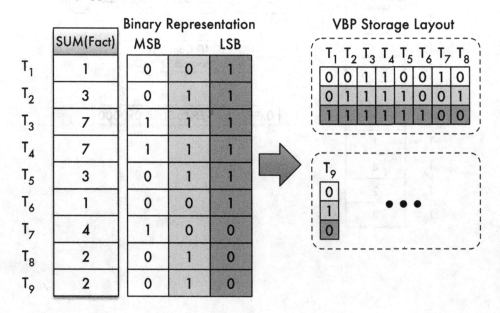

with comparing the most significant bits of the codes, we are able to deduce the result of the comparison from the first two bits that differ in the comparison. If the results of all codes of a processor word are determined, we stop to evaluate these codes and, thus, save computational effort.

Column Imprints

A Column Imprint is a cache-conscious secondary index structure for range queries (Sidirourgos et al, 2013). The idea is to apply a coarse-grained filter indicating whether one can exclude a complete cache line for a given query. To this end, the Column Imprint builds a histogram over all values of a cache line and stores it in a 64-bit integer. The histogram is an equi-width histogram with 64 bins where a bit b = 1 means that at least one value of the corresponding cache line is in the range of the given bin. Notably, the first and the last bin hold values from -∞ to the current smallest value and from the highest value to ∞, respectively.

As an example, we show the bitmap and the Column Imprint for our running example in Figure 6. Assume that our values range from 0 to 7 and we use an 8-bit value to represent the histogram. In this case, we have a direct mapping between the values and bins of the histogram (although in practice, each bin will correspond to a range of values). Furthermore, if a cache line could only hold three values, then our imprint indexes the first three values and is constructed by applying the logical *and* of the bitmaps of the corresponding values.

A further optimization that Sidirourgos & Kersten apply is that if two succeeding imprints are the same, they are compressed using a cache line dictionary (Sidirourgos et al, 2013). Consequently, we only store and scan these repeated cache lines once. To evaluate a selection predicate on a Column Imprint, a bit mask is created where all the bits are set that match the predicate (probably several bits for a range query). If the result of the logical *and* between the bit mask and the current imprint leaves any bit set,

Figure 6. Column imprints

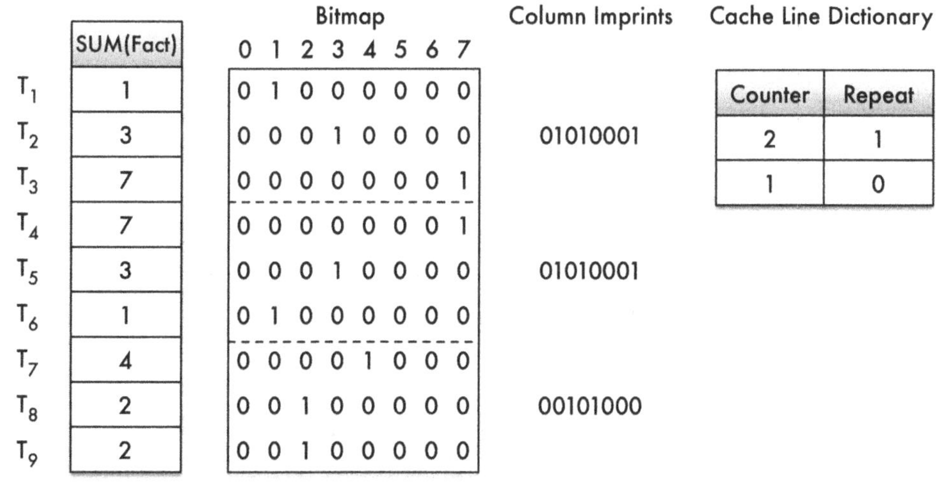

then there is a match and the cache line has to be consulted for filtering out false positives. However, one can skip this filtering step, if the range predicate matches the bin borders, which implies that all values of the cache line are included in the selection.

Group 3: State-of-the-Art Optimized Sequential Scans

In this group, we consider three approaches. The first one is Dwarf introduced to reduce the size of a materialized cube. The second approach is called Sorted Projections and it is implemented in the C-Store system. The final approach, Elf, aims combining efficient memory layout with data compression.

Data Dwarf

The data dwarf is introduced by Sismanis et al. (2002) to store the information of the data cube in a highly compressed manner. This structure is well suited for main memory, but could also be used for data exchange. Note, the compression is realized without loss of information compared to the data cube. The main idea behind this structure is the optimization of redundancies, on the prefix as well as suffix level.

In Figure 7, the data dwarf of our running example is presented. Whereas the data cube requires 576 Bytes, the data dwarf requires only 256 Bytes. This acyclic directed graph differentiates each dimension (column) and stores the facts and their necessary aggregates with Lists, Nodes and Pointers. Lists include information on all stored column attributes dependent on the column attributes in the levels before. Furthermore, in the leaf level, a node within such a list consists of the dimension attribute and the corresponding fact. Nodes in all other levels consist of the dimension attributes and a pointer to the list to the next dimension list. Therefore prefix redundancy is omitted, because in each path a dimension attribute is only stored once. Furthermore, suffix redundancy is eliminated by pointing to already existing paths in the lower levels. The authors Sismanis et al. (2002) state that the data dwarf achieves a compression for a 1 PB data cube to 2.3 GB data dwarf. Nevertheless, the ordering of dimensions is a crucial parameter of the dwarf as well as the algorithmic effort for identifying already existing paths to eliminate suffix redundancy.

Figure 7. Data dwarf

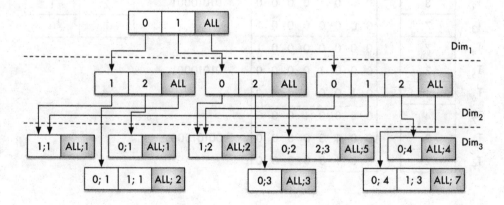

Sorted Projections

C-Store (Stonebreaker, 2005) proposes the concept of projections as an additional index structure. A projection is defined on a set of columns with a predefined order. With respect to this order, column data are replicated and sorted according to the first column in this order. This sorting enables an efficient binary search on the first column. However, it will also alter the position of a tuple in the column that creates the need for an additional TID column (cf. Figure 8) which was implicitly encoded by the tuple position before. Hence, it creates additional storage overhead. The overhead can be reduced by using run-length encoding on the first column being effective due to the sorting criteria. Note, in our example the run-length encoding does not gain any compression. This is due to the fact of the very small data size.

Figure 8. Sorted projection

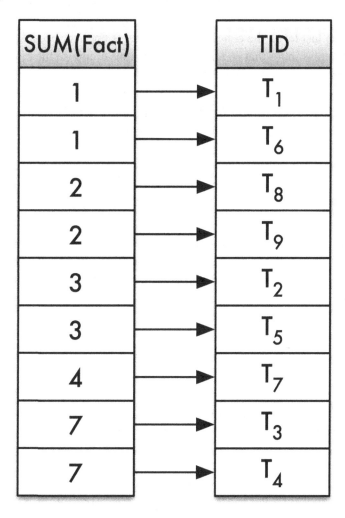

Sorted Projections are very efficient if the query workload is known. Then, the minimal set of necessary projections can be determined to accelerate query execution. However, for frequent updates the more projections are created, the more update propagation has to be done.

Elf

Elf is a tree-based approach that indexes sub-spaces incrementally (Broneske et al, 2017). Elf features a main-memory optimized storage layout that converges to a row-store-like organization, storing each value of some point adjacent to each other in the lower levels of the tree. This results in high data locality, relevant if one needs to scan parts of Elf sequentially circumventing the curse-of-dimensionality. We illustrate the design of Elf with the example in Figure 9. In our example data set, we use all four attributes as columns.

For the first column, two values occur and these build a hash map (1), to directly point to the next level. Both nodes inside are directed via a pointer to two lists of all occurring values for column 2 (dimension 2). In our example at the last level, the concept of monolists is applied, because a differentiation is not necessary anymore. The reason for that is, all three dimensions compose the key. Whereas the first part of the Elf (in our example first two levels) is interpreted as a columnar storage, the concept of monolists uses a storage concept similar to row stores. Therefore, we see this concept as a tradeoff between both architecture representations, whereas the fast lookup on data is beneficial from this layout. Note, for further optimization, Elf also addresses main memory storage layout, which further enhances query processing for multi-dimensional data analytics.

EVALUATION STUDY

In our brief evaluation, we focus on the one side on the TPC-H benchmark We depict the results of the above presented access methods. This means, we do not consider row- and column-store architectures as well as data cube and data dwarf, because of their precomputation the performance mainly depends on the data sizes. In our experiments, we use several different scaling factors, but they all deliver comparable patterns and therefore, we only present results from the scaling factor s = 50, which corresponds to a

Figure 9. Elf

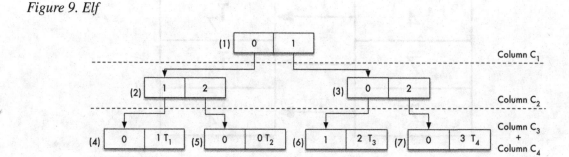

complete data size of all tables with 50GB. Furthermore, we do not present all 22 queries, but a representative selection. We present response times as well as build times of the above presented structures. In the TPC-H benchmark schema, the fact table Lineitem is more than 70% of the complete relational data. Therefore, we select queries based on this table, but also include Queries Q17 and Q19. Note, Query Q17 is based on the table Part and Q19 requires for both tables and consequently two structures for this query. We perform our analysis on an Intel Xeon E5 2609 v2 (ivy Bridge Architecture) with 2.6 GHz clock frequency and 256 GB RAM.

We divide our evaluation into two parts. In the experiment, we investigate the construction time for the different approaches presented before. Note, in an analytical environment, this construction is not often initiated compared to the queries. Therefore, we emphasize the query response times in our second part of the evaluation.

Construction Times

We present the build times for the Lineitem table in Figure 10. Note, this table consumes about 35 GB in the relational data representation. For a fair comparison, we dictionary compress the data before we use the corresponding build algorithms. The construction times for the respected structures vary between 38 seconds for the SIMD approach and 312 seconds for Column Imprints. SIMD requires some time, due to a rearrangement of the data. Nevertheless, this is the fastest approach at construction time and followed by BitWeaving and Sorted Projection. Elf requires four times compared to the SIMD approach. In our presentation, we leave out the sequential scan, because we assume that it is already prepared. Note, in case a row store instead a columnar store layout is given, some reconstruction is necessary, too.

Figure 10. Build Times for lineitem table (s = 50)

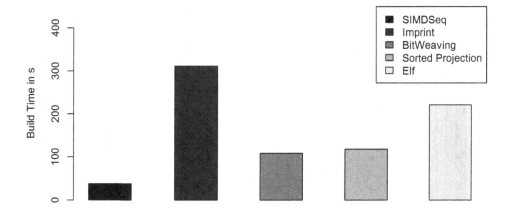

Query Processing Times

More important than the construction times are the query processing times. In multi-dimensional analytical scenarios, a data update is seldom. But queries are more often processed and executed in the corresponding system. In Figure 11, we present the query response times for some selected TPC-H queries. Note, we depict the results of query time responses at a logarithmic scale.

We cluster the queries into two groups, on the one side (Q1, Q10, and Q14) only a single attribute is a selection predicate. Nevertheless, some differences are observable for these queries. For Q6, Q17 and Q19 (presented as part for Lineitem (LQ19) and Part table (PQ19)), two or more selection predicates are involved. These queries address multidimensional analysis.

As a first result, we state that the SIMD approach always outperforms the sequential scan. So, we conclude that applying modern technology is a beneficial effort. Whereas Elf as the slowest approach for Q1 and Q10, in Q6 and Q14 it is one of the fastest. The reason for this behavior lies in the selectivities of theses queries. Q1 has a selectivity of 98%, which means, that almost all data have to be processed, Q10 has a selectivity of about 25%. Q14 instead has a very small selectivity of the data of about 1.3%. Therefore, the addressed query data amount is one crucial factor for efficient access. The authors in (Broneske et al, 2017) state that the tradeoff for index structures is at about a selectivity of 10% to 20%. For multi-dimensional queries, as Q6, Q17, and Q19, it is easily seen, the Elf approach outperforms all

Figure 11. Response times of TPC-H queries for s = 50

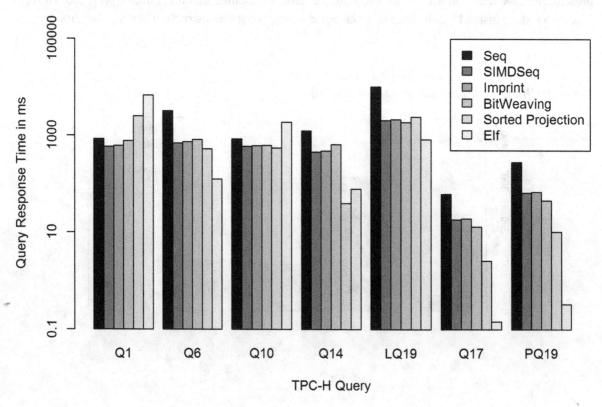

others up to some orders of magnitudes. The second best is Sorted Projections. BitWeaving also outperforms the SIMD sequential scan.

Note, the column imprint approach does not compete with the optimized sequential scan approach for modern hardware. Nevertheless, dependent on the query workload as well as the implementation of the running system a decision for an index structure is necessary. For instance, Sorted Projections are included in the C-Store system, but Elf is not available in an analytical data system at the current state. Finally, an optimization of data access is ongoing research and further potential for efficiency issues might be addressed in the future.

CONCLUSION

The new opportunities that arise from the development of new hardware as well as the evolution of data access approaches enable a significant increase in query response times for multi-dimensional analyses. Multi-dimensional filters build the basis for these analyses and an efficient query response time is therefore very essential. Efficient techniques and architectures enable computational opportunities in the field of data warehousing and big data analytics. Efficient data access requires at data construction time additional effort, which is negligible if many queries have to be processed.

We state that applying a reasonable technique on modern hardware enhances query-processing time. This can be seen in our experiments, where the SIMD approach always outperforms standard sequential scan. Nevertheless, in case different modern approaches are compared, we state that there is no approach that dominates all others. Instead, it is necessary to know or estimate the workload and to select a suitable technique. As a final statement: Use modern hardware with an appropriate data access technique.

REFERENCES

Abadi, Boncz, Harizopoulos, Idreos, & Madden. (2012). The design and implementation of modern column-oriented database systems. *Foundations and Trends in Databases, 5*(3), 197-280.

Abadi, D., Madden, S., & Hachem, N. (2008). Column-stores vs. row-stores: How different are they really? In *SIGMOD* (pp. 967–980). ACM. doi:10.1145/1376616.1376712

Abadi, D., Myers, D., DeWitt, D., & Madden, S. (2007). Materialization strategies in a column-oriented DBMS. In *ICDE* (pp. 466–475). IEEE.

Antoshenkov, G. (1997). Dictionary-based order-preserving string compression. *The VLDB Journal, 6*(1), 26–39. doi:10.1007007780050031

Bayer, R., & McCreight, E. (1972). Organization and Maintenance of Large Ordered Indexes. *Acta Informatica, 1*(3), 173–189. doi:10.1007/BF00288683

Bentley, J. (1975). Multidimensional binary search trees used for associative searching. *Communications of the ACM, 18*(9), 509–517. doi:10.1145/361002.361007

Berchtold, S., Böhm, C., & Kriegel, H.-P. (1998). The Pyramid Technique: Towards Breaking the Curse of Dimensionality. In *SIGMOD* (pp. 142–153). ACM. doi:10.1145/276304.276318

Boncz, P., & Kersten, M. (1999). MIL primitives for querying a fragmented world. *The VLDB Journal, 8*(2), 101–119. doi:10.1007007780050076

Boncz, P., Kersten, M., & Manegold, S. (2008). Breaking the memory wall in MonetDB. *Communications of the ACM, 51*(12), 77–85. doi:10.1145/1409360.1409380

Boncz, P., Zukowski, M., & Nes, N. (2005). *MonetDB/X100: Hyper-Pipelining Query Execution*. CIDR.

Broneske, D., Köppen, V., Saake, G., & Schäler, M. (2017). Accelerating multi-column selection predicates in main-memory – the Elf approach. In ICDE (pp. 647–658). IEEE.

Das, D., Yan, J., Zait, M., Valluri, S. R., Vyas, N., Krishnamachari, R., ... Mukherjee, N. (2015). „Query optimization in Oracle 12c database in-memory. *VLDB, 8*(12), 1770–1781.

Faerber, F., Kemper, A., Larson, P., Levandoski, J., Neumann, T., & Pavlo, A. (2016). „Main Memory Database Systems. *Foundations and Trends in Databases, 8*(1-2), 1–130. doi:10.1561/1900000058

Gray, J., Chaudhuri, S., Bosworth, A., Laymann, A., Reichart, D., Venkatrao, M., ... Pirahesh, H. (1997). Data Cube: A relational aggregation operator generalizing group-by, cross-tab, and sub-totals. *Data Mining and Knowledge Discovery, 1*(1), 29–53. doi:10.1023/A:1009726021843

Guttman, A. (1984). R-Trees: A Dynamic Index Structure for Spatial Searching. In *SIGMOD* (pp. 47–57). ACM. doi:10.1145/602259.602266

Johnson, R., Raman, V., Sidle, R., & Swart, G. (2008). Row-wise parallel predicate evaluation. *PVLDB, 1*(1), 622–634.

Kemper, A., & Neumann, T. (2011). Hyper: A hybrid OLTP & OLAP main memory database system based on virtual memory snapshots. In *ICDE* (pp. 195–206). IEEE. doi:10.1109/ICDE.2011.5767867

Leis, V., Kemper, A., & Neumann, T. (2013). The Adaptive Radix Tree: ARTful Indexing for Main-Memory Databases. In ICDE (pp. 38–49). IEEE.

Li, Y., & Patel, J. (2013). Bitweaving: Fast scans for main memory data processing. In SIGMOD (pp. 289–300). ACM. doi:10.1145/2463676.2465322

Lübcke, A., Schäler, M., Köppen, V., & Saake, G. (2012). *Workload-based Heuristics for Evaluation of Physical Database Architectures*. DB&IS.

Plattner, H. (2009). A common database approach for OLTP and OLAP using an in-memory column database. In *SIGMOD* (pp. 1–2). ACM. doi:10.1145/1559845.1559846

Polychroniou, O., & Ross, K. (2014). Vectorized bloom filters for advanced SIMD processors. In DaMoN. ACM.

Polychroniou, O., & Ross, K. (2015). *Efficient lightweight compression alongside fast scans. In DaMoN*. ACM.

Rao, J., & Ross, K. (2000). *Making B+-Trees cache conscious in main memory. In SIGMOD* (pp. 475–486). ACM.

Schäler, M., Grebhahn, A., Schröter, R., Schulze, S., Köppen, V., & Saake, G. (2013). QuEval: Beyond high- dimensional indexing à la carte. *PVLDB*, *6*(14), 1654–1665.

Sidirourgos, L., & Kersten, M. (2013). Column imprints: A secondary index structure. In SIGMOD (pp. 893–904). ACM. doi:10.1145/2463676.2465306

Sismanis, Y., Deligiannakis, A., Roussopoulos, N., & Kotidis, Y. (2002). Dwarf: Shrinking the PetaCube. In *SIGMOD* (pp. 464–475). ACM.

Sitaridi, E., & Ross, K. (2013). Optimizing select conditions on GPUs. DaMoN, 4:1–4:8. doi:10.1145/2485278.2485282

Stonebraker, M., Abadi, D., Batkin, A., Chen, X., Cherniack, M., Ferreira, M., ... Zdonik, S. (2005). *C-Store: A column-oriented DBMS*. VLDB.

Transaction Processing Performance Council. (2014). *TPC benchmark H (decision support)*. Tech. Rep. 2.17.1. Author.

Willhalm, T., Boshmaf, Y., Plattner, H., Popovici, N., Zeier, A., & Schaffner, J. (2009). SIMDScan: Ultra fast in-memory table scan using on-chip vector processing units. *PVLDB*, *2*(1), 385–394.

Willhalm, T., Oukid, I., Müller, I., & Faerber, F. (2013). Vectorizing database column scans with complex predicates. In ADMS (pp. 1–12). ACM.

Zhou, J., & Ross, K. (2002). Implementing database operations using SIMD instructions. In *SIGMOD* (pp. 145–156). ACM.

Chapter 9
Multidimensional Analysis of Big Data

Salman Ahmed Shaikh
National Institute of Advanced Industrial Science and Technology (AIST), Japan

Kousuke Nakabasami
University of Tsukuba, Japan

Toshiyuki Amagasa
University of Tsukuba, Japan

Hiroyuki Kitagawa
University of Tsukuba, Japan

ABSTRACT

Data warehousing and multidimensional analysis go side by side. Data warehouses provide clean and partially normalized data for fast, consistent, and interactive multidimensional analysis. With the advancement in data generation and collection technologies, businesses and organizations are now generating big data (defined by 3Vs; i.e., volume, variety, and velocity). Since the big data is different from traditional data, it requires different set of tools and techniques for processing and analysis. This chapter discusses multidimensional analysis (also known as on-line analytical processing or OLAP) of big data by focusing particularly on data streams, characterized by huge volume and high velocity. OLAP requires to maintain a number of materialized views corresponding to user queries for interactive analysis. Precisely, this chapter discusses the issues in maintaining the materialized views for data streams, the use of special window for the maintenance of materialized views and the coupling issues of stream processing engine (SPE) with OLAP engine.

DOI: 10.4018/978-1-5225-5516-2.ch009

INTRODUCTION

Due to the increase of stream data sources, such as sensors, GPS, micro blogs, etc., the need to aggregate and analyze stream data has increased. Many organizations require instant decisions exploiting the latest information from the data streams. For instance, timely analysis of business data is required for improving profit, network packets need to be monitored in real time for identifying network attacks, etc. Online analytical processing (OLAP) is a well-known and useful approach to analyse data in a multi-dimensional fashion, initially given for disk-based static data. OLAP requires hierarchical arrangement of dimensional attributes (C.E.F. et al, 1993). For the effective OLAP analysis, the data is converted into a multi-dimensional schema, also known as star schema. The data in star schema is represented as a data cube, where each cube cell contains measure across multiple dimensions. A user may be interested in analysing data across different combination of dimensions or examining different views of it. These are often termed as OLAP operations and to support these operations, data is organized as lattice nodes. Each vertex of lattice corresponds to an aggregate query, called (*OLAP queries*). Materialized views are maintained for the selected lattice vertices. Maintenance of materialized views is handled by OLAP engine, which require clean and structured data stream. Since the raw data stream is inherently unstructured and contains missing values, Stream Processing Engines (SPE) are usually used with OLAP engine to provide it clean and structured stream. There exist many stream processing engines such as STREAM, S4 and Borealis (Arasu et al, 2016; Neumeyer et al, 2010, Cangialosi et al, 2005). These SPEs uses continuous queries to process data streams continuously.

To support OLAP over data streams, SPEs are usually coupled with OLAP engine. J. Han, et al. (2007) in was the first to propose *Stream Cube* architecture to facilitate OLAP for continuous stream data. In order to reduce the query response time and to reduce the storage cost, Stream Cube keeps the distant data at high granularity level, while only very new data at low granularity level. To further reduce the query response time, the stream cube pre-computes some OLAP query results at coarser, intermediate and finer aggregation levels. However, in their work, the use of SPE is not taken into account and it is not possible to perform the fine-grained analysis of the distant data as only the most recent data is available at finer resolution. Moreover, a few *materialized* query results between two layers, i.e., observation layer and minimal interesting layer, are available and users cannot obtain the aggregation results beyond the minimal interesting layer.

In section 4 of this chapter we present a stream OLAP architecture consisting of an SPE and an OLAP engine which is based on our research work. To get the required results, the naive approach is to materialize and maintain OLAP query results of all vertices representing the combinations of dimensions and their hierarchies in a lattice. However, this results in a large number of materialized cubes and will also affect the performance of the SPE. Moreover, all the aggregation results are not needed at all the time. Thus, a cost-based optimization algorithm is discussed. The algorithm decides which queries should be materialized in cooperation with the SPE and which query results should be derived on-demand from other materialized query results. The optimization algorithm tries to minimize the query processing cost by keeping in view the available memory (Nakabasmi et al, 2015).

A number of solutions have been proposed for OLAP analysis on data streams in the near past (Han et al, 2005; Duan eta l, 2011; Sadoghi et al, 2016). The requirement to produce real time OLAP analysis on fast and evolving data streams is not possible unless the data to be analysed reside on primary memory.

However the size of the primary memory is limited and it is volatile. Therefore we need an in-memory compact data structure that can quickly answer user queries in addition to a non-volatile backup of the data streams. Hence section 5 of this chapter discusses an approximate stream OLAP architecture *AOLAP* (Approximate Stream OLAP) which is based on our research work (Shaikh et al, 2017) AOLAP in addition to storing raw data streams to the secondary storage, maintains data streams summaries in a compact memory-based data structure. AOLAP makes use of piece-wise linear approximation (PLA) for storing such data summaries corresponding to each materialized node in the OLAP cube. PLA can store the long data streams' summaries in comparatively smaller space on the primary memory and can give approximate answers to OLAP queries. It provides an impressive data compression ratio and answers user queries with max error guarantees, and has been studied by many researchers (Elmeleegy et al, 2009; Xie et al, 2012).

ESSENTIAL CONCEPTS

In this section we summarize some of the related concepts, which are essentially important in the subsequent discussions.

Online Analytical Processing (OLAP)

OLAP is a technique for interactive analysis over multidimensional data. For efficient OLAP analysis, the underlying database schema is usually converted into a partially-normalized star schema. The data in star schema is represented as a data cube consisting of several dimension tables and a fact table. Dimension tables contain descriptive attributes, while the fact tables contain business facts called measures and foreign keys referring to primary keys in the dimension tables. Some of the dimension attributes are hierarchically connected. A number of dimension hierarchies compose a cube lattice, where each node corresponds to different combination of attributes at different hierarchy levels and an edge between two nodes represents a subsumption relation between them. Hence nodes in a lattice are combinations of dimension attributes and represent OLAP queries.

For instance, consider the star schema benchmark (O'Neil et al, 2009) shown in Figure1a with a fact table *LINEORDER* and four-dimension tables, *PART*, *CUSTOMER*, *SUPPLIER* and *DATE*. Attributes *Quantity*, *ExtendedPrice*, *OrdTotalPrice*, *Discount*, *Revenue*, etc. of the *LINEORDER* are the business facts, while *CustKey*, *PartKey* and *SuppKey* are foreign keys of *CUSTOMER*, *PART* and *SUPPLIER* dimensions respectively. Additionally, each dimension table contains hierarchical relationship among some of its attributes. For example, *SUPPLIER* dimension contains hierarchy among the following attributes: *City* − > *Nation* − > *Region*. If we consider interaction of the *PART*, *CUSTOMER* and *SUPPLIER* dimensions only (without considering their internal hierarchies), the corresponding lattice is given by Figure 1b. In the figure, the nodes with the border are materialized and the associated tables show their tuples. Once an OLAP lattice has been generated, users can register queries and apply OLAP operations to it. The queries registered to non-materialized nodes are computed from the materialized nodes on ad-hoc basis.

Piecewise Linear Approximation (PLA)

PLA is a method of constructing a function to approximate a single valued function of one variable in terms of a sequence of linear segments (O'Rourke et al, 1981). Precisely, let S be a time series of discrete data points (t_i, x_i), where $i \in [1, n]$, t_i is the i-th timestamp, x_i is the i-th value and we wish to approximate x_i with a piece-wise linear function $f(t_i)$, using a small number of segments such that the error $|f(t_i) - x_i| \leq \varepsilon$, where is a user defined error parameter. The goal is to record only the successive line segments, and not the individual data points, to reduce the overhead of recording entire time-series.

Authors in (Aouiche et al, 2009) proposed an online algorithm to construct such an f having the minimum number of line segments. For completeness, the algorithm is described in Algorithm 1. It takes a data point $p = (t_i, x_i)$ and an error parameter . Let P be the set of points processed so far, the algorithm maintains the property that all the points in P can be approximated with a line segment within ε. If $P \cup \{p\}$ can be approximated with a line segment then it is added to P, else the points in P are output as a line segment and a new line segment is started with the point p.

Example 1: A big retail chain collects sales quantities of their stores at the granularity of individual product, store location and promotion (under which the product is sold) dimensions which arrive every minute as an infinite time series data stream. The sales stream arrive as a series of a 5-tuple < t,p,s,m,x >; the timestamp (minute) (t), product (p), store (s), promotion (m) and the sales quantity (x).

$(1, p_1, s_1, m_1, 48)$, $(1, p_2, s_1, m_1, 48)$, $(2, p_1, s_1, m_1, 43)$, $(2, p_2, s_1, m_1, 64)$, $(3, p_1, s_1, m_1, 60)$, $(3, p_2, s_1, m_1, 73)$, $(4, p_1, s_1, m_1, 75)$, $(4, p_2, s_1, m_1, 58)$, $(5, p_1, s_1, m_1, 35)$, $(5, p_2, s_1, m_1, 87)$, $(6, p_1, s_1, m_1, 52)$, $(6, p_2, s_1, m_1, 7)$, $(7, p_1, s_1, m_1, 95)$, $(7, p_2, s_1, m_1, 2)$, ...

Figure 1. Star schema benchmark

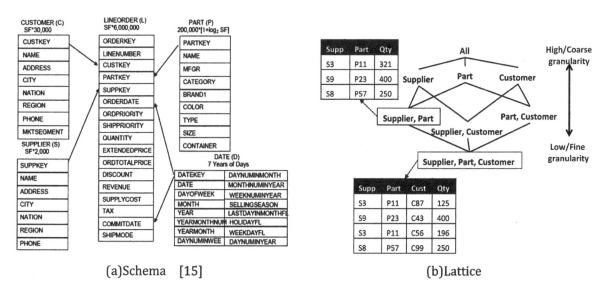

(a)Schema [15]   (b)Lattice

Algorithm 1. PLA

Input: data point p, error parameter
/*P: Set of points processed so far.*/
begin
   if $P \cup \{p\}$ *can be approximated with a line segment within* ϵ **then**
     | Add p to P;
   end
   else
     | **return** a line segment approximating P;
   end
   Set $P \leftarrow \{p\}$;
end

Assuming = 10, the tuples for the dimension keys p_1, s_1 *and* m_1 *in the above time series can be approximated by the following piecewise function.*

$$f_{p_1,s_1,m_1}(t) = \begin{cases} 9.8t + 32 & 1 \le t \le 4 \\ 30t - 119.33 & 5 \le t \le 7 \\ \dots \end{cases}$$

Figure 2 shows the PLA segments of the $f_{p_1},s_1,m_1(t)$. f1(t) and f2(t) are the PLA segments formed by the tuples for timestamps $1 \le t \le 4$ and $5 \le t \le 7$, respectively. The accurate sales quantities are shown in the figure for illustration only, while the approximate sales quantities can be obtained from the PLA segments. Note that when using PLA, we only maintain PLA segments (slopes and intercepts) in memory and not the actual data points, resulting in data size reduction.

Figure 2. Data points approximated by PLA segments

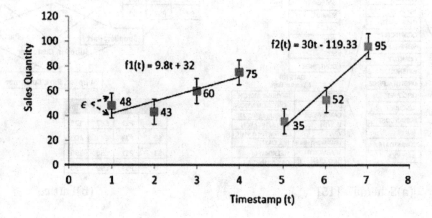

RELATED WORK

Since this chapter is divided into two major parts, we divide the related work section into two sub-sections.

Stream OLAP and View Maintenance

OLAP has been studied for long time in the data engineering arena. In Aouiche, et al (2009) proposed to couple materialized views and index selection to take view-index interaction into account and achieve efficient storage space sharing in OLAP. Talebi, et al (2008) proposed a systematic study of the OLAP view and index-selection problem.

Santos, et al. (2007) linked partitioning and indexing and optimized the data warehouse's performance. Harinarayan et al. (2006) investigated the issue of cells (views) materialization when it is too expensive to materialize all views. They presented a greedy algorithm that determines a good set of views to materialize. Joslyn et al. equipped the view lattice with statistical information and theoretical measures (Joslyn et al, 2009). However, these works target static data and cannot handle data streams.

J. Han, et al (2005) proposed an architecture called Stream Cube to facilitate OLAP for data streams. In order to reduce the query response time and the storage cost, Stream Cube keeps the distant data at high granularity level and very new data is at low granularity level. To further reduce the query response time, the stream cube pre-computes some OLAP query at coarser, intermediate and finer aggregation levels. Yang, et al. (2008) proposed a dynamic data cube for data streams. In their work, dynamic data cube can specify user interesting areas with the support ratio of attribute values. However their work neither address the use of SPE nor cost-based optimization. Zhang, et al (2010) proposed a method to efficiently compute multiple aggregates over stream using Gigascope (Cranor et al, 2003). However, their focus is calculation of multiple aggregates but not OLAP.

The first part of this chapter discusses an stream OLAP architecture consisting of an SPE and an OLAP engine to address the issues discussed above. The OLAP engine collaborates with the SPE and holds the aggregation results in memory to answer the OLAP queries efficiently. Moreover, the aggregation results can be obtained with respect to the time by considering it as one of the dimensions for OLAP. In addition, a cost-based optimization algorithm for stream OLAP is proposed to minimize the query processing cost.

Compact Data Structures and Approximate Querying

Compact data structures have long been utilized to summarize voluminous and velocious data streams and answer queries from them approximately. H. Elmeleegy et al. (2009) proposed two PLA-based stream compression algorithms, swing filters and slide filters, to represent a time-varying numerical signal within some preset error value. The PLA line segments in the swing filter are connected whereas mostly disconnected in the slide filter. The slide filter proposed in their work is almost similar to the one proposed by O'Rourke (1981).

Zhewei et al (2015) proposed sketching techniques that support historical and window queries over summarized data. The data summary is maintained using the count-min sketch and the AMS sketch and the persistence is achieved by utilizing PLAs. Their work can provide persistence for counters only and can support point, heavy hitter and join size queries. (Lou et al, 2015) presented an online algorithm to optimize the representation size of the PLA for streaming time-series data. A PLA function f can be constructed using either only continuous (joint) line segments or only disjoint line segments. To optimize the size of f, the authors gave an adaptive solution that uses a mixture of joint and disjoint PLA segments and they named it *mixed-type* PLA.

Phantoms are intermediate queries to accelerate user queries. Zhang et al (20100 proposed the use of phantoms to reduce the overall cost (processing and data transfer cost) within very limited memory of a network interface card. Although their work can reduce aggregation query cost, but is not capable of answering ad-hoc OLAP queries. M. Sadoghi et al. (2016) presented a lineage-based data store that combines real-time transactional and analytical processing within an engine with the help of the lineage-based storage. However their focus is storage architecture and not the core OLAP. Ahmad et al. (2014) presented *viewlet transforms*, which materializes a query and a set of its higher-order deltas as views resulting in a reduced overall view maintenance cost by trading space.

Wavelet is also a famous technique which is often used for hierarchical data decomposition and summarisation. The technique proposed in (Garofalakis et al, 2004) can effectively perform the wavelet decomposition with maximum error metrics. However, since the technique uses dynamic programming, it is computationally expensive. Therefore it cannot be used effectively for the data streams, which require one-pass methodology in linear time. (Karras et al, 2005) proposed a method for one-pass wavelet synopses with the maximum error metric. (Karras et al, 2005) shows that by using a number of intuitive thresholding techniques, it is possible to approximate the technique discussed in (Karras et al, 2005). However, wavelet summarization can have a number of disadvantages in many situations as many parts of the time series may be approximated very poorly (Rougemont et al, 2012). (Rougemont et al, 2012) used a sampling approach to answer OLAP queries approximately, however they did not consider lattice nodes materialization issue. (Duan et al, 2011) compared different summarization methods on data streams and proved that the PLA is the best data summarization technique as far as querying error is concerned.

SPE AND OLAP ENGINE COUPLING FOR MULTIDIMENSIONAL ANALYSIS OF DATA STREAMS

This work assumes that the data streams consist of relational tuples. Generally in OLAP for static data, a data cube is represented by a star schema consisting of dimension and fact tables. Dimension tables contain descriptive attributes (or fields), while the fact tables contain business facts (or measures) and foreign keys which refer to primary keys in the dimension tables (Figure 3). Dimension tables contain information about dimension hierarchies. A set of dimension hierarchies compose a lattice framework. Within the lattice, vertices are combinations of dimensions and each vertex in a lattice corresponds to an OLAP query. Figure 4 shows a lattice structure constructed by considering the hierarchies in part, supplier and time dimensions.

For example consider the construction of a lattice from the "part", "supplier" and "time" dimensions shown in Figure 3. The root of the lattice is an aggregation of the p name, s name, and minute, which are at the finest granularity level in each dimension's hierarchy. Then the vertices of different granularity levels are added to the lattice, consisting of dimensions' different hierarchy levels. For example (p name, s name, and hour), (p name, minute), (p name, hour), and so on. The lattice has dependence relationship among its vertices. Since a lattice vertex corresponds to an OLAP query, dependence relationship among

Figure 3. Star schema

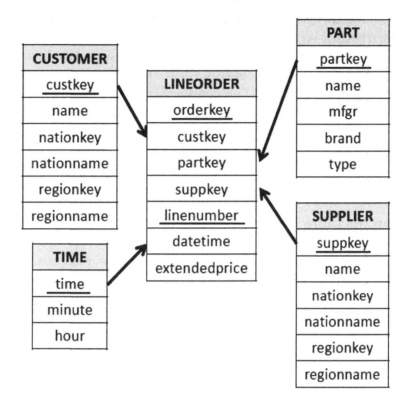

Figure 4. Lattice structure of part, supplier and time dimensions

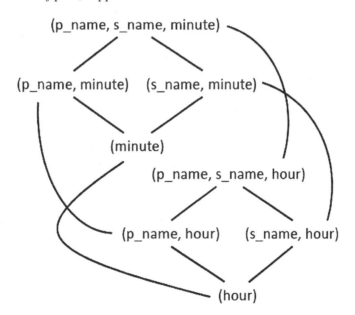

a lattice vertices allows us to obtain query result at high granularity level using the low granularity query results in the lattice, which are linked through edges. In other words, coarser granularity results can be obtained from finer granularity vertices.

Up to this point, the OLAP query processing is similar to that of static data. In stream OLAP, we assume that tuples for the fact table arrive continuously as a stream, while the tuples in the dimension tables are static. Since data streams are infinite, its time domain has no boundaries. Practically it is impossible to query data streams over infinite time, thus we coin a term Interval of Interest (IoI) for querying data streams. IoI is the maximum time duration for which users may query data streams. Namely, each vertex in the lattice contains the OLAP query result obtained from the tuples within an IoI. The IoI duration must be at-least equal to the highest granularity level in the time dimension hierarchy. For the sake of simplicity in this work, we assume that the duration of IoI is same for all the vertices in the lattice.

Stream OLAP Architecture

The stream OLAP architecture is shown in Figure 5. It has two processing engines. 1) A stream processing engine (SPE) and 2) An OLAP engine. The SPE is responsible for generating aggregation results at specified granularity levels from continuous data streams. The OLAP engine holds the aggregation results generated from the SPE in memory for the interval of interest (IoI). When a user requests an OLAP query result, which is not available in memory of the OLAP engine, it computes the result from available aggregation results. In the following, we will discuss the role of each engine in detail.

Stream Processing Engine (SPE)

SPE receives incoming stream tuples and generates aggregate tuples at specified granularity levels. For example in Figure 5, the incoming stream tuples consist of four attributes, three dimensional (part, supplier and time) and one fact (sales) attribute.

The OLAP engine can register CQL queries (Arasu et al, 2003) to the SPE, e.g., aggregation query, join query, etc. as shown in Figure 5. The query in Figure 5 aggregates the fact attribute (sales) of incoming stream tuples with respect to dimension attributes s name and minute. The aggregation is performed for each 1 minute to support the OLAP query (s name, minute).

In the SPE, both the count-based and the time-based windows could be used to perform continuous queries on stream data. A window contains the most recent tuples from a data stream. The query in Figure 5 uses a time-based window, which performs aggregation on the stream tuples which have arrived in last 1 minute. The reason for selecting one minute window is that the temporal granularity of the OLAP query (s name, minute) is *minute*. The RSTREAM operator ("TPC-H", 2017) outputs the query results computed by the aggregation of tuples in the 1 minute window. Thus the result is generated every minute, which corresponds to a new data stream consisting of continuous aggregation results. We assume that the tuples of dimension tables are populated and joined with the incoming fact tuples in the SPE for the generation of aggregation results.

OLAP Engine

The OLAP engine holds the aggregate tuples in memory to answer the OLAP queries efficiently. The OLAP queries are classified into two types in this work. 1) Registered query and 2) On-demand query.

Figure 5. Stream OLAP architecture and process flow

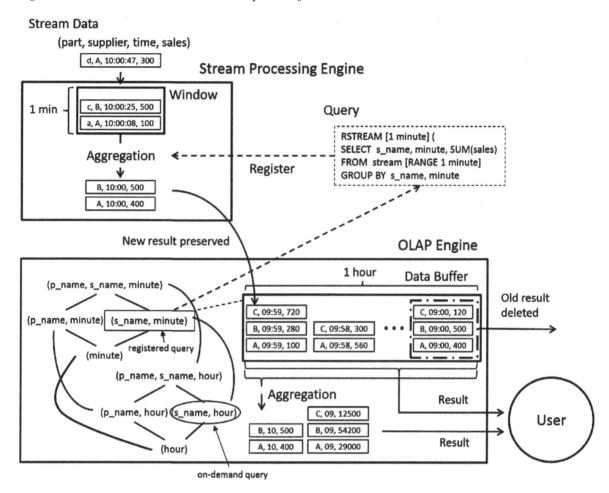

1. **Registered Query:** A registered query is an OLAP query which is submitted to the SPE. The OLAP query is written in CQL and it continuously generates aggregate results at the granularity level specified in the query. The query results are sent to the OLAP engine which are then stored in the *data buffer*. The data buffer is a storage area which is actually an array for storing aggregate tuples generated by the registered query. Since the memory space is limited, the OLAP engine holds the results for the duration of IoI only. Thus, when a user requests an OLAP query, the OLAP engine returns the result from the data buffer directly rather than computing the result from scratch.

For example consider the query (s name, minute) in Figure 5, which is registered to the SPE. Here we assume that the IoI is set to one hour and therefore the data buffer needs to hold data for the recent 1 hour. In Figure 5, the data buffer is shown holding the aggregate tuples from 9:00 to 9:59. When the aggregate tuple of time-stamp 10:00 arrives, the aggregate tuple of time-stamp 9:00 becomes obsolete and is deleted from the data buffer.

2. **On-Demand Query:** Any OLAP query can be submitted as the registered query by a user. However it is not possible to do so for all the vertices in the lattice, as the number of a lattice vertices is huge and materializing them in the data buffer requires a lot of memory. Moreover, users are not always interested in obtaining all the aggregation results.

Hence we propose an on-demand query processing scheme. Using this scheme, only part of the lattice is *materialized*. If a user submits a query which is not registered, the result is computed using the buffered query results for registered queries. Let the query (s name, hour) shown in Figure 5 is an on-demand query. The result of this query can be computed from the finer granularity results available in data buffer, i.e, the registered query result of (s name, minute).

The Time Dimension

In this section, we will discuss how to obtain the aggregation results with respect to the time dimension in Stream OLAP. First of all the granularity and hierarchy of the time dimension must be decided for the lattice construction. For example in Figure 5, the time dimension hierarchy consists of two levels, i.e., *minute* and *hour*. After that, each vertex of the lattice is classified into a registered or on-demand query.

In case of the registered query, the aggregation with respect to the time dimension is available in the data buffer. Therefore, we can obtain the registered query result from it. Here the window size of the registered query is set equivalent to the data output interval of the RSTREAM operator. By doing so, for example, query results are generated every *minute* at the granularity of *minute*. These results are stored in the data buffer for the duration of IoI.

On the other hand, for the on-demand OLAP queries there is no data buffer. However, their results can be obtained by aggregating the results of registered queries available in the data buffer.

Optimization Scheme

In this section we present a cost-based optimization scheme for stream OLAP. Let p_i be the frequency of result look-ups for an OLAP query q_i. Namely, the current aggregated snapshot of query q_i is looked up p_i times per unit time. The proposed optimization scheme decides whether each query q_i should be processed as a registered query or an on-demand query to minimize the query processing cost by keeping in view the limits of spatial cost.

Since this optimization is a combinational problem, we develop a greedy algorithm for it. In the next section we will explain the processing and storage cost models used in the optimization Algorithm 2.

Cost Models

In the following we will discuss the processing and storage costs with respect to the two types of queries, i.e., the registered query and the on-demand query.

Processing Cost

1. **Registered Query:** Since the registered queries results are available in the data buffer, the cost of fetching an OLAP query result is negligible. However, the processing cost is associated with the evaluation of aggregation queries in the SPE. This cost increases in proportion to the number of registered queries. Let n denotes the number of registered queries and C_R denotes the processing cost of a registered query per unit time inside the SPE per unit time. Therefore the total processing cost for n registered queries in the SPE can be expressed as follows.

$$C_R \cdot n \tag{1}$$

2. **On-demand Query:** When an on-demand query q_i is submitted, the OLAP engine searches for its finer granularity registered query q_{ri} inside the data buffer and uses its tuples to answer q_i. Let w_{ri} be the window size of the registered CQL query for q_{ri} and k_{ri} be the average number of tuples in the CQL query result. Then, the CQL query associated with q_{ri} generates k_{ri} tuples per w_{ri} unit times. All the tuples in the data buffer related to q_{ri} are the target of aggregation. Let C_O denotes the aggregation cost per tuple, and I denotes the duration of IoI. Since the data buffer contains $I \cdot \dfrac{k_{r_i}}{w_{r_i}}$ tuples for the query q_{ri}, the processing cost of each invocation of q_i is given by $C_o \cdot I \cdot \dfrac{k_{r_i}}{w_{r_i}}$. Assuming that p_i is the number of times the query result is requested per unit time, the overall on-demand query processing cost of query q_i can be expressed as follows.

$$C_o \cdot I \cdot \frac{k_{r_i}}{w_{r_i}} \cdot p_i \tag{2}$$

There could be multiple q_{ri} candidates for an on-demand query q_i in the data buffer. In such cases, q_{ri} which minimizes the processing time of q_i is chosen.

Assuming that at a unit time, n registered queries and m on-demand queries are submitted to the stream OLAP system, then the overall system processing cost per unit time (C) can be expressed as follows.

$$C = C_R + C_o \cdot I \sum_{i=0}^{m} \frac{k_{r_i}}{w_{r_i}} \cdot p_i \tag{3}$$

Storage Cost

Storage cost mainly depends on the size of the data buffer. Assuming that S_R denotes the storage cost of a registered query. Furthermore, assuming that the size of a tuple in the data buffer for query q_i is s_i, then the total storage cost (S) can be expressed as follows.

$$S = S_R \cdot n + I \sum_{i=0}^{n} \frac{k_i}{w_i} \cdot s_i \qquad (4)$$

Optimization Algorithm

The proposed optimization Algorithm 2 classifies the OLAP queries into registered and on demand queries. The algorithm takes set Q of lattice vertices as input. The root (finest) vertex r of the lattice is always processed as a registered query, since it cannot be an on demand query. The output of the algorithm is a set of registered OLAP queries Q_{out}. Q_r and Q_o represent the sets of registered and on-demand queries, respectively. Initially, Q_r includes only the root r of the lattice, and Q_o includes all the vertices of the lattice except r.

The algorithm calculates the processing cost C_{pre}, by considering all the lattice vertices. The calculation of the total processing cost *processCost*(Q_r,Q_o) is done using Eq. 3. The algorithm selects one vertex at a time from Q_o and calculates the total processing cost C when a lattice vertex (OLAP query) is considered to be registered query. The algorithm then calculates *Benefit*, the difference of C and C_{pre}. The vertex with the maximum *Benefit* is selected and moved to Q_r and its storage cost *storageCost*(Q_r) is also computed using Eq. 4. The process of registered query selection is repeated until the total storage cost exceeds the storage threshold S_{max}. The S_{max} depends on the available memory space. Finally the registered OLAP queries (vertices) with the minimum C values are added to Q_{out}.

Example: Consider an example of the proposed optimization algorithm. The dataset used in the example consists of four attributes, i.e., part, supplier, time, and sales, where the part, supplier and time are dimensions and the sales is the fact. The parameter values assumed for each lattice vertex (OLAP query) are shown in Table 1.

For this example, I (duration of IoI) is set to 3600s and the S_{max} is set to 1GB. Under these conditions, the algorithm decides which OLAP queries (vertices) need to be registered. Firstly, the root (p name, s name, minute) is selected. Secondly, the algorithm selects a vertex from Q_o. Assume that the OLAP query (p name, minute) is selected to be included in Q_r. In order to calculate its processing cost C, we assume that $C_S = 10,000$. Since in this work, the C_o: C_S ratio is 1:10,000, the C_o is set to 1. The data buffer of (p name, s name, minute) is used for on-demand queries (s name, minute), (p name, s name, hour), and

Algorithm 2. Optimization algorithm

Input: V: A set of lattice vertices, S_{max}: Max. available storage
Output: V_m: a set of vertices to be materialized ($V_m \subseteq V$)
begin
    $V_m \leftarrow \{v_f\}$;
    $S_c \leftarrow 0$ (consumed storage) ;
    while $S_c < S_{max}$ **do**
        $C_{min} \leftarrow \infty$;
        $V_{cnd} \leftarrow V \backslash V_m$;
        if $V_{cnd} == \phi$ **then**
            return V_m ;
        end
        for $v \in V_{cnd}$ **do**
            (Let S_v: v's storage cost) ;
            if $S_c + S_v > S_{max}$ **then**
                Continue ;
            end
            $V_{tmp} \leftarrow V_m \cup \{v\}$;
            $C \leftarrow computeCost(V_{tmp})$;
            if $C < C_{min}$ **then**
                $C_{min} \leftarrow C$;
                $v_{min} \leftarrow v$;
            end
        end
        $V_m \leftarrow V_m \cup \{v\}$;
        $S_c \leftarrow S_c + S_v$;
    end
    return V_m
end

Algorithm 3. Querying and maintenance cost

Input: V: A set of lattice vertices, V_{tmp}: A tentative set of lattice vertices for materialization
Output: C: Computed cost for the given V_{tmp}
begin
    for $v \in V$ **do**
        $C_v \leftarrow \infty$
        for $v_t \in V_{tmp}$ **do**
            if *Query v can be answered by* v_t **then**
                $C_{v_t} \leftarrow computeCostViaCostFunction$
                if $C_{v_t} < C_v$ **then**
                    $C_v \leftarrow C_{v_t}$
                end
            end
        end
        $C \leftarrow C + C_v$
    end
    return C
end

Table 1. Parameter values for lattice vertices

Lattice vertex	w_i	k_i	p_i	s_i
p_name, s_name, minute	1	3000	0.7	56
p_name, minute	1	2300	0.4	36
s_name, minute	1	2500	0.8	36
minute	1	60	0.2	16
p_name, s_name, hour	60	2500	0.1	56
p_name, hour	60	2000	0.9	36
s_name, hour	60	2300	0.6	36
hour	60	10	0.3	16

(s name, hour), according to the cost models explained previously. The data buffer of (p name, minute) is used for the other on-demand queries.

$$C = 10000 \times 100 \times 2 + 3000 \times 3600 \times 0.8 / 1 + 2300 \times 3600 \times 0.2 / 1$$

$$+ 3000 \times 3600 \times 0.1 / 1 + 2300 \times 3600 \times 0.9 / 1 + 3000 \times 3600 \times 0.6 / 1 + 2300 \times 3600 \times 0.3 / 1$$

$$= 29792000$$

The processing cost C of other vertices are calculated in a similar fashion and the results are shown in Table 2.

From Table 2, the vertex with the minimum C value is (p name, s name, hour). Thus, this vertex is selected as a registered query and added to Q_r. The algorithm continues in a similar fashion and the vertices (s name, minute) and (p name, minute) are also selected as registered queries and added to Q_r. When (p name, minute) is considered, S value (1.235GB) exceeds the S_{max} and therefore it is dropped.

Next, the algorithm compares the total processing cost of the registered queries, which turned out to be 36,640,000, 17,390,000 and 9,390,000 when vertices (p name, s name, minute), (p name, s name, hour) and (s name, minute) are added to Q_r, respectively. Since the last case has the minimum processing cost, these three vertices are returned by the algorithm to be included in Q_r.

Table 2. Result of C in first iteration

Lattice vertex	C
p_name, minute	27832000
s_name, minute	25060000
minute	30344800
p_name, s_name, hour	15430000
p_name, hour	22756000
s_name, hour	26001400
hour	32440000

EXPERIMENTAL EVALUATION

Experimental Design

The experiments mainly focus on measuring the processing time of the proposed stream OLAP, which consists of an SPE and an OLAP engine.

For the experiments, we used a commercial SPE μCosmi-nexus by Hitachi Ltd. Japan. Since the μCosmi-nexus does not contain an OLAP engine, we implemented a prototype OLAP engine from scratch in Java. The prototype engine can manage data buffers for registered queries, and generate OLAP query results for both registered and on-demand queries. The prototype engine is used to measure the query processing time.

The dataset used in the experiments is the reconstructed version of the TPC-H (2017) dataset, which is one of the benchmark database. For the reconstruction, we referred to the Patrick O'Neil's (2015) work In the experiments, the *lineorder* is used as the fact table which is the combination of two tables i.e., lineitem and order. The lineorder table is used as data stream in this work. Since the lineorder table contains 6,018 tuples, they are repeatedly fed to the SPE. We also include a time dimension table with hierarchy consisting of *minute* and *hour*. Moreover, *customer* and *supplier* tables are used as dimensions with hierarchy consisting of *nation* and *region* attributes. *Part* table is also used as a dimension table and has *mfgr*, *brand*, and *type* in its hierarchy. Figure 3 shows the star schema consisting of these dimension and fact tables. In order to evaluate the effectiveness of the proposed method, we compare it with the following two methods.

- **Random:** The registered queries are selected at random.
- **Frequency-Based:** The registered queries q_i selected depending upon their lookup frequencies. The following six ways are used to decide the frequency p_i of an OLAP query q_i.
- **Rand:** Frequencies are assigned at random to an OLAP query q_i, i.e., p_i is assigned a value in the range [0, 1] at random. (In the experiments, the unit time is *minute*, and $p_i = 1$ means the query result is looked up every minute.)
- **AllHigh:** High frequencies are assigned to all the OLAP queries, i.e., p_i is assigned a value in the range [0.8, 1] at random.
- **AllLow:** Low frequencies are assigned to all the OLAP queries, i.e., p_i is assigned a value in the range [0, 0.2] at random.
- **CoarseHigh:** Higher frequencies are assigned to the coarser granularity OLAP queries, i.e., $p_i = 1$ is assigned to the coarsest granularity OLAP query and the value of p_i is decreased gradually for the finer granularity OLAP queries in the lattice. The frequency is decreased by 0.01 when we move one level up in the lattice.
- **FineHigh:** Higher frequencies are assigned to the finer granularity OLAP queries, i.e., $p_i = 1$ is assigned to the root OLAP query and the value of p_i is decreased gradually for the coarser granularity OLAP queries in the lattice. The frequency is decreased by 0.01 when we move one level down in the lattice.
- **OneDimHigh:** The highest frequency is assigned to the root query. We then assign decreasing frequencies to vertices at coarser granularity levels except for one specific dimension.

The experiments are performed on an Intel(R) Core(TM) i7-3770 CPU with 32GB RAM running CentOS 6.5 (Linux 2.6.32-431.el6.x86 64) OS. For the experiments, we assume that $S_{max} = 1GB$, $C_S = 10,000$ and therefore the value of $C_O = 1$.

The stream OLAP was evaluated for 1 hour using the lineorder data stream, whose arrival rate is 500 tuples/s. In the experiments, following three cases of I (IoI) and S_{max} are used. Case 1: $I = 1$ hour and $S_{max} = 1$ GB are set for all queries, Case 2: $I = 4$ hours and $S_{max} = 1$ GB are set for all queries and Case 3: $I = 4$ hours and $S_{max} = 2$ GB are set for all queries.

Experimental Results

- **Case 1:** I = 60 is allocated to all OLAP queries.
- **Case 2:** I = 60 for the "minute" queries and I = 240 for the "hour" queries

Table 3 shows the number of registered queries for six frequency patterns discussed in Figures 6a and 6b compares the processing cost of the proposed method against the frequency-based and random methods. The x-axis represents the six frequency patterns, whereas the y-axis represents the total processing time

Table 3. Number of registered queries

		Rand	AllHigh	AllLow	CoarseHigh	FineHigh	OneDimHigh
case1	Proposed	13	13	12	16	10	10
	Frequency_based	25	20	20	40	16	10
	Random	27	27	30	35	29	32
case2	Proposed	4	4	4	4	3	3
	Frequency_based	8	4	4	14	2	2
	Random	5	12	4	2	6	3
case3	Proposed	7	9	7	10	5	5
	Frequency_based	14	8	8	24	6	3
	Random	14	12	8	10	6	13

Figure 6. Processing Time

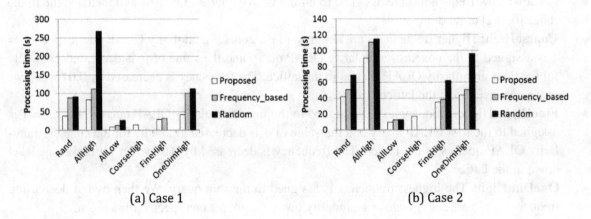

(a) Case 1 (b) Case 2

required for the update (insertions and deletions of tuples) of the data buffers for registered queries and the construction of aggregation results for on-demand queries. The white, gray and black bars are used to represent the proposed, frequency-based and random methods, respectively. The results prove that the query processing plans found by the proposed method are less expensive than the other methods, specially for the "All High" and "Coarse High" frequencies.

MEMORY EFFICIENT MULTIDIMENSIONAL ANALYSIS OF DATA STREAMS

With the increase of stream data sources, such as sensors, GPS, micro blogs, e-business, etc., the need to aggregate and analyze stream data is increasing. Many applications require instant decisions exploiting the latest information from the data streams. For instance, timely analysis of business data is required for improving profit, network packets need to be monitored in real time for identifying network attacks, etc. Online analytical processing (OLAP) is a well-known and useful approach to analyse data in a multi-dimensional fashion, initially given for disk-based static data (we call it *traditional OLAP*). For the effective OLAP analysis, the data is converted into a multi-dimensional schema, also known as star schema. The data in star schema is represented as a data cube, where each cube cell contains measure across multiple dimensions. A user may be interested in analysing data across different combination of dimensions or examining different views of it. These are often termed as OLAP operations and to support these operations, data is organized as lattice nodes.

A number of solutions have been proposed for OLAP analysis on data streams in the near past (Han et al, 2005; Duan et al, 2011; Sadoghi et al, 2016). The requirement to produce real time OLAP analysis on fast and evolving data streams is not possible unless the data to be analysed reside on primary memory. However the size of the primary memory is limited and it is volatile. Therefore we need an in-memory compact data structure that can quickly answer user queries in addition to a non-volatile backup of the data streams. This part of the chapter discusses our novel architecture *AOLAP* (Approximate Stream OLAP) proposed in (Shaikh et al, 2017), which in addition to storing raw data streams to the secondary storage, maintains data stream's summaries in a compact memory-based data structure. To maintain compact summaries, piece-wise linear approximation (PLA) data structure is used. PLA can store the long data streams' summaries in comparatively smaller space on the primary memory and can give approximate answers to OLAP queries. It provides an impressive data compression ratio and answers user queries with max error guarantees, and has been studied by many researchers (Elmeleegy et al, 2009; Xie et al, 2012; Lou et al, 2015; Wei et al, 2015).

PLA-Based Compact Storage

The PLA is a compact data structure and can be used for compact in-memory data summaries. The main idea of this work is to store time series data points as PLA line segments for all the OLAP lattice nodes that need to be materialized, to reduce the overhead of recording complete time-series. This work assumes that only the business facts arrive as time-series stream, while the dimensions are not treated as stream as they are updated less frequently.

Let S be a time-series data stream consisting of tuples $(t_i, k_{1i}, k_{2i}, ..., k_{di}, m_i)$, where t_i is a timestamp, $i \in [1, n]$ and $t_i \leq t_{i+1}$, $k_{1i}, k_{2i}, ..., k_{di}$ constitute a d-dimensional key and m_i is a business fact or measure. To keep the discussion simple, this work assumes that one tuple for every key combination arrives at each time-stamp, however it is easily extendible for the general case. Recall that PLA approximates data points using a piece-wise linear function, such that the error between the approximated and the actual data point is within the user-defined error parameter. For the data points in S, we wish to approximate m_i using a piece-wise linear function $f_{k1i}, ..., k_{di}(t_i)$, such that the $\left| f_{k_{1i}, ..., k_{di}}(t_i) - m_i \right| \leq \varepsilon$. The PLA needs to be maintained for each d-dimensional key. This work, like most of the previous work that discussed this problem in an online setting (Lazaridis et al, 2003; Olston et al, 2003; Elmeleegy et al, 2009; Lou et al, 2015) assumes L_∞-metric for the error computation. This is due to the fact that other error computations are not suitable for online algorithms as they require sum of errors over the entire time series.

The above approach would result in a compact PLA-based storage for each key. The number of line segments required for each PLA and the cost of a PLA line segment computation depend on the choice of error parameter . Larger would result in a smaller number of line segments but larger line segment computation cost and approximation error and vice versa. Also note that for multiple measures, multiple PLA structures need to be maintained per key.

ARCHITECTURE AND QUERY PROCESSING

AOLAP Architecture

This section presents the proposed Approximate Stream OLAP (AOLAP) architecture, shown in Figure 7, that enables users to obtain approximate answer of their OLAP queries. For each materialized node, the AOLAP system maintains a PLA structure discussed previously.

As the time series data arrive, the *Lattice Manager* calls the PLA algorithm (Algorithm 1) for each materialized node and update the corresponding PLA structures (hereafter materialized node is called *PLAV*). In Figure 7, lattice nodes within rectangular boundaries represents PLAVs. The node at the lowest granularity, i.e., the node (*Supplier, Part, Customer*) in the figure, is always materialized to enable the AOLAP system to answer all possible user queries. The raw data stream is also stored in some non-volatile storage to avoid permanent data loss in case of system failure and to enable users to obtain accurate answers of their queries if needed.

In contrast to data stream, primary memory is finite. Since the users are interested in analyzing recent data more frequently than the old or historical data, the *Storage Manager* flushes the old PLA segments to the secondary storage once they reach the memory limits or as specified by end user. These segments may be used to answer the historical queries to avoid computing the results from raw data stream, which is computationally expensive. Since the data is compact, this flushing may be done periodically rather than continuously or when the system is not overloaded by user queries. This also makes the system durable as in the case of system crash, the old segments are not permanently lost while the very new segments, not yet flushed to the secondary storage, can be reconstructed from the raw data stream available in the non-volatile storage.

Figure 7. AOLAP architecture

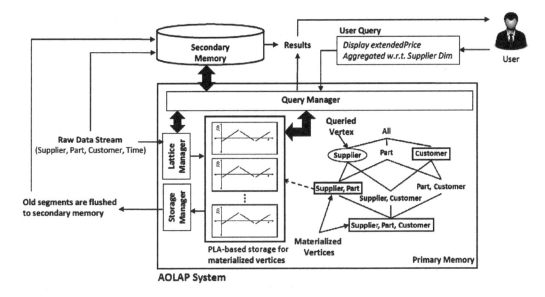

Query Processing

The *Query Manager* in the AOLAP architecture is responsible for accepting user queries, computing the results from the PLAVs and sending the results to the end user. Since a user can query any lattice node, the results are generated using the nearest PLAV to keep the querying error small. The *Lattice Manager*, on the request from *Query Manager*, generates the query results and sends them to the *Query Manager*. For example in Figure 7, the user query (*Supplier*), represented by oval boundary, can be answered using the PLAV (*Supplier, Part*).

OLAP queries over data streams generally involve aggregation operations over current, historical or some window data. Typical OLAP aggregation operations include SUM, MAX, MIN, AVG, etc. Users may also be interested in analyzing raw facts across multiple dimensions. To answer a historical window query for a key k or any combination of keys from d-dimensional key for time range $(t^0, t]$, find the re-

Table 4. Querying PLA

Timestamp (t_i)	m_i	$\hat{m_i}$	$m_i - \hat{m_i}$
t_1	48	41.8	6.2
t_2	43	51.6	-8.6
t_3	60	61.4	-1.4
t_4	75	71.2	3.8
t_5	35	30.67	4.33
t_6	52	60.67	-8.67
t_7	95	90.67	4.33

Table 5. OLAP operation on table 4 data

OLAP Operations	$m_{1,7}$	$\widehat{m_{1,7}}$
MAX	95	90.67
MIN	35	30.67
SUM	408	408.01
AVG	58.286	58.287

corded measures $\hat{}m_i$ for all $t_i \in (t^0, t]$ as an approximation of m_i and perform the requested aggregate operations to obtain $m[t0_{,t}$. Let the average length of a PLA line segment in terms of timestamp is l, then the cost of finding a measure $\hat{}m_i$ can be given by $\frac{n}{l}$, where n is the length of stream.

Querying Error

In a d-dimensional lattice, there exist 2^d nodes (Gray et al, 1997) Let $V = \{v_1, ... v_2 d\}$ denotes the set of all the lattice nodes. The overall querying error is computed by taking into consideration the set of nodes chosen for materialization (V_m) and the number of rows in each node ($|v_i|$). Since the number of rows in a node is not known beforehand, it is estimated using the domain size of dimension attributes.

Consider two nodes $v_i \in V$ and $v_j \in V_m$, then $v_i \preceq v_j$ shows the dependence relationship between the queried node (v_i) and the materialized node (v_j), that is, a query can be answered from a materialized node if the queried node is dependent on the materialized node. Since a query can be answered from more than one materialized nodes, we choose the nearest node which can minimize the fraction $\frac{|v_j|}{|v_i|}$, as the larger $\frac{|v_j|}{|v_i|}$ results in the amplification of the overall querying error. The overall querying error can be expressed as:

$$\sum_{v_i \in V} \min_{\forall v_j \in V_m | v_i \preceq v_j} \left(\frac{|v_j|}{|v_i|} \right) \tag{5}$$

Note that in the Eq. 5, the fraction $\frac{|v_j|}{|v_i|}$ depends on the number of rows in the materialized and the querying nodes. By choosing the smaller fraction we actually choose the node v_j with the smaller number of rows, that is, we need to aggregate a less number of rows to answer a query, resulting in smaller processing time and querying error as each row may contributes to the querying error.

EXPERIMENTS

Experimental Setup

- **Environment:** For the sake of experiments a prototype system corresponding the AOLAP architecture is developed in C++. The experiments are performed on one of the node of HP BladeSystem c7000 with Intel Xeon (ES-2650 v3 @ 2.3GHz) processor and 6 GB RAM running Ubuntu 14.10 OS.
- **Data:** We used TPC-H[1] benchmark for experiments, well-known for OLAP analysis. However its schema is modified according to the Star Schema Benchmark (SSB) (O'Neil et al, 2009) as shown in Figure 1a. The *LINEORDER* fact table contains 6,000,000 tuples and the dimension tables, *PART*, *CUSTOMER* and *SUPPLIER* contains 200,000, 30,000 and 2,000 tuples respectively. We considered the following dimensional hierarchies. *CUSTOMER*: Custkey − > Nation − > Region, *SUPPLIER*: Suppkey − > Nation − > Region, PART: PARTKEY, where NATION and REGION contain 25 and 5 unique tuples, respectively. The hierarchical lattice of the dimensions contain 32 nodes.

The time series is generated by identifying 10K unique dimension keys combinations in the *LINEORDER* fact table and feeding them repeatedly to the system. In order to avoid the repetition of fact values, we only fed the dimension keys repeatedly. The fact values are repeated after every 6,000,000 tuples (which is the size of the fact table) and are quite non-uniform. We selected this business fact to show the usability of the PLA on nonuniform data, as the PLA results in low compression ratio on non-uniform data while high compression ratio on uniform data. The system time is used as the time series timestamp.

Experimental Evaluation

Experimental evaluation is performed for measuring the memory space utilization. The evaluation is done for the worst case SUM operation, i.e., we aggregated the absolute querying error values. Unless otherwise stated, the following default parameter values are used in the experiments: $\eta = 6$ and $= 3\%$ (the value of is set as the percentage of the maximum value in the fact table). Each experiment is performed 5 times and their average values are reported in the graphs.

To evaluate the effectiveness of the PLA, we compared the memory space consumed when using PLA-based storage to that of ordinary storage (which stores the actual data points) in Figures 8 and 9. The storage space is measured in terms of the number of PLA segments for the PLA-based storage and the number of data points for the ordinary storage. Since a PLA segment requires twice memory space than a data point, we divided the total number of data points by a factor of 2 to keep the comparison fair.

The average amount of memory consumed by the PLA-based storage decreases with the increase in PLA error-parameter (ε), as can be observed from Figure 8. This is because as the increases, a PLA segment can approximate a larger number of data points thereby reducing the number of line segments required by the PLA-based storage, which results in reduced memory space consumption. In most of the cases in Figure 8, the memory space used by the PLA-based storage is up to 3 times less than the ordinary storage for $= 4\%$ and higher. This proves that the use of PLA for the materialization of lattice nodes can significantly reduce the memory consumption.

Figure 8. Average memory usage for different η

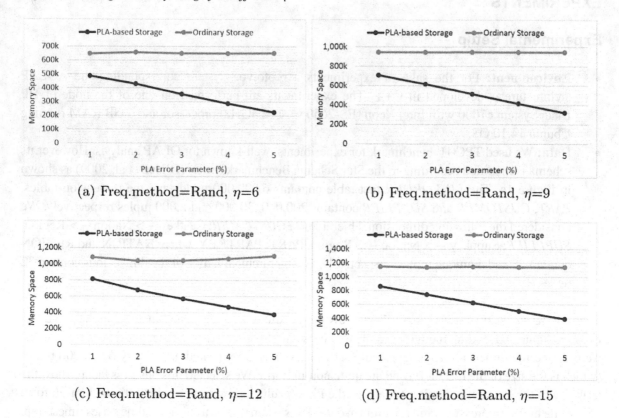

(a) Freq.method=Rand, $\eta=6$ (b) Freq.method=Rand, $\eta=9$

(c) Freq.method=Rand, $\eta=12$ (d) Freq.method=Rand, $\eta=15$

We also measured the memory space consumption by varying the number of materialized lattice nodes (η) as shown in Figure 9. As η increases, the memory space consumption of both the PLA-based storage and the ordinary storage increases because we need to store data at increased number of aggregations levels. However the memory consumption of the PLA based storage is lower than that of ordinary storage for all the η values. Note that we used highly non-uniform data values for the experiments, where it is difficult for the PLA algorithm to approximate the larger number of data points with one line segment. For the uniform time series data, for instance hourly temperature values or stock price data, the PLA-based storage is expected to be far more advantageous.

CONCLUSION AND FUTURE WORK

This chapter discussed the following two issues related to the OLAP/multidimensional analysis of data streams. 1) Coupling of Stream Processing Engine (SPE) and OLAP Engine, 2) Compact Data Structure for the Maintenance of Materialized Views.

In the first part of the chapter discusses Stream OLAP, which couples SPE and OLAP engine for the multidimensional analysis of point cloud. The SPE generates primitive aggregation results from continuous data streams, while the OLAP engine holds the aggregation results in memory to answer

Figure 9. Effect of varying η on space (Freq. method=Rand, $\varepsilon = 3\%$)

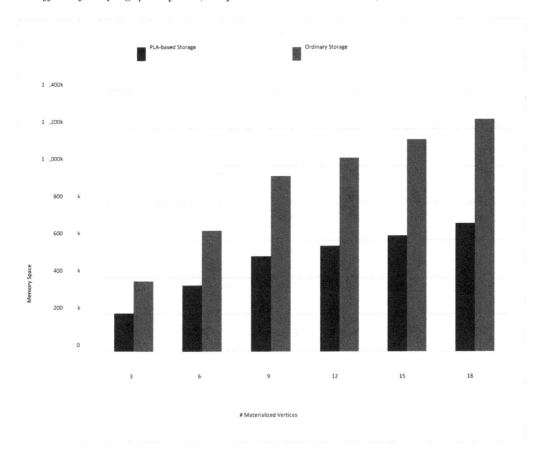

OLAP queries efficiently. The OLAP query results may be obtained either by materializing query results in cooperation with the SPE or by deriving them on-demand from materialized query results. For the stream OLAP, a cost-based optimization algorithm is also presented which decides how to obtain an OLAP query result. The algorithm tries to minimize the query processing cost by keeping in view the limits of memory cost. Experimental study proves that the Stream OLAP method is computationally less expensive than other methods including frequency-based and random methods. A main issue with work is that it requires large memory to hold the aggregation results from the SPE or when the IoI is long. To address this issue, we proposed an Approximate Stream OLAP (AOLAP).

AOLAP maintains time series data streams summaries, corresponding to each materialized lattice node, in a compact memory-based data structure, in addition to storing raw data streams to the secondary storage. For this sake *Piece-wise Linear Approximation* (PLA) is used as an in-memory compact data structure which can answer user queries approximately. Experiments prove that the PLA-based storage can significantly reduce the memory consumption. In future we plan to extend this work to incorporate dependence relation between lattice nodes so that the number of PLA structures need to be maintained can be reduced.

REFERENCES

Aouiche, K., & Darmont, J. (2009, August). Data mining-based materialized view and index selection in data warehouses. *Journal of Intelligent Information Systems*, *33*(1), 65–93. doi:10.100710844-009-0080-0

Arasu, A., Babcock, B., Babu, S., Cieslewicz, J., Datar, M., Ito, K., ... Widom, J. (2016). *STREAM: The Stanford Data Stream Management System*. Springer. doi:10.1007/978-3-540-28608-0_16

Arasu, A., Babu, S., & Widom, J. (2003). *The cql continuous query language: Semantic foundations and query execution. Technical Report*. Stanford InfoLab.

C. E.F. (1993). *Providing olap to user-analysts: An it mandate*. Codd and Date, Inc.

Cangialosi, F. J., Ahmad, Y., Balazinska, M., Cetintemel, U., Cherniack, M., Hwang, J.-H., ... Zdonik, S. (2005). The Design of the Borealis Stream Processing Engine. *Second Biennial Conference on Innovative Data Systems Research (CIDR 2005)*.

Cranor, C., Johnson, T., Spataschek, O., & Shkapenyuk, V. (2003). Gigascope: A stream database for network applications. In *Proceedings of the 2003 ACM SIGMOD International Conference on Management of Data* (pp. 647–651). ACM. 10.1145/872757.872838

De Rougemont, M., & Cao, P. T. (2012). Approximate answers to olap queries on streaming data warehouses. *Proceedings of the Fifteenth International Workshop on Data Warehousing and OLAP*, 121–128. 10.1145/2390045.2390065

Duan, Q., Wang, P., Wu, M., Wang, W., & Huang, S. (2011). *Approximate query on historical stream data*. DEXA.

Duan, Q., Wang, P., Wu, M., Wang, W., & Huang, S. (2011). *Approximate query on historical stream data*. DEXA. doi:10.1007/978-3-642-23091-2_12

Elmeleegy, H., Elmagarmid, A. K., Cecchet, E., Aref, W. G., & Zwaenepoel, W. (2009). Online piecewise linear approximation of numerical streams with precision guarantees. *Proc. VLDB Endow.*, *2*(1), 145–156. 10.14778/1687627.1687645

Garofalakis, M., & Kumar, A. (2004). Deterministic wavelet thresholding for maximum-error metrics. ACM PODS. doi:10.1145/1055558.1055582

Gray, J., Chaudhuri, S., Bosworth, A., Layman, A., Reichart, D., Venkatrao, M., ... Pirahesh, H. (1997). Data cube: A relational aggregation operator generalizing group-by, cross-tab, and sub-totals. *Data Mining and Knowledge Discovery*, *1*(1), 29–53. doi:10.1023/A:1009726021843

Han, J., Cai, Y. D., Chen, Y., Dong, G., Pei, J., Wah, B. W., & Wang, J. (2007). Multidimensional analysis of data streams using stream cubes. In *Data Streams* (pp. 103–125). Models and Algorithms. doi:10.1007/978-0-387-47534-9_6

Han, J., Chen, Y., Dong, G., Pei, J., Wah, B. W., Wang, J., & Cai, Y. D. (2005). Stream cube: An architecture for multi-dimensional analysis of data streams. *Distributed and Parallel Databases*, *18*(2), 173–197. doi:10.100710619-005-3296-1

Han, J., Chen, Y., Dong, G., Pei, J., Wah, B. W., Wang, J., & Cai, Y. D. (2005). Stream cube: An architecture for multi-dimensional analysis of data streams. *Distributed and Parallel Databases, 18*(2), 173–197. doi:10.100710619-005-3296-1

Harinarayan, V., Rajaraman, A., & Ullman, J. D. (1996). Implementing data cubes efficiently. ACM SIGMOD, 205–216. doi:10.1145/233269.233333

Joslyn, C., Burke, J., Critchlow, T., Hengartner, N., & Hogan, E. (2009). View discovery in olap databases through statistical combinatorial optimization. *International Conference, SSDBM, Proceedings*, 37–55. 10.1007/978-3-642-02279-1_4

Karras, P., & Mamoulis, N. (2005). *One-pass wavelet synopses for maximum-error metrics*. PVLDB.

Koch, C., Ahmad, Y., Kennedy, O., Nikolic, M., Nötzli, A., Lupei, D., & Shaikhha, A. (2014). Dbtoaster: Higher-order delta processing for dynamic, frequently fresh views. *The VLDB Journal, 23*(2), 253–278. doi:10.100700778-013-0348-4

Lazaridis, I., & Mehrotra, S. (2003). *Capturing sensor-generated time series with quality guarantees*. ICDE. doi:10.1109/ICDE.2003.1260811

Luo, G., Yi, K., Cheng, S. W., Li, Z., Fan, W., He, C., & Mu, Y. (2015). Piecewise linear approximation of streaming time series data with max-error guarantees. 2015 IEEE 31st ICDE, 173–184. doi:10.1109/ICDE.2015.7113282

Nakabasami, K., Amagasa, T., Shaikh, S. A., Gass, F., & Kitagawa, H. (2015). An architecture for stream olap exploiting spe and olap engine. IEEE BigData, 319–326. doi:10.1109/BigData.2015.7363771

Neumeyer, L., Robbins, B., Nair, A., & Kesari, A. (2010). S4: Distributed stream computing platform. *2010 IEEE International Conference on Data Mining Workshops*, 170–177. 10.1109/ICDMW.2010.172

O'Neil, P., O'Neil, E., Chen, X., & Revilak, S. (2009). *The star schema benchmark and augmented fact table indexing*. TPCTC. doi:10.1007/978-3-642-10424-4_17

O'Rourke, J. (1981). An on-line algorithm for fitting straight lines between data ranges. *Communications of the ACM, 24*(9), 574–578. doi:10.1145/358746.358758

Olston, C., Jiang, J., & Widom, J. (2003). Adaptive filters for continuous queries over distributed data streams. ACM SIGMOD, 563–574. doi:10.1145/872757.872825

Organization, T. (2017). *TPC-H - a Decision Support Benchmark*. Retrieved from http://www.tpc.org/tpch/

R. J. S. (2007). Pin: A partitioning & indexing optimization method for olap. *Proc. 9th International Conference on Enterprise Information Systems (ICEIS 2007)*.

Sadoghi, Bhattacherjee, Bhattacharjee, & Canim. (2016). L-store: A real-time OLTP and OLAP system. *CoRR*.

Shaikh, S. A., & Kitagawa, H. (2017). Approximate olap on sustained data streams. *International Conference on Database Systems for Advanced Applications*, 102–118. 10.1007/978-3-319-55699-4_7

Talebi, Z. A. a. (2008). *Exact and inexact methods for selecting views and indexes for olap performance improvement*. EDBT. doi:10.1145/1353343.1353383

Wei, Z., Luo, G., Yi, K., Du, X., & Wen, J.-R. (2015). Persistent data sketching. In *Proceedings of the 2015 ACM SIGMOD International Conference on Management of Data* (pp. 795–810). ACM. 10.1145/2723372.2749443

Wei, Z., Luo, G., Yi, K., Du, X., & Wen, J.-R. (2015). Persistent data sketching. ACM SIGMOD 2015, 795–810. doi:10.1145/2723372.2749443

Xie, Zhu, Sharaf, Zhou, & Pang. (2012). Efficient buffer management for piecewise linear representation of multiple data streams. ACM CIKM, 2114– 2118.

Yang, W. S., & Lee, W. S. (2008). On-line evaluation of a data cube over a data stream. *Proceedings of the 8th Conference on Applied Computer Scince*, 373–378.

Zhang, R., Koudas, N., Ooi, B. C., Srivastava, D., & Zhou, P. (2010). Streaming multiple aggregations using phantoms. *The VLDB Journal*, *19*(4), 557–583. doi:10.100700778-010-0180-z

ENDNOTE

[1]   TPC-H. http://www.tpc.org/tpch/

Chapter 10
Development of ETL Processes Using the Domain-Specific Modeling Approach

Marko Petrović
University of Belgrade, Serbia

Nina Turajlić
University of Belgrade, Serbia

Milica Vučković
University of Belgrade, Serbia

Sladjan Babarogić
University of Belgrade, Serbia

Nenad Aničić
University of Belgrade, Serbia

ABSTRACT

ETL process development is the most complex and expensive phase of data warehouse development so research is focused on its conceptualization and automation. A new solution (model-driven ETL approach – M-ETL-A), based on domain-specific modeling, is proposed for the formal specification of ETL processes and their implementation. Several domain-specific languages (DSLs) are introduced, each defining concepts relevant for a specific aspect of an ETL process (primarily, languages for specifying the data flow and the control flow). A specific platform (ETL-PL) technologically supports the modeling (using the DSLs) and automated transformation of models into the executable code of a specific application framework. ETL-PL development environment comprises tools for ETL process modeling (tools for defining the abstract and concrete DSL syntax and for creating models in accordance with the DSLs). ETL-PL execution environment consists of services responsible for the automatic generation of executable code from models and execution of the generated code.

DOI: 10.4018/978-1-5225-5516-2.ch010

INTRODUCTION

The aim of data warehouse systems, as a specific type of information system, is to provide the necessary support for decision-making in an increasingly competitive and demanding business environment. To this end they enable the collection of vast amounts of business data and provide the necessary tools for extracting business intelligence from the collected data. As stated in (*Jarke, Lenzerini, Vassiliou, & Vassiliadis, 2003*) such systems are expected to have the right information in the right place at the right time with the right cost in order to support the right decision.

Extract-Transform-Load (ETL) processes are at the core of data warehouse systems as they are responsible for the actual acquisition and integration of business data from a number of different sources, its transformation into strategic business information and the subsequent storage of the transformed data in a format that facilitates business analysis.

It is evident that the development of appropriate ETL processes, in light of the dynamics of modern business systems, faces a number of challenges. Namely, the sheer volume of business data that is to be rapidly gathered, processed, transformed, stored and delivered, imposes strict constraints regarding the performance and scalability of data warehouse systems. Moreover, the accumulated data must somehow be integrated, as it is gathered from diverse, usually very heterogeneous, data sources. Because the data sources may use various data models and be based on different technologies, a wide array of transformations must be performed to first resolve the potential structural and semantic conflicts and then translate such transformed data into a form suitable for its further analysis. On the other hand, the processes must also be agile and flexible so that they are able to easily respond to frequent changes in business requirements and constantly absorb new data sources (and allow for changes in the state and structure of existing data sources). A change in business requirements calls for new business analysis to be conducted, which in turn means that new strategic information must be provided. In other words, according to (*El Akkaoui, Mazón, Vaisman, & Zimányi, 2012*) agile and flexible ETL tools are needed which can quickly produce and modify executable code based on constantly changing needs of the dynamic business environment. It can, thus, be concluded that the development of ETL processes is extremely complex and time-consuming and that, consequently, it requires significant financial resources. Given that it has been estimated that as much as 70% of the time and effort invested in the development of data warehouses is spent on the development of ETL processes (*Kimball & Caserta, 2004; Kimball, Ross, Becker, Mundy, & Thornthwaite, 2010*) it is clear that an appropriate methodological approach to ETL process development has become imperative.

To date, research and practice have led to significant progress being made regarding the formalization and automation of data warehouse development. The methodological approaches, developed during the past couple of decades, are aimed at resolving some of the problems inherent to this process such as: high development and maintenance expenses, low productivity, failure to adequately satisfy user requirements, etc. These issues emanate from the nature of the modern business systems that are to be automated by software solutions. Today's business environment is characterized by rapid organizational and technological changes, and modern business systems are becoming increasingly complex. Furthermore, in light of the pervasiveness of the Internet and the transition to e-business there is a growing need for business integration. It is, thus, evident that the main issues that must be dealt with when developing modern software systems are: overcoming complexity, attaining adaptability to frequent changes and enforcing the interoperability of heterogeneous distributed software systems.

Consequently, the main premise of the presented solution is that ETL process development must be based on abstractions as they are the only valid methodological means for overcoming complexity. Moreover, it is argued that semantically richer abstractions are desired because they can encapsulate greater knowledge thereby increasing productivity and efficiency (*Greenfield, Short, Cook, & Kent, 2004; Kelly & Tolvanen, 2008*). Furthermore, since a greater level of automation is sought, it is necessary to formalize the existing knowledge and experience in such a form that would allow for its reuse (*Greenfield et al., 2004; Kelly & Tolvanen, 2008*). The possibility of reuse additionally increases productivity and efficiency, while at the same time lowering the cost of data warehouse system development. By elevating the semantic level and supporting it technologically development can be significantly automated and fewer steps will be needed to implement the abstract specifications.

A novel approach to ETL process development (Model-driven ETL Approach – *M-ETL-A*) is presented in this chapter. *M-ETL-A* is a research project, conducted at the Faculty of organizational sciences, University of Belgrade. The results of this research project focusing of the implementation details are presented in (*Petrović et al., 2017*). This chapter represents an in-depth, comprehensive, review of the whole solution and includes the details related to the conceptualization aspect.

The aim of the proposed solution is to automate the development to a significant extent. Hence, it was developed in accordance with the leading approach to software development today – Model-Driven Development (MDD). The main goal of MDD is to enable the automation of software development in order to increase development productivity, reduce development time and cost, and improve the quality and flexibility of the obtained solution. To this end it promotes the use of abstractions which enable the analysis of a problem at different levels of detail. MDD is based on the premise that the most important product of software development is not the source code itself but rather the models representing the knowledge about the system that is being developed. In other words, in MDD, models are primary software artifacts and the development process is automated through appropriate model transformations, which should ultimately result in a concrete implementation i.e., executable code. In light of the complexity of ETL processes and the problems related to their development it can be stipulated that they should be developed in accordance with the MDD approach.

More specifically, the Domain-Specific Modeling (DSM) approach has been chosen for the development of ETL process in *M-ETL-A*. Given that DSM introduces models as primary software artifacts it promotes the use of abstractions. Furthermore, in the DSM approach, software development can be fully automated through the application of model transformations (*Kelly & Tolvanen, 2008*). In order to enable such automatic transformations the models must be formal. Thus, the DSM approach has been adopted not only because it allows for the formalization of semantically rich abstractions, in a form which can be reused, but also because it enables the generation of executable code from models representing the specification of the system.

The proposed solution, for the development of ETL processes in the context of a DSM approach, is based on the formal specification of ETL processes and the implementation of such formal specifications. Several new domain-specific languages (DSLs) are introduced, for the formal specification (i.e., modeling) of ETL processes, which define concepts relevant for different aspects of this particular domain. In order to reduce the complexity of the ETL process specification the different aspects of an ETL process would be modeled separately using the appropriate DSLs.

The abstract syntax, concrete syntax and semantics are defined for each of the proposed ETL DSLs. The language models of the abstract syntax are defined by metamodels describing the specific concepts of a particular aspect of an ETL process. In addition, semantic rules are assigned to the defined concepts so that the utilization of these concepts is semantically controlled. The concrete syntax of the proposed ETL DSLs provides graphical elements for representing the concepts defined in the corresponding language models, which are then used in the ETL modeling phase for creating model diagrams.

A specific ETL platform (ETL-PL) has been developed to technologically support both the specification (i.e., creation of models using the graphical or textual notation of the introduced DSLs) and the automated transformation of these models into the executable code of a specific application framework (representing the execution environment of an ETL process). The application framework defines specific implementation concepts which are close to the real domain concepts of the DSLs introduced for the specification of ETL processes. By defining implementation concepts which are close to the real domain concepts the semantic level of the solution is significantly elevated. Furthermore, if both the specification and the application framework use concepts close to the real ETL domain concepts the transformation between them can be fully automated, thus significantly increasing development productivity and efficiency while lowering the development and maintenance costs. In other words, by elevating the semantic level, and supporting it technologically, development can be significantly automated and fewer steps will be needed to implement the abstract specifications. Moreover, the obtained solutions would have good performances and be scalable and maintainable yet, at the same time, flexible (i.e., they could be easily extended to adapt to the constant changes in the environment and new requirements).

The proposed software architecture for implementing ETL-PL is presented, specifying the main components of ETL-PL. The components of ETL-PL are divided into two layers: the development environment and the execution environment.

The development environment is comprised of tools which support the modeling of ETL processes. More specifically, it contains tools for defining the abstract and concrete syntax (in both a graphical and textual notation) of a DSL and tools (syntax editors, graphical and textual) for creating models in accordance with the defined DSL.

The execution environment is responsible for the automatic generation of executable code from the models as well as the actual execution of the generated code. Thus the execution environment consists of code generator components and the components implementing the application framework.

The remainder of the chapter is structured as follows: the *Background* section gives an analysis of the related work on ETL process development. The *Conceptualization* section gives an overview of the conceptual framework for the formal specification of ETL processes. The ETL DSLs are elaborated in the *ETL Process Specification* section. The *ETL Process Modeling* section demonstrates the utilization of the introduced ETL DSLs and provides an illustrative example. The *Automation* section is devoted to the implementation details. The *Requirements* section explains the motivation behind the proposed implementation of ETL process specifications. The proposed ETL platform is outlined in the *ETL Platform* section and the implementation details are presented in the *ETL Platform Implementation* section. Finally, future research opportunities are discussed and a conclusion is given.

The aim of the proposed *M-ETL-A* solution is to formalize and automate the development of ETL processes to a significant extent. *M-ETL-A* it is based on semantically rich abstractions (encapsulating the existing knowledge and experience in the ETL domain in a form which can be reused) which are used for specifying, visualizing, and documenting ETL processes. Furthermore, it enables the automatic generation of executable code from models representing specifications of ETL processes.

BACKGROUND

There is a growing need for the formalization and automation of ETL process development, due to the fact that it is extremely complex and time-consuming and that it requires significant financial resources, and a good deal of research effort has thus far been dedicated to this issue. A detailed analysis of these approaches can be found in a previous paper (*Turajlić, Petrović, & Vučković, 2014*), and only a brief discussion will be presented here in order to justify the proposed approach.

It should first be emphasized that only a few approaches exist which enable the automated development of ETL processes in the context of MDD. In order to enable automated development, MDD requires that the models be formally expressed. Thus far, two distinctive approaches have emerged for realizing MDD in general, which differ primarily in the languages used for the specification of the models. One advocates the use of general purpose modeling languages (GPMLs) and their extension, while the other advocates the use of specially designed domain-specific languages (DSLs). The existing body of research on ETL process development could be classified along the same lines.

The modeling of ETL processes using existing general purpose modeling languages (such as Unified Modeling Language – UML or Business Process Model and Notation – BPMN), which have been extended to incorporate the concepts specific to the ETL process domain, has been proposed in (*Trujillo & Luján-Mora, 2003; Luján-Mora, Vassiliadis, & Trujillo, 2004; Muñoz, Mazón, Pardillo, & Trujillo, 2008; Muñoz, Mazón, & Trujillo, 2009; El Akkaoui & Zimányi, 2009; El Akkaoui, Zimányi, Mazón, & Trujillo, 2011; El Akkaoui et al., 2012*).At the same time, the use of DSLs which are tailored to a particular domain has also been proposed in (*Vassiliadis, Simitsis, & Skiadopoulos, 2002a; Vassiliadis, Simitsis, & Skiadopoulos, 2002b; Vassiliadis, Simitsis, Georgantas, & Terrovitis, 2003; Simitsis & Vassiliadis, 2003; Vassiliadis, Simitsis, Georgantas, Terrovitis, & Skiadopoulos, 2005; Simitsis, Vassiliadis, Terrovitis, & Skiadopoulos, 2005; Simitsis, 2005; Simitsis & Vassiliadis, 2008*).

It can be argued that, since GPMLs were envisaged to support the description of the various aspects of any given business process in any given domain (in order to promote standardization), they include a large number of domain-neutral concepts which are defined at a low level of abstraction. According to (*Kelly & Tolvanen, 2008*) GPMLs do not raise the level of abstraction above code concepts. According to the same authors, the main benefit of DSLs is that, unlike GPMLs, they raise the level of abstraction beyond current programming languages and their abstractions, by specifying the solution in a language that directly uses the concepts and rules from a particular problem domain. Furthermore, the complexity of GPMLs (i.e., too many concepts whose semantics are imprecise) along with the fact that they are often too technical for domain-experts to master, lead to a number of issues related to the acceptance, utilization and value of these languages. Moreover, to extend these languages it is necessary to be familiar with their concepts in order to be able to identify those which can be specialized. Finally, it is up to the designer to know the semantic rules (e.g., the legal connections and structures, the necessary data etc.) and ensure that they are fulfilled when defining the specification. On the other hand, the aim of DSLs is to provide only a minimal set of domain-specific concepts, with clear and precise semantics, along with a set of strict rules controlling their usage and the way in which they can be composed. Since DSLs allow for the inclusion of domain rules (in the form of constraints) both the syntax and the semantics of the concepts can be controlled, thus incorrect or incomplete designs can be prevented by making them impossible to specify.

Therefore, in comparison with GPMLs, DSLs are more expressive (i.e., they enable a precise and unambiguous specification of the problem) while at the same time being more understandable and easier to use by domain experts (since they do not include unnecessary general purpose concepts). In addition, the use of such languages facilitates communication among the various stakeholders (from both the business as well as the technical communities) thereby promoting teamwork which is one of the main principles of current agile approaches to software development.

As a final point it should be noted that some of the approaches do not provide explicit concepts which allow for the formal definition of the semantics of the data transformations. For example, in (*Vassiliadis et al., 2002b; Simitsis & Vassiliadis, 2003; Luján-Mora & Trujillo, 2004*) notes or annotations are used for the explanation of the semantics of the transformations (e.g., type, expression, conditions, constrains etc.), while in (*Trujillo & Luján-Mora, 2003*) even the actual attribute mappings are defined through notes. Since in these approaches the authors allow for the notes to be given in a natural language (and often without any restrictions on their content) they do not represent a formal specification.

However, in order to enable automated development, it is necessary to provide the means for formally specifying the data transformation semantics, and the approaches proposed in (*Muñoz et al., 2008; El Akkaoui & Zimányi, 2009; El Akkaoui et al., 2011; El Akkaoui et al., 2012*) have, to some extent, addressed this issue.

The way in which the actual automation of software development is achieved (Model-Driven Architecture - MDA or Domain-Specific Modeling - DSM) is another point of difference between the general purpose approach and the domain-specific approach. Generally, in order to enable the automation of the development in accordance with MDD, it is necessary to first map the domain concepts to design concepts and then on to programming language concepts.

In the MDA approach, software development can be partially or fully automated through the successive application of model transformations, starting from the model representing the specification of the system (i.e., the conceptual model) and ending in a model representing the detailed description of the physical realization, from which the executable code can ultimately be generated. The development of ETL processes in accordance with the MDA approach is proposed in (*Muñoz et al., 2008; Mazón & Trujillo, 2008*). Thus, the conceptual models are defined as platform independent models – PIM which are then automatically transformed into platform specific models – PSM (through a set of formally defined transformations) from which the code (necessary to create data structures for the ETL process in the corresponding platform) can be derived. However, since the PSMs must be specially designed for a certain technology of ETL processes (i.e., each PSM must be based on the resources of a specific technology) the proposed approach presumes that a metamodel must be manually defined for each specific tool in order to create the transformations from the proposed conceptual model to each deployment platform. Furthermore, the MDA approach in general, is based on the refinement of models through successive model transformations, yet this process usually also requires that the automatically generated models be manually extended with additional details. These manual extensions could lead to a discrepancy between the original and generated models (i.e., the original models would become obsolete). This discrepancy is further emphasized when the modification of models, previously created by partial generation, is required. Since the correct modification of these models remains an unresolved issue, MDA advocates using a single GPML, namely UML, at all the levels (thereby lowering the abstraction levels of models) which not only entails all of the previously discussed issues regarding the use of GPMLs for modeling ETL processes, but also brings additional complexity to the development of model transformations (*Fowler, 2010*). Thus, an improvement of the proposed approach has been suggested in (*El Akkaoui et al., 2011*) to directly obtain the code corresponding to the target platform, bypassing the need for the defining of an intermediate representation (metamodel) of the target tool. The conceptual model can then be automatically transformed into the required vendor-specific code to execute the ETL process on a concrete platform.

Conversely, in the DSM approach the implementation is automatically generated from the specification (which can be modeled using domain-specific concepts) by code generators which specify how the information is extracted from the models and transformed into code. In other words, the generator reads the model based on the metamodel of the language and maps it to code. The generators are also domain-specific (i.e., they produce the code according to the solution domain) since, according to (*Kelly & Tolvanen, 2008*), this is the only way to enable full code generation i.e., the generation of code that does not need to be additionally modified. Usually the code generation is further supported by a domain-specific framework which provides implementation concepts, closer to the domain concepts used in the specification, thus narrowing the gap between the solution domain and the problem domain that would otherwise need to be handled by the code generator. The main benefit of DSM according to (*Kelly & Tolvanen, 2008*) is that generators, along with framework code, provide an automated direct mapping to a lower abstraction level (i.e., there is no need to make error-prone mappings from domain concepts to design concepts and on to programming language concepts) thus providing full code generation instead of resulting in a partial implementation. Because the generated code can be compiled to a finished executable without any additional manual effort, the specification (i.e., model) in fact becomes truly executable.

In summary, it can be concluded that, if the goal is to formalize and automate the development of ETL processes to a significant extent, the DSM approach should be adopted not only, because it allows for the formalization of semantically rich abstractions in a form which can be reused, but also because it enables the automatic generation of executable code from models representing the specification of the system. More precisely put, since DSLs allow for the formalization of semantically rich abstractions (which capture the existing knowledge and experience in the ETL domain) they are more appropriate for the formal specification of ETL processes.

On the other hand, the modeling concepts of GPMLs do not relate to any specific problem domain on the modeling side while on the implementation side, they do not relate to any particular software platform, framework, or component library. However, it is argued that the application framework (supporting the implementation of the ETL process specification in the DSM approach) should define specific implementation concepts which are more close to the real domain concepts introduced in the DSLs used for the specification of ETL processes. If both the specification and the application framework use formal concepts close to the real ETL domain concepts the transformation between them can be fully automated. Furthermore, MDA assumes the existence of several models at different levels of abstraction obtained through progressive refinement (which can be both automatic and manual) thus automation is usually only partially achieved. An additional benefit of the DSM approach is that, both the models and the code generators, can be easily changed (and the code then only needs to be regenerated) which makes the development process more agile. As a final point, according to (*Kelly & Tolvanen, 2008*) domain-specific approaches are reported to be on average 300–1000% more productive than GPMLs or manual coding practices.

The approach, closest to fulfilling all of the posed requirements, is proposed in (*El Akkaoui & Zimányi, 2009; El Akkaoui et al., 2011; El Akkaoui et al., 2012*) in which the authors have even provided built-in mechanisms to validate the syntactic and semantic correctness of the created models. However it is based on the use of a single modeling language which is built by extending a general purpose modeling language, namely BPMN.

Finally, it should be noted, that there is a large number of commercial ETL tools (e.g., Microsoft SQL Server Integration Services, Oracle Data Warehouse Builder, Pentaho Data Integration, etc.) offered by both ETL vendors and Database vendors, and the main rationale for purchasing such a tool is to minimize the development and deployment time and, consequently, development costs. Yet one of the major drawbacks of vendor ETL tools is their extremely high price. Even when it is possible to buy only some of the necessary components of a tool at a smaller price, or even obtain the tool for free (usually from Database vendors as part of a DBMS license) it, almost always, entails some further expenses such as: extra charges for running the tool on a different platform or even on additional CPUs; buying other necessary components; support and maintenance costs; additional fees for providing training, documentation, etc. Furthermore, it takes a significant amount of time for developers to become proficient with the acquired tool even when they are skilled programmers. As stated in (*El Akkaoui & Zimányi, 2009*) each one of these tools provides its own language which often involves implementation level considerations hence they are difficult to understand, optimize, and maintain. Another crucial limitation of most vendor ETL tools is that they do not offer adequate support for complex custom transformations. Since the proprietary source code is rarely available modifications and extensions cannot be easily made. Even if the code is made available, its modification or extension requires significant technical knowledge. Moreover, it is also necessary to ensure that the alterations do not affect the existing functionality. In order to be competitive the vendors constantly improve their tools, and new versions of the tools are deployed. However, this can also present a liability, since it is a question whether the previously implemented functionality will be compatible with the new version. Furthermore, vendors can cease to provide support for previous versions of a tool, or even go out of business.

CONCEPTUALIZATION

One of the most important and demanding phases in the data warehouse development process is the development of the process for transforming the business data into strategic information i.e., the ETL process. An ETL process is comprised of a number of activities which are to be executed in a particular order with the aim of transforming business data into strategic information. The activities in this process represent the actual data operations (i.e., the data flow), while the control flow represents the execution order of these activities.

In *M-ETL-A* the DSM approach has been adopted for the development of ETL process because the aim of the proposed solution is to automate the development to a significant extent and DSM, as discussed in previous section, enables the generation of executable code from models representing the specification of the system. Furthermore, the main premise is that ETL development must be based on semantically rich abstractions which encapsulate the existing knowledge and experience in the ETL domain and DSM allows for the formalization of such abstractions in a form which can be reused.

The first phase in ETL process development is the specification of ETL models. The main goal of this phase is to define "what" the software solution should provide in terms of its basic functionality. Several points where taken into consideration regarding the manner in which the specification should be given. Firstly, since domain experts play a key role in this phase (as they possess an in-depth understanding of the domain i.e., the semantics of the data that is to be transformed) the models should be expressed in terms of concepts specific to the particular domain (i.e., the concepts and terms used by the domain experts). Secondly, the modeling languages should be as simple as possible (i.e., they should provide a minimal set of necessary concepts), but at the same time semantically rich to enable the specification of the various aspects of the problem domain at the appropriate level of abstraction. Thirdly, they should be formal in order to enable automatic model transformations. Thus, for the formal specification of ETL processes, the use of DSLs is preferred over the extension of GPMLs, since they provide only a minimal set of semantically rich domain-specific concepts, which makes them more approachable to domain experts.

Furthermore, taking into account the complexity of ETL processes, it is obvious that the various aspects of an ETL process (e.g., the control flow, the data flow, etc.) should be modeled separately else the specification would lead to an overly complex, convoluted model, in which all of the various aspects of an ETL process are interwoven. However, it can be argued that the use of a single modeling language (be it an extended GPML or a DSL) would not be conducive since it would include a vast amount of disparate concepts and would thus be fairly complicated to use. It is therefore stipulated that each aspect of an ETL process should be modeled by a separate language, which should include only the concepts which are relevant for that particular aspect, thereby keeping the languages straightforward and easy to use. These languages would then constitute a conceptual framework for ETL process specification.

The introduced conceptual framework for ETL process specification defines several novel DSLs for the specification of the different aspects of ETL processes. Primarily, a language for the specification of data operations, i.e., the data flow, (ETL-O) and a language for specification of their execution order, i.e., the control flow, (ETL-P). ETL-D is a language for the specification of source and target data models (which has been simplified for reasons which will be elaborated in the following section). Two supplementary languages are also provided: a language for the specification of various logical and arithmetic expressions (ETL-E), a language for the specification of transformation operation templates (ETL-T). The introduced DSLs define concepts which are relevant for the respective aspects of the ETL processes and they fulfill all of the previously stated requirements regarding modeling languages. Moreover, they are developed as new languages rather than as extensions of generic modeling languages (such as BPMN and UML) which, in light of the discussion in the previous section, makes them extremely appropriate for solving problems in the given domain.

As a final point, it should be noted that, though these ETL DSLs do not constitute a complete set of languages necessary for the specification of every aspect of the ETL process domain, this set could be easily extended to include new languages (Figure 1). Furthermore, the languages themselves were also envisaged to be easily extensible through specialization.

The conceptual framework defining the fundamental concepts of ETL processes and their relationships is given in Figure 2. Only a brief explanation of the conceptual framework is given here, while the elements of the conceptual model are elaborated in the following section. Namely, the *ETL Base* metamodel introduces the set of abstract concepts, which enable the integration of the various ETL modeling languages. The proposed ETL DSLs are defined as extensions of this abstract metamodel, while dependencies also exist between the various DSLs. The metamodels of the introduced DSLs are described using the concepts of a meta meta-language defined by *Microsoft* (as part of *DSL Tools*) and the validity of the DSL metamodels is verified against this meta-language (indicated by the <<*conforms to*>> relationship). Likewise, concrete ETL models are validated against the DSL metamodels (describing these concrete models).

Figure 1. M-ETL-A domain modeling languages

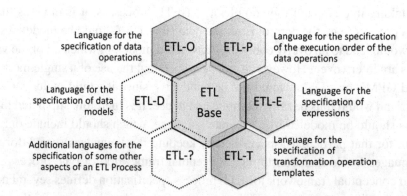

Figure 2. Conceptual M-ETL-A framework

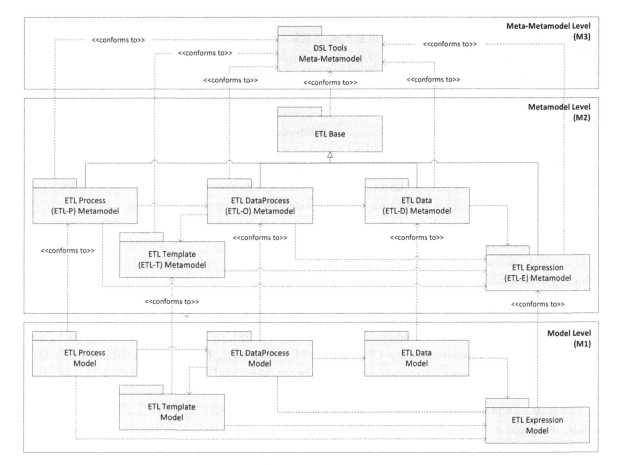

ETL Process Specification

The conceptual ETL framework, presented in the previous section, introduces several ETL modeling languages:

- **ETL-P** defines the fundamental concepts for specifying the execution semantics (i.e., the control flow) of an ETL process;
- **ETL-O** defines the fundamental concepts for defining the semantics of the data operations and the order in which they are to be executed (i.e., the data flows of an ETL process);
- **ETL-E** allows for the formal specification of the semantics of the data operations and the various conditions and restrictions pertaining to the execution of an ETL process;
- **ETL-T** enables the creation of new field transformation operations, in the form of templates which can be reused;
- **ETL-D** provides a uniform representation of the various data models involved in the transformations (either as their inputs or the results of their execution).

In order to define a formal modeling language it is necessary to define its abstract syntax, concrete syntax and semantics. The abstract syntax (metamodel) defines the modeling concepts and their relationships, as well as a set of clear and precise semantic rules determining their proper usage. The concrete syntax provides a visual representation of the modeling language, in a graphical or textual notation.

The specification of the abstract syntax, as a language model, is based on a metamodel that defines specific concepts necessary for modeling a particular DSL. Yet the introduction of several ETL modeling languages, instead of just one, led to the issue of their integration. Hence, first a set of abstract concepts necessary for defining ETL modeling languages is introduced (*ETL Base* metamodel, Figure 2).

The *ETL Base* metamodel introduces the set of abstract concepts which enable the integration of the various ETL modeling languages. The proposed ETL DSLs are then defined as extensions of this abstract metamodel. In other words, each of the proposed DSLs introduces its own concepts (the concepts relevant for the particular aspect which is to be modeled) by extending the base concepts. The metamodel of the base classes for all of the proposed DSLs is given in Figure 3. The abstract concepts of this metamodel are used for specifying the ETL DSL models (the *Model* concept) and their elements (the *ModelElement* concept), as well as for referencing other models (the *ModelRef* concept) and the elements of those models (the *ModelElementRef* concept) in order to track the dependencies (relationships) among various models, wherein the definition of a particular model uses certain definitions given in another model.

As mentioned in the previous section, the metamodels of the introduced DSLs are described using the concepts of a meta-language defined by *Microsoft* (as part of *DSL Tools*) which has thus, as such, been incorporated into the implementation of the proposed ETL platform. Therefore, the validity of the DSL metamodels is verified against this meta-language. On the other hand, the DSL metamodels, describing concrete models, are used for validating the concrete models.

The abstract and concrete syntaxes of the proposed ETL DSLs (ETL-P, ETL-O, ETL-E and ELT-E) will be presented in the remainder of this section.

As an aside, one final remark is given regarding ETL-D. Namely, in order to reconcile the heterogeneity of different data sources, the various local schemata (describing these heterogeneous data sources) must be transformed into equivalent schemata which are uniformly described using the concepts of a consolidated model. However, the problem of designing the consolidated model (with the aim of reconciling the heterogeneity of the different data sources and representing their concepts in a uniform manner) is very complex and is handled in the analysis phase of the data warehouse development process. Nevertheless, ETL-D has been included in order to give a comprehensive overview of the proposed conceptual

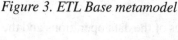

Figure 3. ETL Base metamodel

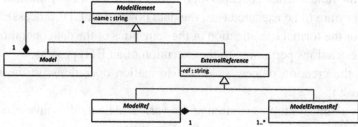

framework (and also because the development and implementation of the proposed solution demands the existence of such a language). Consequently, it will not be further elaborated and a simplified ETL-D metamodel (containing the concept of *Entities* described by *Fields* representing both the atomic and the relationship properties of the entity) is utilized the remainder of this chapter and it is assumed that all of the concrete data models conform to this metamodel. An ETL-D model and its elements will be referenced in other ETL models via *DataModelRef* and *EntityRef* or *FieldRef*.

A Language for Control Flow Specification (ETL-P)

An *ETL process* is comprised of a number of activities which are to be executed in a particular order with the aim of transforming business data into strategic information. The activities in this process represent the actual data transformation operations (which are specified using ETL-O), while the execution order of the activities is specified using ETL-P. In other words ETL-P introduces the fundamental concepts necessary for defining the execution semantics of an ETL process (i.e., the control flow).

Abstract Syntax

The abstract syntax of ETL-P, defined by a metadmodel in the form of a UML class diagram, is given in Figure 4.

The *ETLProcessModel* and *ETLProcessModelElement* are the core classes of ETL-P. The abstract *ExecutableElement* concept is introduced for the specification of the functionality of an ETL process. This abstract class is specialized by the *ETLProcess* and *Activity* classes. The *ETLProcess* class is introduced to represent the control flow of the particular ETL process which is being modeled while the

Figure 4. ETL-P metamodel

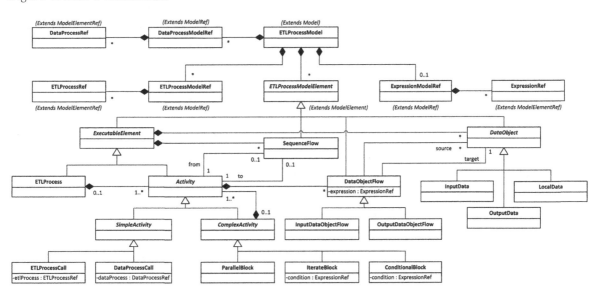

Activity class represents the actual tasks it comprises (depicted by the composition relationship between the *ETLProcess* and *Activity* classes).

The activities can be *SimpleActivities*, such as *ETLProcessCall* and *DataProcessCall* which enable the invocation of other ETL processes (defined in separate ETL-P models and referenced via *ETLProcessRef*) and data processes (defined in separate ETL-O models and referenced via *DataProcessRef*), respectively, or *ComplexActivities* composed of other activities (simple and/or complex).

For specifying the execution order of activities, three concepts are provided representing the basic control structures (i.e., *SequenceFlow*, *ConditionalBlock* and *IterateBlock*). *ConditionalBlock* and *IterateBlock* are derived from the *ComplexActivity* class, thus they can contain other activities (simple and/or complex). An additional concept, the *ParallelBlock*, representing the concurrent execution of activities, is introduced to provide the possibility for optimizing the process execution. The execution semantics of the overall ETL process can be represented through the hierarchical composition of these concepts. Furthermore, the *ExpressionRef* class is used for representing the various conditions (i.e., ETL-E logical expressions) of the activites for example the *IterateBlock* and *ConditionalBlock* conditions.

The *DataObject* class and its specializations *InputData*, *OutputData* and *LocalData* are used for representing the inputs and outputs of the activities, as well as the process and complex activity states.

Finally, the *DataObjectFlow* concept is introduced for specifying the flow of process data between activities (the term "process data", denoting the data necessary for the execution of an ETL process, should be distinguished from the actual data that is being transformed). This abstract class is further specialized into the *InputDataObjectFlow* and *OutputDataObjectFlow* classes to clearly separate the inputs and outputs of an activity. An activity can have multiple input and/or output arguments. In order for the execution of an activity to commence all of the input arguments must be provided, thus an *InputDataObjectFlow* must be defined for each of the input arguments. Likewise, the *OutputDataFlow*s must be defined in order to store the output data once the execution of the activity has terminated. As depicted in the metamodel two additional associations are defined (between the *DataObject* and *DataObjectFlow* classes) in order to specify the *source* and the *target* of the process data flow. The cardinalities of these associations indicate that though each *DataObjectFlow* must have at least one source, it can have only one target. If it is necessary to transform the data on its way from the source to the target, the specification can be further enriched by including the relevant transformations. It should be emphasized that such transformations are mandatory if a process data flow has multiple sources. The necessary transformations would then be specified using ETL-E and referenced via the *ExpressionRef* class.

The *DataProcessModelRef* and *DataProcessRef* classes represent a mechanism for referencing the models and model elements, respectively, representing the actual ETL-O data process models. The *ETLProcessModelRef* and *ETLProcessRef* classes enable the referencing of ETL process models. The expressions for specifying the conditions and constraints, pertaining to the execution of an ETL process, are given in the form of ETL-E expressions (defined in a separate ETL-E model and referenced via *ExpressionModelRef* and *ExpressionRef*).

Concrete Syntax

A graphical notation is adopted for the representation of ETL-P concepts. The graphical element for representing a *SimpleActivity* is the rounded corner rectangle shown in Figure 5-a. The central part of the element contains the *name of the activity*, with its *type* in the upper left corner. The corresponding *activity symbol* (distinguishing the type of the simple activity) is also included and positioned in the upper right corner. Furthermore, an integral part of the graphical element is the symbol for representing the arguments (*InputData* and *OutputData* concepts), i.e., a small square positioned on the outer edge of the rectangle, wherein a white square indicates an input argument and a black square – an output argument. The *activity input argument name* and *activity output argument name* may be omitted.

A *Complex Activity* is represented by the graphical element given in Figure 5-b, i.e., a rounded corner rectangle drawn with a dashed line. The name of the concept that is being represented (the *activity type name*) is given in the upper left corner, while the upper right corner contains the *complex activity symbol*. The central part of the graphical element (i.e., *Child activities*) encloses the graphical elements representing the required activities.

The *SequenceFlow* concept is represented by a solid directed line, while *input data flows* and *output data flows* are represented using dashed directed lines with a circle in the middle (where a filled-in circle indicates that a transformation has been defined), as shown in Figure 5-c.

Figure 5. ETL-P graphical notation

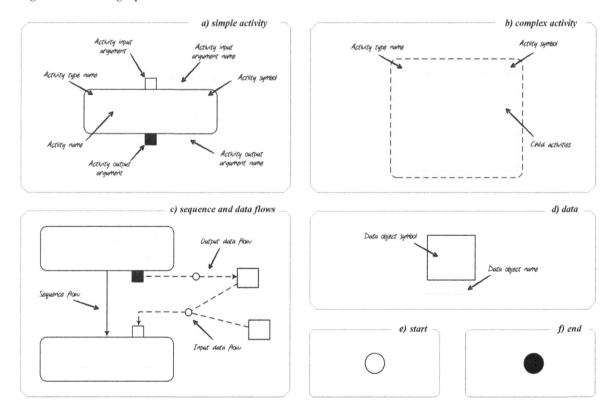

The graphical element, a square (as depicted in Figure 5-d) represents a *DataObject*. The *data object symbol* is located inside the graphical element, while the *data object name* is positioned beneath it.

The symbols in Figure 5-e and 5-f, are used for indicating the start and end of the process, respectively.

A Language for Data Flow Specification (ETL-O)

ETL-O defines the fundamental concepts necessary for the specification of ETL process activities (*DataProcesses*), or more precisely, for defining the semantics of the data operations and the order in which they are to be executed (i.e., the data flows of an ETL process).

Abstract Syntax

The abstract syntax of ETL-O, is defined by the metadmodel, in the form of a UML class diagram, depicted in Figure 6.

The *DataProcessModel* and *DataProcessModelElement* are the base classes of ETL-O. The data flow of a single ETL process activity (i.e., the *DataProcess*), defined using ETL-O concepts, consists of *DataOperations*, representing the atomic data operations, with *DataFlowPaths* composing these operations into a single data flow. Finally, the *DataOperationArgument* class is used for specifying the inputs and outputs of the operations. In other words, the flow of data between the operations, i.e., the execution

Figure 6. ETL-O metamodel

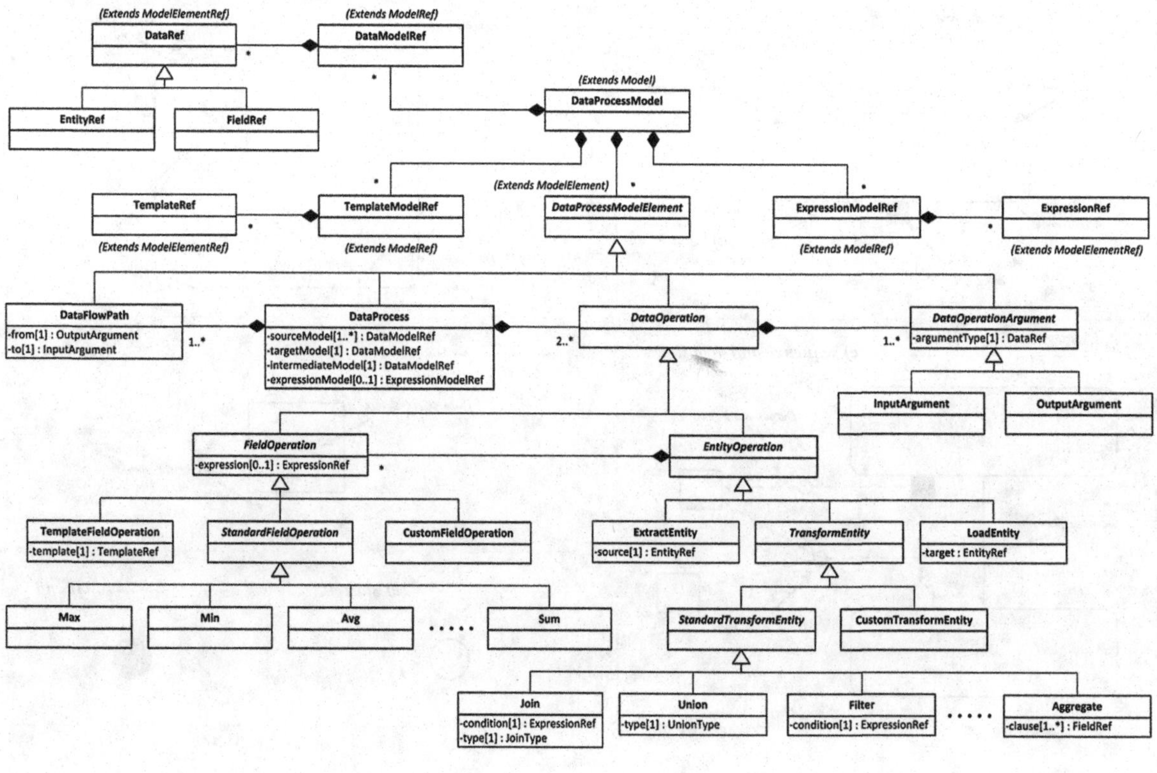

order of the atomic operations, is represented by *DataFlowPaths* (whereby the *OutputArgument* of one operation is related to an *InputArgument* of the following operation).

Furthermore, the specification of a *DataProcess* also requires the specification of the actual data involved in the operations. Given that the source, target and intermediate models, which are referenced in the *DataProcessModel*, are represented using different data models three specific associations are introduced (between the *DataProcess* and *DataModelRef* classes) in order to clearly separate the roles of the referenced models in a particular *DataProcess*. It should be noted that for each data process only a single intermediate data model can be referenced. In addition, for each *DataProcess* it is possible to provide a corresponding expression model which is depicted by the relationship between *DataProcess* and *ExpressionModelRef*.

Since the data involved in the transformations is represented, in separate ETL-D models, by entities which are comprised of fields (referenced via *EntityRef* or *FieldRef*), the transformation of entities also requires the transformation of the corresponding fields i.e., each entity transformation (*EntityOperation*) includes one or more field transformations (*FieldOperations*). The two additional classes (*EntityOperation* and *FieldOperation*) are derived from the abstract *DataOperation* class in order to enable a finer-grained specification at the field level of the entities involved in the transformation, thereby providing a basis for a more precise and comprehensive specification of the data transformation operations.

The semantics of the actual transformation operations are another crucial element of the specification. Therefore, transformation operations at the entity level are further refined in order to introduce more specific concepts i.e., the operations pertaining to the ETL process domain: *ExtractEntity*, *TransformEntity* and *LoadEntity*. Furthermore, the *ExtractEntity* and *LoadEntity* classes are related to the *DataRef* class in order to reference the entities that are to be extracted or loaded, respectively (depicted by the *source* and *target* attributes of the respective classes). On the other hand, the semantics of the transformation operations at the field level are expressed using ETL-E (depicted by *ExpressionRef*).

Likewise, in order to enable a more precise specification of the semantics of the actual transformations, the *TransformEntity* and *FieldOperation* classes have been extended to introduce specific concepts for representing both standard/common and custom transformation operations. The standard operations (e.g., *Join*, *Union*, *Filter*, *Aggregate,* etc., at the entity level, or *Max*, *Min*, *Avg*, *Sum,* etc., at the field level) are defined in accordance with the taxonomy given in (*Vassiliadis, Simitsis, & Baikousi, 2009*)). It should be emphasized that, due to space constraints, only a subset of the most common entity and field transformation operations is depicted, which in no way implies that the proposed language is limited to these operations. For each of these operations the conditions and constraints are specified using ETL-E expressions. In addition *TemplateFieldOperations* provide the necessary support for using transformation templates defined in separate ETL-T models.

The final element of the operation specifications are the inputs and outputs of the operations represented by the *InputArgument* and *OutputArgument* classes, respectively, which are derived from the abstract *DataOperationArgument* class. For each operation multiple inputs and/or outputs can be specified with the restriction that each operation must have at least one input or output argument. More precisely, the *ExtractEntity* and *LoadEntity* operations can have only input or only output arguments, respectively, while the *TransformEntity* operation must have at least one input and at least one output argument. Similarly, each *FieldOperation* must have at least one output argument. Furthermore, a complete specification also requires specifying the data types thus the argument specification is supplemented by introducing a relationship with the *DataRef* concept. However a restriction is imposed so that *EntityOperation* argument types are to be specified using the *EntityRef* class while the argument types of a *FieldOperation* are to be specified using the *FieldRef* class.

The flow of data between the operations, i.e. the execution order of the atomic operations, is represented by the *DataFlowPath* class whereby the *OutputArgument* of one operation is related to an *InputArgument* of another operation with the restriction that these arguments must be of the same type (i.e. reference the same data model element).

The *DataModelRef* class represents a mechanism for referencing the models representing the data involved in the transformations (either as source, target or intermediate data). The *DataRef* class, or more specifically its extensions *EntityRef* and *FieldRef*, enable the referencing of concepts in these data models i.e. entities and fields, respectively. The *TemplateModelRef* and *TemplateRef* classes enable the referencing of transformation operation templates, while *ExpressionModelRef* and *ExpressionRef* are used for referencing the various expressions used in the transformation operations.

Concrete Syntax

A graphical notation is adopted for the representation of ETL-O concepts, as was the case with ETL-P. The rounded corner rectangle (Figure 7-a) is used for representing the various data operations (i.e., the subclasses of the *DataOperation* class). The central part of the element contains the *name of the operation*. The operation's *type* is indicated by its name (i.e., the name of the concept that is being represented) in the upper left corner and the *operation symbol* located in the upper right corner. The arguments of the operation (the *InputArgument* and *OutputArgument* concepts) are depicted by small squares positioned on the outer edges of the rectangle, with white squares representing input arguments and black squares representing output arguments. The *operation input argument name* and *operation output argument name* may be omitted.

The data involved in the transformations, i.e., the referenced data models (*DataModelRef, EntityRef* and *FieldRef* concepts), are represented by the square-cornered rectangle depicted in Figure 7-b. The *data element name* is positioned in the center of the element, while the upper left corner holds the reference type (*data element type name*) with one of the following values: "*Data Model*", "*Entity*" or "*Field*". The upper right corner contains the *data element symbol,* indicating the reference type, while the lower right corner provides *additional information* (for example, the "*group by*" text will be displayed when representing fields of the entities in a grouping condition of an entity aggregation operation).

Solid directed lines are used for indicating dependencies (Figure 7-c), i.e., the operation's *data flow* (*DataFlowPath* concept), wherein the output argument of one operation points to the input argument of the following operation. The inclusion of *data type name* labels, containing the names of the involved entities, is optional. Other relevant dependencies, primarily the *source* entities of extract operations and *target* entities of load operations, are depicted as dashed directed lines.

Several diagrams are used for the specification of data processes. Only an overview of the introduced graphical notation is presented here, while more detailed examples are provided in the *ETL Process Modeling* section.

Figure 7. ETL-O graphical notation

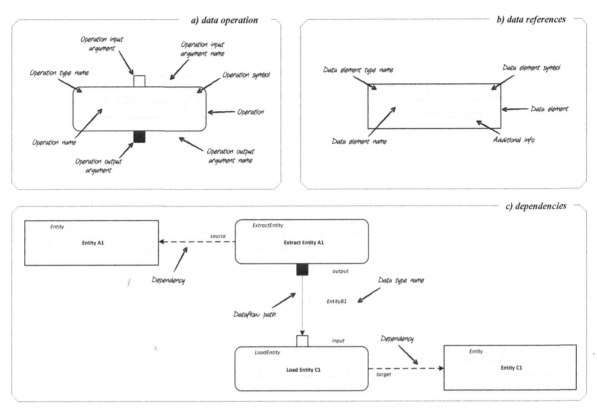

The data process diagram (Figure 8-a) is used for representing the identified data process and the data models that are involved in this process (*DataModelRef* concept). A data process is represented as a rounded corner rectangle, with the *data process name* in the middle and the *data process symbol* in its upper right corner. Links to/from the referenced data models are represented by directed solid lines labeled with the names of the entities that are extracted (*extracted entity name*) or loaded (*loaded entity name*).

The *complex transformation operation diagram* (Figure 8-b) depicts the details of a data process and it is partioned into horizontally stacked compartments. The central compartment (labeled with the *data process name*) is designated for specifying the actual entity transformations (subclasses of the *Entity-Operation* class) that the data process consists of. The referenced data models (*DataModelRef* concept) are depicted on the sides. The roles (*source*, *target* or *intermediate*) and names of each referenced data model are specified at the top of the corresponding compartment, while the relevant entities of these data models (*EntityRef* concept) are represented as nested graphical elements.

The *simple transformation operation diagram* (Figure 8-c) is similar to the previous diagram, except that it specifies *FieldOperations,* instead of entity operations. Consequently, the left part of the diagram contains the *input arguments* of the operation and the right part, its *output arguments*. The name, type and member fields (*FieldRef*) of each argument, are specified. The fields are represented as nested graphical elements.

Figure 8. ETL-O diagrams

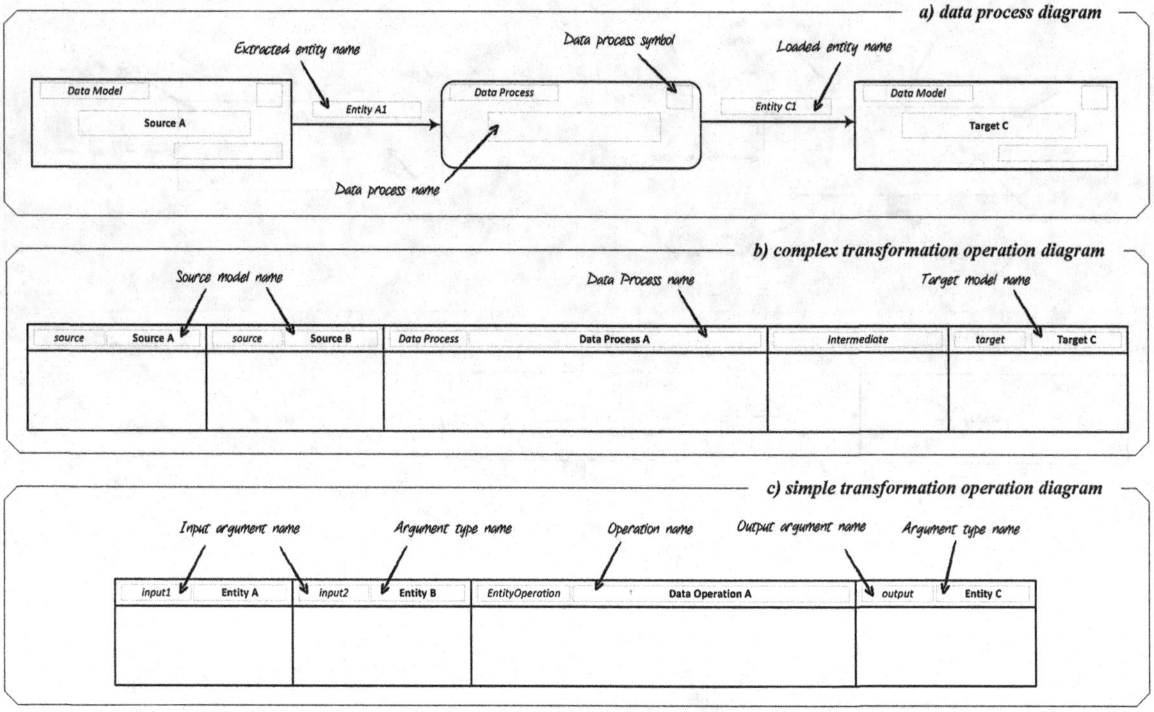

A Language for the Specification of Expressions (ETL-E)

ETL-E supports the formal specification (in a textual notation) of the semantics of the data operations, as well as the various conditions and restrictions pertaining to the execution of an ETL process. To this end, it provides a number of expression types for: primitive expressions (representing variable declarations, numeric and textual constants, method invocations, etc.), methods (which are defined using ETL-E and referenced by the concepts of the other ETL DSLs), statements (corresponding to the basic control structures: sequence, iteration and condition) and operators (for building complex expressions, where the operands can be primitive and/or complex expressions). It should be noted that the evaluation result of every expression must be of a certain data type. A defined ETL-E expression will actually be referenced in other ETL models via an *ExpressionRef*.

Abstract Syntax

The abstract syntax of ETL-E is defined by the metadmodel, in the form of a UML class diagram, given in Figure 9. The central concept is the *ExpressionModel,* while the concepts it comprises are represented as subclasses of the *ExpressionModelElement* class. The ETL-E metadmodel distinguishes several types of expressions (defined as subclasses of the abstract *Expression* class): *ETLMethodExpression, StatementExpression, OperatorExpression* and *PrimitiveExpression.* The *VariableDeclaration* class is used for associating a variable name with a *DataType* (with the *DataType* class representing the predefined data types). Furthermore, every expression evaluates to a certain data type.

Figure 9. ETL-E metamodel (core concepts)

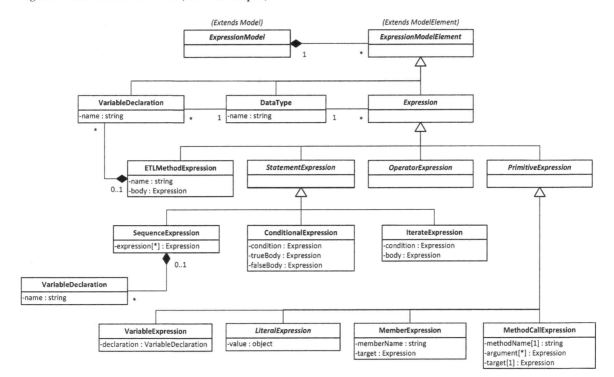

The *ETLMethodExpression* class represents methods, defined using the ETL-E language, which are used by the concepts of the introduced ETL DSLs.

The representation of basic control structures is supported by the abstract *StatementExpression* class or, more precisely, its subclasses: *SequenceExpression*, *ConditionalExpression* and *IterateExpression*.

The *OperatorExpression* class is used for representing complex expressions which can be constructed from primitive expressions and/or other complex expressions. Given that expressions can inherently have other expressions as their operands, the ETL-E metamodel provides two classes for representing operator expressions: *UnaryExpressions* (i.e., expressions with a single operand) and *BinaryExpressions* (with two operands, as indicated by the *leftOperand* and *rightOperand* attributes). The discriminator for the *BinaryExpression* specialization is the type of operator used an expression: assignment, arithmetic operator, relational operator or logical operator. The same criterion, i.e., unary operator type, is applied for the *UnaryExpression* specialization, resulting in the introduction of the *PreDecrementExpression*, *PostDecrementExpression*, *PreIncrementExpression*, *PostIncrementExpression*, *NegateExpression*, *UnaryPlusExpression* and *UnaryMinusExpression* subclasses.

The *PrimitiveExpression* class is extended to distinguish the different primitive expression types: *VariableExpression* (for referencing *VariableDeclarations*), *LiteralExpression* (for representing constants: numerical, string, etc.), *MethodCallExpression* (for representing method invocations) and *MemberExpression* (for accessing the attributes and properties of objects).

Concrete Syntax

A textual notation is adopted for the concrete syntax of ETL-E. A simple illustrative example is given so that the whole object model, corresponding to an ETL-E expression, can be visualized. The defined method *checkCondition* returns a *bool* type result and accepts two input parameters (*x* and *y*), both of type *int*. The body of the method is represented by expressions enclosed in curly braces.

```
ETLMethod checkCondition: bool
    input x: int
    input y: int
{
    x + y > 1000
}
```

The concrete syntax presented in the previous example is represented by the object diagram in Figure 10.

Figure 10. ETL-E concrete syntax object diagram (illustrative example)

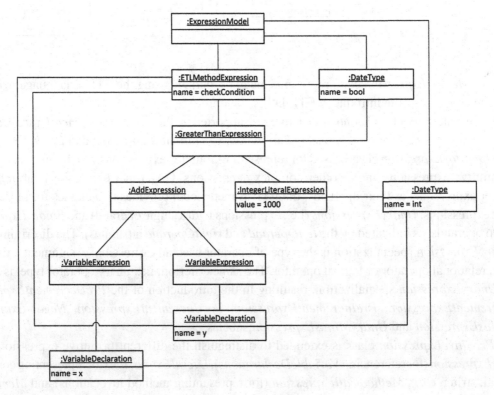

A Language for the Specification of Transformation Operation Templates (ETL-T)

ETL-T enables the creation of new field transformation operations, in the form of templates which can be reused (via a *TemplateRef*). For example, the *ExtractFirstName* template could be defined, for which two arguments would be specified (the full name as the input argument and the first name as the output argument), with the actual operation semantics given in the form of an ETL-E expression.

Abstract Syntax

The ETL-T abstract syntax is represented by the metadmodel, in the form of a UML class diagram, in Figure 11).

The central concepts are the *TemplateModel* (as a container for various templates) and the *TemplateModelElement* (providing the template specifications).

A template for a transformation operation is represented by the *Template* class, with the arguments (involved in the transformation) represented by the *TemplateArgument* class. Separate *InputTemplateArgument* and *OutputTemplateArgument* classes are introduced in order to enable differentiating between the input and output arguments of the transformation operation.

The *ExpressionModelRef* and *ExpressionRef* classes are used for referencing the expression models and their elements, respectively, specifying the semantics of the transformation.

Figure 11. ETL-T metamodel

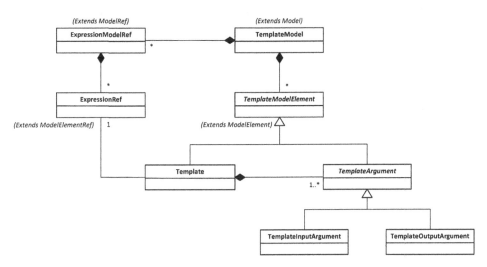

Concrete Syntax

A graphical notation is adopted for the concrete syntax of ETL-T. As shown in Figure 12-a, a transformation operation *Template* is depicted as a rounded corner rectangle, with the *template name* in its center and the *template symbol* in its upper right corner.

A separate graphical element, i.e., a square-cornered rectangle (Figure 12-b), is provided for representing the arguments of the transformation operation (the *InputTemplateArgument* and *OutputTemplateArgument* concepts). The *argument name* is placed in the center of the rectangle, while the upper left corner contains the *argument type* (input or output). The upper right corner is reserved for the argument symbol (a white square indicating an input and a black square an output argument).

A template is connected to its arguments via directed solid lines, which are always directed from the graphical element depicting the template towards the graphical element depicting the argument (regardless of its type, i.e., whether it's an input or output argument).

An example of an ETL-T operation template diagram, illustrating the usage of the introduced graphical elements, is given in Figure 13.

ETL Process Modeling

The proposed approach to ETL process modeling involves the creation of a separate model for each of the different aspects of an ETL process. By separating the different aspects into different models the complexity of an ETL process model is significantly reduced. Each model is created using the concepts of the appropriate DSL (e.g., ETL-O for the specification of data operations – ETL process activities, ETL-P for the specification of the execution order of these activities etc.). Since these models are cre-

Figure 12. ETL-T graphical notation

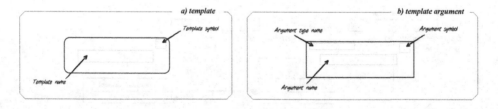

Figure 13. ETL-T diagram

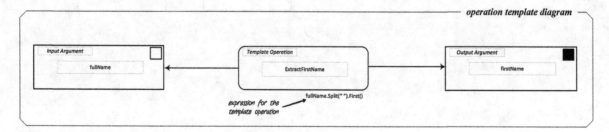

ated independently the actual order of their creation is not predetermined. Thus it is left to the designers to decide (in accordance with their experience, knowledge of the system that is being developed and preferences) which aspect should be modeled first.

However, the models formed in accordance with the proposed ETL-O specification may still be very complex, depending on the complexity of the ETL process that is being modeled, i.e., the number of actual transformations it requires. In order to facilitate the creation of such models it is proposed that it should be done gradually, at different levels of abstraction, with each subsequent level progressively refining the previous i.e., giving a more detailed description of the given ETL process. The hierarchical description of a data process is accomplished by introducing a set of diagrams. Consequently three types of diagrams are introduced: data process diagrams, complex transformation operation diagrams and simple transformation operation diagrams.

Therefore, the proposed approach to the modeling of an ETL process (Figure 14) entails the creation of these diagrams (which are specified using ETL-O concepts) along with an additional diagram (ETL Process execution diagram) depicting the execution of the ETL process (specified using ETL-P concepts). The concrete syntax of the proposed ETL-O and ETL-P DSLs provides the necessary graphical elements (representing the concepts of these languages) for constructing these diagrams. In addition, a complete specification of an ETL process also requires the creation of the data models (both source and target) using the ETL-D DSL, which also provides appropriate graphical elements, as well as the specification of the necessary ETL expressions which are expressed in textual notation using the ETL-E DSL.

In the following subsection an example, illustrating the modeling of a concrete ETL process through these diagrams, is given.

Figure 14. Hierarchical specification of an ETL process

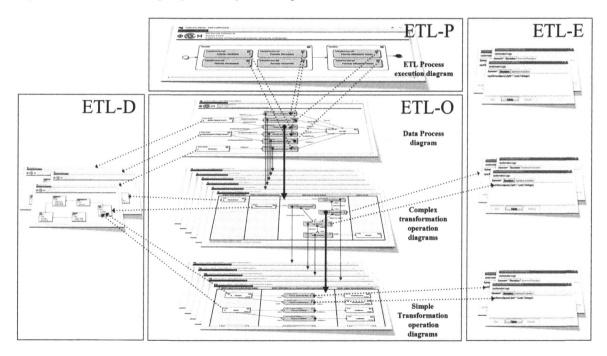

An Illustrative Example

This section illustrates the creation of the models in accordance with the introduced ETL DSLs. A simplified example is given for the development of an ETL process in the context of a data warehouse for the Faculty of Organizational Sciences which integrates data coming from different departments of the faculty. As previously explained, the specification of the ETL process involves the creation of a number of diagrams. For each type of diagram a representative example will be given. The diagrams have been additionally annotated in the presented example in order to clarify the correspondence between the graphical elements and the concepts of the metamodels given in the previous sections.

The specification of the process commences with the creation of the relevant data process diagrams. In Figure 15 an example of a data process diagram is given in which several data processes have been identified.

ProcessStudents, for example, processes data pertaining to students at different study levels i.e., it extracts the *MasterStudents* and *UndergraduateStudents* data from the relevant data sources (*MasterService* and *UndergraduateStudentService*, respectively), then transforms the extracted data into the *Student* entity and finally loads the transformed data into the *FonDW*. For each identified data process a corresponding complex transformation operation diagram is created, representing the semantics of the data process (i.e., the necessary entity transformation operations and the order in which they are to be executed). For example, in Figure 16, the execution of *ProcessStudents* commences with the *ExtractMasterStudents* and *ExtractUndergraduateStudents* operations which extract the necessary data (i.e., *MasterStudents* and *UndergraduateStudents*, respectively) from the *MasterService* and *UndergraduateStudentService* data sources. The result of the execution of these operations is depicted by the *IMasterStudents* and *IUndergraduateStudents* entities.

Figure 15. DataProcess diagram

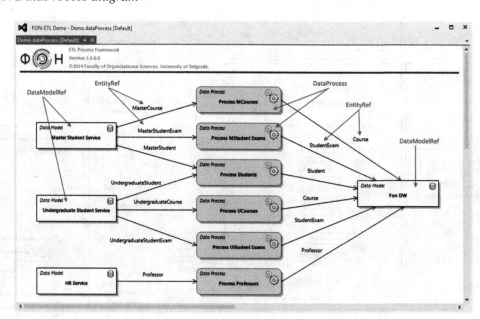

Figure 16. Complex transformation operation diagram for ProcessStudents

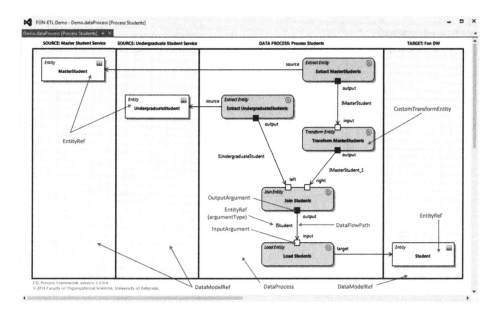

The *TransformMasterStudents* operation performs the necessary transformations on the *IMaster-Student* entities resulting in *IMasterStudent_1* entities which, along with the *IUndergraduateStudent* entities, represent the input of the *JoinStudents* operation. The execution of this operation then results in *IStudent* entities which are finally loaded into the *FonDW* through the *LoadStudents* operation. It should be noted that the *IMasterStudent, IUndergraduateStudent, IMasterStudent_1* and *IStudent* entities are the intermediate results of this data process.

The semantics of the entity transformation operations are represented through simple transformation operation diagrams. In Figure 17 a diagram representing the *TransformMasterStudent* operation is given. For each field of the output entity (*IMasterStudent_1*) the required transformation of one or more fields of the input entity (*IMasterStudent*) is defined. For example, the value of the *StudentNumber* field is obtained by executing the *ProcessStudentNumber* operation which takes the value of the *Number* field as its input.

The semantics of the *ProcessStudentNumber* and *ProcessEnrolmentYear* operations are specified by an ETL-E expression (Figure 18), while the semantics of the *ProcessFirstName* and *ProcessLastName* operations are given by referencing the appropriate templates (i.e., *GetFirstNameTemplate* and *GetLast-NameTemplate*, respectively).

The specification of the execution of the ETL process is given by the ETL process execution diagram in which the identified data processes are represented as ETL process activities. In Figure 19 an ETL process execution diagram for this particular ETL process, which begins with the parallel execution of the *ProcessStudents, ProcessProfessors, ProcessUCourses* and *ProcessMCourses* activities and ends with the parallel execution of the *ProcessUStudentExams* and *ProcessMStudentExams* activities, is given.

Figure 17. Simple transformation operation diagram for TransformMasterStudents

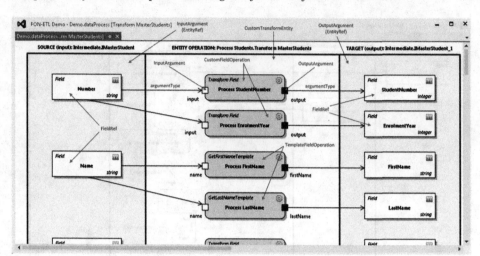

Figure 18. Transformation expression for the ProcessStudentNumber operation

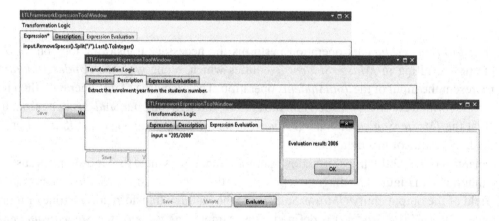

Figure 19. ETL Process execution diagram

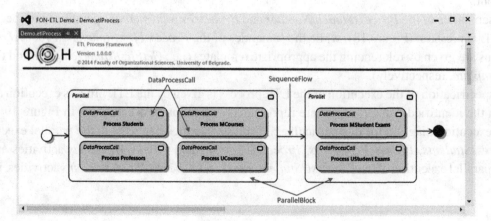

AUTOMATION

Once a DSL has been specified the next step is to provide its actual implementation. The implementation of a DSL is obtained through the automatic transformation of its specification into executable code.

Requirements

On the one hand the aim of this research is to provide a means for fully automating ETL process development in order to significantly increase development productivity and efficiency and lower the development and maintenance costs. In light of the discussion in the *Background* section, it can be concluded that, since the MDA approach (which is based on the refinement of models through successive model transformations) typically requires that the automatically generated models be manually extended with additional details, automation is usually only partially achieved with this approach. Conversely, in the DSM approach the implementation is automatically generated from the specification by code generators which specify how information is extracted from the models and directly transformed into code. Since the code generators are also domain specific, no manual modifications of the generated code are necessary. The code generators should further be supported by a domain-specific framework in order to narrow the gap between the problem domain and the solution domain. If both the specification and the framework use formal concepts close to the real ETL domain concepts, the transformation between them can be fully automated, thus the specification becomes indeed executable.

On the other hand, it is stipulated that, given the nature of ETL processes, several additional requirements should also be fulfilled by the software solution implementing the proposed DSLs:

- It should enable the dynamic execution of ETL process specifications or, more precisely, the automated transformation of ETL models into an executable form at runtime.
- It should provide the necessary flexibility to rapidly respond to changes in business requirements or data sources, by allowing for ETL process specifications to be easily adapted (i.e., modified, extended or even created anew) and immediately executed.
- It should support model versioning, i.e., the execution of different versions of a model.
- It should be easily deployable and scalable without affecting the operation of the execution environment.
- It should enable the execution of ETL processes in a distributed environment and allow for the possibility of parallelizing the execution of different data processes.

In order to meet these requirements, the service-oriented approach to software development (SOA) should be adopted for the development of the supporting software solution, because it results in extremely scalable and flexible solutions and allows for parallelization and distributed execution. In addition, in order to achieve the desired flexibility, the execution of the ETL process should be driven by the relevant metadata, i.e., the ETL-P or ETL-O models that are to be executed (as well as the supplementary ETL-E, ETL-T and ETL-D models) which would all be stored in a model repository.

Moreover, the services, which are to be responsible for the control flow and data flow of an ETL process, should be developed as generic services which would be capable of executing any concrete control flow or data flow model, respectively, and which could easily be installed on each available hardware node (so that every node could handle the execution of any concrete service instance). The functionality of these generic services would then be augmented, at runtime, by the execution semantics, given in the relevant models and interpreted or compiled on demand. For this to be possible a specific application framework should be provided which would include: a set of *implementation concepts* corresponding to each of the introduced language concepts, a specifically developed *Generator* component which would be responsible for interpreting ETL-P and ETL-O models and creating corresponding executable in-memory object models, and a *Compiler* component which would be responsible for dynamically generating executable code from ETL-E models.

The execution semantics would then be obtained as follows (Figure 20): for each concept, specified in an ETL-P or ETL-O model, the corresponding implementation concept is retrieved, instantiated and added to an in-memory object model by the Generator component. If the implementation concepts are close to the DSL concepts, the retrieval of the implementation concept which corresponds to a particular DSL concept would be trivial and could be accomplished by introducing appropriate naming conventions. However, in order to enhance the overall performances of an ETL process it is argued that ETL-E models (giving the specific execution logic) should be dynamically compiled into executable code rather than interpreted. Hence, the ETL-E models, which are referenced in ETL-P and ETL-O models, should be compiled at runtime, resulting in a set of dynamic methods which could then be bound to the corresponding objects, along the lines of the Adaptive model notion (*Fowler, 2010*).

By providing such generic services, the dynamic execution of ETL process models (i.e., the automatic generation, compilation and execution of ETL processes at runtime) would be made possible. This would also allow for ETL process specifications to be easily adapted (i.e., models could be modified,

Figure 20. Proposed implementation of the generic services

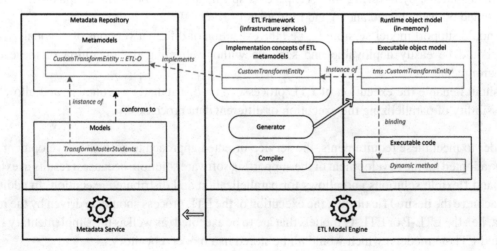

extended or even created anew, and the corresponding executable code would be promptly generated and executed) which would provide the necessary flexibility to quickly respond to the constant changes in business requirements or data sources.

Furthermore, the deployment of a developed ETL process would be straightforward, i.e., it would be accomplished simply by storing the relevant models in the repository. Moreover, the modification of existing models, or the creation of new ones, wouldn't affect the operation of the execution environment. Consequently, such an approach would support model versioning and significantly facilitate the testing of the created ETL processes.

Finally, such an approach would inherently enable the parallelization and distributed execution of an ETL process, thereby making it possible to fully exploit the existing hardware resources. Furthermore, the hardware infrastructure could be easily augmented at runtime by adding additional hardware nodes on which only the generic services need be installed. Those hardware nodes would then be instantly operational, thus increasing the available processing capability.

It can be concluded that by adopting such an approach not only would full automation be supported, but the automation would actually take place in real-time.

The concrete implementation details of a solution which fulfills the posed requirements are given in the following sections.

ETL Platform

M-ETL-A proposes a specific ETL platform to technologically support the ETL process specifications as well as to enable the automated development of ETL processes in accordance with the DSM approach and their subsequent execution. The proposed ETL platform would be an extension of a general purpose platform such as Microsoft .NET or J2EE.

The ETL-PL architecture is characterized by three layers. The bottom layer (*ETL Framework*) represents the execution environment and is comprised of a set of services which are responsible for the execution and management of ETL processes. The introduction of the application framework significantly elevates the semantic level of the solution and supports its automated implementation (i.e., the automatic generation of executable code from the given models).

The middle layer (*ETL Transformations*) is responsible for the automatic transformations of models (which have been created in accordance with the defined DSLs) into executable code. These transformations are supported by specially developed generators.

The final layer (*ETL Tools*), representing the development environment, is comprised of a number of software tools which have been developed to technologically support the modeling of ETL processes.

An overview of the proposed ETL platform is given in Figure 21.

The *Data Environment* represents the relevant, usually very heterogeneous, data sources. All of the data sources (sources as well as targets) are uniformly represented, using the concepts of the ETL-D language.

Figure 21. Overview of the ETL Platform

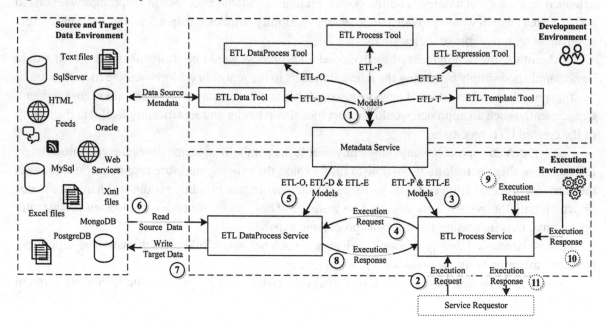

The *Development Environment* is dedicated to domain experts. It provides the supporting infrastructure for efficient ETL process development. Thus, the first step in ETL process development using ETL-PL, would be the modeling of the different aspects of an ETL process using the specially developed tools for each of the introduced ETL DSLs (as depicted in *ETL Process Modeling* section), and the created models would then be stored in the metadata repository (1).

The *Metadata Repository* (governed by the *Metadata Service*) is the central component of ETL-PL. The *Metadata Service* thus represents the communication channel for the automated exchange of metadata (i.e., models) between the development and execution environments. In accordance with contemporary methodological approaches to software development, based on models and MDD standards, models are the central elements of the repository. In other words, models represent the main concept which is to be stored, maintained and searched for by users or software agents (such as components, programs, services). The repository also stores information about model referencing (i.e., when one model uses the definitions given in another model) to track the dependencies among the models. Moreover, in order to achieve the desired flexibility and adaptability of ETL process solutions, ETL-PL also uses the repository to provide model-driven execution. In effect, ETL process execution is actually driven by the repository contents, i.e., the models representing the ETL process. Consequently, changes in business requirements are realized through the adaptation of existing models, or creation of new ones, instead of hard-coding the business logic.

The *Execution Environment* consists of a set of services responsible for the automatic generation of executable code from the models, as well as the actual execution of the generated code along with a number of supporting infrastructure services (e.g., *ETLNotifyingService, ETLLoggingService, ETLSchedulingService*, etc.).

The execution of an ETL process is set into motion upon the receiving an *Execution Request* message (2). The execution can be instigated either by one of the components of ETL-PL (e.g., the *ETLSchedulingService*) or by an external system. Furthermore, the execution can be scheduled or else triggered in response to an event in the environment. In addition, it can also be initiated by a top-level ETL process (9), as is the case when an ETL process coordinates the execution of other ETL processes. Both the Request-Response and One-Way Message Exchange Patterns are supported for requesting the execution of an ETL process. In the case of a Request-Response message exchange, the initiator will receive an *Execution Response* upon the completion of the execution (10 or 11, depending on who initiated the execution).

The execution of an ETL process is driven by the actual models that are to be executed. Thus, following the reception of an execution request, the relevant models (ETL-P and ETL-E models) will be retrieved from the *Metadata Repository* (3). From these models the corresponding executable code will be generated, compiled and finally, executed.

An ETL process is comprised of a number of activities (i.e., data processes) and the execution of data processes is supported by a separate service. Similarly to the execution of an ETL process, the execution of a data process commences upon receiving an *Execution Request* (4). The relevant models (ETL-O, ETL-E, ETL-D and ETL-T) will be retrieved from the *Metadata Repository* (5) and once again the corresponding executable code will be generated, compiled and finally, executed. In the course of the execution of the data process the data is extracted from the data sources (6), transformed and then loaded into the targets (7). Only Request-Response message exchange is supported for data process execution, thus the execution concludes by creating and sending an *Execution Response* (8).

ETL Platform Implementation

In order to develop a high-quality software solution first a stable software architecture must be defined. Since software development can be extremely complex and time-consuming it is necessary to raise the level of abstraction, in order to manage the complexity, and view the solution as a set of components each providing part of the required functionality. The identified components are then organized into layers, on the basis of the functionality they provide, thereby simplifying the solution design. In addition to identifying the necessary structural components, a software architecture also defines the behavior of the system in terms of the collaboration among the identified components. The communication between the components is realized via interfaces (through which the components expose the functionality they provide).

The nature of ETL processes imposes strict requirements regarding the performances and scalability of the supporting software solutions. It is, thus, imperative to define a stable, yet flexible, software architecture which will, on the one hand, fulfill the necessary requirements, while on the other hand, be easily extensible to respond to the constant changes in business requirements.

In accordance with these requirements, a software architecture is proposed, which defines the main components of ETL-PL, their roles and responsibilities, along with a set of rules controlling the way in which they can interact. The main components of ETL-PL are organized into two layers: the development environment (*ETLDevelopment*) and the execution environment (*ETLExecution*).

ETL Development Environment

The development environment is comprised of tools which support the modeling of ETL processes in accordance with the introduced ETL DSLs. Specifically it contains tools for defining the abstract and concrete syntax (in both a graphical and textual notation) of a DSL and tools (syntax editors, graphical and textual) for creating models in accordance with the defined DSL. The developed graphical editors enable the syntax-driven creation of ETL models. More precisely, it consists of a set of tools (*ETLProcessTool, ETLDataProcessTool, ETLExpressionTool, ETLDataTool* and *ETLTemplateTool*) which were developed to technologically support both the introduced DSLs (ETL-P, ETL-O, ETL-E, ETL-D and ETL-T, respectively) and the modeling of an ETL process using these DSLs (Figure 22).

The development environment is also supported by several infrastructure components, among which the *ETLDocumentationTool* (which can automatically generate the ETL process documentation in a *.docx* format) can be singled out.

The component diagrams for each of these tools are similarly structured, so an example pertaining to the *ETLProcessTool* is given in Figure 23. The *ETLProcessEditor* component implements the concrete syntax of ETL-P (i.e., the graphical elements), while the *ETLProcessDomainModel* implements the abstract syntax of ETL-P (i.e., the language concepts). *ETLProcessStore* provides the main functionalities related to the creation of a concrete ETL process execution flow description. *ETLProcessEditor, ETLProcessStore, ETLProcessDomainMododel* and *ETLProcessPersistance* are extensions of the corresponding components provided in *Microsoft DSL Tools* (*Microsoft, 2016*). *ETLMetadataServiceAgent* communicates with the ETL resource repository, while *ETLProcessPersistance* allows for storing and loading models from the local (temporary) *ETLProcessStorage*.

The specification of the abstract and concrete syntax of the proposed DSLs is accomplished using *Microsoft DSL Tools* (*Microsoft, 2016*), along with the open source *Irony* parser generator framework (*Ivantsov, 2009*) for languages which have a textual concrete syntax, while the creation of models using these DSLs is supported by specially developed software tools (primarily graphical editors). The usage of the developed tools for the creation of the models, in accordance with the proposed ETL DSLs, was illustrated in the *ETL Process Modeling* section.

Figure 22. ETLDevelopment component diagram

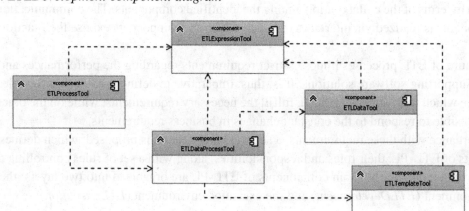

Figure 23. ETLProcessTool component diagram

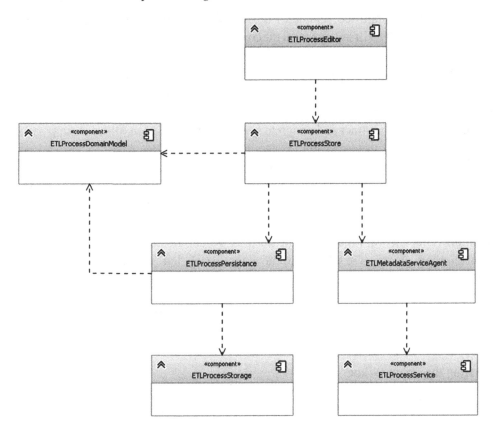

Graphical Editors (for ETL-P, ETL-O and ETL-T)

DSL Tools is a part of the *.NET* platform developed by *Microsoft* to fully support both the development and the utilization of DSLs. Consequently, it provides an environment for the development of graphical DSLs and an environment supporting their utilization i.e., the creation of models and their transformation into different software artefacts (*Cook, Jones, Kent, & Wills, 2007*). The main advantage of *Microsoft DSL Tools* is the fact that it is an integral part of the existing *.NET* development environment. Moreover, the developed DSLs (represented by different specific tools) are automatically integrated into the development environment which significantly facilitates their utilization.

The development of a DSL, using *Microsoft DSL Tools*, is accomplished in two main steps: defining the DSL and implementing the corresponding syntax editor.

1.   Defining the DSL

The development of a DSL begins with its specification, i.e., the defining of an appropriate domain model (*Cook et al., 2007*) which describes the concepts of the language and their relationships, along with the rules governing their usage. In addition to the abstract syntax, the concrete syntax, providing a visual representation of these concepts in the form of graphical elements, is defined.

The *M-ETL-A* DSLs are described using the concepts of the meta-language defined by *Microsoft* (as part of *DSL Tools*) and a simplified version of this meta-language can be found in (*Bézivin, Hillairet, Jouault, Kurtev, & Piers, 2005*). It assumes that the concepts of a DSL are represented by the *DomainClass* meta-concept, while the relationships among these concepts are represented by the *DomainRelationship* meta-concept. The roles the concepts play in a relationship are represented by the *DomainRole* meta-concept, while the *isEmbeding* attribute indicates whether the relationship is composite. The attributes (properties) of the concepts and relationships are represented by the *ValueProperty* meta-concept.

The specification of the abstract and concrete syntax of the *M-ETL-A* DSLs is supported by Microsoft's meta-editor. For each meta-concept (*DomainClass, DomainRelationship*, etc.) a corresponding graphical element is provided. An instance of the meta-concept is created by dragging and dropping the appropriate graphical element onto the diagram. For example, dragging and dropping the graphical element corresponding to the *DomainClass* meta-concept results in the creation of an instance of the *DomainClass*, i.e., the concept of the particular domain model. The ETL-O domain model, created using this meta-editor, is depicted in Figure 24. The abstract syntax, i.e., the ETL-O language concepts and their relationships, are given in the left part of the diagram (labeled "*Classes and Relationships*") while the concrete syntax is defined on the right-hand side (labeled "*Diagram Elements*").

In addition to the abstract and concrete syntax of the DSL, it is also necessary to define the rules which will ensure the validity of the created models. The various rules of the specified DSLs are implemented in the C# programming language.

2.   Generating the syntax editor

Figure 24. DSL Tools meta-editor for creating DSLs

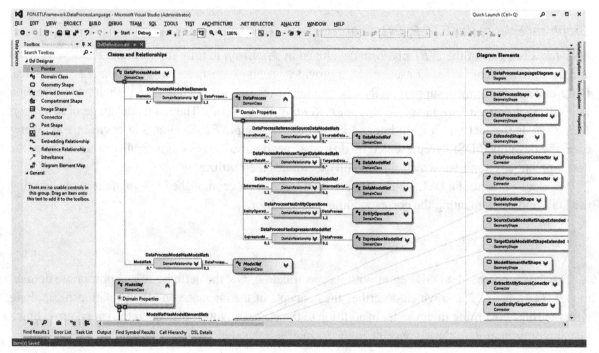

Once a DSL has been specified the next step is the automatic generation of the implementation of a concrete graphical editor (for creating concrete models conforming to the DSL specification). For this purpose *Microsoft DSL Tools* provides a number of *T4* templates (*Text Template Transformation Toolkit – T4*) which enable the automatic transformation of domain models (*Cook et al., 2007*). The end result is a set of specific software modules for the installation of the implemented syntax editor in a particular development environment (i.e., a concrete instance of the MSVS tool).

The flexibility of *Microsoft DSL Tools*, with regard to the possibility of customizing the domain model transformation process, was taken advantage of. Namely, the existing set of *T4* templates can be customized (either by changing existing templates or adding new ones), thereby affecting the implementation of the syntax editors. The set of T4 templates has, thus, been customized to allow for the utilization of multiple models, as per (*Recchia & Guerot, 2009*), in order to enable the representation of an ETL process model at different levels of abstraction.

The *ETLDataProcessTool* is depicted in Figure 25 which shows the developed ETL-O editor and an example of a Complex transformation operation diagram created using the editor. The creation of diagrams is supported by specific components, depicted on the left side of the editor (*Toolbox*). These components implement the graphical elements representing ETL-O language concepts and are grouped into four categories (*Data Process, Data, Entity Operations* and *Field Operations*) for ease of use.

Figure 25. ETL-O graphical editor

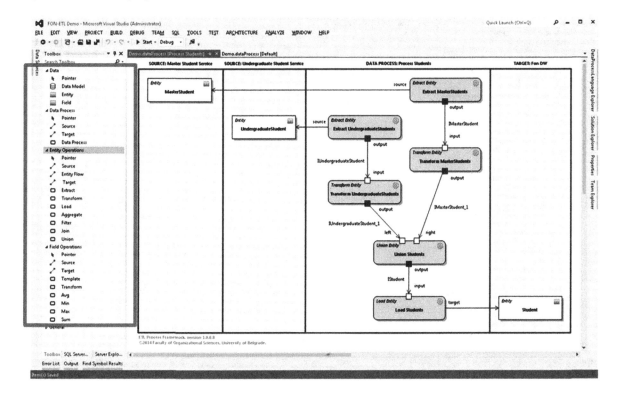

Textual Editor (for ETL-E)

Given that *Microsoft DSL Tools* only provides support for graphical syntaxes, it cannot fully support the development of a DSL which has a textual syntax, such as ETL-E. Consequently, in accordance with the proposed conceptual framework, the abstract syntax of ETL-E is implemented using *DSL Tools*, while the implementation of the concrete syntax is supported by a specific ETL-E language parser developed using the *Irony* tool (*Ivantsov, 2009*). Irony is an open-source tool, implemented in the C# programming language, for the development of textual DSLs using *Microsoft*'s *.NET* platform.

The *Irony* tool was chosen because it is based on an approach that does not require using a separate meta-language for specifying the grammar of the DSL (*Ivantsov, 2009*). Instead, the grammar is defined in the C# programming language, or more precisely, using the C# classes for forming expressions based on *Backus-Naur Form – BNF* production rules (such as: *Terminal, NonTerminal, KeyTerm*, etc.). In addition, this approach does not require the generation of a scanner, nor a parser; a universal parser is used instead (*Ivantsov, 2009*). This universal LALR (*Look-Ahead-Left-to-Right*) parser executes in accordance with the grammar of the language which is represented by a specific object model. The parser creates the corresponding Abstract Syntax Tree (AST). A base *ASTNode* class is provided for representing the tree nodes and it is extended by concrete subclasses specific to the DSL. Figure 26 shows the key elements of the ETL-E parser implementation.

Figure 26. ETL-E parser implementation

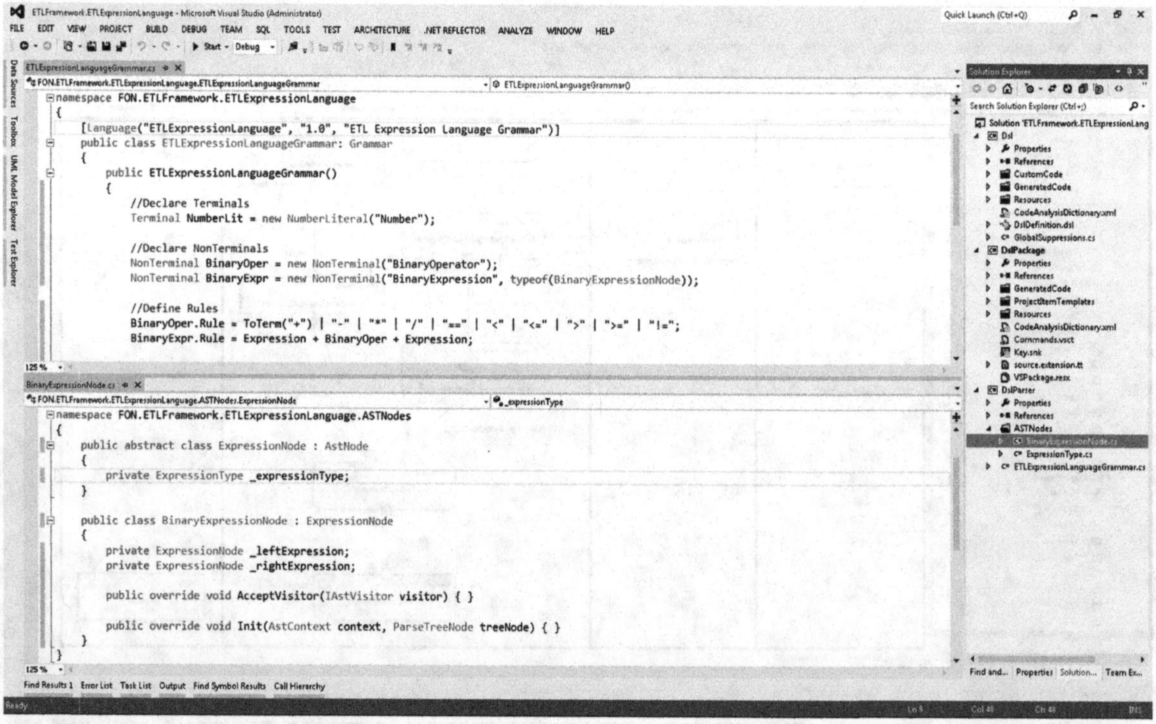

The implementation of the ETL-E parser is the first step in the implementation of ETL-E. The next step is the implementation of the domain model. This is accomplished using *Microsoft DSL Tools,* in the same manner as with the other ETL-DSLs save for the defining of graphical elements, i.e., the concrete syntax.

Figure 27 illustrates the roles of the utilized tools (*Irony* and *Microsoft DSL Tools*) in the implementation of ETL-E. Specifically, the concrete syntax of ETL-E is implemented using the *Irony* tool, while its abstract syntax is implemented using *Microsoft DSL Tools*

ETL Execution Environment

The execution environment is responsible for the automatic generation of executable code from the models as well as the actual execution of the generated code. Thus the execution environment consists of code generator components and the components implementing the application framework.

It is developed in accordance with the service-oriented approach to software development (SOA). Hence it is comprised of a number of independent services (communicating with one another asynchronously, via messages) responsible for the execution and management of the developed ETL processes (or more precisely the executable code generated from the defined models). The SOA approach was adopted because it results in extremely scalable and flexible solutions, which is imperative in light of the frequent changes in business requirements. Since it promotes the loose-coupling of services, the solution can be easily extended, simply by adding new services, or modified without affecting the existing services.

The execution environment consists of four core services (*ETLProcessService, ETLDataProcessService, ETLCompilerService* and *ETLMetadataService*) which are responsible for the execution and management of ETL processes (Figure 28). More precisely, *ETLProcessService* and *ETLDataProcessService* are responsible for executing the control flows and data flows of an ETL process, respectively. The *ETLCompilerService* handles the generation and compilation of executable code, while the *ETLMetadataService* manages the ETL metadata repository. In addition to these core components, the execution environment also contains a number of supporting infrastructure components such as: *ETLNotifyingService, ETLLoggingService, ETLTracingService, ETLSchedulingService*, etc.

Three crucial characteristics of the execution environment should be specially emphasized. First, the developed services enable the dynamic execution of ETL processes or, more precisely, the automated generation and execution of ETL processes at runtime. The execution of a *Process* (be it an *ETLProcess* or an *ETLDataProcess*) is driven by the relevant metadata (i.e., the ETL-P or ETL-O models that are to be executed, respectively, as well as the supplementary ETL-E, ETL-T, ETL-D models). The specially

Figure 27. The roles of Irony and Microsoft DSL Tools in the implementation of ETL-E

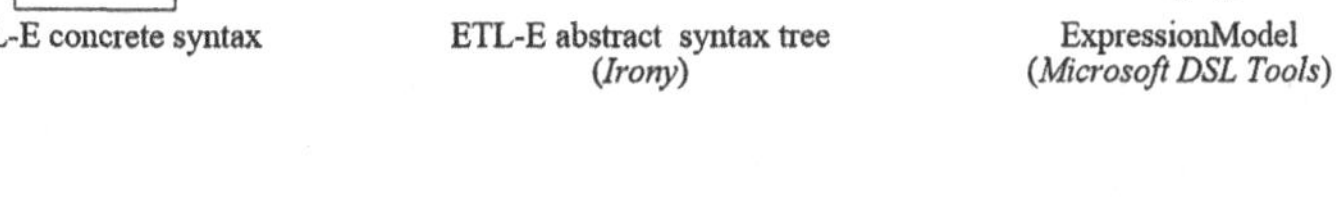

Figure 28. ETLExecution component diagram

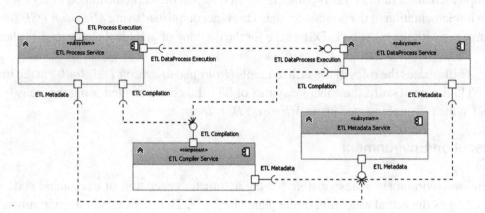

developed *ETLCompilerService* generates the executable code, with the *ETLMetadataService* providing the relevant metadata. Second, the execution environment was developed with the possibility of parallelizing the execution of the different services (responsible for the actual processing of data) in mind. Namely, ETL-PL allows for the independent execution (and specification) of the different aspects of an ETL processes by providing separate services for the execution of the control flows and data flows of an ETL process (*ETLProcessServices* and *ETLDataProcessServices*, respectively). It should be emphasized that these services are actually developed as generic services which are capable of interpreting any concrete control flow and data flow model, respectively. The functionality of these generic services is then augmented, at runtime, by the concrete transformation logic (which is compiled on demand). This opens up the possibility of parallelizing the execution of the different concrete services comprising an ETL process. Finally, that it was designed to enable the execution of ETL processes in a distributed environment. ETL-PL therefore presumes that the generic services are installed on each of the available hardware nodes so that every node can handle the execution of any concrete service instance. By parallelizing the execution of the services, instead of executing them sequentially, the performances of an ETL process are significantly increased. Distributing the execution of the services over the different available hardware nodes leads to yet a further increase in performances.

ETL Process Implementation

An *ETL process* is comprised of a number of activities (data processes) which are to be executed in a particular order with the aim of transforming business data into strategic information. The specification of the control flow (i.e., execution order of the activities) is supported by four main control structures *SequenceFlow*, *ConditionalBlock*, *IterateBlock* and *ParallelBlock*. The activities can be either *SimpleActivities*, such as actual data processes (defined in separate ETL-O models and invoked via the *DataProcessCall*) or other ETL processes (defined in separate ETL-P models and invoked via the *ETLProcessCall*), or *ComplexActivities* (i.e., *ConditionalBlock*, *IterateBlock* and *ParallelBlock*) composed of other activities, simple and/or complex. In this section the different mechanisms, by which the control structures have been implemented, will be elaborated, while the implementation details of the data processes will be given in the next subsection.

The main concepts of the proposed application framework (related to the ETL process implementation) are depicted in Figure 29.

The *ETLProcessExecutor* class is responsible for executing a particular ETL process, while the *ServiceProvider* class is responsible for providing and managing the various components (such as *ETLMetadataService*, *ETLCompilerService*, *ExecutionContextService*, *ExecutionHandlerService*, *ETL-DataProcessService*, *ETLProcessService*, etc.) that are used during the execution of an ETL process.

The *ExecutionContext* class is used for representing the execution context of an ETL process or an ETL process activity. It stores the state of the process or activity that is being executed. A separate execution context is created for the execution of each of the activities comprising an ETL process. Furthermore, if an activity is composite (i.e., *ConditionalBlock*, *IterateBlock* and *ParallelBlock*) separate execution contexts must also be created for the execution of each of its subactivities, and so forth if the subactivities are themselves also composite. Hence, these execution contexts form a parent-child hierarchy, in which the execution context of each composite activity contains the execution contexts of its subactivities, with the execution context of the ETL process as a whole at the root.

Figure 29. ETLProcessService class diagram

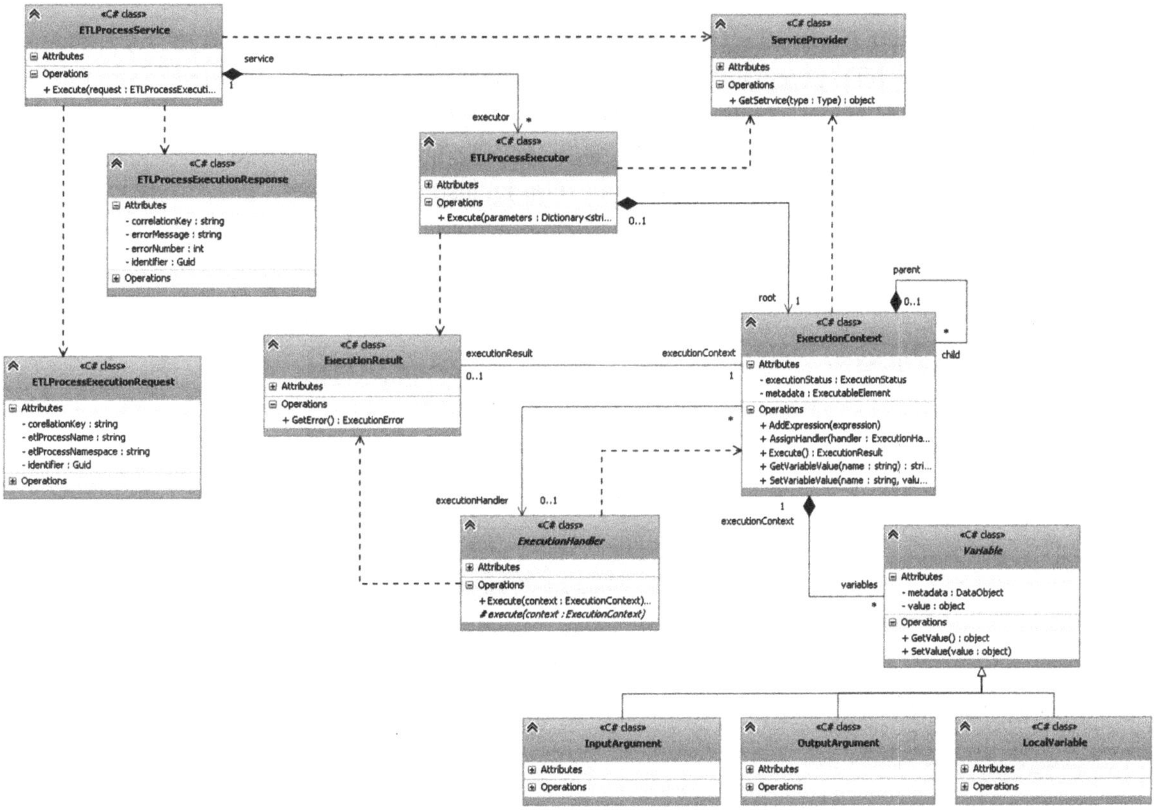

The states are maintained through a set of *InputArguments*, *OutputArguments* and *LocalVariables*. The three different types of *Variables* where introduced in order to provide more control over their usage e.g., the value of an *OutputArgument* is available only after the execution of the activity has been brought to an end (i.e., when its *executionStatus* has been set to *Executed*).

The execution of the activities is supported by the *ExecutionHandler* class. The *ExecutionHandler* class is specialized (Figure 30) to support the different types of activities inherent to the ETL process. Each subclass implements the *execute* method to provide the desired behavior. The public *Execute* method acts as a wrapper for protected *execute* method and implements the behavior common to all of the activities (such as error handling, logging etc.). Both methods expect an *ExecutionContext* as an input parameter, and result in an *ExecutionResult* instance.

As depicted in the sequence diagram, given in Figure 31, the execution of an *ETLProcess* is initiated by invoking the *Execute* method of an *ETLProcessService* instance. In other words the execution commences upon receiving an *ETLProcessExecutionRequest* message and completes by creating and sending an *ETLProcessExecutionResponse* message.

Subsequently, a specific application domain is created (*Hazzard & Bock, 2013; Troelsen, 2012*) and the *ETLProcessExecutor* is instantiated. It should be emphasized that the specific application domain was introduced to support the generation and compilation of executable code during the execution of a process.

Once the *ETLProcessExecutor* has been created, its *Execute* method will be invoked. As previously stated, the execution of ETL processes is metadata driven, so the first step is to retrieve the relevant metadata (i.e., the ETL-P model which is to be executed as well as the ETL-E models it references). To this end the *LoadMetadata* method of an *ETLMetadataService* instance is invoked.

The next step is to create the root execution context (as an instance of the *ExecutionContext* class) for the ETL process, based on the relevant metadata, which is accomplished by invoking the *Create* method of an *ExecutionContextService* instance.

Figure 30. ExecutionHandlers class diagram

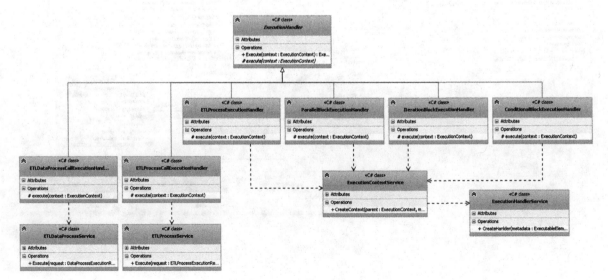

Figure 31. ETLProcessService sequence diagram

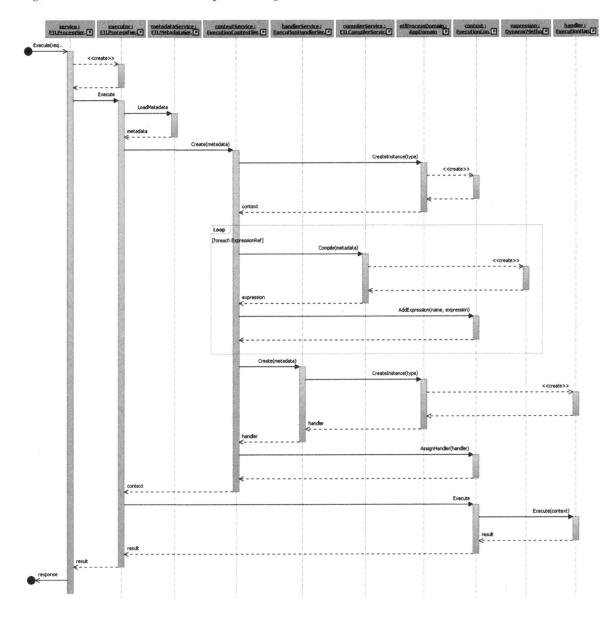

Finally, the *Execute* method of the root *ExecutionContext* (or more precisely, the *ExecutionHandler* assigned to that context) is invoked to execute the ETL process, which actually sets off the execution of the sequence of activities comprising the process. The activities are thus executed one by one. The execution of each activity entails the creation of a new *ExecutionContext* for that activity and the invocation of its *Execute* method. However, if the activity is composite, its execution presumes the creation of individual *ExecutionContexts* for the execution of each of its subactivities. Depending on the activity's type (*Conditional, Iterate* or *Parallel*) the actual execution will be either sequential or parallel.

In order to create an *ExecutionContext* the *Create* method of an *ExecutionContextService* instance is invoked. First the appropriate *ExecutionContext* is instantiated. Then, for each referenced ETL-E expression, the corresponding executable code must be generated and compiled, which is accomplished by invoking the *Compile* method of an *ETLCompilerService* instance. The compilation process (*Hazzard & Bock, 2013; Troelsen, 2012; Microsoft, 2015; Microsoft, 2017*) results in a dynamic method (*DynamicMethod*) which is then attached to the *ExecutionContext* instance. Finally, the appropriate *ExecutionHandler* instance is created (by invoking the *Create* method of an *ExecutionHandlerService* instance) and assigned to the *ExecutionContext*. It should be emphasized that a single *ExecutionHandler* is created for each particular type of activity thus different execution contexts pertaining to the same type of activity will be assigned the same *ExecutionHandler* instance.

ETL DataProcess Implementation

A data process consists of a number of simple data operations (i.e., the data extraction, transformation and loading operations) which are composed into a data flow. The flow of data between the operations (i.e., the execution order of the data operations) is defined by *DataFlowPaths*, with output (*OutputArgument*) of one operation providing the input (*InputArgument*) of the following operation. Thus, the execution flow of a data process is driven by the interdependence of the data operations. However, the actual scheduling of the execution time of these operations is predetermined by the availability of the relevant data. To this end a *push mechanism* has been adopted in the proposed application framework to ensure that each data operation, upon completion, transfers the relevant data to the next operation. The implementation of this mechanism is based on the well-known *Observer* pattern with the output argument of an operation taking the role of the *Subject* and the input argument of the following operation taking the role of the *Observer*. The binding of these arguments is accomplished via the *Subscribe* method of the *IOperationOutputArgument* interface.

An abridged model depicting the main concepts of the proposed application framework (related to the implementation of ETL data processes) is given in Figure 32.

The *DataProcessExecutor* class defines two methods: *Initialize* for configuring the execution environment and *Execute* for initiating the execution of a data process. The data operations comprising a *DataProcess* are represented by the *ExtractEntity*, *TransformEntity* and *LoadEntity* abstract classes, which have been further specialized to introduce concrete data operations (*ExtractEntityFromXml*, *ExtractEntityFromSqlServer*, *ExtractEntityFromOracle*, *JoinEntity*, *UnionEntity*, *SplitEntity*, *SortEntity*, *FilterEntity*, *AggregateEntity*, *LoadEntityIntoText*, *LoadEntityIntoSqlServer*, *LoadEntityIntoOracle*, etc.). The classification of data operations is in accordance with the taxonomy of ETL operations given in (*Vassiliadis et al., 2009; Petrović, 2014*).

The inputs and outputs of a data operation are represented by the *InputArgument* and *OutputArgument* classes, respectively, which, in accordance with the adopted data transfer mechanism, implement the required interfaces (*IOperationInputArgument* and *IOperationOutputArgument*).

The *ServiceProvider* class is responsible for providing and managing the various components (such as *ETLMetadataService*, *ETLCompilerService*, *ETLDataOperationService*, etc.) that are used during the execution of a data process. The *ETLDataProcessService* sequence diagram is given in Figure 33.

Figure 32. ETLDataProcessService class diagram

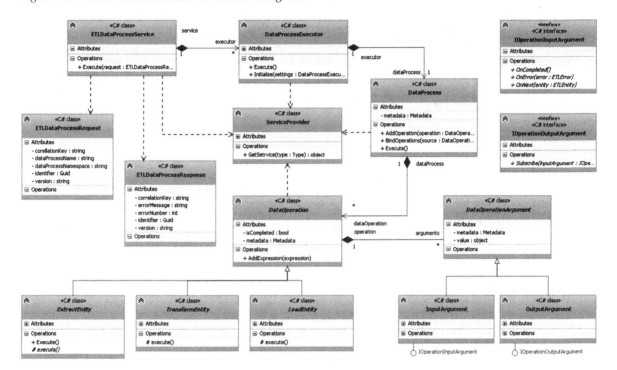

Similarly to the execution of an ETL process, the execution of a *DataProcess* commences upon receiving an *ETLDataProcessExecutionRequest* message and completes by creating and sending an *ETLDataProcessExecutionResponse* message (depicted in Figure 33 by the invocation of the *Execute* method of an *ETLDataProcessService* instance). A specific application domain is then created and the *DataProcessExecutor* is instantiated.

However, contrary to the execution of an ETL process, all of the data operations comprising the data process must be instantiated and bound to each other, before the execution of the data process can commence. Thus once the *DataProcessExecutor* has been created, its *Initialize* method will be invoked to configure the execution environment. Since the execution of a data processes is also metadata driven, it is first necessary to retrieve the relevant metadata (i.e., the ETL-O model which is to be executed as well as the ETL-E models it references) by invoking the *LoadMetadata* method of an *ETLMetadataService* instance. In accordance with the obtained metadata, the appropriate *DataProcess* is instantiated and then configured. The configuration of a data process instance entails the creation of all of the involved data operations.

In order to create a *DataOperation* the *Create* method of a *DataOperationService* instance is invoked. First the appropriate *DataOperation* is instantiated. Then, for each referenced ETL-E expression, the corresponding executable code must be generated and compiled, which is accomplished by invoking the *Compile* method of an *ETLCompilerService* instance. The compilation process (*Hazzard & Bock, 2013; Troelsen, 2012; Microsoft, 2015; Microsoft, 2017*) results in a dynamic method (*DynamicMethod*) which is then attached the *DataOperation* which is subsequently attached to the to the *DataProcess* instance through the *AddOperation* method.

Figure 33. ETLDataProcessService sequence diagram

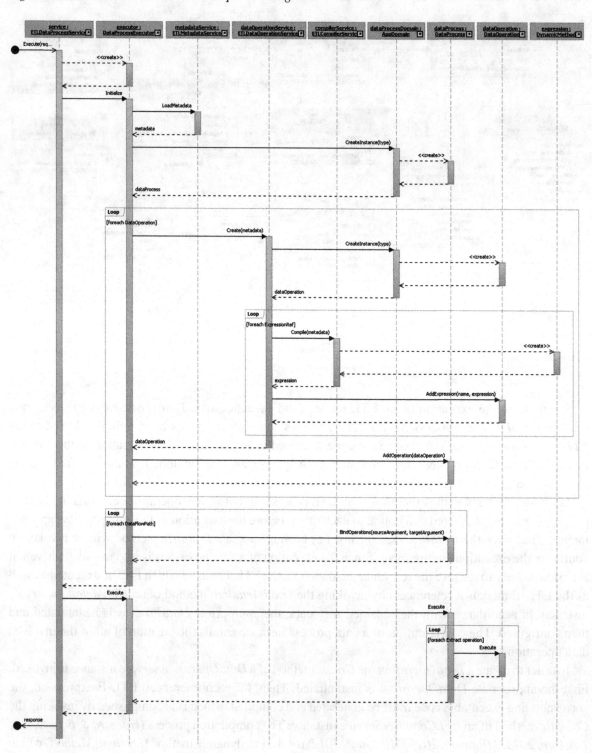

When all of the *DataOperations* have been created, the final step is to bind the operations to each other in order to create the defined data flow. This is accomplished by invoking the *BindOperations* method of the *DataProcess* instance for every *DataFlowPath* in the obtained model.

Once the execution environment has been configured, the *Execute* method of the *DataProcessExecutor* instance is invoked to execute the data process. This entails the creation of a collection of the *Extract* operations and the concurrent invocation of their *Execute* methods. In accordance with the adopted data transfer mechanism, the remaining data operations (i.e., the data transformation and load operations) will automatically be executed as soon as they receive the necessary data. The execution of the data process is completed when all of the data operations have been executed (i.e., once the *isComplete* attribute of every single operation is set to true).

FUTURE RESEARCH DIRECTIONS

One possible future research direction could be exploring the possibility of enhancing the *M-ETL-A* ETL-PL execution environment by introducing a specific *ExecutionOptimizer* service which would be responsible for determining the best possible execution plan for an ETL process on basis of the semantics of the models that are to be executed and the characteristics of hardware infrastructure available at runtime. Given that the dynamics of modern business systems (along with the sheer volume of data to be processed) impose strict constraints on the performances of ETL processes, the potential for increasing the performances of the developed processes lies in the key characteristics of the M-ETL-A ETL-PL execution environment i.e., it is designed to inherently enable the distributed and parallelized execution of an ETL process. Taking advantage of the fact that the generic services (which can easily be installed on any hardware node) are capable of interpreting any concrete ETL model makes it possible to fully exploit the available hardware infrastructure and additionally increase performances by assigning the execution of each of the concrete service instances to the best possible hardware node.

The problem of choosing the particular nodes, on which the concrete service instances should be executed, can be modeled as a multicriteria optimization problem. Namely, if an ETL process model is regarded as a composition of concrete service instances, then the available nodes play the role of possible candidates for executing each of the services. The performances of the generic services will obviously differ from node to node, depending, not only on the volume of data that is to be processed and the semantics of the ETL models, but also on the particular hardware characteristics of the nodes (such as: the number of processors and their type, the number of cores per processor, CPU speed, CPU cache size, available RAM memory, etc.) and each of these characteristics could be assigned a preference indicating its importance. Consequently, the problem of optimizing the execution plan of an ETL process model consists of selecting the particular nodes on which the concrete services instances (comprising the ETL process) should be executed, in such a way that the execution performances of the ETL process, as a whole, are maximized. In addition, the minimal required performance levels of the ETL process may also be given, so the goal would then be to select the best execution plan within the given constraints. Moreover, with the right optimization algorithm, the selection could be truly dynamic (i.e., the actual nodes could be selected just prior to or even during the execution of an ETL process), thereby rendering the execution of the ETL process more reliable and failure resilient.

Further work could also be aimed at extending the proposed *M-ETL-A* conceptual framework to include additional languages. For example, it would be beneficial to introduce a language for representing the hardware infrastructure on which the ETL-PL services are executed. A DSL, with a graphical notation, could be defined for representing the main concepts of the hardware infrastructure.

CONCLUSION

A novel solution – *M-ETL-A*, based on the Domain-Specific Modeling (DSM) approach to software development, is proposed for the conceptualization and automation of ETL process development. A specific platform (ETL-PL) is proposed to technologically support, not only the automated development of ETL processes, but also their subsequent execution.

In comparison with the existing methodological approaches, reviewed in the *Background* section, it should first be emphasized that, as previously stated, only a few approaches exist which enable the automated development of ETL processes in the context of MDD (i.e., which support both the formal specification of ETL processes and the automated transformation of such specifications into executable code), while the remaining approaches only deal with the first aspect i.e., the modeling ETL processes.

On the specification side, building on the identified strengths and weaknesses of the analyzed approaches, the proposed solution provides a means for the formal specification of the different aspects of an ETL process (e.g. the control flow, the data flow, the data structures, etc.), using an extensible set of independent DSLs (each providing only a minimal, yet extensible, set of semantically rich domain-specific concepts pertaining to the relevant aspect) and even more importantly (in order to enable automated development) for the formal definition of the semantics of the actual data transformations. Moreover, the syntax and the semantics of the DSL concepts are controlled, hence incorrect or incomplete designs are prevented by making them impossible to specify. Therefore, one of the main advantages of ETL-PL is that, since it is geared towards ETL domain experts, it doesn't require skilled programmers, or even technical knowledge. The fact that it is based on a minimal set of semantically rich abstractions, which encapsulate the existing knowledge and experience in the ETL domain, makes it possible to fully exploit the knowledge and expertise of domain experts. Consequently, it is easier to learn and use compared to vendor ETL tools and GPML based approaches. Furthermore, by providing a graphical development environment, the ETL processes (which can contain very complex custom transformation operations) are easily specified by domain experts (who need not be technically proficient) and the actual implementation will be automatically obtained from the specification, thus significantly increasing development productivity and efficiency, while lowering the development and maintenance costs. Moreover, by separating the different aspects into different models, and allowing for complex data processes to be gradually defined (through several diagrams at different levels of abstraction) the development of very complex ETL processes is significantly facilitated. Finally, the introduction of a base metamodel makes it possible to easily incorporate new ETL DSLs (created by simply extending the base concepts), while the introduced ETL DSLs are also envisaged to be easily extensible through specialization, thereby providing the desired flexibility.

On the implementation side, it should be noted that, to the best of our knowledge, only two groups of authors deal with this aspect in the context of MDD, yet their specifications are based on extensions of GPMLs. The introduction of ETL DSLs as a means for the formal specification of ETL processes, as well as the automated transformation between the specification and the application framework, significantly elevates the semantic level of the solution whose implementation is supported by the introduced application framework. Since both the specification and the application framework use concepts close to the real ETL domain concepts the transformation between them can be fully automated, thus significantly increasing development productivity and efficiency while lowering the development and maintenance costs. Moreover, the obtained solutions would have good performances and be scalable and maintainable yet, at the same time, flexible (i.e., they could be easily extended to adapt to the constant changes in the environment and new requirements).

It should also be emphasized that an additional advantage of ETL-PL is that it presumes the dynamic execution of ETL process models i.e., the automatic generation, compilation and execution of ETL processes at runtime. More importantly, in light of the constant changes in business requirements, the proposed solution provides the necessary flexibility to quickly respond to these changes since the process specification can easily be adapted (i.e., modified, extended or even created anew) and the corresponding executable code will be promptly generated and executed. In addition, the entire ETL process is well-documented.

The deployment of the developed ETL process is straightforward, since the proposed solution presumes that the generic services (which are capable of interpreting any concrete ETL model and whose implementation is stable) are installed on each of the available hardware nodes, so that every node can handle the execution of any concrete ETL process or data process model. The specific implementation of an ETL process is given in the models, which are stored in the metadata repository, thus the actual deployment is accomplished by simply storing the models in the repository. Furthermore, the modification of existing models, or the creation of new ones, doesn't affect the operation of the execution environment.

Finally, ETL-PL is developed in accordance with the service-oriented approach to software development (SOA). The SOA approach was adopted because it results in extremely scalable and flexible solutions, which is imperative in light of the frequent changes in business requirements. Since it promotes the loose-coupling of services, the solution can be easily extended, simply by adding new services, or modified without affecting the existing services. It was thus designed to enable parallel and distributed execution of an ETL process. By parallelizing the execution of the services, instead of executing them sequentially, the performances of an ETL process are significantly increased. Distributing the execution of the services over the different available hardware nodes leads to yet a further increase in performances. The ever increasing volume of data that is to be processed can, thus, be handled by simply increasing the hardware capabilities (by adding new hardware nodes) and parallelizing the execution.

The main goal of *M-ETL-A* is to introduce a means for supporting executable specifications of ETL processes. It provides a completely integrated solution for ETL process development (integrating both the development and execution environment) which is geared towards ETL domain experts.

REFERENCES

Bézivin, J., Hillairet, G., Jouault, F., Kurtev, I., & Piers, W. (2005). *Bridging the MS/DSL tools and the Eclipse Modeling Framework*. Paper presented at the International Workshop on Software Factories at OOPSLA 2005, San Diego, CA. Retrieved from http://softwarefactories.com/workshops/OOPSLA-2005/Papers/Bezivin.pdf

Cook, S., Jones, G., Kent, S., & Wills, A. C. (2007). *Domain Specific Development with Visual Studio DSL Tools*. Upper Saddle River, NJ: Addison-Wesley Professional/Pearson Education.

El Akkaoui, Z., Mazón, J.-N., Vaisman, A., & Zimányi, E. (2012). BPMN-based conceptual modeling of ETL processes. In A. Cuzzocrea & U. Dayal (Eds.), *Data Warehousing and Knowledge Discovery: Proceedings of the 14th International Conference DaWaK 2012 (LNCS)* (Vol. 7448, pp. 1-14). Berlin, Germany: Springer-Verlag Berlin Heidelberg.

El Akkaoui, Z., & Zimányi, E. (2009). Defining ETL worfklows using BPMN and BPEL. In *Proceedings of the ACM twelfth international workshop on Data warehousing and OLAP –DOLAP'09* (pp. 41-48). New York, NY: ACM. 10.1145/1651291.1651299

El Akkaoui, Z., Zimányi, E., Mazón, J.-N., & Trujillo, J. (2011). A model-driven framework for ETL process development. In *Proceedings of the 14th ACM international workshop on Data warehousing and OLAP –DOLAP'11* (pp. 45-52). New York, NY: ACM. 10.1145/2064676.2064685

Fowler, M. (2010). *Domain-Specific Languages*. Upper Saddle River, NJ: Addison-Wesley Professional/Pearson Education.

Greenfield, J., Short, K., Cook, S., & Kent, S. (2004). *Software Factories: Assembling Applications with Patterns, Models, Frameworks, and Tools*. Indianapolis, IN: Wiley Publishing.

Hazzard, K., & Bock, J. (2013). *Metaprogramming in. NET*. Shelter Island, NY: Manning Publications.

Ivantsov, R. (2009). *Irony -. NET Language Implementation Kit*. Retrieved from: http://irony.codeplex.com/

Jarke, M., Lenzerini, M., Vassiliou, Y., & Vassiliadis, P. (2003). *Fundamentals of Data Warehouses*. Berlin, Germany: Springer-Verlag Berlin Heidelberg. doi:10.1007/978-3-662-05153-5

Kelly, S., & Tolvanen, J.-P. (2008). *Domain-Specific Modeling: Enabling Full Code Generation*. Hoboken, NJ: John Wiley & Sons. doi:10.1002/9780470249260

Kimball, R., & Caserta, J. (2004). *The Data Warehouse ETL Toolkit: Practical Techniques for Extracting, Cleaning, Conforming, and Delivering Data*. Indianapolis, IN: Wiley Publishing.

Kimball, R., Ross, M., Becker, B., Mundy, J., & Thornthwaite, W. (2010). *The Kimball Group Reader: Relentlessly Practical Tools for Data Warehousing and Business Intelligence*. Indianapolis, IN: Wiley Publishing.

Luján-Mora, S., & Trujillo, J. (2004). A data warehouse engineering process. In T. Yakhno (Ed.), *Advances in Information Systems: Proceedings of the Third International Conference ADVIS 2004 (LNCS)* (Vol. 3261, pp. 14-23). Berlin, Germany: Springer-Verlag Berlin Heidelberg. 10.1007/978-3-540-30198-1_3

Luján-Mora, S., Vassiliadis, P., & Trujillo, J. (2004). Data mapping diagrams for data warehouse design with UML. In P. Atzeni, W. Chu., H. Lu, S. Zhou, & T.W. Ling (Eds.), *Conceptual Modeling – ER 2004: Proceedings of the 23rd International Conference on Conceptual Modeling (LNCS)* (*Vol. 3288*, pp. 191-204). Berlin, Germany: Springer-Verlag Berlin Heidelberg. 10.1007/978-3-540-30464-7_16

Mazón, J.-N., & Trujillo, J. (2008). An MDA approach for the development of data warehouses. *Decision Support Systems*, *45*(1), 41–58. doi:10.1016/j.dss.2006.12.003

Microsoft. (2015). *Expression Trees (C#)*. Retrieved from: https://docs.microsoft.com/en-us/dotnet/csharp/programming-guide/concepts/expression-trees/index

Microsoft. (2016). *Modeling SDK for Visual Studio - Domain-Specific Languages*. Retrieved from: https://docs.microsoft.com/en-us/visualstudio/modeling/modeling-sdk-for-visual-studio-domain-specific-languages

Microsoft. (2017). *Emitting Dynamic Methods and Assemblies*. Retrieved from: https://docs.microsoft.com/en-us/dotnet/framework/reflection-and-codedom/emitting-dynamic-methods-and-assemblies

Muñoz, L., Mazón, J.-N., Pardillo, J., & Trujillo, J. (2008). Modelling ETL processes of data warehouses with UML activity diagrams. In R. Meersman, Z. Tari, & P. Herrero (Eds.), *On the Move to Meaningful Internet Systems: OTM 2008 Workshops (LNCS)* (Vol. 5333, pp. 44–53). Berlin, Germany: Springer-Verlag Berlin Heidelberg. doi:10.1007/978-3-540-88875-8_21

Muñoz, L., Mazón, J.-N., & Trujillo, J. (2009). Automatic generation of ETL processes from conceptual models. In *Proceedings of the ACM twelfth international workshop on Data warehousing and OLAP –DOLAP'09* (pp. 33-40). New York, NY: ACM. 10.1145/1651291.1651298

Petrović, M. (2014). *A Model Driven Development Approach for the Data Warehouse Extract, Transform and Load Process* (PhD thesis). Faculty of Organizational Sciences, University of Belgrade, Serbia. (in Serbian)

Petrović, M., Vučković, M., Turajlić, N., Babarogić, S., Aničić, N., & Marjanović, Z. (2017). Automating ETL processes using the domain-specific modeling approach. *Information Systems and e-Business Management*, *15*(2), 425–460. doi:10.100710257-016-0325-8

Recchia, P., & Guerot, A. (2009). Multiply Dsl points of view [Blog post]. Retrieved from: https://mexedge.wordpress.com/2009/01/13/multiply-dsl-points-of-view/

Simitsis, A. (2005). Mapping conceptual to logical models for ETL processes. In *Proceedings of the 8th ACM international workshop on Data warehousing and OLAP –DOLAP'05* (pp. 67-76). New York, NY: ACM. 10.1145/1097002.1097014

Simitsis, A., & Vassiliadis, P. (2003). A methodology for the conceptual modeling of ETL processes. In N. Lammari, N. Prat, & S. Si-Saïd Cherfi (Eds.), *Decision Systems Engineering: Proceedings of the first International Workshop DSE '03 at CAiSE'03 (CEUR Workshop Proceedings – CEUR-WS.org)* (Vol. 75, pp. 305-316). Aachen, Germany: Sun SITE Informatik, RWTH Aachen University.

Simitsis, A., & Vassiliadis, P. (2008). A method for the mapping of conceptual designs to logical blueprints for ETL processes. *Decision Support Systems, 45*(1), 22–40. doi:10.1016/j.dss.2006.12.002

Simitsis, A., Vassiliadis, P., Terrovitis, M., & Skiadopoulos, S. (2005). Graph-based modeling of ETL activities with multi-level transformations and updates. In A. M. Tjoa & J. Trujillo (Eds.), *Data Warehousing and Knowledge Discovery: Proceedings of the 7th International Conference DaWak 2005 (LNCS)* (Vol. 3589, pp. 43-52). Berlin, Germany: Springer-Verlag Berlin Heidelberg. 10.1007/11546849_5

Troelsen, A. (2012). *Pro C# 5.0 and the. NET 4.5 Framework*. New York, NY: Apress. doi:10.1007/978-1-4302-4234-5

Trujillo, J., & Luján-Mora, S. (2003). A UML based approach for modeling ETL processes in data warehouses. In I.-Y. Song, S.W. Liddle, T.W. Ling & P. Scheuermann (Eds.), *Conceptual Modeling – ER 2003: Proceedings of the 22nd International Conference on Conceptual Modeling (LNCS)* (*Vol. 2813,* pp. 307-320). Berlin, Germany: Springer-Verlag Berlin Heidelberg. 10.1007/978-3-540-39648-2_25

Turajlić, N., Petrović, M., & Vučković, M. (2014). Analysis of ETL process development approaches: some open issues. In A. Marković & S. Barjaktarović Rakočević (Eds.), *New Business Models and Sustainable Competitiveness: Proceedings of the XIV International Symposium SymOrg 2014* (pp. 45-51). Belgrade, Serbia: University of Belgrade, Faculty of Organizational Sciences.

Vassiliadis, P., Simitsis, A., & Baikousi, E. (2009). A taxonomy of ETL activities. In *Proceedings of the ACM twelfth international workshop on Data warehousing and OLAP –DOLAP'09* (pp. 25-32). New York, NY: ACM. 10.1145/1651291.1651297

Vassiliadis, P., Simitsis, A., Georgantas, P., & Terrovitis, M. (2003). A framework for the design of ETL scenarios. In J. Eder & M. Missikoff (Eds.), *Advanced Information Systems Engineering: Proceedings of the 15th International Conference CAiSE 2003 (LNCS)* (Vol. 2681, pp. 520-535). Berlin, Germany: Springer-Verlag Berlin Heidelberg. 10.1007/3-540-45017-3_35

Vassiliadis, P., Simitsis, A., Georgantas, P., Terrovitis, M., & Skiadopoulos, S. (2005). A generic and customizable framework for the design of ETL scenarios. *Information Systems, 30*(7), 492–525. doi:10.1016/j.is.2004.11.002

Vassiliadis, P., Simitsis, A., & Skiadopoulos, S. (2002a). Modeling ETL activities as graphs. In L. Lakshmanan (Ed.), *Design and Management of Data Warehouses: Proceedings of the 4th International Workshop DMDW'2002 at CAiSE'02 (CEUR Workshop Proceedings – CEUR-WS.org)* (Vol. 58, pp. 52-61). Aachen, Germany: Sun SITE Informatik, RWTH Aachen University.

Vassiliadis, P., Simitsis, A., & Skiadopoulos, S. (2002b). Conceptual modeling for ETL processes. In *Proceedings of the 5th ACM international workshop on Data warehousing and OLAP –DOLAP'02* (pp. 14-21). New York, NY: ACM. 10.1145/583890.583893

ADDITIONAL READING

Atkinson, C., & Kuhne, T. (2003). Model-driven development: A metamodeling foundation. *IEEE Software*, *20*(5), 36–41. doi:10.1109/MS.2003.1231149

Clark, T., Sammut, P., & Willans, J. (2008). *Applied Metamodelling: a Foundation for Language Driven Development* (2nd ed.). Sheffield, UK: Ceteva.

Cook, S. (2004). Domain-Specific Modeling and Model Driven Architecture. In D. Frankel (Ed.), *MDA Journal*. Retrieved from: https://www.bptrends.com/mda-journal-domain-specific-modeling-and-model-driven-architecture/

France, R., & Rumpe, B. (2005). Domain specific modeling. *Software & Systems Modeling*, *4*(1), 1–3. doi:10.100710270-005-0078-1

France, R., & Rumpe, B. (2007). Model-driven development of complex software: a research roadmap. In *Proceedings of Future of Software Engineering – FOSE'07 at ICSE 2007, Minneapolis, MN, USA* (pp. 37–54). Los Alamitos, CA: IEEE Computer Society. doi:10.1109/FOSE.2007.14

Giordano, A. D. (2010). *Data Integration Blueprint and Modeling: Techniques for a Scalable and Sustainable Architecture*. Boston, MA: Pearson Education.

Golfarelli, M. (2010). From user requirements to conceptual design in warehouse design: a survey. In L. Bellatreche (Ed.), Data Warehousing Design and Advanced Engineering Applications: Methods for Complex Construction (pp. 1-16). Hershey,PA: Information Science Reference, IGI Global. doi:10.4018/978-1-60566-756-0.ch001

Golfarelli, M., & Rizzi, S. (2009). *Data Warehouse Design: Modern Principles and Methodologies*. New York, NY: McGraw-Hill.

Inmon, W. H., Strauss, D., & Neushloss, G. (2010). *DW 2.0: The Architecture for the Next Generation of Data Warehousing*. Burlington, MA: Morgan Kaufmann Publishers.

Mernik, M., Heering, J., & Sloane, A. M. (2005). When and how to develop domain-specific languages. [CSUR]. *ACM Computing Surveys*, *37*(4), 316–344. doi:10.1145/1118890.1118892

Voelter, M., Benz, S., Dietrich, C., Engelmann, B., Helander, M., Kats, L., . . . Wachsmuth, G. (2013). *DSL Engineering: Designing, Implementing and Using Domain-Specific Languages*. http://voelter.de/dslbook/markusvoelter-dslengineering-1.0.pdf

KEY TERMS AND DEFINITIONS

Domain-Specific Modeling (DSM): A modeling approach that allows for the formalization of semantically rich abstractions, in a form which can be reused. It also enables the generation of executable code from models representing the specification of the system.

ETL-D: A language for the specification of source and target data models. It provides a uniform representation of the various data models involved in the transformations (either as their inputs or the results of their execution).

ETL-E: A language for the specification of various logical and arithmetic expressions. It allows for the formal specification of the semantics of the data operations and the various conditions and restrictions pertaining to the execution of an ETL process.

ETL-O: A language for the specification of data operations. It defines the fundamental concepts for defining the semantics of the data operations and the order in which they are to be executed (i.e., the data flows of an ETL process).

ETL-P: A language for specification of the execution order of the data operations. It defines the fundamental concepts for specifying the execution semantics (i.e., the control flow) of an ETL process.

ETL-PL: A specific ETL platform that has been developed to technologically support both the specification and the automated transformation of ETL process models into the executable code of a specific application framework. The components of ETL-PL are divided into two layers: the development environment and the execution environment.

ETL-T: A language for the specification of transformation operation templates. It enables the creation of new field transformation operations, in the form of templates which can be reused.

Extract-Transform-Load (ETL) Process: Process which is responsible for the acquisition and integration of business data from a number of different sources, its transformation into strategic business information and the subsequent storage of the transformed data in a format that facilitates business analysis.

Chapter 11
Introduction of Item Constraints to Discover Characteristic Sequential Patterns

Shigeaki Sakurai
Toshiba Digital Solutions Corporation, Japan

ABSTRACT

This chapter introduces a method that discovers characteristic sequential patterns from sequential data based on background knowledge. The sequential data is composed of rows of items. This chapter focuses on the sequential data based on the tabular structured data. That is, each item is composed of an attribute and an attribute value. Also, this chapter focuses on item constraints in order to describe the background knowledge. The constraints describe the combination of items included in sequential patterns. They can represent the interests of analysts. Therefore, they can easily discover sequential patterns coinciding to the interests of the analysts as characteristic sequential patterns. In addition, this chapter focuses on the special case of the item constraints. It is constrained at the last item of the sequential patterns. The discovered patterns are used to the analysis of cause, and reason and can predict the last item in the case that the sub-sequence is given. This chapter introduces the property of the item constraints for the last item.

INTRODUCTION

Owing to the progress of computer and network environments, it is easy to collect data with time information such as daily business reports, weblog data, and physiological information. This is the context in which methods of analyzing data with time information have been studied. This chapter focuses on a sequential pattern discovery method from discrete sequential data. The research expands the pattern discovery task (Agrawal & Srikant, 1994). The methods proposed by (Garofalakis et al., 2010), (Pei et al., 2001), (Srikant & Agrawal, 1996), and (Zaki, 2001) efficiently discover the frequent patterns as characteristic patterns. However, the discovered patterns do not always correspond to the interests of analysts, because the patterns are common and are not a source of new knowledge for the analysts.

DOI: 10.4018/978-1-5225-5516-2.ch011

The problem has been pointed out in connection with the discovery of associative rules. Blanchard et al. (2005), Brin et al. (1997), Silberschatz et al. (1996), and Suzuki et al. (2005) propose other evaluation criteria in order to discover other kinds of characteristic patterns. The patterns discovered by the criteria are not always frequent but are characteristic with some viewpoints. The criteria may be applicable to discovery methods of sequential patterns. However, these criteria do not satisfy the Apriori property. It is difficult for the methods based on the criteria to efficiently discover the patterns. On the other hand, Sakurai et al. (2008b) proposes sequential interestingness as an evaluation criterion satisfying the Apriori property. It can discover sequential patterns including sub-patterns with relatively small frequency. The sequential patterns are regarded as rules which predict remaining sub-patterns in the case that the sub-sequential patterns are given. We can anticipate that the analysts are interested in the sequential patterns to some degree.

Also, the discovery methods tend to discover a large amount of sequential patterns when the thresholds of evaluation criteria are not appropriate. The thresholds depend on the sequential data. Therefore, the selection of appropriate thresholds are not easy for the analysts. Thus, methods that limit the number of sequential patterns (Fournier-Viger et al, 2013), (Hathi & Ambasana, 2015), (Maciag, 2017), (Sakurai & Nisihizawa, 2015), (Tzvetkov et al., 2003) have been proposed. These methods can discover sequential patterns whose number is appropriate.

In addition, some methods use the background knowledge brought in order to discover sequential patterns corresponding to the interests of analysts (Garofalakis et al., 1999), (Pei et al., 2002), (Sakurai et al., 2008a). Garofalakis et al. (1999) describes the background knowledge based on regular expression constraints. Pei et al. (2002) proposes a framework related to 7 constraints such as the inclusion relation and the length of the patterns, and so on. Sakurai et al. (2008a) deals with seven constraints related to time interval between items in the sequential patterns.

This chapter focuses on item constraints representing the background knowledge (Sakurai et al., 2008c), (Sakurai et al., 2008d). Especially, it focuses on the sequential data described in tabular structured format. In the case of the data, we can deal with the relationships between attributes and attribute values. This chapter introduces the property of the constraints and the discovery method of sequential patterns based on the constraints.

BACKGROUND

This chapter explains basic terminology related to the discovery of sequential patterns. Sequential data is rows of item sets and a sequential pattern is a characteristic sub row extracted from the sequential data. Here, an item is an object, an action, or its evaluation in the analysis target. For example, "beer", "diaper", "milk", and "snack" are items in retail business. Each item set has some items that occur at the same time, but each item set does not have multiple identical items. That is, the data focuses on only whether the items are bought or not by customers. It does not consider the price, the number of buying items, and so on. Formally, a sequential pattern s_x is described as $(l_{x1}, l_{x2}, \cdots, l_{xn_x})$, where l_{xi} is an item set and n_x is the number of the item sets included in the sequential pattern. The number n_x is called length and the sequential pattern is called n_x-th sequential pattern. Also, each l_{xi} is described as $(v_{xi1}, v_{xi2}, \cdots, v_{xim_i})$, where v_{xij} is an item that satisfies the following conditions: $v_{xik_1} \neq v_{xik_2}$ and $k_1 \neq k_2$, and m_i is the number of the items included in the item set l_{xi}. For example, ({"beer", "diaper"}, {"beer", "diaper", "milk"}, {"diaper", "snack"}) is an example of the sequential pattern ($s_{example}$) in the retail business. The pattern is a 3-rd sequential pattern and is composed of three item sets: {"beer", "diaper"}, {"beer", "diaper", "milk"}, and {"diaper", "snack"}. The pattern shows that a person buys "beer" and "diaper" on the first day, buys "beer", "diaper", and "milk" on the second day, and buys "diaper" and "snack" on the third day. The sequential pattern is depicted in Figure 1. In this figure, each circle shows an item, each circle with the same textile shows the same kind of items, items separated by arrow lines show item sets, and this figure shows that an item set at the left side occurs before an item set at the right side.

It is necessary to define the frequency of sequential patterns in order to discover the sequential patterns. In advance of this definition, this chapter explains the concept of the inclusion for sequential patterns. Let two sequential patterns $s_1 (= (l_{11}, l_{12}, \cdots, l_{1n_1}))$ and $s_2 (= (l_{21}, l_{22}, \cdots, l_{2n_2}))$ be given. s_2 is included in s_1, if s_1 and s_2 satisfy the following conditions: $\exists y$ $\{y_1, y_2, \cdots, y_{n_2}\}$ satisfying the conditions $y_1 < y_2 < \cdots < y_{n_2}$, and $l_{21} \subseteq l_{1y_1}$, $l_{22} \subseteq l_{1y_2}$, $\cdots$, and $l_{2n_2} \subseteq l_{1y_{n_2}}$. The inclusion is described as $s_2 \subseteq s_1$. For example, a sequential pattern ({"beer", "diaper"}, {"diaper", "snack"}) is included in $s_{example}$, because {"beer", "diaper"} corresponds to the first item set of $s_{example}$ and {"diaper", "snack"} corresponds to the third item set of $s_{example}$. Also, another pattern ({"diaper"}, {"milk"}) is included in $s_{example}$, because {"diaper"} is included in the first item set of $s_{example}$ and {"milk"} is included in the second item set of $s_{example}$. On the other hand, ({"diaper", "milk"}, {"beer"}) is not included in $s_{example}$, because {"diaper", "milk"} is included in the second item set of $s_{example}$ but {"beer"} is not included in the item set after the second item set.

Each sequential pattern is evaluated to determine whether it is included in each row of sequential data. The number of rows including the sequential pattern is regarded as the frequency of the sequential pattern. For example, sequential data is given as shown in Table 1. The frequency of ({"beer", "diaper"}, {"diaper", "snack"}) is 3, because the sequential pattern is included in D1, D3, and D4. Also, the frequency of ({"diaper", "milk"}, {"beer"}) is 2, because the pattern is included in D1 and D2.

Figure 1.

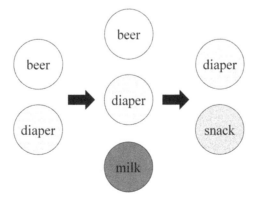

Table 1.

D1	({"beer", "diaper", "milk"}, {"beer", "diaper", "snack"})
D2	({"diaper", "milk"}, {"beer", "diaper"}, {"snack"})
D3	({"beer", "diaper"}, {"beer"}, {"diaper", "snack"})
D4	({"beer", "snack"}, {"beer", "diaper"}, {"diaper", "snack"})
D5	({"beer", "milk"}, {"beer", "diaper"}, {"diaper", "milk"})

Next, this chapter explains the Apriori property, which is the most important property related to the discovery of sequential patterns. The property requires that if a sequential pattern and its sequential sub-pattern are given, a value of an evaluation criterion for the sequential pattern is smaller than or equal to a value of an evaluation criterion for the sequential sub-pattern. For example, if a sequential pattern ({"beer", "milk"}, {"diaper"}), its sub-patterns ({"beer"}, {"diaper"}), and ({"beer", "milk"}) are given, their frequencies are 2, 4, and 2, respectively. An evaluation value of the pattern is smaller than or equal to those of the sub-patterns. The property can reduce the number of candidate sequential patterns generated by sequential pattern discovery methods.

Using these basic concepts, the following sections introduce a method that discovers sequential patterns corresponding to the interests of analysts.

DISCOVERY METHOD

Measures for Evaluating Sequential Patterns

In order to discover sequential patterns, it is necessary to evaluate whether the patterns are characteristic. At first, this section introduces two evaluation criteria for the sequential patterns: the support and the confidence (Agrawal & Srikant, 1995). The support evaluates frequencies of sequential patterns and the confidence evaluates ratios of sequential patterns in the case that sequential sub-patterns are given. These criteria are defined by Formula (1) and Formula (2), respectively.

$$supp(s) = \frac{f(s)}{N} \tag{1}$$

$$conf(s|s_p) = \frac{f(s)}{f(s_p)} \tag{2}$$

Here, s is a sequential pattern, s_p is a sequential sub-pattern of the pattern s, $f(s)$ is frequency of the pattern s, and N is the total number of rows of sequential data.

If the support of a sequential pattern is larger than or equal to the minimum support given by analysts, the pattern is called a frequent pattern. The support satisfies the Apriori property. That is, the support of s_p is larger than or equal to the one of s. The property is used to efficiently discover frequent sequential patterns.

Efficient Sequential Pattern Discovery Methods

This section introduces a discovery method of sequential patterns based on (Srikant & Agrawal, 1996). This is because the following item constraints for the last item use the framework of the discovery method. The discovery method is composed of three processes: frequent item discovery, frequent item set discovery, and frequent sequential pattern discovery.

At first, the frequent item discovery process picks up an item from a row of sequential data. The process calculates the number of rows of sequential data including the item as the frequency of the item. The process judges whether the item is frequent or not by comparing the support with the minimum support given by analysts. That is, if the support is larger than or equal to the minimum support, then the item is regarded as a frequent item. The process stores frequent items. A frequent item is called by 1-st frequent item set. The process can discover all frequent items by evaluating all items included in the rows of the sequential data.

Next, the frequent item set discovery process generates a candidate item set with $i{+}1$ items

$$V_{i+1}(=\{v_1, v_2, \cdots, v_{i-1}, v_i, v_{i+1}\})$$

from two frequent item sets with i items

$$V_{i,1}(=\{v_1, v_2, \cdots, v_{i-1}, v_i\})$$

and

$$V_{i,2}(=\{v_1, v_2, \cdots, v_{i-1}, v_{i+1}\})$$

as shown in Figure 2.

Figure 2.

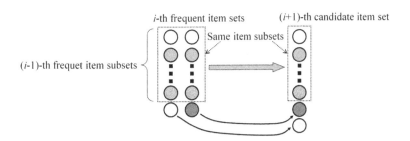

The frequent item set discovery process evaluates whether the candidate item set is frequent or not. The process is repeated until all frequent item sets are discovered. The discovered frequent items and the discovered frequent item sets are regarded as the 1-st frequent sequential patterns.

Next, the frequent sequential pattern discovery process generates a $(k+1)$-th candidate sequential pattern from two k-th frequent sequential patterns as shown in Figure 3.

When the k-th frequent sequential patterns are described as (s_p, l_1) and (s_p, l_2), $(k+1)$-th candidate sequential pattern is described as (s_p, l_1, l_2). The process evaluates whether the $(k+1)$-th candidate sequential pattern is a frequent sequential pattern. Then, it is necessary for the process to calculate the frequency $f((s_p, l_1, l_2))$. The process is repeated until all frequent sequential patterns are discovered.

Based on the above discussions, the discovery method of sequential patterns can efficiently discover all frequent sequential patterns by expanding the number of items and the length of the sequential patterns from discovery of the 1-st frequent sequential patterns with an item.

ITEM CONSTRAINT

Constraint for Attribute and Attribute Value

Originally, the discovery task of sequential patterns dealt with a set of daily purchasing lists for a user and a shop. It gradually expanded to the sequence of tabular structured data. In the case of the data, each item is composed of attribute and its value. If an attribute of an item is equal to the one of other item, the items tend to have relationship. We can discover such characteristic sequential patterns that analysts have interests by using the relationship. Therefore, this section introduces an constraint for attribute and attribute value. The constraint is called by item constraint. It can focus on specific rows of items or specific combinations of items according to the interest of analysts. The constraint is generally described as shown in Formula (3). In this formula, the length of the constraint is m. Also, C_{ij} is an item,

Figure 3.

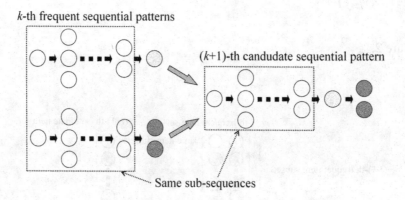

284

an attribute, or an attribute value, and is called a component of an item constraint. Here, x, y, and z are the number of item components included in the constraint.

$$(\{C_{11}, C_{12}, ..., C_{1x}\}, \{C_{21}, C_{22}, ..., C_{2y}\}, ..., \{C_{m1}, C_{m2}, ..., C_{mz}\}) \tag{3}$$

For example, let attributes and attribute values as shown in Table 2 be given. The combination of "Traffic jam" and "Heavy", and the one of "Traffic jam" and "Light" are examples of items in the case of tabular structured data. They are described as "Traffic jam: Heavy" and "Traffic jam: Light". In general, an item composed of an attribute "A" and an attribute value "a" is described as "A:a".

If an item constraint ({Weather: Fine, Day: Weekend}, {Traffic jam:}) is given, the discovery method extracts sequential patterns including either ({Weather: Fine, Day: Weekend}, {Traffic jam: Heavy}) or ({Weather: Fine, Day: Weekend}, {Traffic jam: Light}). On the other hand, if an item constraint ({:Heavy}, {Temperature: Cold}) is given, it does sequential patterns including either ({Traffic jam: Heavy}, {Temperature: Cold} or ({Car weight: Heavy}, {Temperature: Heavy}. An item constraint can represent some combinations of items by using relationships between attributes and their attribute values. The discovery method checks whether candidate sequential patterns satisfy the constraints when the patterns are frequent.

Constraints for the Last Item

It is possible for the above item constraints to discover characteristic patterns by flexibly setting item constraints. The constraints have the effect that decreases the discovery time. This is because we can delete sequences which does not satisfy the constraints in advance. However, the effect is limited in the case that many item constraints are set.

On the other hand, we can set a constraint to the first item (C_{11}) or the last item (C_{m1}) in the sequence as a special case of the item constraint. In the case of the last item, we can regard the last item as the result part of a rule and can regard the remaining sub-sequence as the condition part. The discovered pattern satisfying the constraint for the last item can be used to the analysis of cause and result. Also, it can be done to the prediction of the last item in the case that the sub-sequence corresponding to the condition part is given. Therefore, the analysts tend to be interested in the item constraint for last item.

Table 2.

Attribute	Attribute value
Traffic jam	Heavy, Light
Weather	Fine, Cloud, Rain
Day	Weekday, Weekend
Temperature	Cold, Warm, Hot
Car weight	Heavy, Light

For example, we consider that a sequential pattern as shown in Formula (4) is discovered in order to confirm the effect of the constraint.

({Weather: Fine, Temperature: Warm}, {Day: Weekend}, {Traffic jam: Heavy})   (4)

The pattern is interpreted as such a rule that if weather is fine and temperature is warm in a day, and the next day is weekend, then the traffic jam is heavy in the day after the next day. The pattern shows the heavy traffic jam related to coming back home. In the present, a sub-sequence {Weather: Fine, Temperature: Warm}, {Day: Weekend} is given. Then, we can predict an item {Traffic jam: Heavy} in the next day. The pattern is discovered by using the constraint for the last item. In the case that the analysts try to analyze amount of the traffic, they can set the constraint for the last item {Traffic jam: }.

The item constraint for the last item can discover characteristic sequential patterns. In addition, it has good property for the efficient discovery of sequential patterns. It can restrict the growth of item set and the one of sequential pattern. That is, it can decrease the candidate of both item set and sequential pattern. In the following, the chapter introduces how the decrease is performed.

Firstly, we consider the discovery process of the 1-st frequent item sets. The item sets are required to include an item satisfying the item constraint for the last item. In the following, the item is called as the last item. If there is not an item set satisfying the constraint, the discovery process of frequent sequential patterns stops. Next, we consider the discovery process of the 2-nd frequent item sets. Figure 4 explains that the 2-nd candidate item sets cannot include the last item. In this figure, 2-nd candidate item sets assigned X signs are not generated. This is because the last item appears only the last part of frequent sequential patterns. It is not necessary for the process to generate 2-nd candidate item sets including the last item. The remaining 2-nd candidate item sets are investigated the frequency. If they are frequent, the item sets are regarded as the 2-nd frequent item sets. In the following discovery process of the 3-rd or more candidate item sets, the item sets do not have the last item. The usual expansion process is repeated. We can acquire all 1-st frequent sequential patterns considering the constraints.

Next, we consider the discovery process of the 2-nd frequent sequential pattern. The process combines two 1-st frequent sequential patterns. Then, the item constraints for the last item require that one of the patterns is the last item and it is positioned at the next of the other pattern. Therefore, it is not necessary for the process to generate 2-nd candidate sequential patterns which do not satisfy the two conditions. Figure 5 shows the unnecessary combinations of the 1-st frequent sequential patterns are gotten rid of the candidate sets.

Figure 4.

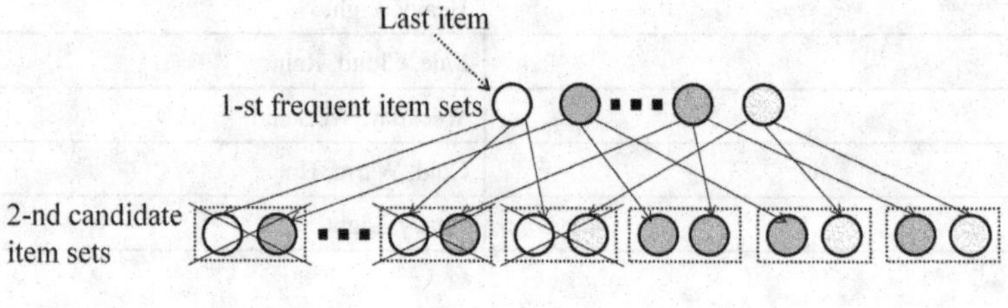

Figure 5.

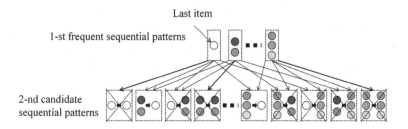

Lastly, the discovery method dealing with the item constraints for the last item is expanded backward in order to keep the last item of sequential patterns. The expansion is called the backward expansion. It is similar to the expansion shown in Figure 3. The latter expansion is called the forward expansion hereafter. In the case of the backward expansion, two k-th frequent sequential patterns are selected. The patterns have the same sub-sequence whose length is $k-1$ and is extracted from respective k-th frequent sequential patterns by cutting their most left item sets. The cut item sets are arranged before the same sub-sequence. The combination of the cut item sets and the same sub-sequence is $(k+1)$-th candidate sequential pattern. Figure 6 shows an example of the backward expansion. In this figure, the cut item set from the top left follows the cut item set from the bottom left. Also, the process can generate such $(k+1)$-th candidate sequential pattern that the one from the bottom left does the one from the top left. The backward expansion is repeated until all sequential patterns are discovered.

The discovery process can restrict the generation of the 2-nd candidate item sets and the 2-nd candidate sequential patterns. Therefore, it is possible to more efficiently discover all frequent sequential patters satisfying the constraints for the last item.

Figure 6.

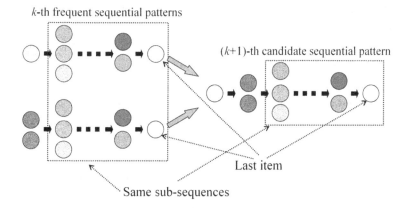

FUTURE TRENDS

This chapter focuses on item constraints in order to acquire characteristic sequential patterns by reflecting on the interests of analysts, and introduces an efficient discovery method of sequential patterns based on the constraints. Even if the method is powerful in the analysis of real sequential data, there are many other techniques related to the discovery methods. For example, Yan et al. (2003) proposes a method that discovers only sequential patterns not including super-pattern with the same support. Fournier-Viger et al. (2016a), Kiran et al. (2016), and Tanbeer (2009) propose methods that discover periodic-frequent patterns. Parthasarathy et al. (1999) proposes a method that discovers sequential patterns from dynamic databases. Fiot et al. (2007) proposes a method that discovers frequent sequential patterns from sequential data whose parts are missed.

Instead of simple discrete sequential data, the author expects methods seamlessly dealing with various types of sequential data. Chiang et al. (2004) proposes a method that discovers fuzzy sequential sentence patterns representing relationships between genes from literatures in the biomedical field. Huang and Kao (2005) proposes a method that represents numerical sequential data by fuzzy sets and discovers association rules from the data. Fiot et al. (2008) proposes a method that discovers fuzzy sequential patterns from sequential data including items and their volume. Also, our other research (Sakurai et al., 2017) proposes a ranking method of evaluation objects. It deals with numerical sequential data and textual sequential data related to evaluation objects. A ranking model is constructed from these data. In the case of the prediction of attractive stock brands, the model is constructed from stock price sequences and news headline sequences. In addition, Sakurai et al. (2014a) and Sakurai et al. (2014b) discover trend rules from the numerical data and the textual data. The trend rules represent relationships among the change of numerical data, keywords, and evaluation objects. They are used in order to explain the reason why predicted evaluation objects are attractive.

On the other hand, even if we have many methods which directly uses the numerical sequential data, we can transform the data to discrete sequential data by using the pre-process methods. SAX(Symbolic Aggregate approXimation) (Lin et al., 2003) is a representative one of the transformation methods. The method transforms numerical values to representative numerical values by referring to average value in the specified time interval. The representative ones are regarded as discrete values. Then, the method equalizes the frequency of the discrete values by assuming Gaussian distribution and adjusting the threshold for the transformation. Many researchers have tried to revise the method. Lkhagava et al. (2006) proposes a method considering the minimum value and the maximum value. Malinowski et al. (2013) and Zalewski et al. (2012) propose methods reflecting on the direction of the change. We can acquire discrete sequential data from numerical sequential data by using these methods.

In other research directions, the author expects methods that adaptively update the model acquired from the sequential data. This is because previous model is not always valid when the time passes. On-line learning techniques are one of key technologies for the adaptive update. Also, the author expects a framework to be established that includes pre-process method, discovery method, post-process method, and user interaction, because all these elements are indispensable for the discovery of new knowledge from sequential data. For example, Fournier-Viger et al. (2014a) and Fournier-Viger et al. (2016b) introduce a open-source based data mining library including many algorithms specialized in pattern mining.

Lastly, the author notes that application fields of discovery methods from the data are expanding more and more by the arrival of Big Data age (Kusnetzky, 2010) (White, 2012). For example, the author expects methods to be used for sequential data collected from ubiquitous computing environments, that is Internet of Things. In near future, many sensors will be embedded in such environments where people live and work, and much sensor information will be collected. The data will be used in order to improve health care, smart community and other aspects of people's lives. Also, the author expects the methods to be applied to sequential data related to bioinformatics. Much gene information of various species is stored in databases. The analysis of the information may lead to advances in animal and plant breeding, veterinary medicine, and medical treatment for human beings. The discovery methods of sequential patterns will be extended to additional research and application fields.

CONCLUSION

This chapter introduced some techniques related to the discovery of sequential patterns. At first, it introduced basic terminology and basic definitions in this field. Next, it introduced item constraints in order to flexibly use the background knowledge brought by analysts. In addition, an efficient discovery method based on the background knowledge is introduced in the special case of item constraints. Lastly, this chapter described the future direction of this research field.

REFERENCES

Agrawal, R., & Srikant, R. (1994). Fast Algorithms for Mining Association Rules. *Proceedings of the 20th International Conference on Very Large Data Bases*, 487-499.

Agrawal, R., & Srikant, R. (1995). Mining Sequential Patterns. *Proceedings of the 11th International Conference on Data Engineering*, 3-14. 10.1109/ICDE.1995.380415

Blanchard, J. (2005). Assessing Rule Interestingness with a Probabilistic Measure of Deviation from Equilibrium. *Proceedings of the 11th International Symposium on Applied Stochastic Models and Data Analysis*, 191-200.

Brin, S. (1997). Beyond Market Baskets: Generalizing Association Rules to Correlations. *Proceedings of the 1997 ACM SIGMOD International Conference on Management of Data*, 265-276. 10.1145/253260.253327

Chiang, J.-H. (2004). Discovering Gene-gene Relations form Fuzzy Sequential Sentence Patterns in Biomedical Literature. *Proceedings of the 13th IEEE International Conference on Fuzzy Systems*, 2, 1165-1168.

Fiot, C. (2007). Approximate Sequential Patterns for Incomplete Sequence Database Mining. *Proceedings of the 16th IEEE International Conference on Fuzzy Systems*, 1-6. 10.1109/FUZZY.2007.4295445

Fiot, C. (2008). TED and EVA: Expressing Temporal Tendencies among Quantitative Variables using Fuzzy Sequential Patterns. *Proceedings of the 17th IEEE International Conference on Fuzzy Systems*, 1861-1868.

Fournier-Viger, P. (2013). TKS: Efficient Mining of Top-K Sequential Patterns. *Proceedings of the International Conference on Advanced Data Mining and Applications*, 109-120. 10.1007/978-3-642-53914-5_10

Fournier-Viger, P. (2014). SPMF: A Java Open-source Pattern Mining Library. *Journal of Machine Learning Research, 15*, 3389–3393.

Fournier-Viger, P. (2016a). PHM: Mining Periodic High-utility Itemsets. *Proceedings of the 16th Industrial Conference on Data Mining*, 64-79.

Fournier-Viger, P. (2016b). The SPMF Open-source Data Mining Library Version 2. *Proceedings of the European Conference on Principles of Data Mining and Knowledge Discovery*, 36-40. 10.1007/978-3-319-46131-1_8

Garofalakis, M. N. (1999). SPIRIT: Sequential Pattern Mining with Regular Expression Constraints. *Proceedings of the 25th International Conference on Very Large Data Bases Conference*, 223-234.

Garofalakis, M. N. (2010). PRISM: An Effective Approach for Frequent Sequence Mining via Prime-block Encoding. *Journal of Computer and System Sciences, 76*(1), 88-102.

Hathi, K. B., & Ambasana, J. R. (2015). Top K Sequential Pattern Mining Algorithm. *Proceedings of the International Conference on Information Engineering, Management and Security*, 113-120.

Huang, Y.-P., & Kao, L.-J. (2005). A Novel Approach to Mining Inter-transaction Fuzzy Association Rules from Stock Price Variation Data. *Proceedings of the 14th IEEE International Conference on Fuzzy Systems*, 791-796. 10.1109/FUZZY.2005.1452495

Kiran, R. U., Kitsuregawa, M., & Reddy, P. K. (2016). Efficient Discovery of Periodic-frequent Patterns in Very Large Databases. *Journal of Systems and Software, 112*, 110–121. doi:10.1016/j.jss.2015.10.035

Kusnetzky, D. (2010). What is "Big Data?" *ZDNet*. Retrieved from http://www.zdnet.com/blog/virtualization/ what-is-big-data/1708

Lin, J. (2003). A Symbolic Representation of Time Series, with Implications for Streaming Algorithms. *Proceedings of the 8th ACM SIGMOD Workshop on Research Issues in Data Mining and Knowledge Discovery*, 2-11.

Lkhagava, B. (2006). Extended SAX: Extension of Symbolic Aggregate Approximation for Financial Time Series Data Representation. *Proceedings of the Data Engineering Workshop 2006*, 4A0-8.

Maciag, P. S. (2017). *Efficient Discovery of Top-K Sequential Patterns in Event-based Spatial-temporal Data*. Retrieved from https://arxiv.org/pdf/1707.00670.pdf

Malinowski, S., Guyet, T., Quiniou, R., & Tavenard, R. (2013). 1d-SAX: A Novel Symbolic Representation for Time Series. *Lecture Notes in Computer Science, 8207*, 273–284. doi:10.1007/978-3-642-41398-8_24

Parthasarathy, S. (1999). Incremental and Interactive Sequence Mining. *Proceedings of the 8th International Conference on Information and Knowledge Management*, 251-258.

Pei, J. (2001). PrefixSpan: Mining Sequential Patterns Efficiently by Prefix-Projected Pattern Growth. *Proceedings of the 2001 International Conference on Data Engineering*, 215-224.

Pei, J. (2002). Mining Sequential Patterns with Constraints in Large Databases. *Proceedings of the 11th ACM International Conference on Information and Knowledge Management*, 18-25. 10.1145/584792.584799

Sakurai, S. (2008a). Discovery of Time Series Event Patterns based on Time Constraints from Textual Data. *International Journal of Information and Mathematical Sciences*, 4(2), 144–151.

Sakurai, S. (2008b). A Sequential Pattern Mining Method based on Sequential Interestingness. *International Journal of Information and Mathematical Sciences*, 4(4), 252–260.

Sakurai, S. (2008d). Discovery of Sequential Patterns based on Constraint Patterns. *International Journal of Computer, Electrical, Automation. Control and Information Engineering*, 2(11), 3758–3764.

Sakurai, S. (2014a). A Prediction of Attractive Evaluation Objects based on Complex Sequential Data, *World Academy of Science, Engineering and Technology, International Journal of Computer. Quantum and Information Engineering*, 8(2), 88–96.

Sakurai, S. (2014b). An Activation Method of Topic Dictionary to Expand Training Data for Trend Rule Discovery. *Applied Computational Intelligence and Soft Computing*, 871412.

Sakurai, S. (2017). Ranking of Evaluation Targets based on Complex Sequential Data. *International Journal of Data Warehousing and Mining*, 13(4), 19–32. doi:10.4018/IJDWM.2017100102

Sakurai, S., Kitahara, Y., Orihara, R., Iwata, K., Honda, N., & Hayashi, T. (2008c). Discovery of Sequential Patterns Coinciding with Analysts' Interests. *Journal of Computers*, 3(7), 1–8. doi:10.4304/jcp.3.7.1-8

Sakurai, S., & Nishizawa, M. (2015). A New Approach for Discovering Top-K Sequential Patterns based on the Variety of Items. *Journal of Artificial Intelligence and Soft Computing Research*, 5(2), 141–153. doi:10.1515/jaiscr-2015-0025

Silberschatz, A., & Tuzhilin, A. (1996). What Makes Patterns Interesting in Knowledge Discovery Systems. *IEEE Transactions on Knowledge and Data Engineering*, 8(6), 970–974. doi:10.1109/69.553165

Srikant, R., & Agrawal, R. (1996). Mining Sequential Patterns: Generalizations and Performance Improvements. *Proceedings of the 5th International Conference on Extending Database Technology*, 3-17. 10.1007/BFb0014140

Suzuki, E., & Zytkow, J. M. (2005). Unified Algorithm for Undirected Discovery of Exception Rules. *International Journal of Intelligent Systems*, 20(7), 673–691. doi:10.1002/int.20090

Tanbeer, S. K. (2009). Discovering Periodic-frequent Patterns in Transactional Databases, *Proceedings of the Pacific-Asia Conference on Knowledge Discovery and Data Mining*, 242-253. 10.1007/978-3-642-01307-2_24

Tzvetkov, P. (2003). TSP: Mining Top-k Closed Sequential Patterns. *Proceedings of the 2003 International Conference on Data Mining*, 347-354.

White, T. (2012). *Hadoop: The Definitive Guide*. O'Reilly Media.

Yan, X. (2003). CloSpan: Mining Closed Sequential Patterns in Large Datasets. *Proceedings of the SIAM International Conference on Data Mining*, 166-177. 10.1137/1.9781611972733.15

Zaki, M. J. (2001). SPADE: An Efficient Algorithm for Mining Frequent Sequences. *Machine Learning*, *42*(1/2), 31–60. doi:10.1023/A:1007652502315

Zalewski, W. (2012). Time Series Discretization based on the Approximation of the Local Slope Information. *Proceedings of the 13th Ibero-American Conference on AI, Lecture Notes in Computer Science*, *7367*, 91-100. 10.1007/978-3-642-34654-5_10

Compilation of References

Abadi, Boncz, Harizopoulos, Idreos, & Madden. (2012). The design and implementation of modern column-oriented database systems. *Foundations and Trends in Databases, 5*(3), 197-280.

Abadi, D., Madden, S., & Hachem, N. (2008). Column stores vs. row stores: how different are they really? *Proceedings of the 2008 Special Interest Group on Management of Data international conference*, 967-980. 10.1145/1376616.1376712

Abadi, D., Myers, D., DeWitt, D., & Madden, S. (2007). Materialization strategies in a column-oriented DBMS. In *ICDE* (pp. 466–475). IEEE.

Abello, A., Ferrarons, F., & Romero, O. (2011). Building cubes with MapReduce. *14th international workshop on Data Warehousing and OLAP*, 17-24.

Adamala, S., & Cidrin, L. (2011). Key Success Factors in Business Intelligence. *Journal of Intelligence Studies in Business, 1*(1), 107–127.

Agrawal, R., & Srikant, R. (1994). Fast Algorithms for Mining Association Rules. *Proceedings of the 20th International Conference on Very Large Data Bases*, 487-499.

Agrawal, R., & Srikant, R. (1995). Mining Sequential Patterns. *Proceedings of the 11th International Conference on Data Engineering*, 3-14. 10.1109/ICDE.1995.380415

Aissi, S., Gouider, M., Sboui, T., & Bensaid, L. (2014). *Enhancing spatial datacube exploitation: A spatio-semantic similarity perspective*. Academic Press.

Ajtai, M., & Gurevich, Y. (1994). Datalog vs first-order logic. *Journal of Computer and System Sciences, 49*(3), 562–588. doi:10.1016/S0022-0000(05)80071-6

Aligon, J., Golfarelli, M., Marcel, P., Rizzi, S., & Turricchia, E. (2014). Similarity measures for olap sessions. *Knowledge and Information Systems, 39*(2), 463–489. doi:10.100710115-013-0614-1

Aligon, J., Marcel, P., & Negre, E. (2013). Summarizing and Querying Logs of OLAP Queries. *Advances in Knowledge Discovery and Management. Studies in Computational Intelligence, 471*, 99–124.

Allen, J. F. (1983). Maintaining knowledge about temporal intervals. *Communications of the ACM, 26*(11), 832–843. doi:10.1145/182.358434

Alvares, L. O., Bogorny, V., Kuijpers, B., de Macedo, J. A. F., Moelans, B., & Vaisman, A. (2007). A model for enriching trajectories with semantic geographical information. *Proceedings of the 15th Annual ACM International Symposium on Advances in Geographic Information Systems GIS*, 22:1–22:8. 10.1145/1341012.1341041

Antoshenkov, G. (1997). Dictionary-based order-preserving string compression. *The VLDB Journal*, 6(1), 26–39. doi:10.1007007780050031

Aouiche, K., & Darmont, J. (2009, August). Data mining-based materialized view and index selection in data warehouses. *Journal of Intelligent Information Systems*, 33(1), 65–93. doi:10.100710844-009-0080-0

Arasu, A., Babcock, B., Babu, S., Cieslewicz, J., Datar, M., Ito, K., ... Widom, J. (2016). *STREAM: The Stanford Data Stream Management System*. Springer. doi:10.1007/978-3-540-28608-0_16

Arasu, A., Babu, S., & Widom, J. (2003). *The cql continuous query language: Semantic foundations and query execution. Technical Report*. Stanford InfoLab.

Aufaure, M., Kuchmann-Beauger, N., Marcel, P., Rizzi, S., & Vanrompay, Y. (2013). Predicting your next OLAP query based on recent analytical sessions. *Data Warehousing and Knowledge Discovery - 15th International Conference, Proceedings*, 134-145. 10.1007/978-3-642-40131-2_12

Bach, M., & Werner, A. (2014). Standardization of NoSQL database languages. In *International Conference: Beyond Databases, Architectures and Structures* (pp. 50–60). Academic Press.

Badard, T. (2011). *L'open source au service du géospatial et de l'intelligence D'affaires*. Geomatics Sciences Department.

Badia, A. (2006). Text Warehousing: Present and Future. In *Processing and Managing Complex Data for Decision Support*. Idea Group Publishing. doi:10.4018/978-1-59140-655-6.ch004

Baglioni, M., de Macêdo, J. A. F., Renso, C., & Wachowicz, M. (2008). An ontology-based approach for the semantic modelling and reasoning on trajectories. Academic Press. doi:10.1007/978-3-540-87991-6_41

Bank, J., & Cole, B. (2008). *Calculating the jaccard similarity coefficient with map reduce for entity pairs in Wikipedia*. Academic Press.

Barber, R., Bendel, P., Czech, M., Draese, O., Ho, F., Hrle, N., ... Lee, J. (2012). Business analytics in (a) blink. *A Quarterly Bulletin of the Computer Society of the IEEE Technical Committee on Data Engineering*, 35(1), 9–14.

Bayer, R., & McCreight, E. (1972). Organization and Maintenance of Large Ordered Indexes. *Acta Informatica*, 1(3), 173–189. doi:10.1007/BF00288683

Beaulieu, A. (2009). Learning SQL. *Database*. doi:10.1017/CBO9781107415324.004

Behrend, A., & Jörg, T. (2010). Optimized Incremental ETL Jobs for Maintaining Data Warehouses. *Proc. of IDEAS*, 1–9. 10.1145/1866480.1866511

Bellatreche, L., Giacometti, A., Marcel, P., Mouloudi, H., & Laurent, D. (2005). A personalization framework for OLAP queries. *DOLAP 2005, ACM 8th International Workshop on Data Warehousing and OLAP Proceedings*, 9-18. 10.1145/1097002.1097005

Bellatreche, L., Mouloudi, H., Giacometti, A., & Marcel, P. (2006). Personalizationof MDX queries. 22_emes Journées Bases de Données Avancées, BDA2006, Lille, 17-20 octobre 2006, Actes (Informal Proceedings).

Bentley, J. (1975). Multidimensional binary search trees used for associative searching. *Communications of the ACM, 18*(9), 509–517. doi:10.1145/361002.361007

Berchtold, S., Böhm, C., & Kriegel, H.-P. (1998). The Pyramid Technique: Towards Breaking the Curse of Dimensionality. In *SIGMOD* (pp. 142–153). ACM. doi:10.1145/276304.276318

Bernardino, J. (2013). Open Business Intelligence for Better Decision-Making. *International Journal of Information Communication Technologies and Human Development, 5*(2), 20–36. doi:10.4018/jic-thd.2013040102

Beyer, K., & Ramakrishnan, R. (1999). Bottom up computation of sparse and iceberg cube. In *International Conference on Management Of Data* (vol. 28, pp.359-370). Philadelphia, PA: Academic Press. 10.1145/304182.304214

Bézivin, J., Hillairet, G., Jouault, F., Kurtev, I., & Piers, W. (2005). *Bridging the MS/DSL tools and the Eclipse Modeling Framework.* Paper presented at the International Workshop on Software Factories at OOPSLA 2005, San Diego, CA. Retrieved from http://softwarefactories.com/workshops/OOPSLA-2005/Papers/Bezivin.pdf

Bhogal, J., & Choksi, I. (2015). Handling big data using NoSQL. *29th International Conference on Advanced Information Networking and Applications Workshops*, 393-398.

Blanchard, J. (2005). Assessing Rule Interestingness with a Probabilistic Measure of Deviation from Equilibrium. *Proceedings of the 11th International Symposium on Applied Stochastic Models and Data Analysis*, 191-200.

Bliujute, R., Saltenis, S., Slivinskas, G., & Jensen, C. S. (1998). *Systematic Change Management in Dimensional Data Warehousing.* Time Center Technical Report TR-23.

Bogorny, V., Kuijpers, B., & Alvares, L. O. (2009). ST-DMQL: A Semantic Trajectory Data Mining Query Language. *International Journal of Geographical Information Science, 23*(10), 1245–1276. doi:10.1080/13658810802231449

Boncz, P., & Kersten, M. (1999). MIL primitives for querying a fragmented world. *The VLDB Journal, 8*(2), 101–119. doi:10.1007007780050076

Boncz, P., Kersten, M., & Manegold, S. (2008). Breaking the memory wall in MonetDB. *Communications of the ACM, 51*(12), 77–85. doi:10.1145/1409360.1409380

Boncz, P., Zukowski, M., & Nes, N. (2005). *MonetDB/X100: Hyper-Pipelining Query Execution.* CIDR.

Boulicaut, J. F., Marcel, P., & Rigotti, C. (2001). Query driven knowledge discovery via OLAP manipulations. *17èmes Journées Bases de Données Avancées (BDA 2001)*, 311 – 323. Retrieved June 13, 2013, from http://liris.cnrs.fr/~jboulica/bda01.pdf

Braz, F. J. (2007). *Trajectory data warehouses: Proposal of design and application to exploit data.* GeoInfo.

Brin, S. (1997). Beyond Market Baskets: Generalizing Association Rules to Correlations. *Proceedings of the 1997 ACM SIGMOD International Conference on Management of Data*, 265-276. 10.1145/253260.253327

Broneske, D., Köppen, V., Saake, G., & Schäler, M. (2017). Accelerating multi-column selection predicates in main-memory – the Elf approach. In ICDE (pp. 647–658). IEEE.

Bruckner, R. M., List, B., & Schiefer, J. (2002). Striving towards Near Real-Time Data Integration for Data Warehouses. In Y. Kambayashi, W. Winiwarter, & M. Arikawa (Eds.), *Data Warehousing and Knowledge Discovery* (pp. 317–326). Berlin: Springer Berlin Heidelberg; doi:10.1007/3-540-46145-0_31

C. E.F. (1993). *Providing olap to user-analysts: An it mandate.* Codd and Date, Inc.

Cangialosi, F. J., Ahmad, Y., Balazinska, M., Cetintemel, U., Cherniack, M., Hwang, J.-H., ... Zdonik, S. (2005). The Design of the Borealis Stream Processing Engine. *Second Biennial Conference on Innovative Data Systems Research (CIDR 2005)*.

Cao, H., Jiang, D., Pei, J., He, Q., Liao, Z., Chen, E., & Li, H. (2008, August). Context-aware query suggestion by mining click-through and session data. In *Proceedings of the 14th ACM SIGKDD international conference on Knowledge discovery and data mining* (pp. 875-883). ACM. 10.1145/1401890.1401995

Carral, D., Scheider, S., Janowicz, K., Vardeman, C., Krisnadhi, A. A., & Hitzler, P. (2013). An ontology design pattern for cartographic map scaling. *The Semantic Web: Semantics and Big Data, 10th International Conference, ESWC.* 10.1007/978-3-642-38288-8_6

Casters, M., Bouman, R., & Dongen, J. V. (2010). *Pentaho Kettle Solutions: Building Open Source ETL Solutions With Pentaho Data Integration.* John Wiley & Sons.

Cattell, R. (2011). Scalable SQL and NoSQL data stores. *Special Interest Group on Management of Data Record Journal., 39*(4), 12–27.

Celko, J. (2005). *Joe Celko's SQL programming style.* Joe Celko's SQL Programming Style; doi:10.1016/B978-012088797-2/50000-5

Chang, J.-W., Bista, R., Kim, Y.-C., & Kim, Y.-K. (2007). Spatio-temporal similarity measure algorithm for moving objects on spatial networks. In *Proceedings of the 2007 International Conference on Computational Science and Its Applications - Volume Part III, ICCSA'07* (pp. 1165-1178). Berlin, Germany: Springer-Verlag. 10.1007/978-3-540-74484-9_102

Chang, F., Dean, S., Ghemawat, W. C., Hsieh, D., Wallach, M., Burrows, T., ... Gruber, R. (2008). Bigtable: A distributed storage system for structured data. *ACM Transactions on Computer Systems Journal, 26*(2), 4–26.

Chaudhuri, S., & Dayal, U. (1997). An overview of data warehousing and olap technology. *Special Interest Group on Management of Data Record Journal, 26*(2), 65–74.

Chavan, V., & Phursule, R. (2014). Survey paper on big data. *International Journal of Computer Science and Information Technologies, 5*(6), 7932–7939.

Chebotko, A., Kashlev, A., & Lu, S. (2015). A Big Data Modeling Methodology for Apache Cassandra. In *Proceedings of the 2015 IEEE International Congress on Big Data* (pp. 238–245). Washington, DC: IEEE Computer Society. 10.1109/BigDataCongress.2015.41

Chen, G. J., Wiener, J. L., Iyer, S., Jaiswal, A., Lei, R., & Simha, N., ... Yilmaz, S. (2016). Realtime Data Processing at Facebook. In *Proceedings of the 2016 International Conference on Management of Data* (pp. 1087–1098). New York, NY: ACM. 10.1145/2882903.2904441

Chen, H., Chiang, R. H. L., & Storey, V. C. (2012). Business Intelligence and Analytics: From Big Data to Big Impact. *Management Information Systems Quarterly, 36*(4), 1165–1188. doi:10.2307/41703503

Chen, M., Mao, S., & Liu, Y. (2014). Big Data: A Survey. *Mobile Networks and Applications, 19*(2), 171–209. doi:10.100711036-013-0489-0

Chen, W., Hao, Z., Shao, T., & Chen, H. (2018). Personalized query suggestion based on user behavior. *International Journal of Modern Physics C, 29*(04), 1850036. doi:10.1142/S0129183118500365

Chevalier, R., Malki, M., Kopliku, A., Teste, O., & Tournier, R. (2015). Implementation of multidimensional databases in column-oriented NoSQL systems. In *Conference on Advances in Databases and Information Systems* (*vol. 9282*, pp. 79-91). Academic Press. 10.1007/978-3-319-23135-8_6

Chiang, J.-H. (2004). Discovering Gene-gene Relations form Fuzzy Sequential Sentence Patterns in Biomedical Literature. *Proceedings of the 13th IEEE International Conference on Fuzzy Systems, 2,* 1165-1168.

Clementini, E., & Felice, P. D. (1995). A comparison of methods for representing topological relationships. *Information Sciences - Applications, 3*(3), 149-178.

Colomb, R. M. (2005). *Deductive databases and their applications*. London, UK: Taylor & Francis.

Compton, M., Barnaghi, P. M., Bermudez, L., Garcia-Castro, R., Corcho, Ó., Cox, S. J. D., ... Taylor, K. (2012). The SSN ontology of the W3C semantic sensor network incubator group. *Journal of Web Semantics, 17*, 25–32. doi:10.1016/j.websem.2012.05.003

Cook, S., Jones, G., Kent, S., & Wills, A. C. (2007). *Domain Specific Development with Visual Studio DSL Tools*. Upper Saddle River, NJ: Addison-Wesley Professional/Pearson Education.

Coronel, C., & Morris, S. (2016). *Database systems: design, implementation, & management*. Cengage Learning.

Costa, E., Costa, C., & Santos, M. Y. (2017). Efficient Big Data Modelling and Organization for Hadoop Hive-Based Data Warehouses. In M. Themistocleous & V. Morabito (Eds.), *Information Systems: 14th European, Mediterranean, and Middle Eastern Conference, EMCIS 2017, Coimbra, Portugal, September 7-8, 2017, Proceedings* (pp. 3–16). Cham: Springer International Publishing. 10.1007/978-3-319-65930-5_1

Cranor, C., Johnson, T., Spataschek, O., & Shkapenyuk, V. (2003). Gigascope: A stream database for network applications. In *Proceedings of the 2003 ACM SIGMOD International Conference on Management of Data* (pp. 647–651). ACM. 10.1145/872757.872838

Cuzzocrea, A., Ferreira, N., & Furtado, P. (2014). Enhancing Traditional Data Warehousing Architectures with Real-Time Capabilities. *Proc. of ISMIS*, 456–465. 10.1007/978-3-319-08326-1_46

Cuzzocrea, A., Song, I.-Y., & Davis, K. C. (2011). Analytics over Large-Scale Multidimensional Data: The Big Data Revolution! *Proceedings of the ACM 14th International Workshop on Data Warehousing and OLAP*, 101–104. 10.1145/2064676.2064695

Damiani, M. L., & Spaccapietra, S. (2006). Spatial Data Warehouse Modelling. In *Processing and Managing Complex Data for Decision Support*. Idea Group Publishing. doi:10.4018/978-1-59140-655-6.ch001

Darmont, J., & Boussaïd, O. (2006). *Processing and Managing Complex Data for Decision Support*. Idea Group Publishing. doi:10.4018/978-1-59140-655-6

Das, D., Yan, J., Zait, M., Valluri, S. R., Vyas, N., Krishnamachari, R., ... Mukherjee, N. (2015). „Query optimization in Oracle 12c database in-memory. *VLDB*, *8*(12), 1770–1781.

Date, C. (2000). *What Not How: The Business Rules Approach to Application Development*. Reading, MA: Addison-Wesley.

Date, C. (2004). *An Introduction to Database Systems*. Boston, MA: Addison-Wesley.

Date, C. (2012). *Database Design and Relational Theory: Normal Forms and All That Jazz*. Sebastopol, CA: O'Reilly Media.

De Rougemont, M., & Cao, P. T. (2012). Approximate answers to olap queries on streaming data warehouses. *Proceedings of the Fifteenth International Workshop on Data Warehousing and OLAP*, 121–128. 10.1145/2390045.2390065

Dean, J., & Ghemawat, S. (2004). Mapreduce: simplified data processing on large clusters. In *Proceedings of the 6th conference on Symposium on Opearting Systems Design & Implementation* (vol. 6, pp. 137-149). USENIX Association.

Dean, J., & Ghemawat, S. (2008). MapReduce: Simplified Data Processing on Large Clusters. *Communications of the ACM*, *51*(1), 107–113. doi:10.1145/1327452.1327492

Dehdouh, K., Bentayeb, F., Boussaid, O., & Kabachi, N. (2015). Using the column oriented NoSQL model for implementing big data warehouses. *The 21ˢᵗ International Conference on Parallel and Distributed Processing Techniques and Applications*, 469-475.

Dehdouh, K., Bentayeb, F., Boussaid, O., & Kabachi, N. (2014). Columnar NoSQL cube: Agregation operator for columnar NoSQL data warehouse. In *IEEE International Conference on Systems, Man, and Cybernetics* (pp. 3828-3833). San Diego, CA: IEEE. 10.1109/SMC.2014.6974527

Design Tip #57: Early Arriving Facts. (n.d.). Retrieved from www.kimballgroup.com/2004/08/design-tip-57-early-arriving-facts

Di Tria, F., Lefons, E., & Tangorra, F. (2014a). Big Data Warehouse Automatic Design Methodology. In Big Data Management, Technologies, and Applications (pp. 115–149). IGI Global. doi:10.4018/978-1-4666-4699-5.ch006

Di Tria, F., Lefons, E., & Tangorra, F. (2014b). Design Process for Big Data Warehouses. *2014 International Conference on Data Science and Advanced Analytics (DSAA)*, 512–518. 10.1109/DSAA.2014.7058120

Diamantini, C., & Potena, D. (2008). Semantic enrichment of strategic datacubes. *ACM 11th International Workshop on Data Warehousing and OLAP, DOLAP*. 10.1145/1458432.1458447

Dijkstra, E. W. (1959). A note on two problems in connexion with graphs. *Numerische Mathematik*, *1*(1), 269–271. doi:10.1007/BF01386390

Duan, Q., Wang, P., Wu, M., Wang, W., & Huang, S. (2011). *Approximate query on historical stream data*. DEXA.

E2 WebCast. (2013). *Building on Early Successes in UBM's Social Business Strategy*. Retrieved from http://event.on24.com

Egenhofer, M. J., & Al-Taha, K. K. (1992). Reasoning about gradual changes of topological relationships. In *Theories and Methods of Spatio-Temporal Reasoning in Geographic Space: Proc. of the International Conference GIS*, (pp. 196-219). Springer. 10.1007/3-540-55966-3_12

Egenhofer, M. J. (2002). Toward the semantic geospatial web. In *Proceedings of the 10th ACM International Symposium on Advances in Geographic Information Systems, GIS '02* (pp. 1-4). New York, NY: ACM.

Egenhofer, M. J., & Franzosa, R. D. (1991). Point-set topological spatial relations. *International Journal of Geographical Information Systems*, *2*(5), 161–174. doi:10.1080/02693799108927841

Eiter, T., Gottlob, G., & Mannila, H. (1997). Disjunctive Datalog. *ACM Transactions on Database Systems*, *22*(3), 364–418. doi:10.1145/261124.261126

El Akkaoui, Z., Mazón, J.-N., Vaisman, A., & Zimányi, E. (2012). BPMN-based conceptual modeling of ETL processes. In A. Cuzzocrea & U. Dayal (Eds.), *Data Warehousing and Knowledge Discovery: Proceedings of the 14th International Conference DaWaK 2012 (LNCS)* (Vol. 7448, pp. 1-14). Berlin, Germany: Springer-Verlag Berlin Heidelberg.

El Akkaoui, Z., & Zimányi, E. (2009). Defining ETL worfklows using BPMN and BPEL. In *Proceedings of the ACM twelfth international workshop on Data warehousing and OLAP –DOLAP'09* (pp. 41-48). New York, NY: ACM. 10.1145/1651291.1651299

El Akkaoui, Z., Zimányi, E., Mazón, J.-N., & Trujillo, J. (2011). A model-driven framework for ETL process development. In *Proceedings of the 14th ACM international workshop on Data warehousing and OLAP –DOLAP'11* (pp. 45-52). New York, NY: ACM. 10.1145/2064676.2064685

Elmasri, R., & Navathe, S. B. (2003). Fundamentals of Database Systems. *Database, 28*, 1029. doi:10.1016/S0026-2692(97)80960-3

Elmeleegy, H., Elmagarmid, A. K., Cecchet, E., Aref, W. G., & Zwaenepoel, W. (2009). Online piece-wise linear approximation of numerical streams with precision guarantees. *Proc. VLDB Endow., 2*(1), 145–156. 10.14778/1687627.1687645

Faerber, F., Kemper, A., Larson, P., Levandoski, J., Neumann, T., & Pavlo, A. (2016). „Main Memory Database Systems. *Foundations and Trends in Databases, 8*(1-2), 1–130. doi:10.1561/1900000058

Farber, F., Cha, S., Primsch, J., Bornhovd, C., Sigg, S., & Lehner, W. (2012). SAP HANA database: Data management for modern business applications. *Special Interest Group on Management of Data Record Journal, 40*(4), 45–51.

Feuerstein, S., & Pribyl, B. (2015). *Oracle PL SQL Programming*, 867. Retrieved from http://www.amazon.com/s/ref=nb_sb_noss?url=search-alias%3Daps&field-keywords=9781449324452

Fidalgo, R. N., Times, V. C., Silva, J., & Souza, F. (2004), GeoDWFrame: a framework for guiding the design of geographical dimensional schemas. *Proceedings of the 6th International Conference on Data Warehousing and Knowledge Discovery (DaWaK 2004), 3181*, 26-37. 10.1007/978-3-540-30076-2_3

Fiot, C. (2007). Approximate Sequential Patterns for Incomplete Sequence Database Mining. *Proceedings of the 16th IEEE International Conference on Fuzzy Systems*, 1-6. 10.1109/FUZZY.2007.4295445

Fiot, C. (2008). TED and EVA: Expressing Temporal Tendencies among Quantitative Variables using Fuzzy Sequential Patterns. *Proceedings of the 17th IEEE International Conference on Fuzzy Systems*, 1861-1868.

Floratou, A., Minhas, U. F., & Özcan, F. (2014). SQL-on-Hadoop: Full circle back to shared-nothing database architectures. *Proceedings of the VLDB Endowment International Conference on Very Large Data Bases, 7*(12), 1295–1306. doi:10.14778/2732977.2733002

Fournier-Viger, P. (2013). TKS: Efficient Mining of Top-K Sequential Patterns. *Proceedings of the International Conference on Advanced Data Mining and Applications*, 109-120. 10.1007/978-3-642-53914-5_10

Fournier-Viger, P. (2014). SPMF: A Java Open-source Pattern Mining Library. *Journal of Machine Learning Research, 15*, 3389–3393.

Fournier-Viger, P. (2016a). PHM: Mining Periodic High-utility Itemsets. *Proceedings of the 16th Industrial Conference on Data Mining*, 64-79.

Fournier-Viger, P. (2016b). The SPMF Open-source Data Mining Library Version 2. *Proceedings of the European Conference on Principles of Data Mining and Knowledge Discovery*, 36-40. 10.1007/978-3-319-46131-1_8

Fowler, M. (2010). *Domain-Specific Languages*. Upper Saddle River, NJ: Addison-Wesley Professional/Pearson Education.

Frank, A. U. (1996). *Qualitative spatial reasoning: Cardinal directions as an example*. Academic Press.

Freudenreich, T., Furtado, P., Koncilia, C., Thiele, M., Waas, F., & Wrembel, R. (2013). An On-Demand ELT Architecture for Real-Time BI. In M. Castellanos, U. Dayal, & E. A. Rundensteiner (Eds.), *Enabling Real-Time Business Intelligence* (pp. 50–59). Berlin: Springer Berlin Heidelberg; doi:10.1007/978-3-642-39872-8_4

Gandomi, A., & Haider, M. (2015). Beyond the hype: Big data concepts, methods, and analytics. *International Journal of Information Management*, *35*(2), 137–144. doi:10.1016/j.ijinfomgt.2014.10.007

Gangemi, A. (2005). Ontology design patterns for semantic web content. *Proceedings of the 4th International Semantic Web Conference, ISWC*. 10.1007/11574620_21

Gangemi, A., Fisseha, F., Keizer, J., Lehmann, J., Liang, A., Pettman, I., ... Taconet, M. (2004). A core ontology of fishery and its use in the fos project. *Proceedings of the EKAW Workshop on Core Ontologies in Ontology Engineering*.

Garcia-Molina, H., Labio, W. J., Wiener, J. L., & Zhuge, Y. (1998). Distributed and Parallel Computing Issues in Data Warehousing (Invited Talk). *Proc. of SPAA/PODC*.

Garcia-Molina, H., Ullman, J., & Widom, J. (2009). *Database Systems: The Complete Book*. London, UK: Pearson Education.

Garofalakis, M. N. (2010). PRISM: An Effective Approach for Frequent Sequence Mining via Prime-block Encoding. *Journal of Computer and System Sciences*, *76*(1), 88-102.

Garofalakis, M., & Kumar, A. (2004). Deterministic wavelet thresholding for maximum-error metrics. ACM PODS. doi:10.1145/1055558.1055582

Garofalakis, M. N. (1999). SPIRIT: Sequential Pattern Mining with Regular Expression Constraints. *Proceedings of the 25th International Conference on Very Large Data Bases Conference*, 223-234.

Gartner. (2014). *Magic Quadrant for Business Intelligence and Analytics Platforms*. Author.

Ghapanchi, A. H., & Aurum, A. (2011). The impact of project license and operating system on the effectiveness of the defect-fixing process in open source software projects. *IJBIS*, *8*(4), 413–424. doi:10.1504/IJBIS.2011.042398

Giacometti, A., Marcel, P., Negre, E., & Soulet, A. (2011). Query recommendations for OLAP discovery-driven analysis. *International Journal of Data Warehousing and Mining*, 7(2), 1–25. doi:10.4018/jdwm.2011040101

Giannotti, F., Nanni, M., Pinelli, F., & Pedreschi, D. (2007). Trajectory pattern mining. In *13th ACM SIGKDD International Conference on Knowledge Discovery and Data Mining* (pp. 330–339). ACM.

Glorio, O., Mazon, J.-N., Garrigos, I., & Trujillo, J. (2012). A personalization process for spatial data warehouse development. *Decision Support Systems*, 52(4), 884–898. doi:10.1016/j.dss.2011.11.010

Golab, L., & Johnson, T. (2014). Data Stream Warehousing. In *International Conference on Data Engineering* (pp. 1290–1293). IEEE Computer Society. 10.1109/ICDE.2014.6816763

Goss, R. G., & Veeramuthu, K. (2013). Heading Towards Big Data Building A Better Data Warehouse For More Data, More Speed, And More Users. In ASMC (Advanced Semiconductor Manufacturing Conference) (pp. 220–225). Academic Press. doi:10.1109/ASMC.2013.6552808

Goyal, R., & Egenhofer, M. (2001). Similarity of cardinal directions. Lecture Notes in Computer Science, 2121, 36-55. doi:10.1007/3-540-47724-1_3

Gray, J., Chaudhuri, S., Bosworth, A., Layman, A., Reichart, D., Venkatrao, M., … Pirahesh, H. (1997). Data cube: A relational aggregation operator generalizing group by, crosstab, and sub-totals. *Data Mining and Knowledge Discovery*, 1(1), 29–53. doi:10.1023/A:1009726021843

Green, T. J. (2012). Datalog and Recursive Query Processing. *Foundations and Trends® in Databases*, 5(2), 105–195. doi:10.1561/1900000017

Greenfield, J., Short, K., Cook, S., & Kent, S. (2004). *Software Factories: Assembling Applications with Patterns, Models, Frameworks, and Tools*. Indianapolis, IN: Wiley Publishing.

Gurevich, Y. (2012). Datalog: A perspective and the potential. Lecture Notes in Computer Science, 7494, 9–20. doi:10.1007/978-3-642-32925-8_2

Guttman, A. (1984). R-Trees: A Dynamic Index Structure for Spatial Searching. In *SIGMOD* (pp. 47–57). ACM. doi:10.1145/602259.602266

Han, J. (1997). OLAP mining: An integration of OLAP with data mining. *Proceedings of the 7th IFIP*, 2, 1–9.

Han, J., Cai, Y. D., Chen, Y., Dong, G., Pei, J., Wah, B. W., & Wang, J. (2007). Multidimensional analysis of data streams using stream cubes. In *Data Streams* (pp. 103–125). Models and Algorithms. doi:10.1007/978-0-387-47534-9_6

Han, J., Chen, Y., Dong, G., Pei, J., Wah, B. W., Wang, J., & Cai, Y. D. (2005). Stream cube: An architecture for multi-dimensional analysis of data streams. *Distributed and Parallel Databases*, 18(2), 173–197. doi:10.100710619-005-3296-1

Harinarayan, V., Rajaraman, A., & Ullman, J. D. (1996). Implementing data cubes efficiently. ACM SIGMOD, 205–216. doi:10.1145/233269.233333

Hasanah, G. U., & Trisminingsih, R. (2016). Multidimensional analysis and location intelligence application for spatial data warehouse hotspot in indonesia using spagobi. *IOP Conference Series: Earth and Environmental Science, 31*(1). 10.1088/1755-1315/31/1/012011

Hathi, K. B., & Ambasana, J. R. (2015). Top K Sequential Pattern Mining Algorithm. *Proceedings of the International Conference on Information Engineering, Management and Security*, 113-120.

Hazzard, K., & Bock, J. (2013). *Metaprogramming in. NET*. Shelter Island, NY: Manning Publications.

He, H., & Singh, A. K. (2008). Graphs-at-a-time: query language and access methods for graph databases. In *Proceedings of the 2008 ACM SIGMOD international conference on Management of data* (pp. 405–418). ACM. 10.1145/1376616.1376660

Hellerstein, J. M. (2009). Dedalus: Datalog in Time and Space. *Office*, (UCB/EECS-2009-173), 262–281. doi:10.1007/978-3-642-24206-9_16

Hernandez, M. J. (2013). *Database design for mere mortals: a hands-on guide to relational database design*. Pearson Education.

Hewitt, E., & Carpenter, J. (2016). *Cassandra: The Definitive Guide* (2nd ed.). O'Reilly Media, Inc.

Holanda, M., & Souza, J. A. (2015). Query languages in nosql databases. Handbook of Research on Innovative Database Query Processing Techniques, 415.

Holzschuher, F., & Peinl, R. (2013). Performance of graph query languages: comparison of cypher, gremlin and native access in Neo4j. In *Proceedings of the Joint EDBT/ICDT 2013 Workshops* (pp. 195–204). Academic Press. 10.1145/2457317.2457351

Hu, Y., Janowicz, K., Carral, D., Scheider, S., Kuhn, W., Berg-Cross, G., . . . Kolas, D. (2013). A geo-ontology design pattern for semantic trajectories. *Spatial Information Theory - 11th International Conference, COSIT*, 438–456. 10.1007/978-3-319-01790-7_24

Huang, S. S., Green, T. J., & Loo, B. T. (2011). Datalog and Emerging Applications: An Interactive Tutorial. In *Proceedings of the 2011 international conference on Management of data - SIGMOD '11* (p. 1213). ACM. 10.1145/1989323.1989456

Huang, Y.-P., & Kao, L.-J. (2005). A Novel Approach to Mining Inter-transaction Fuzzy Association Rules from Stock Price Variation Data. *Proceedings of the 14th IEEE International Conference on Fuzzy Systems*, 791-796. 10.1109/FUZZY.2005.1452495

Idreos, S., Groen, F., Nes, N., Manegold, S., Mullender, S., & Kersten, M. (2012). Monetdb: Two decades of research in column-oriented database architectures. *A Quarterly Bulletin of the Computer Society of the IEEE Technical Committee on Data Engineering, 35*(1), 40–45.

Imho, C., Geiger, J., & Galemmo, N. (2003). *Relational Modeling and Data Warehouse Design.* New York: John Wiley & Sons.

Information Week. (2006). *Connecting the Business Technology Community. "Q&A: BI Visionary Howard Dresner".* Author.

Inmon, W. (1992). *Building the data warehouse.* New York: John Wiley & Sons.

Inmon, W. H. (2002). *Building the Data Warehouse.* John Wiley and Sons.

Inmon, W. H. (2003). The System of Record in the Global Data Warehouse. *Information & Management.*

Intel. (n.d.). *Business Intelligence.* Intel - Diálogo TI - Next Generation Center.

Ivantsov, R. (2009). *Irony -. NET Language Implementation Kit.* Retrieved from: http://irony.codeplex.com/

Jarke, M., Lenzerini, M., Vassiliou, Y., & Vassiliadis, P. (2003). *Fundamentals of Data Warehouses.* Berlin, Germany: Springer-Verlag Berlin Heidelberg. doi:10.1007/978-3-662-05153-5

Jerbi, H. (2012). *Personnalisation d'analyses décisionnelles sur des donnes multidimensionnelles* (PhD thesis). Institut de Recherche en Informatique de Toulouse UMR 5505, France.

Jerzy, D. (2012). Business intelligence and NoSQL databases. *Information Systems Management, 1*(1), 25–37.

Jiang, D., Leung, K. W. T., Vosecky, J., & Ng, W. (2014, March). Personalized query suggestion with diversity awareness. In *Data Engineering (ICDE), 2014 IEEE 30th International Conference on* (pp. 400-411). IEEE. 10.1109/ICDE.2014.6816668

Johnson, R., Raman, V., Sidle, R., & Swart, G. (2008). Row-wise parallel predicate evaluation. *PVLDB, 1*(1), 622–634.

Joslyn, C., Burke, J., Critchlow, T., Hengartner, N., & Hogan, E. (2009). View discovery in olap databases through statistical combinatorial optimization. *International Conference, SSDBM, Proceedings*, 37–55. 10.1007/978-3-642-02279-1_4

Karras, P., & Mamoulis, N. (2005). *One-pass wavelet synopses for maximum-error metrics.* PVLDB.

Kelly, S., & Tolvanen, J.-P. (2008). *Domain-Specific Modeling: Enabling Full Code Generation.* Hoboken, NJ: John Wiley & Sons. doi:10.1002/9780470249260

Kemper, A., & Neumann, T. (2011). Hyper: A hybrid OLTP & OLAP main memory database system based on virtual memory snapshots. In *ICDE* (pp. 195–206). IEEE. doi:10.1109/ICDE.2011.5767867

Kharitonov, E., Macdonald, C., Serdyukov, P., & Ounis, I. (2013, October). Intent models for contextualising and diversifying query suggestions. In *Proceedings of the 22nd ACM international conference on Conference on information & knowledge management* (pp. 2303-2308). ACM. 10.1145/2505515.2505661

Kimball, R. (1996). *The Data Warehouse Toolkit.* Wiley & Sons.

Kimball, R., & Caserta, J. (2004). *The Data Warehouse ETL Toolkit: Practical Techniques for Extracting, Cleaning, Conforming, and Delivering Data*. Wiley.

Kimball, R., & Ross, M. (2002). *The data warehouse toolkit: the complete guide to dimensional modeling*. New York: Wiley.

Kimball, R., & Ross, M. (2013). *The Data Warehouse Toolkit, The Definitive Guide to Dimensional Modeling* (3rd ed.). John Wiley & Sons, Inc.

Kimball, R., & Ross, M. (2013). *The Data Warehouse Toolkit: The Definitive Guide to Dimensional Modeling*. John Wiley & Sons.

Kimball, R., Ross, M., Becker, B., Mundy, J., & Thornthwaite, W. (2010). *The Kimball Group Reader: Relentlessly Practical Tools for Data Warehousing and Business Intelligence*. Indianapolis, IN: Wiley Publishing.

Kimball, R., Ross, M., Thornthwaite, W., Mundy, J., & Becker, B. (2008). *The Data Warehouse Lifecycle Toolkit*. Indianapolis, IN: Wiley.

King, W. R. (2009). Knowledge Management and Organizational Learning. *Annals of Information Systems, 4*. doi:10.1007/978-1-4419-0011-1_1

Kiran, R. U., Kitsuregawa, M., & Reddy, P. K. (2016). Efficient Discovery of Periodic-frequent Patterns in Very Large Databases. *Journal of Systems and Software, 112*, 110–121. doi:10.1016/j.jss.2015.10.035

Koch, C., Ahmad, Y., Kennedy, O., Nikolic, M., No¨tzli, A., Lupei, D., & Shaikhha, A. (2014). Dbtoaster: Higher-order delta processing for dynamic, frequently fresh views. *The VLDB Journal, 23*(2), 253–278. doi:10.100700778-013-0348-4

Krishnan, K. (2013). *Data Warehousing in the Age of Big Data*. Elsevier Inc. doi:10.1016/B978-0-12-405891-0.00001-5

Kruschwitz, U., Lungley, D., Albakour, M. D., & Song, D. (2013). Deriving query suggestions for site search. *Journal of the American Society for Information Science and Technology, 64*(10), 1975–1994. doi:10.1002/asi.22901

Kusnetzky, D. (2010). What is "Big Data?" *ZDNet*. Retrieved from http://www.zdnet.com/blog/virtualization/ what-is-big-data/1708

Lamb, A., Fuller, M., Varadarajan, R., Tran, N., Vandiver, B., & Doshi, L. (2012). The vertica analytic database: C-store 7 years later. *Proceedings of the Very Large Database Endowment, 5*(12), 1790–1801.

Langseth, J., & Vivatrat, N. (2003). Why Proactive Business Intelligence is a Hallmark of the Real-Time Enterprise: Outward Bound. *Intelligent Enterprise, 5*(18), 34–41.

Lapa, J., Bernardino, J., & Figueiredo, A. (2015). Commercial Business Intelligence Suites Comparison. In *WorldCIST'15 - 3rd World Conference on Information Systems and Technologies*. Ponta Delgada, Portugal: Springer. 10.1007/978-3-319-16486-1_24

Larson, A., Hanson, E., & Price, S. (2012). Columnar storage in SQL server. *A Quarterly Bulletin of the Computer Society of the IEEE Technical Committee on Data Engineering, 35*, 15–20.

Layouni, O., & Akaichi, J. (2014). A novel approach for a collaborative exploration of a spatial data cube. IJCCE. *International Journal of Computer and Communication Engineering, 3*(1), 63–68. doi:10.7763/IJCCE.2014.V3.293

Lazaridis, I., & Mehrotra, S. (2003). *Capturing sensor-generated time series with quality guarantees.* ICDE. doi:10.1109/ICDE.2003.1260811

Leis, V., Kemper, A., & Neumann, T. (2013). The Adaptive Radix Tree: ARTful Indexing for Main-Memory Databases. In ICDE (pp. 38–49). IEEE.

Leonardi, L., Orlando, S., Raffaetà, A., Roncato, A., Silvestri, C., Andrienko, G., & Andrienko, N. (2014). A general framework for trajectory data warehousing and visual olap. *GeoInformatica, 18*(2), 273–312. doi:10.100710707-013-0181-3

Levene, M., & Loizou, G. (1999). *A guided tour of relational databases and beyond.* Springer. Retrieved from https://books.google.hr/books?id=CkYpI7QsLlQC&dq=datalog+is&hl=hr&source=gbs_navlinks_s

Lezak, D., & Eastwood, V. (2009). Data warehouse technology by infobright. *Special Interest Group on Management of Data international conference*, 841-846.

Lezak, D., Wrblewski, J., Eastwood, V., & Synak, P. (2008). Brighthouse: an analytic data warehouse for adhoc queries. *Proceedings of the Very Large Database Endowment, 1*(2), 1337-1345.

Li, N., & Mitchell, J. C. (2002). Datalog with Constraints: A Foundation for Trust Management Languages. PADL, 2562, 58–73. doi:10.1007/3-540-36388-2_6

Li, Y., & Patel, J. (2013). Bitweaving: Fast scans for main memory data processing. In SIGMOD (pp. 289–300). ACM. doi:10.1145/2463676.2465322

Li, B., & Fonseca, F. (2006). Tdd: A comprehensive model for qualitative spatial similarity assessment. *Spatial Cognition and Computation, 6*(1), 31–62. doi:10.120715427633scc0601_2

Li, H., & Zhan, D. (2005). Workflow Timed Critical Path Optimization. *Nature and Science, 3*(2), 65–74.

Lim, E.-P., Chen, H., & Chen, G. (2012). Business intelligence and analytics: Research directions. ACM Trans. Manage. Inf. Syst., 3(4).

Lin, J. (2003). A Symbolic Representation of Time Series, with Implications for Streaming Algorithms. *Proceedings of the 8th ACM SIGMOD Workshop on Research Issues in Data Mining and Knowledge Discovery*, 2-11.

Liu, J. G., Zhou, T., Wang, B. H., Zhang, Y. C., & Guo, Q. (2009). Effects of user's tastes on personalized recommendation. *International Journal of Modern Physics C, 20*(12), 1925–1932. doi:10.1142/S0129183109014825

Liu, X., Thomsen, C., & Pedersen, T. B. (2011). *ETLMR: A Highly Scalable Dimensional ETL Framework Based on MapReduce. Proc. of DaWak.*

Liu, X., Thomsen, C., & Pedersen, T. B. (2014). CloudETL: Scalable Dimensional ETL for Hive. *Proc. of the 18th International Database Engineering & Applications Symposium*, 195–206. 10.1145/2628194.2628249

Li, X., & Mao, Y. (2015). Real-Time Data ETL Framework for Big Real-Time Data Analysis. In *2015 IEEE International Conference on Information and Automation* (pp. 1289–1294). Institute of Electrical and Electronics Engineers Inc. 10.1109/ICInfA.2015.7279485

Lkhagava, B. (2006). Extended SAX: Extension of Symbolic Aggregate Approximation for Financial Time Series Data Representation. *Proceedings of the Data Engineering Workshop 2006*, 4A0-8.

Lübcke, A., Schäler, M., Köppen, V., & Saake, G. (2012). *Workload-based Heuristics for Evaluation of Physical Database Architectures.* DB&IS.

Luján-Mora, S., & Trujillo, J. (2004). A data warehouse engineering process. In T. Yakhno (Ed.), *Advances in Information Systems: Proceedings of the Third International Conference ADVIS 2004 (LNCS)* (Vol. 3261, pp. 14-23). Berlin, Germany: Springer-Verlag Berlin Heidelberg. 10.1007/978-3-540-30198-1_3

Luján-Mora, S., Vassiliadis, P., & Trujillo, J. (2004). Data mapping diagrams for data warehouse design with UML. In P. Atzeni, W. Chu., H. Lu, S. Zhou, & T.W. Ling (Eds.), *Conceptual Modeling – ER 2004: Proceedings of the 23rd International Conference on Conceptual Modeling (LNCS)* (*Vol. 3288*, pp. 191-204). Berlin, Germany: Springer-Verlag Berlin Heidelberg. 10.1007/978-3-540-30464-7_16

Luo, G., Yi, K., Cheng, S. W., Li, Z., Fan, W., He, C., & Mu, Y. (2015). Piecewise linear approximation of streaming time series data with max-error guarantees. 2015 IEEE 31st ICDE, 173–184. doi:10.1109/ICDE.2015.7113282

Maciag, P. S. (2017). *Efficient Discovery of Top-K Sequential Patterns in Event-based Spatial-temporal Data.* Retrieved from https://arxiv.org/pdf/1707.00670.pdf

Majecka, B. (2009). *Statistical models of pedestrian behaviour in the forum* (Master's thesis). University of Edinburgh.

Malinowski, E., & Zimányi, E. (2005). Spatial hierarchies and topological relationships in the spatial multidimer model. *Database: Enterprise, Skills and Innovation, 22nd British National Conference on Databases, BNCOD.* 10.1007/11511854_2

Malinowski, S., Guyet, T., Quiniou, R., & Tavenard, R. (2013). 1d-SAX: A Novel Symbolic Representation for Time Series. *Lecture Notes in Computer Science, 8207*, 273–284. doi:10.1007/978-3-642-41398-8_24

Malki, J., Bouju, A., & Mefteh, W. (2012). *An ontological approach for modeling and reasoning on trajectories taking into account thematic, temporal and spatial rules.* Technique et Science Informatiques.

Manaa, M., & Akaichi, J. (2016). Ontology-based trajectory data warehouse conceptual model. *Big Data Analytics and Knowledge Discovery - 18th International Conference, DAWAK.* 10.1007/978-3-319-43946-4_22

Manaa, M., & Akaichi, J. (2017). Ontology-based modeling and querying of trajectory data. *Data & Knowledge Engineering*, *111*, 58–72. doi:10.1016/j.datak.2017.06.005

Mapelsden, D., Hosking, J., & Grundy, J. (2002). Design pattern modelling and instantiation using dpml. *Proceedings of the Fortieth International Conference on Tools Pacific: Objects for Internet, Mobile and Embedded Applications.*

Marakas, G. M. (2003). *Modern Data Warehousing, Mining, and Visualisation*. Prentice-Hall.

Marcel, P., Missaoui, R., & Rizzi, S. (2012). Towards intensional answers to OLAP queries for analytical sessions. *DOLAP 2012, ACM 15th International Workshop on Data Warehousing and OLAP Proceedings*, 49-56. 10.1145/2390045.2390054

March, S. T., & Hevner, A. R. (2007). Integrated Decision Support Systems: A Data Warehousing Perspective. *Decision Support Systems*, *43*(3), 1031–1043. doi:10.1016/j.dss.2005.05.029

Marinheiro, A. & Bernardino, J. (2015). Experimental Evaluation of Open Source Business Intelligence Suites using OpenBRR. *IEEE Latin America Transactions*, *13*(3), 810-817. doi:10.1109/TLA.2015.7069109

Marketos, G. D. (2009). *Data Warehousing and Mining Techniques for Moving Object Databases* (PhD thesis). University of Piraeus.

Marz, N., & Warren, J. (2015). *Big Data: Principles and best practices of scalable real-time data systems* (1st ed.). Greenwich, CT: Manning Publications Co.

Matthew, P. (2008). *A Framework to Support Spatial, Temporal and Thematic Analytics over Semantic Web Data* (PhD thesis). Wright State University.

Mazón, J.-N., & Trujillo, J. (2008). An MDA approach for the development of data warehouses. *Decision Support Systems*, *45*(1), 41–58. doi:10.1016/j.dss.2006.12.003

Meehan, P. (2011). *Gartner Business Intelligence Summit 2011*. Retrieved from http://link.brightcove.com/services/player/bcpid1156010110?bctid=741282639001

Mell, P. & Grance, T. (2011). *The NIST Definition of Cloud Computing*. National Institute of Standards and Technology Special Publication 800-145.

Meng, X., Bradley, J., Yavuz, B., Sparks, E., Venkataraman, S., Liu, D., ... Xin, D. (2016). Mllib: Machine learning in Apache Spark. *Journal of Machine Learning Research*, *17*(1), 1235–1241.

Microsoft. (2015). *Expression Trees (C#)*. Retrieved from: https://docs.microsoft.com/en-us/dotnet/csharp/programming-guide/concepts/expression-trees/index

Microsoft. (2016). *Modeling SDK for Visual Studio - Domain-Specific Languages*. Retrieved from: https://docs.microsoft.com/en-us/visualstudio/modeling/modeling-sdk-for-visual-studio-domain-specific-languages

Microsoft. (2017). *Emitting Dynamic Methods and Assemblies*. Retrieved from: https://docs.microsoft.com/en-us/dotnet/framework/reflection-and-codedom/emitting-dynamic-methods-and-assemblies

Mignet, L., Barbosa, D., & Veltri, P. (2003). The XML Web: A first study. In *Proceed. of the 12ᵗʰ International World Wide Web Conference (WWW 2003)* (pp. 500-510). ACM. 10.1145/775152.775223

Mohamed, N., & Al-Jaroodi, J. (2014). Real-Time Big Data Analytics: Applications and Challenges. In *2014 International Conference on High Performance Computing Simulation (HPCS)* (pp. 305–310). Academic Press. 10.1109/HPCSim.2014.6903700

Moreau, E., Yvon, F., & Cappé, O. (2008). Robust similarity measures for named entities matching. In *Proceedings of the 22Nd International Conference on Computational Linguistics - Volume 1, COLING '08*, (pp. 593-600). Stroudsburg, PA: Association for Computational Linguistics. 10.3115/1599081.1599156

Muñoz, L., Mazón, J.-N., Pardillo, J., & Trujillo, J. (2008). Modelling ETL processes of data warehouses with UML activity diagrams. In R. Meersman, Z. Tari, & P. Herrero (Eds.), *On the Move to Meaningful Internet Systems: OTM 2008 Workshops (LNCS)* (Vol. 5333, pp. 44–53). Berlin, Germany: Springer-Verlag Berlin Heidelberg. doi:10.1007/978-3-540-88875-8_21

Muñoz, L., Mazón, J.-N., & Trujillo, J. (2009). Automatic generation of ETL processes from conceptual models. In *Proceedings of the ACM twelfth international workshop on Data warehousing and OLAP –DOLAP'09* (pp. 33-40). New York, NY: ACM. 10.1145/1651291.1651298

Nakabasami, K., Amagasa, T., Shaikh, S. A., Gass, F., & Kitagawa, H. (2015). An architecture for stream olap exploiting spe and olap engine. IEEE BigData, 319–326. doi:10.1109/BigData.2015.7363771

Negash, S., & Gray, P. (2003). Business Intelligence. *Ninth Americas Conference on Information Systems*.

Neil, P. O., Neil, E. O., & Chen, X. (2007). *The star schema benchmark*. Retrieved from http://www.cs.umb.edu/ ~poneil/StarSchemaB.pdf

Neumayr, B., Anderlik, S., & Schrefl, M. (2012). Towards ontology-based OLAP: datalog-based reasoning over multidimensional ontologies. In *DOLAP '12 Proceedings of the fifteenth international workshop on Data warehousing and OLAP* (pp. 41-48). New York: ACM.

Neumeyer, L., Robbins, B., Nair, A., & Kesari, A. (2010). S4: Distributed stream computing platform. *2010 IEEE International Conference on Data Mining Workshops*, 170–177. 10.1109/ICDMW.2010.172

O'Neil, P., O'Neil, B., & Chen, X. (2007). *The star schema benchmark (SSB)*. Retrieved from http://www.cs.umb.edu/~poneil/StarSchemaB.PDF

O'Neil, P., O'Neil, E., Chen, X., & Revilak, S. (2009). *The star schema benchmark and augmented fact table indexing*. TPCTC. doi:10.1007/978-3-642-10424-4_17

O'Rourke, J. (1981). An on-line algorithm for fitting straight lines between data ranges. *Communications of the ACM*, 24(9), 574–578. doi:10.1145/358746.358758

Olston, C., Jiang, J., & Widom, J. (2003). Adaptive filters for continuous queries over distributed data streams. ACM SIGMOD, 563–574. doi:10.1145/872757.872825

Olston, C., Reed, B., Srivastava, U., Kumar, R., & Tomkins, A. (2008). Pig latin: a Not-so-foreign Language for Data Processing. *Proc. of SIGMOD*, 1099–1110. 10.1145/1376616.1376726

Organization, T. (2017). *TPC-H - a Decision Support Benchmark*. Retrieved from http://www.tpc.org/tpch/

Pardede, E. (2007). *eXtensible Markup Language (XML) Document Update in XML Database Storages* (PhD thesis). LaTrobe University, Australia.

Parthasarathy, S. (1999). Incremental and Interactive Sequence Mining. *Proceedings of the 8th International Conference on Information and Knowledge Management*, 251-258.

Paton, N. W. (1998). *Active rules in database systems*. New York: Springer.

Pei, J. (2001). PrefixSpan: Mining Sequential Patterns Efficiently by Prefix-Projected Pattern Growth. *Proceedings of the 2001 International Conference on Data Engineering*, 215-224.

Pei, J. (2002). Mining Sequential Patterns with Constraints in Large Databases. *Proceedings of the 11th ACM International Conference on Information and Knowledge Management*, 18-25. 10.1145/584792.584799

Pentaho. (2015). Retrieved from http://wiki.pentaho.com/display/EAI/eradata+TPT+Insert+Upsert+Bulk+Loader

Petrović, M. (2014). *A Model Driven Development Approach for the Data Warehouse Extract, Transform and Load Process* (PhD thesis). Faculty of Organizational Sciences, University of Belgrade, Serbia. (in Serbian)

Petrović, M., Vučković, M., Turajlić, N., Babarogić, S., Aničić, N., & Marjanović, Z. (2017). Automating ETL processes using the domain-specific modeling approach. *Information Systems and e-Business Management*, 15(2), 425–460. doi:10.100710257-016-0325-8

Piattini, M., & Diaz, O. (2000). *Advanced Database Technology and Design*. Boston: Artech House.

Plattner, H. (2009). A common database approach for OLTP and OLAP using an in-memory column database. In *SIGMOD* (pp. 1–2). ACM. doi:10.1145/1559845.1559846

Polychroniou, O., & Ross, K. (2014). Vectorized bloom filters for advanced SIMD processors. In DaMoN. ACM.

Polychroniou, O., & Ross, K. (2015). *Efficient lightweight compression alongside fast scans. In DaMoN.* ACM.

Ponniah, P. (2001). *Data Warehousing Fundamentals*. Chichester, UK: Wiley. doi:10.1002/0471221627

R. J. S. (2007). Pin: A partitioning & indexing optimization method for olap. *Proc. 9th International Conference on Enterprise Information Systems (ICEIS 2007)*.

Rabuzin, K., Maleković, M., & Lovrenčić, A. (2007). The Theory of Active Databases vs. The SQL Standard. In *The Proceedings of 18th International Conference on Information and Intelligent Systems* (pp. 49–54). Academic Press.

Rabuzin, K. (2014). Deductive Data Warehouses. *International Journal of Data Warehousing and Mining*, *10*(1), 16–31. doi:10.4018/ijdwm.2014010102

Rabuzin, K., Maleković, M., & Šestak, M. (2016). Gremlin By Example. In H. R. Arabnia, F. G. Tinetti, & M. Yang (Eds.), *Proceedings of the 2016 International Conference on Advances in Big Data Analytics* (pp. 144–149). Las Vegas, NV: CSREA Press. Retrieved from http://www.worldcomp-proceedings. com/proc/proc2016/ABDA16_Final_Edition/ABDA16_Papers.pdf

Rabuzin, K., & Modruan, N. (2014). Business intelligence and column-oriented databases. *Central European Conference on Information and Intelligent Systems*, 12-16.

Rao, J., & Ross, K. (2000). *Making B+-Trees cache conscious in main memory. In SIGMOD* (pp. 475–486). ACM.

Recchia, P., & Guerot, A. (2009). Multiply Dsl points of view [Blog post]. Retrieved from: https:// mexedge.wordpress.com/2009/01/13/multiply-dsl-points-of-view/

Reddy, G., Srinivasu, R., Rao, M., & Rikkula, S. (2010). Data Warehousing, Data Mining, OLAP and OLTP Technologies are Essential Elements to Support Decision-Making Process in Industries. *International Journal on Computer Science and Engineering*, *2*(9), 88–93.

Redmond, E., & Wilson, J. R. (2012). *Seven databases in seven weeks: a guide to modern databases and the NoSQL movement*. Dallas, TX: Pragmatic Bookshelf.

Reinschmidt, J., & Francoise, A. (1999). *Business Intelligence Certification Guide*. IBM International Technical Support Organization.

Richter, K.F., Schmid, F., & Laube, P. (2015). Semantic trajectory compression: Representing urban movement in a nutshell. *Journal of Spatial Information Science*, (4), 3–30.

Rivest, S., Bdard, Y., Proulx, M., Nadeau, M., Hubert, F., & Pastor, J. (2005). Solap technology: Merging business intelligence with geospatial technology for interactive spatio-temporal exploration and analysis of data. *ISPRS Journal of Photogrammetry and Remote Sensing*, *60*(1), 17–33. doi:10.1016/j. isprsjprs.2005.10.002

Rivest, S., Bedard, Y., & Marchand, P. (2001). Towards better support for spatial decision making: Defining the characteristics of spatial on-line analytical processing (SOLAP). *Geomatica*, *55*(4), 539–555.

Robinson, J., Webber, J., & Eifrem, E. (2013). *Graph Databases*. Sebastopol, CA: O'Reilly.

Ross, R. G. (2003). *Principles of the business rule approach*. Boston: Addison Wesley.

Rutherglen, J., Wampler, D., & Capriolo, E. (2012). *Programming Hive* (1st ed.). O'Reilly Media, Inc.

Sadoghi, Bhattacherjee, Bhattacharjee, & Canim. (2016). L-store: A real-time OLTP and OLAP system. *CoRR*.

Sakouhi, T., Akaichi, J., Malki, J., Bouju, A., & Wannous, R. (2014). Inference on semantic trajectory data warehouse using an ontological approach. *Foundations of Intelligent Systems - 21st International Symposium, ISMIS*. 10.1007/978-3-319-08326-1_47

Sakurai, S. (2008a). Discovery of Time Series Event Patterns based on Time Constraints from Textual Data. *International Journal of Information and Mathematical Sciences, 4*(2), 144–151.

Sakurai, S. (2008b). A Sequential Pattern Mining Method based on Sequential Interestingness. *International Journal of Information and Mathematical Sciences, 4*(4), 252–260.

Sakurai, S. (2008d). Discovery of Sequential Patterns based on Constraint Patterns. *International Journal of Computer, Electrical, Automation. Control and Information Engineering, 2*(11), 3758–3764.

Sakurai, S. (2014a). A Prediction of Attractive Evaluation Objects based on Complex Sequential Data, *World Academy of Science, Engineering and Technology, International Journal of Computer. Quantum and Information Engineering, 8*(2), 88–96.

Sakurai, S. (2014b). An Activation Method of Topic Dictionary to Expand Training Data for Trend Rule Discovery. *Applied Computational Intelligence and Soft Computing*, 871412.

Sakurai, S. (2017). Ranking of Evaluation Targets based on Complex Sequential Data. *International Journal of Data Warehousing and Mining, 13*(4), 19–32. doi:10.4018/IJDWM.2017100102

Sakurai, S., Kitahara, Y., Orihara, R., Iwata, K., Honda, N., & Hayashi, T. (2008c). Discovery of Sequential Patterns Coinciding with Analysts' Interests. *Journal of Computers, 3*(7), 1–8. doi:10.4304/jcp.3.7.1-8

Sakurai, S., & Nishizawa, M. (2015). A New Approach for Discovering Top-K Sequential Patterns based on the Variety of Items. *Journal of Artificial Intelligence and Soft Computing Research, 5*(2), 141–153. doi:10.1515/jaiscr-2015-0025

Santos, M. Y., Oliveira e Sá, J., Andrade, C., Vale Lima, F., Costa, E., Costa, C., … Galvão, J. (2017). A Big Data system supporting Bosch Braga Industry 4.0 strategy. *International Journal of Information Management*.

Santos, R. J., Bernardino, J., & Vieira, M. (2011). 24/7 Real-Time Data Warehousing: A Tool for Continuous Actionable Knowledge. In *2011 IEEE 35th Annual Computer Software and Applications Conference* (pp. 279–288). IEEE. 10.1109/COMPSAC.2011.44

Santos, M. Y., Costa, C., Galvão, J., Andrade, C., Martinho, B. A., Vale Lima, F., & Costa, E. (2017). Evaluating SQL-on-Hadoop for Big Data Warehousing on Not-So-Good Hardware. In *Proceedings of the 21st International Database Engineering & Applications Symposium* (pp. 242–252). New York, NY: ACM. 10.1145/3105831.3105842

Santos, R. J., & Bernardino, J. (2008). Real-time Data Warehouse Loading Methodology. In *Proceedings of the 2008 International Symposium on Database Engineering & Applications* (pp. 49–58). New York, NY: ACM. 10.1145/1451940.1451949

Sapia, C. (1999). On modeling and predicting query behavior in olap systems. Proc. Intl Workshop on Design and Management of Data Warehouses (DMDW 99), 1-10.

Sapia, C. (2000). Promise: Predicting query behavior to enable predictive caching strategies for olap systems. Lecture Notes in Computer Science, 1874, 224-233.

Sapia, C., Alexander, F., & Erlangen-nrnberg, U. (2001). *Promise: Modeling and predicting user behavior for online analytical processing applications* (PhD thesis). Technische Universitt Mnchen.

Sarawagi, S. (1999). Explaining differences in multidimensional aggregates. In *Proceedings of the 25th International Conference on Very Large Data Bases, VLDB '99*, (pp. 42-53). San Francisco, CA: Morgan Kaufmann Publishers Inc.

Sarawagi, S. (2000). User-adaptive exploration of multidimensional data. In *VLDB* (pp. 307–316). Morgan Kaufmann.

Sathe, G., & Sarawagi, S. (2001). Intelligent rollups in multidimensional olap data. In *Proceedings of the 27th International Conference on Very Large Data Bases, VLDB '01*, (pp. 531-540). San Francisco, CA: Morgan Kaufmann Publishers Inc.

Schäler, M., Grebhahn, A., Schröter, R., Schulze, S., Köppen, V., & Saake, G. (2013). QuEval: Beyond high- dimensional indexing à la carte. *PVLDB*, *6*(14), 1654–1665.

Scotch, M., & Parmantoa, B. (2005). SOVAT: Spatial OLAP visualisation and analysis tool. *Proceedings of the 38th Hawaii International Conference on System Sciences.*

Sedgewick, R. (1978). Implementing quicksort programs. *Communications of the ACM, 21*(10), 847–857. doi:10.1145/359619.359631

Shaikh, S. A., & Kitagawa, H. (2017). Approximate olap on sustained data streams. *International Conference on Database Systems for Advanced Applications*, 102–118. 10.1007/978-3-319-55699-4_7

Sidirourgos, L., & Kersten, M. (2013). Column imprints: A secondary index structure. In SIGMOD (pp. 893–904). ACM. doi:10.1145/2463676.2465306

Silberschatz, A., Korth, H. F., & Sudarshan, S. (2011). *Database System Concepts* (6th ed.; Vol. 4). Database; doi:10.1145/253671.253760

Silberschatz, A., & Tuzhilin, A. (1996). What Makes Patterns Interesting in Knowledge Discovery Systems. *IEEE Transactions on Knowledge and Data Engineering, 8*(6), 970–974. doi:10.1109/69.553165

Silvers, F. (2008). *Building and Maintaining a Data Warehouse*. Boca Raton, FL: CRC Press. doi:10.1201/9781420064636

Simitsis, A., & Vassiliadis, P. (2003). A methodology for the conceptual modeling of ETL processes. In N. Lammari, N. Prat, & S. Si-Saïd Cherfi (Eds.), *Decision Systems Engineering: Proceedings of the first International Workshop DSE '03 at CAiSE'03 (CEUR Workshop Proceedings – CEUR-WS.org)* (Vol. 75, pp. 305-316). Aachen, Germany: Sun SITE Informatik, RWTH Aachen University.

Simitsis, A., Vassiliadis, P., & Sellis, T. (2005). State-space Optimization of ETL Workflows. *TKDE*, *17*(10), 1404–1419.

Simitsis, A., Vassiliadis, P., Terrovitis, M., & Skiadopoulos, S. (2005). Graph-based modeling of ETL activities with multi-level transformations and updates. In A. M. Tjoa & J. Trujillo (Eds.), *Data Warehousing and Knowledge Discovery: Proceedings of the 7th International Conference DaWak 2005 (LNCS)* (Vol. 3589, pp. 43-52). Berlin, Germany: Springer-Verlag Berlin Heidelberg. 10.1007/11546849_5

Simitsis, A. (2005). Mapping conceptual to logical models for ETL processes. In *Proceedings of the 8th ACM international workshop on Data warehousing and OLAP –DOLAP'05* (pp. 67-76). New York, NY: ACM. 10.1145/1097002.1097014

Simitsis, A., & Vassiliadis, P. (2008). A method for the mapping of conceptual designs to logical blueprints for ETL processes. *Decision Support Systems*, *45*(1), 22–40. doi:10.1016/j.dss.2006.12.002

Simitsis, A., Vassiliadis, P., & Sellis, T. (2005) Optimizing ETL Processes in Data Warehouses. *Proc. of ICDE*, 564–575.

Simitsis, A., Wilkinson, K., Castellanos, M., & Dayal, U. (2009). QoX-driven ETL Design: Reducing the Cost of ETL Consulting Engagements. *Proc. of SIGMOD*, 953–960. 10.1145/1559845.1559954

Sismanis, Y., Deligiannakis, A., Roussopoulos, N., & Kotidis, Y. (2002). Dwarf: Shrinking the PetaCube. In *SIGMOD* (pp. 464–475). ACM.

Sitaridi, E., & Ross, K. (2013). Optimizing select conditions on GPUs. DaMoN, 4:1–4:8. doi:10.1145/2485278.2485282

Spaccapietra, S., Parent, C., Damiani, M. L., de Macedo, J. A., Porto, F., & Vangenot, C. (2008). A conceptual view on trajectories. *Data & Knowledge Engineering*, *65*(1), 126–146. doi:10.1016/j.datak.2007.10.008

Srikant, R., & Agrawal, R. (1996). Mining Sequential Patterns: Generalizations and Performance Improvements. *Proceedings of the 5th International Conference on Extending Database Technology*, 3-17. 10.1007/BFb0014140

Stonebraker, M. (2010). SQL databases v. NoSQL databases. *Communications of the ACM*, *53*(4), 10. doi:10.1145/1721654.1721659

Stonebraker, M., Abadi, D., Batkin, A., Chen, X., Cherniack, M., Ferreira, M., ... Zdonik, S. (2005). *C-Store: A column-oriented DBMS*. VLDB.

Sundstrom, D. (2010). *Star schema benchmark dbgen*. Retrieved from https://github.com/electrum/ssb-dbgen

Suzuki, E., & Zytkow, J. M. (2005). Unified Algorithm for Undirected Discovery of Exception Rules. *International Journal of Intelligent Systems*, *20*(7), 673–691. doi:10.1002/int.20090

Talebi, Z. A. a. (2008). *Exact and inexact methods for selecting views and indexes for olap performance improvement*. EDBT. doi:10.1145/1353343.1353383

Tanbeer, S. K. (2009). Discovering Periodic-frequent Patterns in Transactional Databases, *Proceedings of the Pacific-Asia Conference on Knowledge Discovery and Data Mining*, 242-253. 10.1007/978-3-642-01307-2_24

Thomsen, C., & Pedersen, T. B. (2009). A Survey of Open Source Tools for Business Intelligence. *International Journal of Data Warehousing and Mining*, *5*(3), 56–75. doi:10.4018/jdwm.2009070103

Thomsen, C., & Pedersen, T. B. (2011). Easy and Effective Parallel Programmable ETL. *Proc. of DOLAP*, 37–44.

Thomsen, C., Pedersen, T. B., & Lehner, W. (2008). RiTE: Providing On-demand Data for Right-time Data Warehousing. *Proc. of ICDE*, 456–465. 10.1109/ICDE.2008.4497454

Thusoo, A., Sen Sarma, J., Jain, N., Shao, Z., Chakka, P., & Anthony, S., ... Murthy, R. (2009). Hive - A Warehousing Solution Over a Map-Reduce Framework. In *Proceedings of the VLDB Endowment (Vol. 2*, pp. 1626–1629). Academic Press. 10.14778/1687553.1687609

Thusoo, A., Sen Sarma, J., Jain, N., Shao, Z., Chakka, P., & Zhang, N., ... Murthy, R. (2010). Hive - A Petabyte Scale Data Warehouse Using Hadoop. In *International Conference on Data Engineering* (pp. 996–1005). Academic Press. 10.1109/ICDE.2010.5447738

Thusoo, A. (2009). Hive: A Warehousing Solution Over a Map-Reduce Framework. *PVLDB*, *2*(2), 1626–1629.

Tjioe, H. C., & Taniar, D. (2005). Mining Association Rules in Data Warehouses. *International Journal of Data Warehousing and Mining*, *1*(3), 28–62. doi:10.4018/jdwm.2005070103

TPC-H. (2015). Retrieved from http://tpc.org/tpch/

Tranchant, M. (2011). *Capacités des outils solap en termes de requêtes spatiales, temporelles et spatio-temporelles. Technical report*. Conservatoire National Des Arts Et Metiers Centre Regional Rhone- Alpes Centre Denseignement De Grenoble.

Transaction Processing Performance Council. (2014). *TPC benchmark H (decision support)*. Tech. Rep. 2.17.1. Author.

Troelsen, A. (2012). *Pro C# 5.0 and the. NET 4.5 Framework*. New York, NY: Apress. doi:10.1007/978-1-4302-4234-5

Trujillo, J., & Luján-Mora, S. (2003). A UML based approach for modeling ETL processes in data warehouses. In I.-Y. Song, S.W. Liddle, T.W. Ling & P. Scheuermann (Eds.), *Conceptual Modeling – ER 2003: Proceedings of the 22nd International Conference on Conceptual Modeling (LNCS) (Vol. 2813*, pp. 307-320). Berlin, Germany: Springer-Verlag Berlin Heidelberg. 10.1007/978-3-540-39648-2_25

Turajlić, N., Petrović, M., & Vučković, M. (2014). Analysis of ETL process development approaches: some open issues. In A. Marković & S. Barjaktarović Rakočević (Eds.), *New Business Models and Sustainable Competitiveness: Proceedings of the XIV International Symposium SymOrg 2014* (pp. 45-51). Belgrade, Serbia: University of Belgrade, Faculty of Organizational Sciences.

Tzvetkov, P. (2003). TSP: Mining Top-k Closed Sequential Patterns. *Proceedings of the 2003 International Conference on Data Mining*, 347-354.

Vaisman, A., & Zimányi, E. (2012). Data warehouses: Next Challenges. *Lecture Notes in Business Information Processing*, 1–26. doi:10.1007/978-3-642-27358-2_1

Vaisman, A., & Zimányi, E. (2014). *Data Warehouse Systems: Design and Implementation*. Heidelberg, Germany: Springer. doi:10.1007/978-3-642-54655-6

Vandecasteele, A., Devillers, R., & Napoli, A. (2014). From movement data to objects behavior using semantic trajectory and semantic events. *Marine Geodesy*, *37*(2), 126–144. doi:10.1080/01490419.2014.902885

Vassiliadis, P., Simitsis, A., & Skiadopoulos, S. (2002a). Modeling ETL activities as graphs. In L. Lakshmanan (Ed.), *Design and Management of Data Warehouses: Proceedings of the 4th International Workshop DMDW'2002 at CAiSE'02 (CEUR Workshop Proceedings – CEUR-WS.org)* (Vol. 58, pp. 52-61). Aachen, Germany: Sun SITE Informatik, RWTH Aachen University.

Vassiliadis, P., Simitsis, A., Georgantas, P., & Terrovitis, M. (2003). A framework for the design of ETL scenarios. In J. Eder & M. Missikoff (Eds.), *Advanced Information Systems Engineering: Proceedings of the 15th International Conference CAiSE 2003 (LNCS)* (Vol. 2681, pp. 520-535). Berlin, Germany: Springer-Verlag Berlin Heidelberg. 10.1007/3-540-45017-3_35

Vassiliadis, P., Simitsis, A., & Baikousi, E. (2009). A taxonomy of ETL activities. In *Proceedings of the ACM twelfth international workshop on Data warehousing and OLAP –DOLAP'09* (pp. 25-32). New York, NY: ACM. 10.1145/1651291.1651297

Vassiliadis, P., Simitsis, A., Georgantas, P., Terrovitis, M., & Skiadopoulos, S. (2005). A generic and customizable framework for the design of ETL scenarios. *Information Systems*, *30*(7), 492–525. doi:10.1016/j.is.2004.11.002

Vassiliadis, P., Simitsis, A., & Skiadopoulos, S. (2002b). Conceptual modeling for ETL processes. In *Proceedings of the 5th ACM international workshop on Data warehousing and OLAP –DOLAP'02* (pp. 14-21). New York, NY: ACM. 10.1145/583890.583893

Verberne, S., Sappelli, M., Järvelin, K., & Kraaij, W. (2015, March). User simulations for interactive search: Evaluating personalized query suggestion. In *European Conference on Information Retrieval* (pp. 678-690). Springer. 10.1007/978-3-319-16354-3_75

Vidakovic, B. (1998). Nonlinear wavelet shrinkage with Bayes rules and Bayes factors. *Journal of the American Statistical Association*, *93*(441), 173–179. doi:10.1080/01621459.1998.10474099

W., K. M. (2010). SQL vs. NoSQL. *Linux Journal.*

Wagner, R., de Macêdo, J. A. F., Raffaetà, A., Renso, C., Roncato, A., & Trasarti, R. (2013). Mob-warehouse: A semantic approach for mobility analysis with a trajectory data warehouse. Advances in Conceptual Modeling - ER 2013 Workshops.

Wannous, R., Malki, J., Bouju, A., & Vincent, C. (2012). Time integration in semantic trajectories using an ontological modelling approach. *New Trends in Databases and Information Systems, Workshop Proceedings of the 16th East European Conference, ADBIS.*

Wannous, R., Malki, J., Bouju, A., & Vincent, C. (2013). Modelling Mobile Object Activities Based on Trajectory Ontology Rules Considering Spatial Relationship Rules. *Studies in Computational Intelligence, 488,* 249–258.

Ward, J. S., & Barker, A. (2013). Undefined By Data: A Survey of Big Data Definitions. *arXiv.org, 2.*

Wei, Z., Luo, G., Yi, K., Du, X., & Wen, J.-R. (2015). Persistent data sketching. In *Proceedings of the 2015 ACM SIGMOD International Conference on Management of Data* (pp. 795–810). ACM. 10.1145/2723372.2749443

White, T. (2012). *Hadoop: The Definitive Guide* (4th ed.; Vol. 54). O'Reilly Media, Inc.;

Willems, N., van Hage, W. R., de Vries, G., Janssens, J. H. M., & Malaise, V. (2010). An integrated approach for visual analysis of a multisource moving objects knowledge base. *International Journal of Geographical Information Science, 24*(10), 1543–1558. doi:10.1080/13658816.2010.515029

Willhalm, T., Oukid, I., Müller, I., & Faerber, F. (2013). Vectorizing database column scans with complex predicates. In ADMS (pp. 1–12). ACM.

Willhalm, T., Boshmaf, Y., Plattner, H., Popovici, N., Zeier, A., & Schaffner, J. (2009). SIMDScan: Ultra fast in-memory table scan using on-chip vector processing units. *PVLDB, 2*(1), 385–394.

Wood, P. T. (2012). Query languages for graph databases. *SIGMOD Record, 41*(1), 50–60. doi:10.1145/2206869.2206879

Wurst, K., Postner, L., & Jackson, S. (2014). Teaching open source (software). In *Proceedings of the 45th ACM technical symposium on Computer science education.* ACM. 10.1145/2538862.2544248

Xie, Zhu, Sharaf, Zhou, & Pang. (2012). Efficient buffer management for piecewise linear representation of multiple data streams. ACM CIKM, 2114–2118.

Yan, Z. (2009). Towards semantic trajectory data analysis: A conceptual and computational approach. *Proceedings of the VLDB PhD Workshop. Co-located with the 35th International Conference on Very Large Data Bases.*

Yang, W. S., & Lee, W. S. (2008). On-line evaluation of a data cube over a data stream. *Proceedings of the 8th Conference on Applied Computer Scince,* 373–378.

Yan, X. (2003). CloSpan: Mining Closed Sequential Patterns in Large Datasets. *Proceedings of the SIAM International Conference on Data Mining*, 166-177. 10.1137/1.9781611972733.15

Yan, Z., & Chakraborty, D. (2014). *Semantics in mobile sensing*. Morgan & Claypool Publishers. doi:10.2200/S00577ED1V01Y201404WBE008

Yan, Z., Macedo, J., Parent, C., & Spaccapietra, S. (2008). Trajectory ontologies and queries. *Transactions in GIS*, *12*, s1. doi:10.1111/j.1467-9671.2008.01137.x

Yeoh, W., & Koronios, A. (2010). Critical Success Factors for Business Intelligence Systems. *Journal of Computer Information Systems*, *50*(3), 23–32.

Zaki, M. J. (2001). SPADE: An Efficient Algorithm for Mining Frequent Sequences. *Machine Learning*, *42*(1/2), 31–60. doi:10.1023/A:1007652502315

Zalewski, W. (2012). Time Series Discretization based on the Approximation of the Local Slope Information. *Proceedings of the 13th Ibero-American Conference on AI, Lecture Notes in Computer Science*, *7367*, 91-100. 10.1007/978-3-642-34654-5_10

Zhang, R., Koudas, N., Ooi, B. C., Srivastava, D., & Zhou, P. (2010). Streaming multiple aggregations using phantoms. *The VLDB Journal*, *19*(4), 557–583. doi:10.100700778-010-0180-z

Zhou, J., & Ross, K. (2002). Implementing database operations using SIMD instructions. In *SIGMOD* (pp. 145–156). ACM.

Zikopoulos, P., Eaton, C., DeRoos, D., Deutsch, T., & Lapis, G. (2011). *Understanding Big Data: Analytics for Enterprise Class Hadoop and Streaming Data* (1st ed.). McGraw-Hill Osborne Media.

Zimányi, E. (2012). Spatio-temporal data warehouses and mobility data: Current status and research issues. *19th International Symposium on Temporal Representation and Reasoning*, 6–9.

Zukowski, M., & van de Wiel, M., & Boncz, P. A. (2012). Vectorwise: A vectorized analytical dbms. *28th International Conference on Data Engineering*, 1349-1350.

Related References

To continue our tradition of advancing information science and technology research, we have compiled a list of recommended IGI Global readings. These references will provide additional information and guidance to further enrich your knowledge and assist you with your own research and future publications.

Aasi, P., Rusu, L., & Vieru, D. (2017). The Role of Culture in IT Governance Five Focus Areas: A Literature Review. *International Journal of IT/Business Alignment and Governance, 8*(2), 42-61. doi:10.4018/IJITBAG.2017070103

Abdrabo, A. A. (2018). Egypt's Knowledge-Based Development: Opportunities, Challenges, and Future Possibilities. In A. Alraouf (Ed.), *Knowledge-Based Urban Development in the Middle East* (pp. 80–101). Hershey, PA: IGI Global. doi:10.4018/978-1-5225-3734-2.ch005

Abu Doush, I., & Alhami, I. (2018). Evaluating the Accessibility of Computer Laboratories, Libraries, and Websites in Jordanian Universities and Colleges. *International Journal of Information Systems and Social Change, 9*(2), 44–60. doi:10.4018/IJISSC.2018040104

Adeboye, A. (2016). Perceived Use and Acceptance of Cloud Enterprise Resource Planning (ERP) Implementation in the Manufacturing Industries. *International Journal of Strategic Information Technology and Applications, 7*(3), 24–40. doi:10.4018/IJSITA.2016070102

Adegbore, A. M., Quadri, M. O., & Oyewo, O. R. (2018). A Theoretical Approach to the Adoption of Electronic Resource Management Systems (ERMS) in Nigerian University Libraries. In A. Tella & T. Kwanya (Eds.), *Handbook of Research on Managing Intellectual Property in Digital Libraries* (pp. 292–311). Hershey, PA: IGI Global. doi:10.4018/978-1-5225-3093-0.ch015

Adhikari, M., & Roy, D. (2016). Green Computing. In G. Deka, G. Siddesh, K. Srinivasa, & L. Patnaik (Eds.), *Emerging Research Surrounding Power Consumption and Performance Issues in Utility Computing* (pp. 84–108). Hershey, PA: IGI Global. doi:10.4018/978-1-4666-8853-7.ch005

Afolabi, O. A. (2018). Myths and Challenges of Building an Effective Digital Library in Developing Nations: An African Perspective. In A. Tella & T. Kwanya (Eds.), *Handbook of Research on Managing Intellectual Property in Digital Libraries* (pp. 51–79). Hershey, PA: IGI Global. doi:10.4018/978-1-5225-3093-0.ch004

Agarwal, R., Singh, A., & Sen, S. (2016). Role of Molecular Docking in Computer-Aided Drug Design and Development. In S. Dastmalchi, M. Hamzeh-Mivehroud, & B. Sokouti (Eds.), *Applied Case Studies and Solutions in Molecular Docking-Based Drug Design* (pp. 1–28). Hershey, PA: IGI Global. doi:10.4018/978-1-5225-0362-0.ch001

Ali, O., & Soar, J. (2016). Technology Innovation Adoption Theories. In L. Al-Hakim, X. Wu, A. Koronios, & Y. Shou (Eds.), *Handbook of Research on Driving Competitive Advantage through Sustainable, Lean, and Disruptive Innovation* (pp. 1–38). Hershey, PA: IGI Global. doi:10.4018/978-1-5225-0135-0.ch001

Alsharo, M. (2017). Attitudes Towards Cloud Computing Adoption in Emerging Economies. *International Journal of Cloud Applications and Computing*, 7(3), 44–58. doi:10.4018/IJCAC.2017070102

Amer, T. S., & Johnson, T. L. (2016). Information Technology Progress Indicators: Temporal Expectancy, User Preference, and the Perception of Process Duration. *International Journal of Technology and Human Interaction*, 12(4), 1–14. doi:10.4018/IJTHI.2016100101

Amer, T. S., & Johnson, T. L. (2017). Information Technology Progress Indicators: Research Employing Psychological Frameworks. In A. Mesquita (Ed.), *Research Paradigms and Contemporary Perspectives on Human-Technology Interaction* (pp. 168–186). Hershey, PA: IGI Global. doi:10.4018/978-1-5225-1868-6.ch008

Anchugam, C. V., & Thangadurai, K. (2016). Introduction to Network Security. In D. G., M. Singh, & M. Jayanthi (Eds.), *Network Security Attacks and Countermeasures* (pp. 1-48). Hershey, PA: IGI Global. doi:10.4018/978-1-4666-8761-5.ch001

Anchugam, C. V., & Thangadurai, K. (2016). Classification of Network Attacks and Countermeasures of Different Attacks. In D. G., M. Singh, & M. Jayanthi (Eds.), *Network Security Attacks and Countermeasures* (pp. 115-156). Hershey, PA: IGI Global. doi:10.4018/978-1-4666-8761-5.ch004

Anohah, E. (2016). Pedagogy and Design of Online Learning Environment in Computer Science Education for High Schools. *International Journal of Online Pedagogy and Course Design*, 6(3), 39–51. doi:10.4018/IJOPCD.2016070104

Anohah, E. (2017). Paradigm and Architecture of Computing Augmented Learning Management System for Computer Science Education. *International Journal of Online Pedagogy and Course Design*, 7(2), 60–70. doi:10.4018/IJOPCD.2017040105

Anohah, E., & Suhonen, J. (2017). Trends of Mobile Learning in Computing Education from 2006 to 2014: A Systematic Review of Research Publications. *International Journal of Mobile and Blended Learning*, 9(1), 16–33. doi:10.4018/IJMBL.2017010102

Assis-Hassid, S., Heart, T., Reychav, I., & Pliskin, J. S. (2016). Modelling Factors Affecting Patient-Doctor-Computer Communication in Primary Care. *International Journal of Reliable and Quality E-Healthcare, 5*(1), 1–17. doi:10.4018/IJRQEH.2016010101

Bailey, E. K. (2017). Applying Learning Theories to Computer Technology Supported Instruction. In M. Grassetti & S. Brookby (Eds.), *Advancing Next-Generation Teacher Education through Digital Tools and Applications* (pp. 61–81). Hershey, PA: IGI Global. doi:10.4018/978-1-5225-0965-3.ch004

Balasubramanian, K. (2016). Attacks on Online Banking and Commerce. In K. Balasubramanian, K. Mala, & M. Rajakani (Eds.), *Cryptographic Solutions for Secure Online Banking and Commerce* (pp. 1–19). Hershey, PA: IGI Global. doi:10.4018/978-1-5225-0273-9.ch001

Baldwin, S., Opoku-Agyemang, K., & Roy, D. (2016). Games People Play: A Trilateral Collaboration Researching Computer Gaming across Cultures. In K. Valentine & L. Jensen (Eds.), *Examining the Evolution of Gaming and Its Impact on Social, Cultural, and Political Perspectives* (pp. 364–376). Hershey, PA: IGI Global. doi:10.4018/978-1-5225-0261-6.ch017

Banerjee, S., Sing, T. Y., Chowdhury, A. R., & Anwar, H. (2018). Let's Go Green: Towards a Taxonomy of Green Computing Enablers for Business Sustainability. In M. Khosrow-Pour (Ed.), *Green Computing Strategies for Competitive Advantage and Business Sustainability* (pp. 89–109). Hershey, PA: IGI Global. doi:10.4018/978-1-5225-5017-4.ch005

Basham, R. (2018). Information Science and Technology in Crisis Response and Management. In M. Khosrow-Pour, D.B.A. (Ed.), Encyclopedia of Information Science and Technology, Fourth Edition (pp. 1407-1418). Hershey, PA: IGI Global. doi:10.4018/978-1-5225-2255-3.ch121

Batyashe, T., & Iyamu, T. (2018). Architectural Framework for the Implementation of Information Technology Governance in Organisations. In M. Khosrow-Pour, D.B.A. (Ed.), Encyclopedia of Information Science and Technology, Fourth Edition (pp. 810-819). Hershey, PA: IGI Global. doi:10.4018/978-1-5225-2255-3.ch070

Bekleyen, N., & Çelik, S. (2017). Attitudes of Adult EFL Learners towards Preparing for a Language Test via CALL. In D. Tafazoli & M. Romero (Eds.), *Multiculturalism and Technology-Enhanced Language Learning* (pp. 214–229). Hershey, PA: IGI Global. doi:10.4018/978-1-5225-1882-2.ch013

Bennett, A., Eglash, R., Lachney, M., & Babbitt, W. (2016). Design Agency: Diversifying Computer Science at the Intersections of Creativity and Culture. In M. Raisinghani (Ed.), *Revolutionizing Education through Web-Based Instruction* (pp. 35–56). Hershey, PA: IGI Global. doi:10.4018/978-1-4666-9932-8.ch003

Bergeron, F., Croteau, A., Uwizeyemungu, S., & Raymond, L. (2017). A Framework for Research on Information Technology Governance in SMEs. In S. De Haes & W. Van Grembergen (Eds.), *Strategic IT Governance and Alignment in Business Settings* (pp. 53–81). Hershey, PA: IGI Global. doi:10.4018/978-1-5225-0861-8.ch003

Bhatt, G. D., Wang, Z., & Rodger, J. A. (2017). Information Systems Capabilities and Their Effects on Competitive Advantages: A Study of Chinese Companies. *Information Resources Management Journal, 30*(3), 41–57. doi:10.4018/IRMJ.2017070103

Bogdanoski, M., Stoilkovski, M., & Risteski, A. (2016). Novel First Responder Digital Forensics Tool as a Support to Law Enforcement. In M. Hadji-Janev & M. Bogdanoski (Eds.), *Handbook of Research on Civil Society and National Security in the Era of Cyber Warfare* (pp. 352–376). Hershey, PA: IGI Global. doi:10.4018/978-1-4666-8793-6.ch016

Boontarig, W., Papasratorn, B., & Chutimaskul, W. (2016). The Unified Model for Acceptance and Use of Health Information on Online Social Networks: Evidence from Thailand. *International Journal of E-Health and Medical Communications, 7*(1), 31–47. doi:10.4018/IJEHMC.2016010102

Brown, S., & Yuan, X. (2016). Techniques for Retaining Computer Science Students at Historical Black Colleges and Universities. In C. Prince & R. Ford (Eds.), *Setting a New Agenda for Student Engagement and Retention in Historically Black Colleges and Universities* (pp. 251–268). Hershey, PA: IGI Global. doi:10.4018/978-1-5225-0308-8.ch014

Burcoff, A., & Shamir, L. (2017). Computer Analysis of Pablo Picasso's Artistic Style. *International Journal of Art, Culture and Design Technologies, 6*(1), 1–18. doi:10.4018/IJACDT.2017010101

Byker, E. J. (2017). I Play I Learn: Introducing Technological Play Theory. In C. Martin & D. Polly (Eds.), *Handbook of Research on Teacher Education and Professional Development* (pp. 297–306). Hershey, PA: IGI Global. doi:10.4018/978-1-5225-1067-3.ch016

Calongne, C. M., Stricker, A. G., Truman, B., & Arenas, F. J. (2017). Cognitive Apprenticeship and Computer Science Education in Cyberspace: Reimagining the Past. In A. Stricker, C. Calongne, B. Truman, & F. Arenas (Eds.), *Integrating an Awareness of Selfhood and Society into Virtual Learning* (pp. 180–197). Hershey, PA: IGI Global. doi:10.4018/978-1-5225-2182-2.ch013

Carlton, E. L., Holsinger, J. W. Jr, & Anunobi, N. (2016). Physician Engagement with Health Information Technology: Implications for Practice and Professionalism. *International Journal of Computers in Clinical Practice, 1*(2), 51–73. doi:10.4018/IJCCP.2016070103

Carneiro, A. D. (2017). Defending Information Networks in Cyberspace: Some Notes on Security Needs. In M. Dawson, D. Kisku, P. Gupta, J. Sing, & W. Li (Eds.), Developing Next-Generation Countermeasures for Homeland Security Threat Prevention (pp. 354-375). Hershey, PA: IGI Global. doi:10.4018/978-1-5225-0703-1.ch016

Cavalcanti, J. C. (2016). The New "ABC" of ICTs (Analytics + Big Data + Cloud Computing): A Complex Trade-Off between IT and CT Costs. In J. Martins & A. Molnar (Eds.), *Handbook of Research on Innovations in Information Retrieval, Analysis, and Management* (pp. 152–186). Hershey, PA: IGI Global. doi:10.4018/978-1-4666-8833-9.ch006

Chase, J. P., & Yan, Z. (2017). Affect in Statistics Cognition. In *Assessing and Measuring Statistics Cognition in Higher Education Online Environments: Emerging Research and Opportunities* (pp. 144–187). Hershey, PA: IGI Global. doi:10.4018/978-1-5225-2420-5.ch005

Chen, C. (2016). Effective Learning Strategies for the 21st Century: Implications for the E-Learning. In M. Anderson & C. Gavan (Eds.), *Developing Effective Educational Experiences through Learning Analytics* (pp. 143–169). Hershey, PA: IGI Global. doi:10.4018/978-1-4666-9983-0.ch006

Chen, E. T. (2016). Examining the Influence of Information Technology on Modern Health Care. In P. Manolitzas, E. Grigoroudis, N. Matsatsinis, & D. Yannacopoulos (Eds.), *Effective Methods for Modern Healthcare Service Quality and Evaluation* (pp. 110–136). Hershey, PA: IGI Global. doi:10.4018/978-1-4666-9961-8.ch006

Cimermanova, I. (2017). Computer-Assisted Learning in Slovakia. In D. Tafazoli & M. Romero (Eds.), *Multiculturalism and Technology-Enhanced Language Learning* (pp. 252–270). Hershey, PA: IGI Global. doi:10.4018/978-1-5225-1882-2.ch015

Cipolla-Ficarra, F. V., & Cipolla-Ficarra, M. (2018). Computer Animation for Ingenious Revival. In F. Cipolla-Ficarra, M. Ficarra, M. Cipolla-Ficarra, A. Quiroga, J. Alma, & J. Carré (Eds.), *Technology-Enhanced Human Interaction in Modern Society* (pp. 159–181). Hershey, PA: IGI Global. doi:10.4018/978-1-5225-3437-2.ch008

Cockrell, S., Damron, T. S., Melton, A. M., & Smith, A. D. (2018). Offshoring IT. In M. Khosrow-Pour, D.B.A. (Ed.), Encyclopedia of Information Science and Technology, Fourth Edition (pp. 5476-5489). Hershey, PA: IGI Global. doi:10.4018/978-1-5225-2255-3.ch476

Coffey, J. W. (2018). Logic and Proof in Computer Science: Categories and Limits of Proof Techniques. In J. Horne (Ed.), *Philosophical Perceptions on Logic and Order* (pp. 218–240). Hershey, PA: IGI Global. doi:10.4018/978-1-5225-2443-4.ch007

Dale, M. (2017). Re-Thinking the Challenges of Enterprise Architecture Implementation. In M. Tavana (Ed.), *Enterprise Information Systems and the Digitalization of Business Functions* (pp. 205–221). Hershey, PA: IGI Global. doi:10.4018/978-1-5225-2382-6.ch009

Das, A., Dasgupta, R., & Bagchi, A. (2016). Overview of Cellular Computing-Basic Principles and Applications. In J. Mandal, S. Mukhopadhyay, & T. Pal (Eds.), *Handbook of Research on Natural Computing for Optimization Problems* (pp. 637–662). Hershey, PA: IGI Global. doi:10.4018/978-1-5225-0058-2.ch026

De Maere, K., De Haes, S., & von Kutzschenbach, M. (2017). CIO Perspectives on Organizational Learning within the Context of IT Governance. *International Journal of IT/Business Alignment and Governance, 8*(1), 32-47. doi:10.4018/IJITBAG.2017010103

Demir, K., Çaka, C., Yaman, N. D., İslamoğlu, H., & Kuzu, A. (2018). Examining the Current Definitions of Computational Thinking. In H. Ozcinar, G. Wong, & H. Ozturk (Eds.), *Teaching Computational Thinking in Primary Education* (pp. 36–64). Hershey, PA: IGI Global. doi:10.4018/978-1-5225-3200-2.ch003

Deng, X., Hung, Y., & Lin, C. D. (2017). Design and Analysis of Computer Experiments. In S. Saha, A. Mandal, A. Narasimhamurthy, S. V, & S. Sangam (Eds.), Handbook of Research on Applied Cybernetics and Systems Science (pp. 264-279). Hershey, PA: IGI Global. doi:10.4018/978-1-5225-2498-4.ch013

Denner, J., Martinez, J., & Thiry, H. (2017). Strategies for Engaging Hispanic/Latino Youth in the US in Computer Science. In Y. Rankin & J. Thomas (Eds.), *Moving Students of Color from Consumers to Producers of Technology* (pp. 24–48). Hershey, PA: IGI Global. doi:10.4018/978-1-5225-2005-4.ch002

Devi, A. (2017). Cyber Crime and Cyber Security: A Quick Glance. In R. Kumar, P. Pattnaik, & P. Pandey (Eds.), *Detecting and Mitigating Robotic Cyber Security Risks* (pp. 160–171). Hershey, PA: IGI Global. doi:10.4018/978-1-5225-2154-9.ch011

Dores, A. R., Barbosa, F., Guerreiro, S., Almeida, I., & Carvalho, I. P. (2016). Computer-Based Neuropsychological Rehabilitation: Virtual Reality and Serious Games. In M. Cruz-Cunha, I. Miranda, R. Martinho, & R. Rijo (Eds.), *Encyclopedia of E-Health and Telemedicine* (pp. 473–485). Hershey, PA: IGI Global. doi:10.4018/978-1-4666-9978-6.ch037

Doshi, N., & Schaefer, G. (2016). Computer-Aided Analysis of Nailfold Capillaroscopy Images. In D. Fotiadis (Ed.), *Handbook of Research on Trends in the Diagnosis and Treatment of Chronic Conditions* (pp. 146–158). Hershey, PA: IGI Global. doi:10.4018/978-1-4666-8828-5.ch007

Doyle, D. J., & Fahy, P. J. (2018). Interactivity in Distance Education and Computer-Aided Learning, With Medical Education Examples. In M. Khosrow-Pour, D.B.A. (Ed.), Encyclopedia of Information Science and Technology, Fourth Edition (pp. 5829-5840). Hershey, PA: IGI Global. doi:10.4018/978-1-5225-2255-3.ch507

Elias, N. I., & Walker, T. W. (2017). Factors that Contribute to Continued Use of E-Training among Healthcare Professionals. In F. Topor (Ed.), *Handbook of Research on Individualism and Identity in the Globalized Digital Age* (pp. 403–429). Hershey, PA: IGI Global. doi:10.4018/978-1-5225-0522-8.ch018

Eloy, S., Dias, M. S., Lopes, P. F., & Vilar, E. (2016). Digital Technologies in Architecture and Engineering: Exploring an Engaged Interaction within Curricula. In D. Fonseca & E. Redondo (Eds.), *Handbook of Research on Applied E-Learning in Engineering and Architecture Education* (pp. 368–402). Hershey, PA: IGI Global. doi:10.4018/978-1-4666-8803-2.ch017

Estrela, V. V., Magalhães, H. A., & Saotome, O. (2016). Total Variation Applications in Computer Vision. In N. Kamila (Ed.), *Handbook of Research on Emerging Perspectives in Intelligent Pattern Recognition, Analysis, and Image Processing* (pp. 41–64). Hershey, PA: IGI Global. doi:10.4018/978-1-4666-8654-0.ch002

Filipovic, N., Radovic, M., Nikolic, D. D., Saveljic, I., Milosevic, Z., Exarchos, T. P., ... Parodi, O. (2016). Computer Predictive Model for Plaque Formation and Progression in the Artery. In D. Fotiadis (Ed.), *Handbook of Research on Trends in the Diagnosis and Treatment of Chronic Conditions* (pp. 279–300). Hershey, PA: IGI Global. doi:10.4018/978-1-4666-8828-5.ch013

Fisher, R. L. (2018). Computer-Assisted Indian Matrimonial Services. In M. Khosrow-Pour, D.B.A. (Ed.), Encyclopedia of Information Science and Technology, Fourth Edition (pp. 4136-4145). Hershey, PA: IGI Global. doi:10.4018/978-1-5225-2255-3.ch358

Fleenor, H. G., & Hodhod, R. (2016). Assessment of Learning and Technology: Computer Science Education. In V. Wang (Ed.), *Handbook of Research on Learning Outcomes and Opportunities in the Digital Age* (pp. 51–78). Hershey, PA: IGI Global. doi:10.4018/978-1-4666-9577-1.ch003

García-Valcárcel, A., & Mena, J. (2016). Information Technology as a Way To Support Collaborative Learning: What In-Service Teachers Think, Know and Do. *Journal of Information Technology Research*, *9*(1), 1–17. doi:10.4018/JITR.2016010101

Gardner-McCune, C., & Jimenez, Y. (2017). Historical App Developers: Integrating CS into K-12 through Cross-Disciplinary Projects. In Y. Rankin & J. Thomas (Eds.), *Moving Students of Color from Consumers to Producers of Technology* (pp. 85–112). Hershey, PA: IGI Global. doi:10.4018/978-1-5225-2005-4.ch005

Garvey, G. P. (2016). Exploring Perception, Cognition, and Neural Pathways of Stereo Vision and the Split–Brain Human Computer Interface. In A. Ursyn (Ed.), *Knowledge Visualization and Visual Literacy in Science Education* (pp. 28–76). Hershey, PA: IGI Global. doi:10.4018/978-1-5225-0480-1.ch002

Ghafele, R., & Gibert, B. (2018). Open Growth: The Economic Impact of Open Source Software in the USA. In M. Khosrow-Pour (Ed.), *Optimizing Contemporary Application and Processes in Open Source Software* (pp. 164–197). Hershey, PA: IGI Global. doi:10.4018/978-1-5225-5314-4.ch007

Ghobakhloo, M., & Azar, A. (2018). Information Technology Resources, the Organizational Capability of Lean-Agile Manufacturing, and Business Performance. *Information Resources Management Journal*, *31*(2), 47–74. doi:10.4018/IRMJ.2018040103

Gianni, M., & Gotzamani, K. (2016). Integrated Management Systems and Information Management Systems: Common Threads. In P. Papajorgji, F. Pinet, A. Guimarães, & J. Papathanasiou (Eds.), *Automated Enterprise Systems for Maximizing Business Performance* (pp. 195–214). Hershey, PA: IGI Global. doi:10.4018/978-1-4666-8841-4.ch011

Gikandi, J. W. (2017). Computer-Supported Collaborative Learning and Assessment: A Strategy for Developing Online Learning Communities in Continuing Education. In J. Keengwe & G. Onchwari (Eds.), *Handbook of Research on Learner-Centered Pedagogy in Teacher Education and Professional Development* (pp. 309–333). Hershey, PA: IGI Global. doi:10.4018/978-1-5225-0892-2.ch017

Gokhale, A. A., & Machina, K. F. (2017). Development of a Scale to Measure Attitudes toward Information Technology. In L. Tomei (Ed.), *Exploring the New Era of Technology-Infused Education* (pp. 49–64). Hershey, PA: IGI Global. doi:10.4018/978-1-5225-1709-2.ch004

Grace, A., O'Donoghue, J., Mahony, C., Heffernan, T., Molony, D., & Carroll, T. (2016). Computerized Decision Support Systems for Multimorbidity Care: An Urgent Call for Research and Development. In M. Cruz-Cunha, I. Miranda, R. Martinho, & R. Rijo (Eds.), *Encyclopedia of E-Health and Telemedicine* (pp. 486–494). Hershey, PA: IGI Global. doi:10.4018/978-1-4666-9978-6.ch038

Gupta, A., & Singh, O. (2016). Computer Aided Modeling and Finite Element Analysis of Human Elbow. *International Journal of Biomedical and Clinical Engineering, 5*(1), 31–38. doi:10.4018/IJBCE.2016010104

H., S. K. (2016). Classification of Cybercrimes and Punishments under the Information Technology Act, 2000. In S. Geetha, & A. Phamila (Eds.), *Combating Security Breaches and Criminal Activity in the Digital Sphere* (pp. 57-66). Hershey, PA: IGI Global. doi:10.4018/978-1-5225-0193-0.ch004

Hafeez-Baig, A., Gururajan, R., & Wickramasinghe, N. (2017). Readiness as a Novel Construct of Readiness Acceptance Model (RAM) for the Wireless Handheld Technology. In N. Wickramasinghe (Ed.), *Handbook of Research on Healthcare Administration and Management* (pp. 578–595). Hershey, PA: IGI Global. doi:10.4018/978-1-5225-0920-2.ch035

Hanafizadeh, P., Ghandchi, S., & Asgarimehr, M. (2017). Impact of Information Technology on Lifestyle: A Literature Review and Classification. *International Journal of Virtual Communities and Social Networking, 9*(2), 1–23. doi:10.4018/IJVCSN.2017040101

Harlow, D. B., Dwyer, H., Hansen, A. K., Hill, C., Iveland, A., Leak, A. E., & Franklin, D. M. (2016). Computer Programming in Elementary and Middle School: Connections across Content. In M. Urban & D. Falvo (Eds.), *Improving K-12 STEM Education Outcomes through Technological Integration* (pp. 337–361). Hershey, PA: IGI Global. doi:10.4018/978-1-4666-9616-7.ch015

Haseski, H. İ., Ilic, U., & Tuğtekin, U. (2018). Computational Thinking in Educational Digital Games: An Assessment Tool Proposal. In H. Ozcinar, G. Wong, & H. Ozturk (Eds.), *Teaching Computational Thinking in Primary Education* (pp. 256–287). Hershey, PA: IGI Global. doi:10.4018/978-1-5225-3200-2.ch013

Hee, W. J., Jalleh, G., Lai, H., & Lin, C. (2017). E-Commerce and IT Projects: Evaluation and Management Issues in Australian and Taiwanese Hospitals. *International Journal of Public Health Management and Ethics, 2*(1), 69–90. doi:10.4018/IJPHME.2017010104

Hernandez, A. A. (2017). Green Information Technology Usage: Awareness and Practices of Philippine IT Professionals. *International Journal of Enterprise Information Systems, 13*(4), 90–103. doi:10.4018/IJEIS.2017100106

Hernandez, A. A., & Ona, S. E. (2016). Green IT Adoption: Lessons from the Philippines Business Process Outsourcing Industry. *International Journal of Social Ecology and Sustainable Development, 7*(1), 1–34. doi:10.4018/IJSESD.2016010101

Hernandez, M. A., Marin, E. C., Garcia-Rodriguez, J., Azorin-Lopez, J., & Cazorla, M. (2017). Automatic Learning Improves Human-Robot Interaction in Productive Environments: A Review. *International Journal of Computer Vision and Image Processing, 7*(3), 65–75. doi:10.4018/IJCVIP.2017070106

Horne-Popp, L. M., Tessone, E. B., & Welker, J. (2018). If You Build It, They Will Come: Creating a Library Statistics Dashboard for Decision-Making. In L. Costello & M. Powers (Eds.), *Developing In-House Digital Tools in Library Spaces* (pp. 177–203). Hershey, PA: IGI Global. doi:10.4018/978-1-5225-2676-6.ch009

Hossan, C. G., & Ryan, J. C. (2016). Factors Affecting e-Government Technology Adoption Behaviour in a Voluntary Environment. *International Journal of Electronic Government Research*, *12*(1), 24–49. doi:10.4018/IJEGR.2016010102

Hu, H., Hu, P. J., & Al-Gahtani, S. S. (2017). User Acceptance of Computer Technology at Work in Arabian Culture: A Model Comparison Approach. In M. Khosrow-Pour (Ed.), *Handbook of Research on Technology Adoption, Social Policy, and Global Integration* (pp. 205–228). Hershey, PA: IGI Global. doi:10.4018/978-1-5225-2668-1.ch011

Huie, C. P. (2016). Perceptions of Business Intelligence Professionals about Factors Related to Business Intelligence input in Decision Making. *International Journal of Business Analytics*, *3*(3), 1–24. doi:10.4018/IJBAN.2016070101

Hung, S., Huang, W., Yen, D. C., Chang, S., & Lu, C. (2016). Effect of Information Service Competence and Contextual Factors on the Effectiveness of Strategic Information Systems Planning in Hospitals. *Journal of Global Information Management*, *24*(1), 14–36. doi:10.4018/JGIM.2016010102

Ifinedo, P. (2017). Using an Extended Theory of Planned Behavior to Study Nurses' Adoption of Healthcare Information Systems in Nova Scotia. *International Journal of Technology Diffusion*, *8*(1), 1–17. doi:10.4018/IJTD.2017010101

Ilie, V., & Sneha, S. (2018). A Three Country Study for Understanding Physicians' Engagement With Electronic Information Resources Pre and Post System Implementation. *Journal of Global Information Management*, *26*(2), 48–73. doi:10.4018/JGIM.2018040103

Inoue-Smith, Y. (2017). Perceived Ease in Using Technology Predicts Teacher Candidates' Preferences for Online Resources. *International Journal of Online Pedagogy and Course Design*, *7*(3), 17–28. doi:10.4018/IJOPCD.2017070102

Islam, A. A. (2016). Development and Validation of the Technology Adoption and Gratification (TAG) Model in Higher Education: A Cross-Cultural Study Between Malaysia and China. *International Journal of Technology and Human Interaction*, *12*(3), 78–105. doi:10.4018/IJTHI.2016070106

Islam, A. Y. (2017). Technology Satisfaction in an Academic Context: Moderating Effect of Gender. In A. Mesquita (Ed.), *Research Paradigms and Contemporary Perspectives on Human-Technology Interaction* (pp. 187–211). Hershey, PA: IGI Global. doi:10.4018/978-1-5225-1868-6.ch009

Jamil, G. L., & Jamil, C. C. (2017). Information and Knowledge Management Perspective Contributions for Fashion Studies: Observing Logistics and Supply Chain Management Processes. In G. Jamil, A. Soares, & C. Pessoa (Eds.), *Handbook of Research on Information Management for Effective Logistics and Supply Chains* (pp. 199–221). Hershey, PA: IGI Global. doi:10.4018/978-1-5225-0973-8.ch011

Jamil, G. L., Jamil, L. C., Vieira, A. A., & Xavier, A. J. (2016). Challenges in Modelling Healthcare Services: A Study Case of Information Architecture Perspectives. In G. Jamil, J. Poças Rascão, F. Ribeiro, & A. Malheiro da Silva (Eds.), *Handbook of Research on Information Architecture and Management in Modern Organizations* (pp. 1–23). Hershey, PA: IGI Global. doi:10.4018/978-1-4666-8637-3.ch001

Janakova, M. (2018). Big Data and Simulations for the Solution of Controversies in Small Businesses. In M. Khosrow-Pour, D.B.A. (Ed.), Encyclopedia of Information Science and Technology, Fourth Edition (pp. 6907-6915). Hershey, PA: IGI Global. doi:10.4018/978-1-5225-2255-3.ch598

Jha, D. G. (2016). Preparing for Information Technology Driven Changes. In S. Tiwari & L. Nafees (Eds.), *Innovative Management Education Pedagogies for Preparing Next-Generation Leaders* (pp. 258–274). Hershey, PA: IGI Global. doi:10.4018/978-1-4666-9691-4.ch015

Jhawar, A., & Garg, S. K. (2018). Logistics Improvement by Investment in Information Technology Using System Dynamics. In A. Azar & S. Vaidyanathan (Eds.), *Advances in System Dynamics and Control* (pp. 528–567). Hershey, PA: IGI Global. doi:10.4018/978-1-5225-4077-9.ch017

Kalelioğlu, F., Gülbahar, Y., & Doğan, D. (2018). Teaching How to Think Like a Programmer: Emerging Insights. In H. Ozcinar, G. Wong, & H. Ozturk (Eds.), *Teaching Computational Thinking in Primary Education* (pp. 18–35). Hershey, PA: IGI Global. doi:10.4018/978-1-5225-3200-2.ch002

Kamberi, S. (2017). A Girls-Only Online Virtual World Environment and its Implications for Game-Based Learning. In A. Stricker, C. Calongne, B. Truman, & F. Arenas (Eds.), *Integrating an Awareness of Selfhood and Society into Virtual Learning* (pp. 74–95). Hershey, PA: IGI Global. doi:10.4018/978-1-5225-2182-2.ch006

Kamel, S., & Rizk, N. (2017). ICT Strategy Development: From Design to Implementation – Case of Egypt. In C. Howard & K. Hargiss (Eds.), *Strategic Information Systems and Technologies in Modern Organizations* (pp. 239–257). Hershey, PA: IGI Global. doi:10.4018/978-1-5225-1680-4.ch010

Kamel, S. H. (2018). The Potential Role of the Software Industry in Supporting Economic Development. In M. Khosrow-Pour, D.B.A. (Ed.), Encyclopedia of Information Science and Technology, Fourth Edition (pp. 7259-7269). Hershey, PA: IGI Global. doi:10.4018/978-1-5225-2255-3.ch631

Karon, R. (2016). Utilisation of Health Information Systems for Service Delivery in the Namibian Environment. In T. Iyamu & A. Tatnall (Eds.), *Maximizing Healthcare Delivery and Management through Technology Integration* (pp. 169–183). Hershey, PA: IGI Global. doi:10.4018/978-1-4666-9446-0.ch011

Kawata, S. (2018). Computer-Assisted Parallel Program Generation. In M. Khosrow-Pour, D.B.A. (Ed.), Encyclopedia of Information Science and Technology, Fourth Edition (pp. 4583-4593). Hershey, PA: IGI Global. doi:10.4018/978-1-5225-2255-3.ch398

Khanam, S., Siddiqui, J., & Talib, F. (2016). A DEMATEL Approach for Prioritizing the TQM Enablers and IT Resources in the Indian ICT Industry. *International Journal of Applied Management Sciences and Engineering*, 3(1), 11–29. doi:10.4018/IJAMSE.2016010102

Khari, M., Shrivastava, G., Gupta, S., & Gupta, R. (2017). Role of Cyber Security in Today's Scenario. In R. Kumar, P. Pattnaik, & P. Pandey (Eds.), *Detecting and Mitigating Robotic Cyber Security Risks* (pp. 177–191). Hershey, PA: IGI Global. doi:10.4018/978-1-5225-2154-9.ch013

Khouja, M., Rodriguez, I. B., Ben Halima, Y., & Moalla, S. (2018). IT Governance in Higher Education Institutions: A Systematic Literature Review. *International Journal of Human Capital and Information Technology Professionals*, 9(2), 52–67. doi:10.4018/IJHCITP.2018040104

Kim, S., Chang, M., Choi, N., Park, J., & Kim, H. (2016). The Direct and Indirect Effects of Computer Uses on Student Success in Math. *International Journal of Cyber Behavior, Psychology and Learning*, 6(3), 48–64. doi:10.4018/IJCBPL.2016070104

Kiourt, C., Pavlidis, G., Koutsoudis, A., & Kalles, D. (2017). Realistic Simulation of Cultural Heritage. *International Journal of Computational Methods in Heritage Science*, 1(1), 10–40. doi:10.4018/IJCMHS.2017010102

Korikov, A., & Krivtsov, O. (2016). System of People-Computer: On the Way of Creation of Human-Oriented Interface. In V. Mkrttchian, A. Bershadsky, A. Bozhday, M. Kataev, & S. Kataev (Eds.), *Handbook of Research on Estimation and Control Techniques in E-Learning Systems* (pp. 458–470). Hershey, PA: IGI Global. doi:10.4018/978-1-4666-9489-7.ch032

Köse, U. (2017). An Augmented-Reality-Based Intelligent Mobile Application for Open Computer Education. In G. Kurubacak & H. Altinpulluk (Eds.), *Mobile Technologies and Augmented Reality in Open Education* (pp. 154–174). Hershey, PA: IGI Global. doi:10.4018/978-1-5225-2110-5.ch008

Lahmiri, S. (2018). Information Technology Outsourcing Risk Factors and Provider Selection. In M. Gupta, R. Sharman, J. Walp, & P. Mulgund (Eds.), *Information Technology Risk Management and Compliance in Modern Organizations* (pp. 214–228). Hershey, PA: IGI Global. doi:10.4018/978-1-5225-2604-9.ch008

Landriscina, F. (2017). Computer-Supported Imagination: The Interplay Between Computer and Mental Simulation in Understanding Scientific Concepts. In I. Levin & D. Tsybulsky (Eds.), *Digital Tools and Solutions for Inquiry-Based STEM Learning* (pp. 33–60). Hershey, PA: IGI Global. doi:10.4018/978-1-5225-2525-7.ch002

Lau, S. K., Winley, G. K., Leung, N. K., Tsang, N., & Lau, S. Y. (2016). An Exploratory Study of Expectation in IT Skills in a Developing Nation: Vietnam. *Journal of Global Information Management*, 24(1), 1–13. doi:10.4018/JGIM.2016010101

Lavranos, C., Kostagiolas, P., & Papadatos, J. (2016). Information Retrieval Technologies and the "Realities" of Music Information Seeking. In I. Deliyannis, P. Kostagiolas, & C. Banou (Eds.), *Experimental Multimedia Systems for Interactivity and Strategic Innovation* (pp. 102–121). Hershey, PA: IGI Global. doi:10.4018/978-1-4666-8659-5.ch005

Lee, W. W. (2018). Ethical Computing Continues From Problem to Solution. In M. Khosrow-Pour, D.B.A. (Ed.), Encyclopedia of Information Science and Technology, Fourth Edition (pp. 4884-4897). Hershey, PA: IGI Global. doi:10.4018/978-1-5225-2255-3.ch423

Lehto, M. (2016). Cyber Security Education and Research in the Finland's Universities and Universities of Applied Sciences. *International Journal of Cyber Warfare & Terrorism*, 6(2), 15–31. doi:10.4018/IJCWT.2016040102

Lin, C., Jalleh, G., & Huang, Y. (2016). Evaluating and Managing Electronic Commerce and Outsourcing Projects in Hospitals. In A. Dwivedi (Ed.), *Reshaping Medical Practice and Care with Health Information Systems* (pp. 132–172). Hershey, PA: IGI Global. doi:10.4018/978-1-4666-9870-3.ch005

Lin, S., Chen, S., & Chuang, S. (2017). Perceived Innovation and Quick Response Codes in an Online-to-Offline E-Commerce Service Model. *International Journal of E-Adoption*, 9(2), 1–16. doi:10.4018/IJEA.2017070101

Liu, M., Wang, Y., Xu, W., & Liu, L. (2017). Automated Scoring of Chinese Engineering Students' English Essays. *International Journal of Distance Education Technologies*, 15(1), 52–68. doi:10.4018/IJDET.2017010104

Luciano, E. M., Wiedenhöft, G. C., Macadar, M. A., & Pinheiro dos Santos, F. (2016). Information Technology Governance Adoption: Understanding its Expectations Through the Lens of Organizational Citizenship. *International Journal of IT/Business Alignment and Governance, 7*(2), 22-32. doi:10.4018/IJITBAG.2016070102

Mabe, L. K., & Oladele, O. I. (2017). Application of Information Communication Technologies for Agricultural Development through Extension Services: A Review. In T. Tossy (Ed.), *Information Technology Integration for Socio-Economic Development* (pp. 52–101). Hershey, PA: IGI Global. doi:10.4018/978-1-5225-0539-6.ch003

Manogaran, G., Thota, C., & Lopez, D. (2018). Human-Computer Interaction With Big Data Analytics. In D. Lopez & M. Durai (Eds.), *HCI Challenges and Privacy Preservation in Big Data Security* (pp. 1–22). Hershey, PA: IGI Global. doi:10.4018/978-1-5225-2863-0.ch001

Margolis, J., Goode, J., & Flapan, J. (2017). A Critical Crossroads for Computer Science for All: "Identifying Talent" or "Building Talent," and What Difference Does It Make? In Y. Rankin & J. Thomas (Eds.), *Moving Students of Color from Consumers to Producers of Technology* (pp. 1–23). Hershey, PA: IGI Global. doi:10.4018/978-1-5225-2005-4.ch001

Mbale, J. (2018). Computer Centres Resource Cloud Elasticity-Scalability (CRECES): Copperbelt University Case Study. In S. Aljawarneh & M. Malhotra (Eds.), *Critical Research on Scalability and Security Issues in Virtual Cloud Environments* (pp. 48–70). Hershey, PA: IGI Global. doi:10.4018/978-1-5225-3029-9.ch003

McKee, J. (2018). The Right Information: The Key to Effective Business Planning. In *Business Architectures for Risk Assessment and Strategic Planning: Emerging Research and Opportunities* (pp. 38–52). Hershey, PA: IGI Global. doi:10.4018/978-1-5225-3392-4.ch003

Mensah, I. K., & Mi, J. (2018). Determinants of Intention to Use Local E-Government Services in Ghana: The Perspective of Local Government Workers. *International Journal of Technology Diffusion*, 9(2), 41–60. doi:10.4018/IJTD.2018040103

Mohamed, J. H. (2018). Scientograph-Based Visualization of Computer Forensics Research Literature. In J. Jeyasekar & P. Saravanan (Eds.), *Innovations in Measuring and Evaluating Scientific Information* (pp. 148–162). Hershey, PA: IGI Global. doi:10.4018/978-1-5225-3457-0.ch010

Moore, R. L., & Johnson, N. (2017). Earning a Seat at the Table: How IT Departments Can Partner in Organizational Change and Innovation. *International Journal of Knowledge-Based Organizations*, *7*(2), 1–12. doi:10.4018/IJKBO.2017040101

Mtebe, J. S., & Kissaka, M. M. (2016). Enhancing the Quality of Computer Science Education with MOOCs in Sub-Saharan Africa. In J. Keengwe & G. Onchwari (Eds.), *Handbook of Research on Active Learning and the Flipped Classroom Model in the Digital Age* (pp. 366–377). Hershey, PA: IGI Global. doi:10.4018/978-1-4666-9680-8.ch019

Mukul, M. K., & Bhattaharyya, S. (2017). Brain-Machine Interface: Human-Computer Interaction. In E. Noughabi, B. Raahemi, A. Albadvi, & B. Far (Eds.), *Handbook of Research on Data Science for Effective Healthcare Practice and Administration* (pp. 417–443). Hershey, PA: IGI Global. doi:10.4018/978-1-5225-2515-8.ch018

Na, L. (2017). Library and Information Science Education and Graduate Programs in Academic Libraries. In L. Ruan, Q. Zhu, & Y. Ye (Eds.), *Academic Library Development and Administration in China* (pp. 218–229). Hershey, PA: IGI Global. doi:10.4018/978-1-5225-0550-1.ch013

Nabavi, A., Taghavi-Fard, M. T., Hanafizadeh, P., & Taghva, M. R. (2016). Information Technology Continuance Intention: A Systematic Literature Review. *International Journal of E-Business Research*, *12*(1), 58–95. doi:10.4018/IJEBR.2016010104

Nath, R., & Murthy, V. N. (2018). What Accounts for the Differences in Internet Diffusion Rates Around the World? In M. Khosrow-Pour, D.B.A. (Ed.), Encyclopedia of Information Science and Technology, Fourth Edition (pp. 8095-8104). Hershey, PA: IGI Global. doi:10.4018/978-1-5225-2255-3.ch705

Nedelko, Z., & Potocan, V. (2018). The Role of Emerging Information Technologies for Supporting Supply Chain Management. In M. Khosrow-Pour, D.B.A. (Ed.), Encyclopedia of Information Science and Technology, Fourth Edition (pp. 5559-5569). Hershey, PA: IGI Global. doi:10.4018/978-1-5225-2255-3.ch483

Ngafeeson, M. N. (2018). User Resistance to Health Information Technology. In M. Khosrow-Pour, D.B.A. (Ed.), Encyclopedia of Information Science and Technology, Fourth Edition (pp. 3816-3825). Hershey, PA: IGI Global. doi:10.4018/978-1-5225-2255-3.ch331

Nozari, H., Najafi, S. E., Jafari-Eskandari, M., & Aliahmadi, A. (2016). Providing a Model for Virtual Project Management with an Emphasis on IT Projects. In C. Graham (Ed.), *Strategic Management and Leadership for Systems Development in Virtual Spaces* (pp. 43–63). Hershey, PA: IGI Global. doi:10.4018/978-1-4666-9688-4.ch003

Nurdin, N., Stockdale, R., & Scheepers, H. (2016). Influence of Organizational Factors in the Sustainability of E-Government: A Case Study of Local E-Government in Indonesia. In I. Sodhi (Ed.), *Trends, Prospects, and Challenges in Asian E-Governance* (pp. 281–323). Hershey, PA: IGI Global. doi:10.4018/978-1-4666-9536-8.ch014

Odagiri, K. (2017). Introduction of Individual Technology to Constitute the Current Internet. In *Strategic Policy-Based Network Management in Contemporary Organizations* (pp. 20–96). Hershey, PA: IGI Global. doi:10.4018/978-1-68318-003-6.ch003

Okike, E. U. (2018). Computer Science and Prison Education. In I. Biao (Ed.), *Strategic Learning Ideologies in Prison Education Programs* (pp. 246–264). Hershey, PA: IGI Global. doi:10.4018/978-1-5225-2909-5.ch012

Olelewe, C. J., & Nwafor, I. P. (2017). Level of Computer Appreciation Skills Acquired for Sustainable Development by Secondary School Students in Nsukka LGA of Enugu State, Nigeria. In C. Ayo & V. Mbarika (Eds.), *Sustainable ICT Adoption and Integration for Socio-Economic Development* (pp. 214–233). Hershey, PA: IGI Global. doi:10.4018/978-1-5225-2565-3.ch010

Oliveira, M., Maçada, A. C., Curado, C., & Nodari, F. (2017). Infrastructure Profiles and Knowledge Sharing. *International Journal of Technology and Human Interaction*, *13*(3), 1–12. doi:10.4018/IJTHI.2017070101

Otarkhani, A., Shokouhyar, S., & Pour, S. S. (2017). Analyzing the Impact of Governance of Enterprise IT on Hospital Performance: Tehran's (Iran) Hospitals – A Case Study. *International Journal of Healthcare Information Systems and Informatics*, *12*(3), 1–20. doi:10.4018/IJHISI.2017070101

Otunla, A. O., & Amuda, C. O. (2018). Nigerian Undergraduate Students' Computer Competencies and Use of Information Technology Tools and Resources for Study Skills and Habits' Enhancement. In M. Khosrow-Pour, D.B.A. (Ed.), Encyclopedia of Information Science and Technology, Fourth Edition (pp. 2303-2313). Hershey, PA: IGI Global. doi:10.4018/978-1-5225-2255-3.ch200

Özçınar, H. (2018). A Brief Discussion on Incentives and Barriers to Computational Thinking Education. In H. Ozcinar, G. Wong, & H. Ozturk (Eds.), *Teaching Computational Thinking in Primary Education* (pp. 1–17). Hershey, PA: IGI Global. doi:10.4018/978-1-5225-3200-2.ch001

Pandey, J. M., Garg, S., Mishra, P., & Mishra, B. P. (2017). Computer Based Psychological Interventions: Subject to the Efficacy of Psychological Services. *International Journal of Computers in Clinical Practice*, *2*(1), 25–33. doi:10.4018/IJCCP.2017010102

Parry, V. K., & Lind, M. L. (2016). Alignment of Business Strategy and Information Technology Considering Information Technology Governance, Project Portfolio Control, and Risk Management. *International Journal of Information Technology Project Management*, *7*(4), 21–37. doi:10.4018/IJITPM.2016100102

Patro, C. (2017). Impulsion of Information Technology on Human Resource Practices. In P. Ordóñez de Pablos (Ed.), *Managerial Strategies and Solutions for Business Success in Asia* (pp. 231–254). Hershey, PA: IGI Global. doi:10.4018/978-1-5225-1886-0.ch013

Patro, C. S., & Raghunath, K. M. (2017). Information Technology Paraphernalia for Supply Chain Management Decisions. In M. Tavana (Ed.), *Enterprise Information Systems and the Digitalization of Business Functions* (pp. 294–320). Hershey, PA: IGI Global. doi:10.4018/978-1-5225-2382-6.ch014

Paul, P. K. (2016). Cloud Computing: An Agent of Promoting Interdisciplinary Sciences, Especially Information Science and I-Schools – Emerging Techno-Educational Scenario. In L. Chao (Ed.), *Handbook of Research on Cloud-Based STEM Education for Improved Learning Outcomes* (pp. 247–258). Hershey, PA: IGI Global. doi:10.4018/978-1-4666-9924-3.ch016

Paul, P. K. (2018). The Context of IST for Solid Information Retrieval and Infrastructure Building: Study of Developing Country. *International Journal of Information Retrieval Research*, *8*(1), 86–100. doi:10.4018/IJIRR.2018010106

Paul, P. K., & Chatterjee, D. (2018). iSchools Promoting "Information Science and Technology" (IST) Domain Towards Community, Business, and Society With Contemporary Worldwide Trend and Emerging Potentialities in India. In M. Khosrow-Pour, D.B.A. (Ed.), Encyclopedia of Information Science and Technology, Fourth Edition (pp. 4723-4735). Hershey, PA: IGI Global. doi:10.4018/978-1-5225-2255-3.ch410

Pessoa, C. R., & Marques, M. E. (2017). Information Technology and Communication Management in Supply Chain Management. In G. Jamil, A. Soares, & C. Pessoa (Eds.), *Handbook of Research on Information Management for Effective Logistics and Supply Chains* (pp. 23–33). Hershey, PA: IGI Global. doi:10.4018/978-1-5225-0973-8.ch002

Pineda, R. G. (2016). Where the Interaction Is Not: Reflections on the Philosophy of Human-Computer Interaction. *International Journal of Art, Culture and Design Technologies*, *5*(1), 1–12. doi:10.4018/IJACDT.2016010101

Pineda, R. G. (2018). Remediating Interaction: Towards a Philosophy of Human-Computer Relationship. In M. Khosrow-Pour (Ed.), *Enhancing Art, Culture, and Design With Technological Integration* (pp. 75–98). Hershey, PA: IGI Global. doi:10.4018/978-1-5225-5023-5.ch004

Poikela, P., & Vuojärvi, H. (2016). Learning ICT-Mediated Communication through Computer-Based Simulations. In M. Cruz-Cunha, I. Miranda, R. Martinho, & R. Rijo (Eds.), *Encyclopedia of E-Health and Telemedicine* (pp. 674–687). Hershey, PA: IGI Global. doi:10.4018/978-1-4666-9978-6.ch052

Qian, Y. (2017). Computer Simulation in Higher Education: Affordances, Opportunities, and Outcomes. In P. Vu, S. Fredrickson, & C. Moore (Eds.), *Handbook of Research on Innovative Pedagogies and Technologies for Online Learning in Higher Education* (pp. 236–262). Hershey, PA: IGI Global. doi:10.4018/978-1-5225-1851-8.ch011

Radant, O., Colomo-Palacios, R., & Stantchev, V. (2016). Factors for the Management of Scarce Human Resources and Highly Skilled Employees in IT-Departments: A Systematic Review. *Journal of Information Technology Research*, *9*(1), 65–82. doi:10.4018/JITR.2016010105

Rahman, N. (2016). Toward Achieving Environmental Sustainability in the Computer Industry. *International Journal of Green Computing*, 7(1), 37–54. doi:10.4018/IJGC.2016010103

Rahman, N. (2017). Lessons from a Successful Data Warehousing Project Management. *International Journal of Information Technology Project Management*, 8(4), 30–45. doi:10.4018/IJITPM.2017100103

Rahman, N. (2018). Environmental Sustainability in the Computer Industry for Competitive Advantage. In M. Khosrow-Pour (Ed.), *Green Computing Strategies for Competitive Advantage and Business Sustainability* (pp. 110–130). Hershey, PA: IGI Global. doi:10.4018/978-1-5225-5017-4.ch006

Rajh, A., & Pavetic, T. (2017). Computer Generated Description as the Required Digital Competence in Archival Profession. *International Journal of Digital Literacy and Digital Competence*, 8(1), 36–49. doi:10.4018/IJDLDC.2017010103

Raman, A., & Goyal, D. P. (2017). Extending IMPLEMENT Framework for Enterprise Information Systems Implementation to Information System Innovation. In M. Tavana (Ed.), *Enterprise Information Systems and the Digitalization of Business Functions* (pp. 137–177). Hershey, PA: IGI Global. doi:10.4018/978-1-5225-2382-6.ch007

Rao, Y. S., Rauta, A. K., Saini, H., & Panda, T. C. (2017). Mathematical Model for Cyber Attack in Computer Network. *International Journal of Business Data Communications and Networking*, 13(1), 58–65. doi:10.4018/IJBDCN.2017010105

Rapaport, W. J. (2018). Syntactic Semantics and the Proper Treatment of Computationalism. In M. Danesi (Ed.), *Empirical Research on Semiotics and Visual Rhetoric* (pp. 128–176). Hershey, PA: IGI Global. doi:10.4018/978-1-5225-5622-0.ch007

Raut, R., Priyadarshinee, P., & Jha, M. (2017). Understanding the Mediation Effect of Cloud Computing Adoption in Indian Organization: Integrating TAM-TOE- Risk Model. *International Journal of Service Science, Management, Engineering, and Technology*, 8(3), 40–59. doi:10.4018/IJSSMET.2017070103

Regan, E. A., & Wang, J. (2016). Realizing the Value of EHR Systems Critical Success Factors. *International Journal of Healthcare Information Systems and Informatics*, 11(3), 1–18. doi:10.4018/IJHISI.2016070101

Rezaie, S., Mirabedini, S. J., & Abtahi, A. (2018). Designing a Model for Implementation of Business Intelligence in the Banking Industry. *International Journal of Enterprise Information Systems*, 14(1), 77–103. doi:10.4018/IJEIS.2018010105

Rezende, D. A. (2016). Digital City Projects: Information and Public Services Offered by Chicago (USA) and Curitiba (Brazil). *International Journal of Knowledge Society Research*, 7(3), 16–30. doi:10.4018/IJKSR.2016070102

Rezende, D. A. (2018). Strategic Digital City Projects: Innovative Information and Public Services Offered by Chicago (USA) and Curitiba (Brazil). In M. Lytras, L. Daniela, & A. Visvizi (Eds.), *Enhancing Knowledge Discovery and Innovation in the Digital Era* (pp. 204–223). Hershey, PA: IGI Global. doi:10.4018/978-1-5225-4191-2.ch012

Riabov, V. V. (2016). Teaching Online Computer-Science Courses in LMS and Cloud Environment. *International Journal of Quality Assurance in Engineering and Technology Education, 5*(4), 12–41. doi:10.4018/IJQAETE.2016100102

Ricordel, V., Wang, J., Da Silva, M. P., & Le Callet, P. (2016). 2D and 3D Visual Attention for Computer Vision: Concepts, Measurement, and Modeling. In R. Pal (Ed.), *Innovative Research in Attention Modeling and Computer Vision Applications* (pp. 1–44). Hershey, PA: IGI Global. doi:10.4018/978-1-4666-8723-3.ch001

Rodriguez, A., Rico-Diaz, A. J., Rabuñal, J. R., & Gestal, M. (2017). Fish Tracking with Computer Vision Techniques: An Application to Vertical Slot Fishways. In M. S., & V. V. (Eds.), Multi-Core Computer Vision and Image Processing for Intelligent Applications (pp. 74-104). Hershey, PA: IGI Global. doi:10.4018/978-1-5225-0889-2.ch003

Romero, J. A. (2018). Sustainable Advantages of Business Value of Information Technology. In M. Khosrow-Pour, D.B.A. (Ed.), Encyclopedia of Information Science and Technology, Fourth Edition (pp. 923-929). Hershey, PA: IGI Global. doi:10.4018/978-1-5225-2255-3.ch079

Romero, J. A. (2018). The Always-On Business Model and Competitive Advantage. In N. Bajgoric (Ed.), *Always-On Enterprise Information Systems for Modern Organizations* (pp. 23–40). Hershey, PA: IGI Global. doi:10.4018/978-1-5225-3704-5.ch002

Rosen, Y. (2018). Computer Agent Technologies in Collaborative Learning and Assessment. In M. Khosrow-Pour, D.B.A. (Ed.), Encyclopedia of Information Science and Technology, Fourth Edition (pp. 2402-2410). Hershey, PA: IGI Global. doi:10.4018/978-1-5225-2255-3.ch209

Rosen, Y., & Mosharraf, M. (2016). Computer Agent Technologies in Collaborative Assessments. In Y. Rosen, S. Ferrara, & M. Mosharraf (Eds.), *Handbook of Research on Technology Tools for Real-World Skill Development* (pp. 319–343). Hershey, PA: IGI Global. doi:10.4018/978-1-4666-9441-5.ch012

Roy, D. (2018). Success Factors of Adoption of Mobile Applications in Rural India: Effect of Service Characteristics on Conceptual Model. In M. Khosrow-Pour (Ed.), *Green Computing Strategies for Competitive Advantage and Business Sustainability* (pp. 211–238). Hershey, PA: IGI Global. doi:10.4018/978-1-5225-5017-4.ch010

Ruffin, T. R. (2016). Health Information Technology and Change. In V. Wang (Ed.), *Handbook of Research on Advancing Health Education through Technology* (pp. 259–285). Hershey, PA: IGI Global. doi:10.4018/978-1-4666-9494-1.ch012

Ruffin, T. R. (2016). Health Information Technology and Quality Management. *International Journal of Information Communication Technologies and Human Development, 8*(4), 56–72. doi:10.4018/IJICTHD.2016100105

Ruffin, T. R., & Hawkins, D. P. (2018). Trends in Health Care Information Technology and Informatics. In M. Khosrow-Pour, D.B.A. (Ed.), Encyclopedia of Information Science and Technology, Fourth Edition (pp. 3805-3815). Hershey, PA: IGI Global. doi:10.4018/978-1-5225-2255-3.ch330

Safari, M. R., & Jiang, Q. (2018). The Theory and Practice of IT Governance Maturity and Strategies Alignment: Evidence From Banking Industry. *Journal of Global Information Management, 26*(2), 127–146. doi:10.4018/JGIM.2018040106

Sahin, H. B., & Anagun, S. S. (2018). Educational Computer Games in Math Teaching: A Learning Culture. In E. Toprak & E. Kumtepe (Eds.), *Supporting Multiculturalism in Open and Distance Learning Spaces* (pp. 249–280). Hershey, PA: IGI Global. doi:10.4018/978-1-5225-3076-3.ch013

Sanna, A., & Valpreda, F. (2017). An Assessment of the Impact of a Collaborative Didactic Approach and Students' Background in Teaching Computer Animation. *International Journal of Information and Communication Technology Education, 13*(4), 1–16. doi:10.4018/IJICTE.2017100101

Savita, K., Dominic, P., & Ramayah, T. (2016). The Drivers, Practices and Outcomes of Green Supply Chain Management: Insights from ISO14001 Manufacturing Firms in Malaysia. *International Journal of Information Systems and Supply Chain Management, 9*(2), 35–60. doi:10.4018/IJISSCM.2016040103

Scott, A., Martin, A., & McAlear, F. (2017). Enhancing Participation in Computer Science among Girls of Color: An Examination of a Preparatory AP Computer Science Intervention. In Y. Rankin & J. Thomas (Eds.), *Moving Students of Color from Consumers to Producers of Technology* (pp. 62–84). Hershey, PA: IGI Global. doi:10.4018/978-1-5225-2005-4.ch004

Shahsavandi, E., Mayah, G., & Rahbari, H. (2016). Impact of E-Government on Transparency and Corruption in Iran. In I. Sodhi (Ed.), *Trends, Prospects, and Challenges in Asian E-Governance* (pp. 75–94). Hershey, PA: IGI Global. doi:10.4018/978-1-4666-9536-8.ch004

Siddoo, V., & Wongsai, N. (2017). Factors Influencing the Adoption of ISO/IEC 29110 in Thai Government Projects: A Case Study. *International Journal of Information Technologies and Systems Approach, 10*(1), 22–44. doi:10.4018/IJITSA.2017010102

Sidorkina, I., & Rybakov, A. (2016). Computer-Aided Design as Carrier of Set Development Changes System in E-Course Engineering. In V. Mkrttchian, A. Bershadsky, A. Bozhday, M. Kataev, & S. Kataev (Eds.), *Handbook of Research on Estimation and Control Techniques in E-Learning Systems* (pp. 500–515). Hershey, PA: IGI Global. doi:10.4018/978-1-4666-9489-7.ch035

Sidorkina, I., & Rybakov, A. (2016). Creating Model of E-Course: As an Object of Computer-Aided Design. In V. Mkrttchian, A. Bershadsky, A. Bozhday, M. Kataev, & S. Kataev (Eds.), *Handbook of Research on Estimation and Control Techniques in E-Learning Systems* (pp. 286–297). Hershey, PA: IGI Global. doi:10.4018/978-1-4666-9489-7.ch019

Simões, A. (2017). Using Game Frameworks to Teach Computer Programming. In R. Alexandre Peixoto de Queirós & M. Pinto (Eds.), *Gamification-Based E-Learning Strategies for Computer Programming Education* (pp. 221–236). Hershey, PA: IGI Global. doi:10.4018/978-1-5225-1034-5.ch010

Sllame, A. M. (2017). Integrating LAB Work With Classes in Computer Network Courses. In H. Alphin Jr, R. Chan, & J. Lavine (Eds.), *The Future of Accessibility in International Higher Education* (pp. 253–275). Hershey, PA: IGI Global. doi:10.4018/978-1-5225-2560-8.ch015

Smirnov, A., Ponomarev, A., Shilov, N., Kashevnik, A., & Teslya, N. (2018). Ontology-Based Human-Computer Cloud for Decision Support: Architecture and Applications in Tourism. *International Journal of Embedded and Real-Time Communication Systems*, *9*(1), 1–19. doi:10.4018/IJERTCS.2018010101

Smith-Ditizio, A. A., & Smith, A. D. (2018). Computer Fraud Challenges and Its Legal Implications. In M. Khosrow-Pour, D.B.A. (Ed.), Encyclopedia of Information Science and Technology, Fourth Edition (pp. 4837-4848). Hershey, PA: IGI Global. doi:10.4018/978-1-5225-2255-3.ch419

Sohani, S. S. (2016). Job Shadowing in Information Technology Projects: A Source of Competitive Advantage. *International Journal of Information Technology Project Management*, *7*(1), 47–57. doi:10.4018/IJITPM.2016010104

Sosnin, P. (2018). Figuratively Semantic Support of Human-Computer Interactions. In *Experience-Based Human-Computer Interactions: Emerging Research and Opportunities* (pp. 244–272). Hershey, PA: IGI Global. doi:10.4018/978-1-5225-2987-3.ch008

Spinelli, R., & Benevolo, C. (2016). From Healthcare Services to E-Health Applications: A Delivery System-Based Taxonomy. In A. Dwivedi (Ed.), *Reshaping Medical Practice and Care with Health Information Systems* (pp. 205–245). Hershey, PA: IGI Global. doi:10.4018/978-1-4666-9870-3.ch007

Srinivasan, S. (2016). Overview of Clinical Trial and Pharmacovigilance Process and Areas of Application of Computer System. In P. Chakraborty & A. Nagal (Eds.), *Software Innovations in Clinical Drug Development and Safety* (pp. 1–13). Hershey, PA: IGI Global. doi:10.4018/978-1-4666-8726-4.ch001

Srisawasdi, N. (2016). Motivating Inquiry-Based Learning Through a Combination of Physical and Virtual Computer-Based Laboratory Experiments in High School Science. In M. Urban & D. Falvo (Eds.), *Improving K-12 STEM Education Outcomes through Technological Integration* (pp. 108–134). Hershey, PA: IGI Global. doi:10.4018/978-1-4666-9616-7.ch006

Stavridi, S. V., & Hamada, D. R. (2016). Children and Youth Librarians: Competencies Required in Technology-Based Environment. In J. Yap, M. Perez, M. Ayson, & G. Entico (Eds.), *Special Library Administration, Standardization and Technological Integration* (pp. 25–50). Hershey, PA: IGI Global. doi:10.4018/978-1-4666-9542-9.ch002

Sung, W., Ahn, J., Kai, S. M., Choi, A., & Black, J. B. (2016). Incorporating Touch-Based Tablets into Classroom Activities: Fostering Children's Computational Thinking through iPad Integrated Instruction. In D. Mentor (Ed.), *Handbook of Research on Mobile Learning in Contemporary Classrooms* (pp. 378–406). Hershey, PA: IGI Global. doi:10.4018/978-1-5225-0251-7.ch019

Syväjärvi, A., Leinonen, J., Kivivirta, V., & Kesti, M. (2017). The Latitude of Information Management in Local Government: Views of Local Government Managers. *International Journal of Electronic Government Research*, *13*(1), 69–85. doi:10.4018/IJEGR.2017010105

Tanque, M., & Foxwell, H. J. (2018). Big Data and Cloud Computing: A Review of Supply Chain Capabilities and Challenges. In A. Prasad (Ed.), *Exploring the Convergence of Big Data and the Internet of Things* (pp. 1–28). Hershey, PA: IGI Global. doi:10.4018/978-1-5225-2947-7.ch001

Teixeira, A., Gomes, A., & Orvalho, J. G. (2017). Auditory Feedback in a Computer Game for Blind People. In T. Issa, P. Kommers, T. Issa, P. Isaías, & T. Issa (Eds.), *Smart Technology Applications in Business Environments* (pp. 134–158). Hershey, PA: IGI Global. doi:10.4018/978-1-5225-2492-2.ch007

Thompson, N., McGill, T., & Murray, D. (2018). Affect-Sensitive Computer Systems. In M. Khosrow-Pour, D.B.A. (Ed.), Encyclopedia of Information Science and Technology, Fourth Edition (pp. 4124-4135). Hershey, PA: IGI Global. doi:10.4018/978-1-5225-2255-3.ch357

Trad, A., & Kalpić, D. (2016). The E-Business Transformation Framework for E-Commerce Control and Monitoring Pattern. In I. Lee (Ed.), *Encyclopedia of E-Commerce Development, Implementation, and Management* (pp. 754–777). Hershey, PA: IGI Global. doi:10.4018/978-1-4666-9787-4.ch053

Triberti, S., Brivio, E., & Galimberti, C. (2018). On Social Presence: Theories, Methodologies, and Guidelines for the Innovative Contexts of Computer-Mediated Learning. In M. Marmon (Ed.), *Enhancing Social Presence in Online Learning Environments* (pp. 20–41). Hershey, PA: IGI Global. doi:10.4018/978-1-5225-3229-3.ch002

Tripathy, B. K. T. R., S., & Mohanty, R. K. (2018). Memetic Algorithms and Their Applications in Computer Science. In S. Dash, B. Tripathy, & A. Rahman (Eds.), Handbook of Research on Modeling, Analysis, and Application of Nature-Inspired Metaheuristic Algorithms (pp. 73-93). Hershey, PA: IGI Global. doi:10.4018/978-1-5225-2857-9.ch004

Turulja, L., & Bajgoric, N. (2017). Human Resource Management IT and Global Economy Perspective: Global Human Resource Information Systems. In M. Khosrow-Pour (Ed.), *Handbook of Research on Technology Adoption, Social Policy, and Global Integration* (pp. 377–394). Hershey, PA: IGI Global. doi:10.4018/978-1-5225-2668-1.ch018

Unwin, D. W., Sanzogni, L., & Sandhu, K. (2017). Developing and Measuring the Business Case for Health Information Technology. In K. Moahi, K. Bwalya, & P. Sebina (Eds.), *Health Information Systems and the Advancement of Medical Practice in Developing Countries* (pp. 262–290). Hershey, PA: IGI Global. doi:10.4018/978-1-5225-2262-1.ch015

Vadhanam, B. R. S., M., Sugumaran, V., V., V., & Ramalingam, V. V. (2017). Computer Vision Based Classification on Commercial Videos. In M. S., & V. V. (Eds.), Multi-Core Computer Vision and Image Processing for Intelligent Applications (pp. 105-135). Hershey, PA: IGI Global. doi:10.4018/978-1-5225-0889-2.ch004

Valverde, R., Torres, B., & Motaghi, H. (2018). A Quantum NeuroIS Data Analytics Architecture for the Usability Evaluation of Learning Management Systems. In S. Bhattacharyya (Ed.), *Quantum-Inspired Intelligent Systems for Multimedia Data Analysis* (pp. 277–299). Hershey, PA: IGI Global. doi:10.4018/978-1-5225-5219-2.ch009

Vassilis, E. (2018). Learning and Teaching Methodology: "1:1 Educational Computing. In K. Koutsopoulos, K. Doukas, & Y. Kotsanis (Eds.), *Handbook of Research on Educational Design and Cloud Computing in Modern Classroom Settings* (pp. 122–155). Hershey, PA: IGI Global. doi:10.4018/978-1-5225-3053-4.ch007

Wadhwani, A. K., Wadhwani, S., & Singh, T. (2016). Computer Aided Diagnosis System for Breast Cancer Detection. In Y. Morsi, A. Shukla, & C. Rathore (Eds.), *Optimizing Assistive Technologies for Aging Populations* (pp. 378–395). Hershey, PA: IGI Global. doi:10.4018/978-1-4666-9530-6.ch015

Wang, L., Wu, Y., & Hu, C. (2016). English Teachers' Practice and Perspectives on Using Educational Computer Games in EIL Context. *International Journal of Technology and Human Interaction*, *12*(3), 33–46. doi:10.4018/IJTHI.2016070103

Watfa, M. K., Majeed, H., & Salahuddin, T. (2016). Computer Based E-Healthcare Clinical Systems: A Comprehensive Survey. *International Journal of Privacy and Health Information Management*, *4*(1), 50–69. doi:10.4018/IJPHIM.2016010104

Weeger, A., & Haase, U. (2016). Taking up Three Challenges to Business-IT Alignment Research by the Use of Activity Theory. *International Journal of IT/Business Alignment and Governance, 7*(2), 1-21. doi:10.4018/IJITBAG.2016070101

Wexler, B. E. (2017). Computer-Presented and Physical Brain-Training Exercises for School Children: Improving Executive Functions and Learning. In B. Dubbels (Ed.), *Transforming Gaming and Computer Simulation Technologies across Industries* (pp. 206–224). Hershey, PA: IGI Global. doi:10.4018/978-1-5225-1817-4.ch012

Williams, D. M., Gani, M. O., Addo, I. D., Majumder, A. J., Tamma, C. P., Wang, M., ... Chu, C. (2016). Challenges in Developing Applications for Aging Populations. In Y. Morsi, A. Shukla, & C. Rathore (Eds.), *Optimizing Assistive Technologies for Aging Populations* (pp. 1–21). Hershey, PA: IGI Global. doi:10.4018/978-1-4666-9530-6.ch001

Wimble, M., Singh, H., & Phillips, B. (2018). Understanding Cross-Level Interactions of Firm-Level Information Technology and Industry Environment: A Multilevel Model of Business Value. *Information Resources Management Journal*, *31*(1), 1–20. doi:10.4018/IRMJ.2018010101

Wimmer, H., Powell, L., Kilgus, L., & Force, C. (2017). Improving Course Assessment via Web-based Homework. *International Journal of Online Pedagogy and Course Design*, *7*(2), 1–19. doi:10.4018/IJOPCD.2017040101

Wong, Y. L., & Siu, K. W. (2018). Assessing Computer-Aided Design Skills. In M. Khosrow-Pour, D.B.A. (Ed.), Encyclopedia of Information Science and Technology, Fourth Edition (pp. 7382-7391). Hershey, PA: IGI Global. doi:10.4018/978-1-5225-2255-3.ch642

Wongsurawat, W., & Shrestha, V. (2018). Information Technology, Globalization, and Local Conditions: Implications for Entrepreneurs in Southeast Asia. In P. Ordóñez de Pablos (Ed.), *Management Strategies and Technology Fluidity in the Asian Business Sector* (pp. 163–176). Hershey, PA: IGI Global. doi:10.4018/978-1-5225-4056-4.ch010

Yang, Y., Zhu, X., Jin, C., & Li, J. J. (2018). Reforming Classroom Education Through a QQ Group: A Pilot Experiment at a Primary School in Shanghai. In H. Spires (Ed.), *Digital Transformation and Innovation in Chinese Education* (pp. 211–231). Hershey, PA: IGI Global. doi:10.4018/978-1-5225-2924-8.ch012

Yilmaz, R., Sezgin, A., Kurnaz, S., & Arslan, Y. Z. (2018). Object-Oriented Programming in Computer Science. In M. Khosrow-Pour, D.B.A. (Ed.), Encyclopedia of Information Science and Technology, Fourth Edition (pp. 7470-7480). Hershey, PA: IGI Global. doi:10.4018/978-1-5225-2255-3.ch650

Yu, L. (2018). From Teaching Software Engineering Locally and Globally to Devising an International-ized Computer Science Curriculum. In S. Dikli, B. Etheridge, & R. Rawls (Eds.), *Curriculum Internationalization and the Future of Education* (pp. 293–320). Hershey, PA: IGI Global. doi:10.4018/978-1-5225-2791-6.ch016

Yuhua, F. (2018). Computer Information Library Clusters. In M. Khosrow-Pour, D.B.A. (Ed.), Encyclopedia of Information Science and Technology, Fourth Edition (pp. 4399-4403). Hershey, PA: IGI Global. doi:10.4018/978-1-5225-2255-3.ch382

Zare, M. A., Taghavi Fard, M. T., & Hanafizadeh, P. (2016). The Assessment of Outsourcing IT Services using DEA Technique: A Study of Application Outsourcing in Research Centers. *International Journal of Operations Research and Information Systems*, 7(1), 45–57. doi:10.4018/IJORIS.2016010104

Zhao, J., Wang, Q., Guo, J., Gao, L., & Yang, F. (2016). An Overview on Passive Image Forensics Technology for Automatic Computer Forgery. *International Journal of Digital Crime and Forensics*, 8(4), 14–25. doi:10.4018/IJDCF.2016100102

Zimeras, S. (2016). Computer Virus Models and Analysis in M-Health IT Systems: Computer Virus Models. In A. Moumtzoglou (Ed.), *M-Health Innovations for Patient-Centered Care* (pp. 284–297). Hershey, PA: IGI Global. doi:10.4018/978-1-4666-9861-1.ch014

Zlatanovska, K. (2016). Hacking and Hacktivism as an Information Communication System Threat. In M. Hadji-Janev & M. Bogdanoski (Eds.), *Handbook of Research on Civil Society and National Security in the Era of Cyber Warfare* (pp. 68–101). Hershey, PA: IGI Global. doi:10.4018/978-1-4666-8793-6.ch004

About the Contributors

David Taniar is the editor-in-chief of the *International Journal of Data Warehousing and Mining.*

* * *

Jalel Akaichi received his PhD's degree, in the computer science and engineering field, from the University of Sciences and Technologies of Lille 1. He is currently a Full Professor at the University of Tunis and the University of Bisha. His research interests include, mainly, business intelligence, knowledge discovery in databases, data warehousing and mining, big data and data science, social networks, etc. He is the leader and the founder of the Business Intelligence Research Team and had multiple grants and positions for visiting and working in various international universities. He published numerous book chapters, and many papers in international journals and conferences, served in different program committees related to international conferences and journals, and provided international courses and tutorials.

Nenad Aničić received the M.Sc. and Ph.D. degrees in Information Systems from Belgrade University, Serbia in 2001 and 2006, respectively. He is currently a full professor in the Department of Information System and Technologies at the Faculty of Organizational Sciences, Belgrade University. He teaches courses in Business Process Modeling, Databases, XML Technologies and Applications, and Information Systems Design. His research interests include information systems development methodologies, model driven development, semantic technologies, and interoperable application systems.

Sladjan Babarogić received his B.Sc. degree in Information Systems from the Faculty of Organizational Sciences in Belgrade in 1996. He completed his M.Sc. and Ph.D. in Information systems at the University of Belgrade, Faculty of Organizational Sciences in 2004 and 2011, respectively. Currently, he works as Associate Professor at the Faculty of Organizational Sciences at the University of Belgrade, where he lectures in several Information Systems courses, and the most important among them Information System Design and Databases. His research interests are related to Model Driven Development, Business Analysis and Business Process Modeling, Information System Development Methodologies and Database Systems. He is the author or co-author of over 40 papers and co-author of two books in the ICT area.

Jorge Bernardino received the PhD degree in computer science from the University of Coimbra in 2002. He is a Coordinator Professor at ISEC (Instituto Superior de Engenharia de Coimbra) of the Polytechnic of Coimbra, Portugal. His main research fields are big data, data warehousing, business intelligence, open source tools, and software engineering, subjects in which he has authored or co-authored more than a hundred papers in refereed conferences and journals. Jorge Bernardino has served on program committees of many conferences and acted as referee for many international conferences and journals. He was President of ISEC from 2005–2010. During 2014 he was a visiting professor at Carnegie Mellon University (CMU). He is actually President of Scientific Council of ISEC.

David Broneske studied Computer Science at the University of Magdeburg (Bachelor of Science 2012, Master of Science 2013). Currently, he is a PhD student at the Databases and Software Engineering Group of Gunter Saake. His research interests include hardware-sensitive database operations and data structures.

Carlos Costa is an Invited Lecturer in the field of Information Systems, at the University of Minho. His current interests include Big Data, Data Warehousing, Data-driven Software Development, Data Science (e.g., Machine Learning and Data Visualization), and Information Systems Architectures and Administration. Regarding his technological skills, the following can be highlighted: Hadoop, Spark, SQL-on-Hadoop (e.g., Hive and Presto), NoSQL/NewSQL databases (e.g., Cassandra, HBase, and Apache Ignite), Kafka, Data Integration tools (e.g., Talend Open Studio for Big Data), Java, Python, HTML, CSS, JavaScript, Linux, Cloud Infrastructures (e.g., GCP), among others. He is the (co)-author of more than 25 scientific publications related to Big Data and Data Science, having several certificates and courses focusing on these topics. He participated in several events and conferences as a presenter, organizer, keynote, or spectator. He won several honors and awards, either due to his merit as a student (e.g., Caixa Geral de Depósitos Award and DGES/UMinho Merit Scholarship), or as a pro-active individual (e.g., Microsoft Power BI Contest 2014 and Deloitte ChallengeIT@Braga 2014). Furthermore, he is constantly looking to contribute to the scientific community and, therefore, he already collaborates in the review process of some journal/conference publications (e.g., Journal of Grid Computing, AMCIS, and IDEAS).

Khaled Dehdouh is a university lecturer at the Military Academy of Cherchell, Algeria Ex-researcher at the university of Lyon 2,France . Currently, he is the Head of the Computer Engineering Department, at the military Academy of Cherchell. He received his doctorate Degree in Business Intelligence (BI) information system (2015) from the university of Lyon 2, Lyon, France. His interest in research focuses on the evolution of BI in BIG DATA, analysis of social graphs cubes, community detection &evaluation, designing distributed data warehouses using NoSQL databases &MapReduce paradigm for parallel processing and massive data analysis . He is a member of "Big data & Cloud Computing" team in the Military Academy of Cherchell Laboratory. Also, he collaborated in some research projects with different universities: University of Lyon 2 (ERIC Laboratory), France, The Polytechnic Military School of El Bordj-El-Bahri (Algiers) and Saad Dahleb University, Blida 1, Algeria. Concerning his activity in the educational field, he delivers lectures and teaches different modules; mainly, "Decision Support Systems" for Master 2 and "Object-oriented Programming" for Bachelor's classes.

Huan Huo receives her Ph.D. in Computer Software and Theory from Northeastern University, and she is working as a senior lecturer in the University of Technology Sydney. Her research interests include cloud data management technology, data stream query optimization, XML data management technology, etc.

Nadeem Iftikhar is an Associate Professor at University College of Northern Denmark. He received the BS degree in Applied Mathematics and Computer Science from Eastern Mediterranean University, Famagusta, Turkish Republic of Northern Cyprus, in 1994, followed by the MS degree in Information Science from University of New South Wales, Sydney, Australia, in 1997 and the Ph.D. degree in Computer Science from Aalborg University, Aalborg, Denmark, in 2011. His research activity and published work concerns the area of data warehousing, with a particular emphasis on OLAP and ETL, as well as big data analytics. He is an IEEE member.

Veit Köppen received his Master degree from the Humboldt University Berlin in 2003. Afterwards he was employed as a research assistant at the Freie University Berlin receiving his Ph.D. degree in 2008. From 2008 to 2015 he was a scientific coordinator and post-doctoral researcher at the DBSE working group of Prof. Saake at the Otto-von-Guericke University Magdeburg. Since 2016, he is the head of the IT department at the university library in Magdeburg. His research interests include Scientific Data Management, Business Intelligence, Big Data Analytics, and Data Warehousing.

Xiufeng Liu received his PhD in Computer Science from Aalborg University, Denmark in 2012. Between 2013 and 2014, he worked as a Postdoctoral researcher at Waterloo University, Canada, and since January 2015 he has been working as a Postdoctoral researcher in Technical University of Denmark. His research areas are smart meter data analytics, data warehousing, and big data.

Per Nielsen has been working in the energy modelling and sustainability area since 1990. He is senior researcher in the System Analysis Division at the Department of Management Engineering at the Technical University of Denmark. He has participated in a range of international research programmes and multi-disciplinary research programmes. Currently Per is working on various projects in energy systems integration in particular "smart cities" development. He is currently supervisor of three PhD students and Co-supervisor of another two PhD students.

Marko Petrović is an assistant professor at the Department of Information Systems, Faculty of Organizational Sciences, University of Belgrade. His key research interests are: Domain-specific languages and approaches; Software development; Software development automation; Integration and interoperability of heterogeneous distributed resources; ETL process automation.

Kornelije Rabuzin is Full Professor in the Faculty of Organization and Informatics at the University of Zagreb.

Shigeaki Sakurai has been born in 1966. He has acquired bachelor degree, master degree, and doctor degree in 1989, 1991, and 2000 from Tokyo University of Science. In 1991, he took part in Toshiba Corporation. In 1998, he was temporally loaned to Real World Computing Partnership from Toshiba Corporation. The partnership was organized to develop new information processing technology by Japanese government. He returned to Toshiba Corporation in 2000. In 2010, he was loaned to the Business Intelligent Laboratory of Toshiba Solutions Corporation. Presently, he is a senior specialist at Software & AI Technology Center of Toshiba Digital Solutions Corporation. On the other hand, he was a visiting professor of Tokyo Institute of Technology from 2009 to 2013. Also, he became a professional engineer of the information technology department in Japan in 2004. His research topic is data mining, Web intelligence, machine learning, soft computing, healthcare data analysis, and so on.

Maribel Yasmina Santos is an Associate Professor at the Department of Information Systems, University of Minho, Portugal, where she is also a Senior Researcher at the ALGORITMI Research Centre (http://algoritmi.uminho.pt) and at the Engineering Process Maturity and Quality (EPMQ) domain of the Computer Graphics Centre (http://www.ccg.pt). She was the Secretary-General of the Association of Geographic Information Laboratories for Europe (www.agile-online.org) from May 2013 to June 2015 and Associate Director of the Department of Information Systems, University of Minho, from May 2010 to July 2014. Currently, she is the leader of the Software-based Information Systems Engineering and Management Group at the ALGORITMI Research Centre. Her research interests include Business Intelligence and Analytics, Big Data Analytics, (Big) Data Warehousing and Online Analytical Processing.

Martin Schäler was born in 1985 in Havelberg (Germany). He received his Master degree from the Otto-von-Guericke University Magdeburg in 2010. Afterwards he was employed as a research assistant and scientific coordinator at the Otto-von-Guericke University Magdeburg receiving his Ph.D. degree in 2014. Since August 2015 he is a post-doctoral researcher at the DBIS working group of Prof. Böhm at the Karlsruhe Institute of Technology. His research interests include Scientific Data Management, Hardware-sensitive Database Tuning, Time Series Analytics, and Provenance.

Salman Ahmed Shaikh received the B.E. degree in computer systems, the M.E. degree in communication systems and networks, from the Mehran University of Engineering and Technology, Pakistan, and the Ph.D. degree in computer science, from the University of Tsukuba, Japan, in 2005, 2008 and 2014, respectively. He is currently working as a postdoc researcher at the Center for Computational Sciences, University of Tsukuba, Japan. His research interests include stream processing, big data manipulation and multidimensional analysis, transaction processing, uncertain data and data mining. He is a member of the Database Society of Japan (DBSJ), International Association of Computer Science and Information Technology (IACSIT) and Pakistan Engineering Council (PEC).

Nina Turajlić is an assistant professor at the Department of Information Systems, Faculty of Organizational Sciences, University of Belgrade. Her key research interests are: Programming languages and compilers; Domain-specific languages and approaches; Optimization methods and operations research; Information systems design and implementation; ETL process automation.

Francisca Vale Lima completed her master's degree in Information Systems in 2017. She is currently a Big Data Analyst/Developer and formerly a researcher at the University of Minho, Portugal. Her interests are in Business Intelligence, Data Analytics, Big Data, Big Data Warehousing and Real-Time.

Milica Vučković is an associate professor at the Department of Information Systems, Faculty of Organizational Sciences, University of Belgrade. Her key research interests are: Programming languages and compilers; Domain-specific languages and approaches; Information systems design and implementation; ETL process automation.

Index

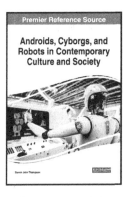

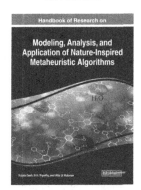

Ensure Quality Research is Introduced to the Academic Community

Become an IGI Global Reviewer for Authored Book Projects

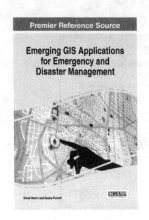

Premier Reference Source

Emerging GIS Applications for Emergency and Disaster Management

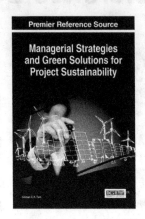

Premier Reference Source

Managerial Strategies and Green Solutions for Project Sustainability

Premier Reference Source

Comparative Approaches to Using R and Python for Statistical Data Analysis

Premier Reference Source

Solutions for High-Touch Communications in a High-Tech World

The overall success of an authored book project is dependent on quality and timely reviews.

In this competitive age of scholarly publishing, constructive and timely feedback significantly expedites the turnaround time of manuscripts from submission to acceptance, allowing the publication and discovery of forward-thinking research at a much more expeditious rate. Several IGI Global authored book projects are currently seeking highly qualified experts in the field to fill vacancies on their respective editorial review boards:

Applications may be sent to:
development@igi-global.com

Applicants must have a doctorate (or an equivalent degree) as well as publishing and reviewing experience. Reviewers are asked to write reviews in a timely, collegial, and constructive manner. All reviewers will begin their role on an ad-hoc basis for a period of one year, and upon successful completion of this term can be considered for full editorial review board status, with the potential for a subsequent promotion to Associate Editor.

If you have a colleague that may be interested in this opportunity, we encourage you to share this information with them.

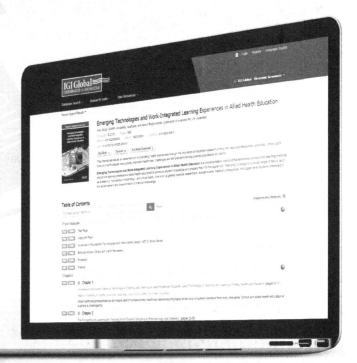